HIKING,

CYCLING, *and*

CANOEING

in MARYLAND

A Family Guide

HIKING,

CYCLING, *and*

CANOEING

in MARYLAND

A Family Guide

Bryan MacKay

Illustrations by Sandra Glover

The Johns Hopkins University Press

Baltimore and London

This book has been brought to publication with the generous assistance of the Laurence Hall Fowler Fund.

The Johns Hopkins University Press
2715 North Charles Street
Baltimore, Maryland 21218-4319
The Johns Hopkins Press Ltd., London

ISBN 0-8018-5033-9
ISBN 0-8018-5035-5 (pbk.)

Library of Congress Cataloging-in-Publication Data will be found at the end of this book.
A catalog record for this book is available from the British Library.

CONTENTS

CYCLING

CANOEING

PREFACE

WELCOME TO *Hiking, Cycling, and Canoeing in Maryland: A Family Guide!* I decided to write this guidebook because so many people have asked me where to go for a good family-oriented outdoor recreational experience. Almost everyone who asks wants to go on a walk or a hike, many like to bicycle, and a substantial number want to canoe. It seems that the two most important requirements are that the destination be suitable for kids and that it be an attractive place in a natural setting. I've tried to meet these two criteria in selecting a variety of destinations across the state.

Fortunately, Maryland is the perfect state for outdoor activities like walking, cycling, and canoeing. Maryland extends from the ocean to the mountains, and both are within a three-hour drive for the majority of its residents. Its waters include the tidal tributaries of Chesapeake Bay as well as whitewater rivers draining rolling uplands. Maryland has a great diversity of natural habitats and is home to a large variety of plants and animals. The variety of outdoor experiences available to citizens is nothing short of amazing.

This book is specifically oriented toward *family* outdoor recreation—that is, recreation in which children of all ages accompany adults. I have selected destinations that can be toured without strenuous exercise by people who may not be in peak physical condition. For this reason, children will be able to participate as well. There are no long hikes up steep mountains, no bike rides over a procession of endless hills, and no canoe trips down roaring whitewater. Of course, Maryland has no shortage of these possibilities, and I have tried to indicate places where such opportunities are available as options.

For this book, I have selected the *best* natural areas in Maryland for your outdoor excursions. The selection of places to visit is not meant to be complete or even comprehensive. It reflects my personal favorite places, a list accumulated over a dozen years of weekends walking, riding, and paddling throughout the state. I believe that each venue recommends itself in some outstanding way and is sure to please and delight you when you visit.

This book deals only with *natural areas*. There are no amusement parks, festival sites, museums, quaint villages, resorts, or restaurants listed. Such day-trip destinations have already been well covered by other authors. Many of the venues are state or national parks, typically established for their scenic beauty. A few are privately owned reserves, generously open to the public. All feature aspects of nature that deserve a wider appreciation.

The destinations were selected using certain specific criteria. Walking and hiking sites had to be in safe, beautiful natural places, but ones where there were no steep hills to climb. Most feature flat to gently rolling terrain that can be handled by younger children without difficulty. A special effort was made to locate acceptable trails in mountainous regions of the state, so that hikers could get a feel for the land without exhausting themselves on steep climbs. A few venues traverse rocky, uneven terrain; although they are more difficult, I've seen children having a great time on all such trails listed.

Sites for cycling are either off-road or on roads where vehicular traffic is very light and speeds are limited by law. Most are designated bike trails. Although many avid bicyclists ride on public roads, such roads are no place for children, and adults run a risk of injury that to me is unacceptable. Judging by the rapidly increasing popularity of designated off-road bike trails, many others agree. Not every bike trail in Maryland is included, however; in order for it to be listed, I required that a trail traverse an interesting or unique natural area. Furthermore, I have included three bike trails from just outside the borders of Maryland because of the paucity of such off-road trails.

Many of these designated bike trails are used by walkers, joggers, runners, and, more recently, in-line skaters. They are actually more appropriate than the destinations listed in the hiking section for families with toddlers or children in strollers. Citizens confined to wheelchairs or with other physical disabilities may find these paved trails of value as well.

Criteria for canoeing rivers included the requirement that they could be paddled on any day of the year (as long as they were not frozen). Most nontidal creeks and streams in Maryland dry up in summer and fall and cannot be canoed when the weather is most benign. Rivers requiring intermediate or advanced whitewater skills were eliminated, since they are inappropriate for children. I have included one river from just beyond Maryland's borders because it offers reliable summertime elementary whitewater.

Each trip description includes information on the natural history and ecology of the site. I have found that many people are curious about the natural world around them, but most other guidebooks have a strictly anthropocentric focus. In addition to a listing of some of the more obvious and interesting plants and animals found at the site, in many cases I try to explain their presence. I call this interpreting the landscape, but it is nothing more than using an understanding of basic ecology to make hypotheses about distributions and abundances of organisms. I believe that observing the natural world with an analytical eye helps in the appreciation of it.

Accompanying each destination is a sidebar that considers a relevant organism or related concept in greater detail. I have tried to enhance descriptions of life histories with interesting new findings gleaned from the recent scientific literature. A number of these essays provide a closer look at some aspect of conservation in Maryland and frequently provide a perspective on controversial questions and a suggestion for future action on the part of society.

A map accompanies each destination. Nearby roads, especially those that give access, are shown. The key for each map is the same:

Highway	=========
Hard-surfaced road	_____
Limited-traffic road	_____
Trail	··········
Parking area	P
Area of interest	*

Written directions at the end of each trip description will get you from the Washington-Baltimore metropolitan area to at least one road on the map.

A number of the trails recommended here are suitable for wheelchairs and strollers. The principal criterion for inclusion is that such trails have an asphalt or other sufficiently hard surface so that wheels can turn with a minimum of effort. Hills must be minimal or nonexistent. Not all of the individual trails delineated in the trip description may be suitable, but at least a significant segment is. These trails are Great Falls Tavern Walk, C & O Canal Towpath (portions), Assateague Island Bike Trail, Quiet Waters Park, Baltimore and Annapolis Trail, Rock Creek Trail, Patapsco Valley State Park, (Avalon–Orange Grove Area), Northern Central Trail, Chincoteague National Wildlife Refuge, and Mount Vernon Trail.

Finally, each venue is graced by a pen and ink sketch by Sandy Glover. Each sketch portrays a plant or animal you might encounter at that destination. Sandy's wonderful sketches capture the essence of these organisms and greatly enrich this book.

I hope you enjoy using this book to explore Maryland. May you have many safe and memorable experiences.

ACKNOWLEDGMENTS

THIS GUIDEBOOK would not have been possible without the knowledgeable assistance and friendly companionship of a great many people.

Fellow hikers, cyclists, and paddlers on some of the exploratory excursions were Warren, Anne, and Christopher Heppding; Tom, Christy, and Lisa Gianniccinni; Steve, Susan, Katie, Joe, and Tom Meyer; Art, Chris, Lauren, and Connor Grace; Tricia Precht; Ken and Taryn Bruette; Charley Stine; John Bulger; and Chris Riegel. Their enthusiasm, good cheer, and willingness to act as test subjects made each trip a joy, and I value their friendship.

A number of scientists and colleagues provided well-chosen advice or had useful general discussions with me on some of the ecological material found in this book. They include Charley Stine, Rodger Waldman, Dave Flaim, Bob Platt, Carl Weber, Roger Davis, José Barata, Stuart Strahl, and Bill Richkus. In addition, two anonymous reviewers provided constructive criticism. Among the professional staff members at managing agencies who supplied specific information were Bob Chance, Larry Lubbers, Bob Lunsford, Tom Mathews, Theresa Moore, Rachel Newhouse, Roger Rector, and John Schroer. My thanks to all.

Use of the facilities of the Department of Biological Sciences and the Albin O. Kuhn Library, University of Maryland, Baltimore County, is gratefully acknowledged. Audrey Ellis and Dave Flaim were invaluable resources when problems arose with computer hardware or software. Tom Rabenhorst and

Joe School of the Geography Department provided much helpful advice with cartography.

I have long admired the line drawings of Sandy Glover, and I feel fortunate that she was willing to enrich this book with her sketches. Sandy, in turn, wishes to thank her employer, the Irvine Natural Science Center, Stevenson, Maryland, for its support.

Thanks to Bob Brugger of the Johns Hopkins University Press for his interest in this project and his faith in seeing it through to completion.

Finally, completion of this book would not have been possible without the love, understanding, and support of my Mom and Dad. Thanks—for everything.

The author will donate a share of his royalties from this book for the support of environmental education programs at the Pickering Creek Environmental Center, Easton, Maryland, and the Irvine Natural Science Center.

OUTDOOR ACTIVITIES WITH KIDS

O NE OF THE GREATEST joys of life with children is the opportunity to expose them to activities that give you pleasure. Children learn best from their parents, and they appreciate the chance to spend time with the people they most admire and love. Outdoor recreation, including hiking, cycling, and canoeing, is a perfect opportunity for parents, children, and friends to enjoy one another in a healthful and relaxing setting. In addition, all parents want to impart a set of ethical precepts to their children which can be used throughout life, and a natural setting is the perfect place for this to happen. By setting the sort of example that you feel is appropriate you can teach these patterns of proper behavior effortlessly and thoroughly.

Nevertheless, doing things outdoors with children does require a bit more effort and planning than sending them out to play with neighborhood kids, sitting them in front of the VCR, or signing them up for Little League. Here are a number of tips, obtained from parents whose families are active hikers, cyclists, or paddlers. Not every bit of advice may apply to your family, but surely some will; temper it with your own ideas and experience.

Specific advice for a given sport, including tips on equipment and clothing, may be found in the introduction to the appropriate section of this book. The tips below are more general and apply to any outdoor activity. Perhaps surprisingly, most of them deal with mental preparation and attitudes rather than hardware.

Possibly the single most important factor in ensuring that children will have a good time hiking, cycling, or canoeing is attitude. Not theirs—yours. If you look upon these activities as competitive sports, with success or failure dependent upon achieving some particular goal, then everyone concerned would be better served if the kids were left at home. Say that you decide beforehand that the family will bicycle to Grand Vista Point in time to eat lunch there. That's a worthwhile goal for an adult, but younger children rarely appreciate scenic panoramas and may not understand why that goal has to be achieved. Distractd by a scattering of mushrooms on the forest floor, a stream perfect for throwing stones into, and a playground, children will want to stop to enjoy the moment. And when kids get hungry or thirsty, they need to eat or drink *now*, not at Grandview Point. Adults must above all be flexible on a trip with kids. Remember, the successful outdoor experience is not a parental trip on which kids come along, but a family trip in which kids are full and equal partners. Stop frequently to enjoy whatever catches the attention and interest of children; such stops are opportunities for you to spend some quality time with them in an unstructured setting. Hiking, cycling, and canoeing should be fun, with an emphasis on these activities as enjoyable play for the whole family.

If the trip itself should be unstructured and open to an appreciation of the moment, planning for the trip needs to be careful, thoughtful, and ongoing. If this is your first trip out with the kids, or you go out only rarely, the advice in this book should be helpful. More experienced parents can temper this counsel with their own experience with their own kids. After all, every child is different, and no set of recommendations can possibly apply to all children. In general, however, involve your children as much as possible in planning an outdoor activity. Older kids can be assigned to pack some of their own gear, and you should go over the route with them in advance. Familiarize young children with equipment that you expect to use. For a canoe trip, put the boat in the backyard as a plaything; if the weather is hot, fill it up with water and use it as a splash pool. For biking trips, do a few shakedown cruises through the neighborhood to get in shape and to make sure that all mechanical parts are functioning properly. Hikers may want to don boots or a small pack for a trial walk. If you're going to camp, have the children help you set the tent up in the backyard, sleep out in it one night, and cook a meal outside. Most important, discuss the trip in advance with the kids so they will be mentally prepared for it. Tell them what the trip will be like and what will be expected of them. Establish rules for acceptable behavior and review what to do in an emergency: what to do if separated, what to do if the canoe capsizes, and so forth. But don't worry about kids; children are more adaptable than adults to novel experiences, since so much of their world is still new to them.

Occasionally parents new to outdoor experiences may be overly protective of their children. Yes, there are all sorts of potential dangers out there, but don't panic. Kids invariably do better than their parents expect them to. Instill in them a healthy respect for objective dangers like cliffs, snakes, and fire. But there's no need to scare them. Make children increasingly responsible for their own actions in the outdoors as they grow. Keep them in sight at all times, but let your invisible leash lengthen in safe areas. Think about whether it's really important to say "don't" *before* you say it. Consider putting some of your normal household rules (regarding diet, for example) in abeyance for trips so that children will associate the experience with special, pleasurable occasions.

Of course, no parent would ever knowingly put a child in a dangerous situation. Know your kids: what their strengths and weaknesses are, what scares them, where their physical and emotional limits lie. Take these factors into account when you plan the trip. Realize that the unforeseen is a frequent occurrence on outdoors trips; expect the unexpected, and be flexible enough to adapt to a new situation. This requires you to know yourself as well as your kids. Honestly evaluate your skills: can you carry an injured child out of the woods on your back, fix a flat tire, or rescue a swamped canoe? Work to remedy any deficiencies; it will do wonders for your self-confidence even if you never have occasion to use your newfound skills. Take along a guidebook (preferably this one!) on your trip. Make sure that you have appropriate, high-quality gear. Know the basics of first aid in a setting where calling 911 is not an immediate option. Know the location of the hospital nearest your destination. Review in your mind scenarios that might occur requiring emergency skills and what you would do; this visualization training is recognized as one of the most effective preparation methods.

All of the foregoing advice involves preparation that is mental. It is of paramount importance. But there are also some practical pieces of advice that will make your trip more successful. Most seem obvious, but it's surprisingly easy to overlook some of them.

- Start with short, easy trips close to home and work up to the longer, more difficult ones.
- Consider going with other families, or inviting along favorite playmates of your own kids. (If you invite other children along without their parents or guardians, you should obtain a signed release that allows you to give permission for their treatment at a hospital.)
- Have kids carry something in a small fanny pack or backpack in order to increase their sense of full partnership in the trip. It can be a favorite toy, stuffed animal, storybook, tissue, or water bottle.
- Feed children frequently, more often than at home. Although all children should be fed a nutritious, healthy diet, bring along some sweets for outdoor trips. The simple sugars in these treats can often jump start a tired child in ways that complex carbohydrates cannot. Parents experienced in outdoor activities invariably emphasize one rule: never, *ever*, run out of food!
- Drink copiously. Dehydration is a real threat in the outdoors and is more common than is generally recognized. Children are especially susceptible given their smaller body size. If you and your kids aren't urinating about every two

hours, you can probably use more liquids. Water is best, but never drink from natural sources like rivers, streams, and springs. Electrolyte replacement liquids are acceptable, but dilute them in half for kids. Fruit juices provide sugar and vitamins in addition to water.

° What goes in must come out, so carry toilet paper and a small plastic shovel. Solid waste should be buried under six inches to a foot of soil, where soil bacteria can decompose the waste. Place a branch, log, or rock over the site to prevent disturbance by animals.

° Wear clothes appropriate to the weather, and carry extra clothes in case it gets colder. Bring along rain gear, including a rain hat. Brightly colored clothes make lost children easier to find. Clothing specific to a given sport is discussed in the introduction to the appropriate section of this book.

° Each child should have a whistle on a lanyard, to be blown *only* in case of emergency.

° Adults should carry a Swiss Army knife, sun block, bug spray, a small first aid kit, a reflective blanket, paper and pencil, extra money, and identification, in addition to extra food, water, and clothing. However, your most important gear is your common sense, intelligence, experience, and preparedness.

° Two common hazards on outdoor trips are poison ivy and ticks. Be able to recognize poison ivy, and teach your kids to do so as well. Ticks are harder to avoid, but in general avoid brushy and unmanaged grassy areas, especially east of a line extending from Baltimore to Washington. Be sure to check the skin, especially the scalp, for ticks at the end of an outdoor excursion.

Good luck!

WALKING AND HIKING

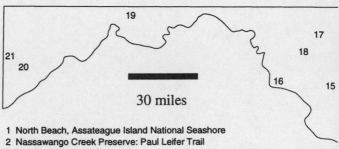

30 miles

1 North Beach, Assateague Island National Seashore
2 Nassawango Creek Preserve: Paul Leifer Trail
3 Calvert Cliffs State Park
4 Flag Ponds Nature Park
5 Elk Neck State Park
6 Susquehanna River Trail
7 North Point State Park (Black Marsh)
8 Great Falls Tavern Walk and Billy Goat Trail
9 Lake Roland Trail
10 Oregon Ridge Park
11 Soldiers Delight Natural Environmental Area
12 Patapsco Valley State Park: McKeldin area
13 Gunpowder South Trail
14 Little Bennett Regional Park
15 Sugarloaf Mountain
16 Harpers Ferry and the C & O Canal Towpath
17 Blue Ridge Duo
18 The Appalachian Trail
19 Rocky Gap State Park
20 Swallow Falls State Park
21 Cranesville Swamp Preserve

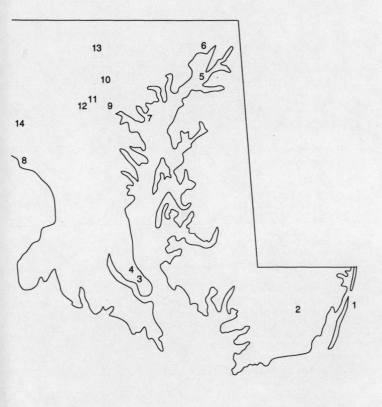

WALKING AND
HIKING WITH KIDS

WHETHER IT'S A STROLL through the local playground or a brisk hike along a state park trail, walking for health and pleasure is Maryland's most popular participatory sport. The benefits of regular, moderate exercise are well known, and walking in a beautiful natural area only enhances these gains. Walking is the best way (and sometimes the only way) to visit many of Maryland's unique landscapes and to view some of its most attractive flora and interesting fauna. Hiking requires no special equipment, no advanced knowledge, no acquired skills. It is truly a democratic activity.

Parents take children along on walks and hikes for many of these same reasons. Children are natural explorers, and their presence can open an adult's jaded eyes to new ways of seeing. Curious children are great hiking companions; their vitality and exuberance lend an energy to the experience that cannot be duplicated. But hikes with children are different, and their participation must be taken into account.

The purpose of this chapter is to address those aspects of walking and hiking that are specifically different because children are along. It is not a comprehensive treatment of hiking in general. A number of good books can supply you with more information regarding the sport of hiking; consult your public library or bookstore.

PLANNING

Any activity that includes children requires more planning than one that does not. Perhaps the most important aspect is to plan a hiking trip that is well within the physical capabilities of the children who participate. Start children young so that a hike will become a familiar activity, and go regularly so that children can build up their stamina. However, walks with young children should be short, perhaps less than a mile in length for toddlers. Children are inquisitive and can find plenty to see and do in just a short stretch of trail. Remember that for younger children the activity rather than the final destination is the objective, and you will need to devote lots of time to exploring whatever is interesting along the trail.

As children get older and stronger, you can select longer and more difficult trails. Look for routes that have diversity: a stream into which they can throw stones, a rock outcrop to explore, different habitats to pass through. Set destination goals that have value for kids: a playground, a swimming lake, a snack bar, a fishing hole. Let older children participate in route planning and decisionmaking; an experienced teenager can probably do just as good a job as an adult and should be offered the opportunity to direct a family outing.

Proper planning also involves assembling the appropriate clothes and gear for a hike. Bring along rain gear and an extra jacket for everyone on the walk. Hiking on a damp, drizzly day isn't nearly as bad as bicycling or canoeing, but proper protection from the elements adds greatly to the enjoyment.

EQUIPMENT

The single most important piece of gear for a child on a hike is footwear. Shoes that fit poorly or are insufficiently sturdy will quickly cause blisters, and blisters soon turn a pleasant stroll into something resembling the Bataan death march. Children are especially susceptible to blisters because their feet grow so fast that shoes rarely fit properly. If you're going to go hiking with some regularity, spend the money to buy shoes that fit rather than shoes the child will "grow into." In addition to fitting correctly, shoes should be sturdy enough to provide proper support. Some of the athletic shoes on the market today are carefully designed with such criteria in mind (although many others are merely cosmetic imitations). A knowledgeable, experienced salesperson at an athletic shoe store can help with solid advice. Finally, good shoes for hiking should have laces rather than Velcro closures, and they should have a nonskid pattern on the sole. Good-quality athletic shoes are sufficient for most walking; I believe that hiking boots are necessary only when backpacking over rocky, broken ground. Hiking boots also take time to break in, so that by the time a boot is really comfortable, the child will have outgrown it.

Children should be encouraged to become full partners in a walk by carrying some personal and group gear. Day hikes do not typically require a knapsack; I prefer a fanny pack that buckles around the waist and transfers weight to the hips. Such packs are so light that the wearer soon forgets that he or she has one on. Young children can carry some identification, a few coins, some tissues, a snack, and whatever else they choose. Older children may want to add a camera, windbreaker, or game.

Every child should carry a whistle for emergency use attached to his or her belt by a lanyard. Review with your kids what to do if they lose sight of the group: stop immediately, hug a tree, and blow the whistle. Obviously you must impress upon children that the whistle is not a toy and that it must be blown only in an emergency.

Adults should carry some emergency gear: a first aid kit with a manual for its use, knife, matches, flashlight, duct tape, toilet paper, plastic shovel, reflective blanket, extra money, and identification. If you invite other children along without their parents or guardians, you should have a signed release for each one that allows you to give permission for his or her treatment at a hospital.

ON THE TRAIL

Once you have selected a hike, planned for it, and arrived at the trailhead, the success of the hike depends in large measure on the attitude of the adults participating. A walk with children is an opportunity for a family or group of friends to be together and to enjoy each other's company in an outdoor setting. Keep in mind that achieving a particular destination in a given amount of time is unimportant, and probably irrelevant to kids. Focus on the process of hiking itself and the chances it offers for exploration, learning, and personal growth. Take the time to examine the insects found on a goldenrod flower, to search under wet logs for salamanders, and to compare the shapes of tree leaves. Stop frequently to play games, snack, or watch clouds. Be flexible; if someone is not having a good time, change the game plan so that he or she will.

Make sure you stop to eat and drink with regularity. Children exercising outdoors expend energy faster than at home, so bring plenty of food and drink along on the trail. Have a snack about every two hours and a drink every hour or so, although this advice should obviously be adapted to the specific needs of your children. Nevertheless, it is worthwhile to offer food and drink frequently; children do not always tell you that they're hungry or thirsty, and they may be so involved with something that they themselves fail to realize it.

All of this is fine advice, but much of it is common sense. After all, you don't have to be an expert to take kids for a walk. The most important thing is to get out and hike, frequently and in all seasons, to enjoy natural Maryland.

North Beach, Assateague Island National Seashore

County: Worcester

Distance: Up to 10 miles

Difficulty: Flat; sandy terrain

Highlights: Ocean beach, wildlife (especially birds)

More Information: Assateague Island State Park, (410) 641-2120. Assateague Island National Seashore, (410) 641-3030

ASSATEAGUE ISLAND forms the easternmost boundary of Maryland. A barrier island separated from the mainland by a shallow coastal bay, Assateague is a study in contrasts. To the north is Ocean City, an intensively developed vacation destination with the highest population density in the state on holiday summer weekends. Just across the inlet, much of the upper five miles of Assateague exists as de facto wilderness, where visitors are few in number and minimal in their impact. Protected by Assateague Island National Seashore and Assateague Island State Park, this land of sand and sea is a special and enticing place.

Beachwalking is a familiar seashore activity, but few places on the east coast have as long a stretch of truly deserted beach as Assateague. For this reason, a natural community of plants and animals dominates the life of Assateague, and we humans are only temporary visitors and observers. For anyone interested in the natural world, especially birds, there are few better places in Maryland. Even if you just want to get away from it all, Assateague is a great place to hike.

North Beach, Assateague Island National Seashore

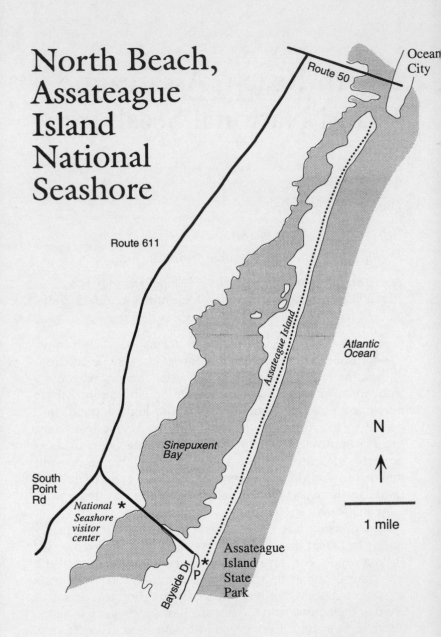

Route 50

Ocean City

Route 611

Assateague Island

Atlantic Ocean

Sinepuxent Bay

N

↑

1 mile

South Point Rd

National Seashore visitor center *

Bayside Dr

P *

Assateague Island State Park

A note of caution: this ten-mile walk is a long and difficult hike if completed in its entirety. Walking over sand is more tiring than walking over almost any other type of surface. In summer the beach can be very hot, although heatstroke can be easily avoided by taking occasional swims in the ocean. Bring lots of sunblock to avoid burning. Be sure to carry at least a quart of drinking water per person; in addition to the heat and lack of shade, salt spray and a constant breeze can be desiccating. Insect repellent is a must if you plan to explore the area behind the dunes; the regular southerly breeze usually keeps the winged hordes at bay on the forebeach. So come prepared, especially if you bring children.

TRIP DESCRIPTION

Begin your hike from the day-use parking lot of Assateague Island State Park, operated by Maryland's Department of Natural Resources. There is parking here for hundreds of cars, usually sufficient if you arrive before 11 A.M. or after 4 P.M. in beach season and always ample at other times of the year. An entrance fee is charged. Changing houses with cold-water showers, flush toilets, drinking water, and a snack bar are available.

Unlike most of the other hikes in this book, this one offers you the chance to see lots of wildlife even before you leave the parking lot. A small contingent of the Assateague pony herd patrols the parking lot for handouts at all hours and in all seasons, soliciting donations of food as their own special token of admission and leaving the unwary with a fragrant reminder of their visit wedged in shoe soles, on sandal bottoms, or between the toes. Most visitors are enchanted by the famous ponies, and a few minutes of observation will reveal the degree of poor judgment of which humans are capable in their effort to experience wildlife up close and personal. Although the ponies are generally docile, they can become quite persistent in their pursuit of food and may be short-tempered and even aggressive on occasion. Ponies kick and bite, so avoid feeding

them and keep your distance. The parking lot is also frequented by gulls (mostly laughing gulls in the summer and
ring-billed gulls in the winter), crows, and grackles, all of
whom will scavenge shamelessly through the accumulated
trash discarded by your fellow visitors. Although all of this
animal activity is artifically induced by us humans, the parking
lot is nevertheless a great place to observe behavior. Students
of ethology will have few other opportunities to ply their trade
from the comfort of an air-conditioned automobile.

Walk toward the beach, crossing the dunes on the boardwalk provided. Despite the presence of this boardwalk, a few
thoughtless people have created their own footpaths over the
dunes. Such actions compact the shallow soil, kill the fragile
vegetation, and make the dune more susceptible to erosion by
wind and water.

At the ocean's edge, turn left (north). Five miles of ocean
beach stretch in front of you, becoming increasingly less populated the farther you walk. Indeed, in colder weather, you
may be the only person in sight. As you walk north, notice the
substantial dunes that have been built up near the bathing
beach. This continuous battlement, known as the primary
dune, protects the inner stretches of the island from the
pounding surf during storm events. These dunes are not natural. Bulldozers built them up years ago, and the dunes are
repaired whenever a breakthrough occurs. In the winter, when
strong winds may erode the dunes, snow fences are erected to
catch the airborne sand.

The tops of well-established dunes have been colonized by
vegetation, dominated by dunegrass, *Ammophila breviligu-
lata*. The most important plant on Assateague Island, this
insignificant-looking grass acts as a living snow fence, combing
sand out of the air. Grains that hit the blade are funneled
downward by the shallow V shape and accumulate around the
base. In most plants, this act of self-burial would be suicidal,
but dunegrass thrives in this situation. In fact, it grows vigorously only when continually buried, spreading via underground rhizomes. Roots reach downward to the water table far
below, further stabilizing the plant. If you look closely at the

stem, you'll see that crystals of salt accumulate here. In many less hardy plants, this would be the literal kiss of death, as the salt would draw water out of the plant's tissues. In *Ammophila,* however, the blade is composed of parallel ridges of impervious tissue where the salt crystals accumulate, while the more sensitive soft tissues occupy the hollows. Dunegrass is a common food plant for the Assateague ponies.

The dunes are actively maintained only where they protect man-made structures in the state park and national seashore. Elsewhere, the dunes are allowed to erode, build up, or migrate, as the vagaries of nature dictate. For this reason, the solid wall of dunes soon gives way to occasional breakouts, and then single isolated dunes, as you hike northward.

Visible on the horizon, just behind the primary dune, is a large and beautiful beach home, known as the McCabe house. It is the last remnant of the days before Assateague was bought for the public domain. Having thus far resisted the erosive action of waves and wind, the McCabe house is occasionally used by researchers and Park Service staff.

As you walk along the beach, you will no doubt see an assortment of small shorebirds foraging at the water's edge. These amusing little animals scurry along just out of reach of advancing waves and follow retreating waves seaward for a few moments until the next wave arrives. Identification of the shorebirds is rarely easy, even for experienced birders, and mixed flocks of sandpiperlike birds are often just called "peeps," for their distinctive calls. The two largest shorebirds you are likely to see in summer, however, are easy to recognize. Both are about the size of crows. The willet is rather nondescript until it flies, revealing a distinctive black and white banding pattern on the underside of the wing and almost invariably uttering its "pill-will-willet" call. Willets nest in the salt marshes behind Assateague. The other distinctive large shorebird, the oystercatcher, is far less common, so count it as a real find when you see one. Oystercatchers are mostly black but have neon-orange bills and a yellow eye ring. As their name suggests, they are most often found feeding in shallow oyster beds like those off Chincoteague, but on occasion they will stray out onto the beach. Although shorebirds are present at Assateague year-round, diversity and numbers are greatest during the spring and fall migrations. May is the peak month for spring migrations, whereas fall migrants arrive as early as mid-August and continue arriving for the next two months. Mid-September is probably the peak.

Shorebirds are the most distinctive animals you're likely to see on this walk, but other, smaller life forms are found in the zone between the ocean and dune. The intertidal zone, where the shorebirds feed, has some interesting residents. The mole crab is a common one. This small crustacean swims in on the leading edge of a wave; as the wave recedes, it rapidly buries itself in the wet sand, facing the beach. The mole crab then raises its periscopes: a pair of eyes on the ends of long stalks, a set of antennae that forms a snorkel for breathing, and a feathery set of appendages that seine the next incoming wave for animal and vegetable matter. On occasion, you may see another resident of the intertidal zone: *Donax,* the coquina clam. These tiny, brightly colored clams glisten in the sun momentarily before they, too, burrow in the sand. They siphon the incoming waves for food. Coquina clams may be rare or incredibly abundant, depending on their demographics and the abundance of their parasites and predators at any given time.

The sun-blasted beach above the high tide mark is an even harsher environment for plants and animals than the intertidal zone. Fresh water is all but nonexistent, and the food supply can be highly variable. You're likely to run across only two kinds of animals here, both of whom feed on detritus—dead plant and animal matter. If you lie down on the beach, especially in late afternoon and while you're wet, you may notice tiny animals that hop about on your skin like jumping beans. These are beach hoppers (also known as beach fleas). They are amphipod crustaceans, with blue eyes and well-developed forelegs for jumping.

By far the most interesting resident of the forebeach, however, is the ghost crab. This drab, sand-colored crab ranges in size from immature, thumbnail-size specimens to husky indi-

viduals three inches across the shell. Ghost crabs live in burrows on the forebeach, notable for the scrabbling tracks in the
vicinity laid down by the occupant. These burrows may be
several feet deep, providing the crab with the cool, moist
environment needed for survival. Although you may see ghost
crabs during the day, scurrying sideways over the sand, night is
when they are most active and most easily observed. By late
summer, when the year's crop of juveniles swell the
population, an evening stroll along the beach will reveal a
density of several crabs per square foot, as far as the eye can see.
They will (almost) always avoid your footfall, but will crawl
across your foot if you stand in place. Ghost crabs feed on
almost anything they can find, alive or dead; they are true
omnivores.

After about two miles of walking, you may note a signpost
with the design of a tent on it, just visible over the low primary
dune. This is Sinepuxent, a designated backcountry campsite
for backpacking campers. It is the only one on the North
Beach, although two others may be found south of the developed area of Assateague.

The northern mile or two of Assateague Island is almost
devoid of dunes. Large areas of hard-packed sand, studded
with cobbles and flotsam, stretch from ocean to bayside. These
are known as washover flats and, as their name implies, result
from salt water incursions during major storms. The salt water
kills the sparse vegetation, making the sand more susceptible
to wind and water erosion. Once a washover flat is established,
it is very difficult to convert it into a dune-protected beach.

Washover flats are, however, important habitats for some
species of nesting shorebirds. Mixed colonies of terns, gulls,
plovers, and skimmers nest communally here, taking advantage of the lack of human traffic and the long sight lines along
which predators can be spotted and driven off. Nevertheless,
these species are extraordinarily sensitive to disturbance, and a
casual stroll through one of these colonies may be enough to
kill many nestlings by trampling and nest abandonment. Predatory gulls often hover nearby, waiting for the opportunity to
swoop down on unprotected eggs and nestlings. Therefore,

confine your walking to the intertidal zone when hiking here in the nesting season, late April through early August.

At last, after five miles of walking, you will run out of beach almost in the shadow of Ocean City. The contrast is remarkable. You are separated from Ocean City by a channelized inlet only a few hundred yards across. Created by the great storm of 1933, it must be regularly dredged to keep it open for the fishing and recreational fleet of West Ocean City. Currents here are swift and irregular, so avoid swimming anywhere near this end of the island.

The northern end of Assateague Island is several hundred feet west of the southern tip of Ocean City and is considerably narrower in width. The huge jetty at Ocean City interrupts the southerly flow of sand in the Atlantic, depositing it on the bathing beaches but robbing Assateague of its sandy lifeblood. Barrier islands like Assateague are dynamic, shifting landward or seaward depending on whether the forces of erosion or sand accumulation dominate. But the northern tip of Assateague has moved only westward toward the mainland in the last 40 years, and scientists expect that the island may fuse with the mainland sometime in the next 100 years.

As with all out-and-back hikes, you have now reached only the halfway point, so retrace your steps back to the state park. Fortunately, there are always new sights to see and novel discoveries to make on the return trip.

DIRECTIONS

From Baltimore or Washington, cross the Bay Bridge and continue south on Route 50 through Easton, Cambridge, and Salisbury. Just before the bridge to Ocean City, turn right on Route 611 at the prominent sign marking the Assateague Island National Seashore. Follow Route 611 for 5.8 miles, crossing the bridge onto Assateague Island. Continue straight ahead to the entrance kiosk for Assateague Island State Park. A fee is charged. Park in the bathing beach parking lot straight ahead.

OTHER OUTDOOR RECREATIONAL
OPPORTUNITIES NEARBY

Camping facilities are available at both the state park and the national seashore. The state park has hot-water showers and flush toilets; it is so popular that reservations are a must. The national seashore sites have only portable toilets and cold-water showers. In hot weather, a screen house is a virtual necessity, providing refuge from the sun and bugs. Because of the physical discomfort of camping on the beach, consider camping at the Shad Landing area of Pocomoke River State Park, about a 45-minute commute away.

Backpackers on North Beach must obtain a permit from the national seashore, which administers the island north of the offical state park bathing beach. Backpackers' vehicles cannot be left in the closer state park parking lot; they must be left at the national seashore entrance station, which is south of the state park.

It is possible to walk the many miles of beach south of the state park. If you're interested in solitude or nature, however, forget it. Bathers dominate the beach near campgrounds, while surf fishermen in oversand vehicles occupy the beach at regular intervals south to the Virginia line.

For bicyclists, a paved bike path traverses the length of the developed part of Assateague Island. It is described beginning on page 207 in this book.

Assateague Ponies

If there is one species that the public associates with Assateague Island, it is the feral ponies that have long been a part of the life and lore of Maryland's only natural barrier island. Legend has it that Assateague ponies are the descendants of the survivors of a shipwrecked seventeenth-century Spanish galleon. There is, however, no evidence that this romantic tale is true; the facts are far more pedestrian. Early colonists grazed their horses on Assateague because no fences were required, and natural forage was sufficient if not abundant.

There are two distinct pony herds on Assateague, separated by a fence crossing the island from ocean to bay at the Maryland-Virginia border. The Virginia herd is owned by the Chincoteague Volunteer Fire Company and managed with the assistance of the Chincoteague National Wildlife Refuge. Each year, excess foals are removed from the herd and sold in the famous Chincoteague "pony penning." The Maryland herd is treated as a wild population, receiving little or no veterinary care, forage supplements, or management.

Assateague ponies

When Assateague Island National Seashore was established in 1965, only about 20 ponies belonging to a landowner were found north of the Virginia line. These were bought by the National Park Service and are the progenitors of the present herd. In 1975, there were still only 27 horses, but by 1982 there were 80, and the population peaked in 1991 at 170 ponies. Scientific studies pegged the carrying capacity of the seashore at approximately 150 animals. For this reason, much effort has been expended in controlling the population by nonlethal methods.

The National Park Service herd is now controlled in two ways. First, excess ponies are rounded up and taken south to the National Wildlife Refuge, where they become part of the Chincoteague Volunteer Fire Company herd. This management strategy has the advantage of allowing ponies to remain on the island and visible to visitors. Second and more interestingly, the Assateague herd has been the subject of several experimental studies of artificial fertility control.

In 1986–87, chemical contraceptives were administered by dart gun to both mares and stallions. The drugs administered to mares were completely unsuccessful in preventing foaling; in fact, treated mares appeared to be *more* fertile than untreated mares! Male contraceptives proved difficult to administer, as stallions were very wary, and the darts often fell out before the full dose of drug was delivered. Clearly another approach was required.

In 1988, mares were injected with a vaccine that prevents pregnancy. This proved highly effective; only 1 out of the 26 mares treated foaled that year. The treatment was reversible, as about half of these mares gave birth the next year (when they were not vaccinated), a ratio similar to the pregnancy rates before the study began. In addition to being relatively inexpensive, effective, and reversible, this method did not affect pregnancies already in progress, did not affect pony behavior, and did not stress animals as do techniques requiring capture and surgery. This represented the first successful application of the technique of immunocontraception to uncaptured, free-roaming wild animals.

Although the population size of the Assateague pony herd has now stabilized, the horses do have significant effects on the native vegetation of the island. Large grazing animals process a great deal of vegetation, and urine and manure deposition may affect local soil and water chemistry. Visible effects of grazing and trampling can already be seen and may variably affect the many endemic, unusual, and endangered plant species on the island. Horses often graze the beach grass atop primary dunes, a process that accelerates erosion of the island's main protection against storm damage. Yet despite these negative effects, the ponies remain an intrinsic part of the Assateague experience, and visitors are the richer for their encounters with this most interesting species. ⚘

Nassawango Creek Preserve: Paul Leifer Trail and Furnace Town

County: Worcester

Distance: About 1 mile

Difficulty: Flat; sandy to muddy terain

Highlights: Bald cypress swamp, historic village

More Information: The Nature Conservancy (Maryland), (301) 656-8673. Furnace Town, (410) 632-2032

T HE CYPRESS SWAMPS of the Pocomoke River watershed are best explored by canoe, but for those who want to visit this unique habitat on foot, The Nature Conservancy has established the Paul Leifer Nature Trail. This woodchip and boardwalk path leads through the forest along the edge of Nassawango Creek, a major tributary of the Pocomoke. The trail is adjacent to Furnace Town, a partially restored iron smelter village dating from the early 1800s. Exhibits at Furnace Town portray daily life in this now remote but once busy and well-populated corner of Maryland.

Because of the difficulty of cutting trail through the boggy soil and tangled growth of swamps like this one, and the desire to disturb the swamp to the smallest extent possible, the Paul Leifer Trail is only about a mile in length. It is flat but can have puddles and muddy spots underfoot. Birdwatchers and wildflower lovers will want to go slowly, however, especially in late

Nassawango Creek Preserve: Paul Leifer Trail and Furnace Town

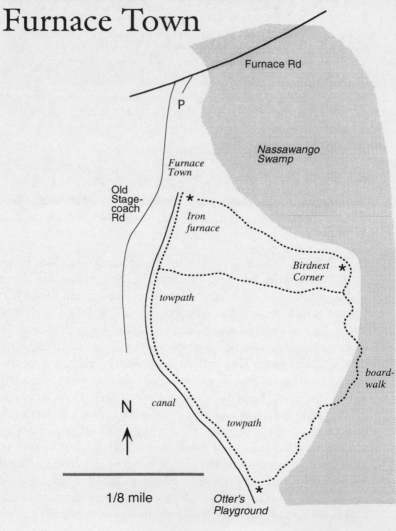

Furnace Rd

Nassawango
Swamp

P

Furnace
Town

Old
Stage-
coach
Rd

*
Iron
furnace

Birdnest
Corner *

towpath

board-
walk

N

canal

towpath

↑

Otter's
Playground *

1/8 mile

spring when flora and fauna are at their peak diversity. Combined with a tour of Furnace Town, the trail described here makes an easy half-day exploration.

TRIP DESCRIPTION

Access to the Paul Leifer Trail is across the property of Furnace Town. The nonprofit group operating and restoring the village asks you to register with them first, and an admission fee is charged. A small museum documenting life at the iron furnace is next door. Several other exhibits are scattered about the property in separate buildings. Restrooms, water, picnic tables, trash cans, and a soda machine are available here.

From the museum, walk toward the remains of the iron furnace. Made of brick, it is 35 feet high and 24 feet square at the base. Hot blast tubes at the top were a later addition, meant to increase the efficiency of burning. The furnace was loaded with a layer of charcoal, then a layer of bog iron, then oyster shells as a flux. This layering was repeated many times. A bellows run by a waterwheel provided oxygen to the mixture. When fired, the melted bog ore was let out at the casting hearth, the oyster shells removing impurities. Between 1828 and 1850, the iron furnace produced about 700 tons of pig iron annually.

The source of ore for the furnace was a peculiar complex of iron found in certain coastal plain streams and known as bog iron. As rainwater filters through the decaying vegetable matter of bogs, it assumes greater acidity. This acid water dissolves iron in the soil, which emerges as bluish slicks on the surface of still water, and in complex with sand as bog iron. This was the source of much of the iron smelted in the colonies and in the United States until about 1850, when purer sources of iron ore became available.

Begin at a bulletin board in back of the smelter. The trail is roughly in the shape of a figure eight; casual visitors generally prefer the shorter circuit. The first portion of the trail runs along the edge of the swamp. To the left, the land is about a foot lower in elevation, putting it in the floodplain of Nassawango Creek. The black, mucky soil, rich in organic matter, is also relatively poor in oxygen. For this reason, anaerobic bacteria lend the characteristic "rotten egg" smell associated with wet areas.

The hydric soil conditions limit the kinds of plants that can grow there; almost all of them are specific to wetlands. Look for sphagnum moss lying directly on the substrate. Although it is not as deep or as widespread here as in a true bog like Cranesville in western Maryland, sphagnum is an obligate wetland plant. Its foliage was used to dress wounds during the Civil War because bacteria could not live in the acidic water trapped among the leaves. The bright red spike of the cardinal flower decorates these wetlands in late summer. Cinnamon ferns are very common here—large, graceful ferns easily identified by "hairy armpits": the base of each leaflet where it joins the stalk has a tuft of brown "hairs."

The wetland forest is dominated by bald cypress, coniferous trees that shed their needles each autumn. They are easily identified by their stringy, fibrous, reddish brown bark and the many "knees" that often surround the trunks. Other trees in the swamp include sweetgum and holly on higher sites and the ubiquitous red maple. These forests have been cut repeatedly since colonial times, supplying charcoal for the operation of the furnace.

At the first sharp turn, known as Birdnest Corner, look for woodpeckers and, in spring, prothonotary warblers nesting in cavities in several swamp trees. The latter, with bright yellow chests and heads and bluish wings, are both spectacular and engaging, chasing each other in territorial displays during the month of May. Prothonotaries may be the defining bird of wooded swamps in southern Maryland, and they are a favorite of birdwatchers everywhere. At least 14 species of warblers raise their young in this dense swamp.

Just a bit farther up the trail, look for depressions in the swamp. These are the sites where bog ore was mined more than 150 years ago, and they indicate the slow rate of the recovery that some fragile lands make from human insults.

River otter

Just ahead are a trail junction and a sign dedicating the path to Paul Leifer, a longtime member of The Nature Conservancy. The Nature Conservancy owns nearly 3,000 acres in the Nassawango Creek watershed, constituting its largest property in Maryland. The right fork returns you promptly to Furnace Town. You should bear left.

The trail now enters a more broken part of the forest, where upland hammocks alternate with wetland swamps. Accordingly, frequent boardwalks link the stretches of dry ground so that foot traffic does not trample the fragile vegetation and soils and so that you can view the swamp closely and with dry feet.

After at least a half mile, the trail reaches its deepest penetration into the woods. Ahead the trail turns right to parallel the remains of an old canal. This canal allowed pig iron to be floated from the furnace to Nassawango Creek, and thence down the Pocomoke to distant ports. This point is known as the Otter's Playground; in winter, river otters slide down the bank into the icy water over and over again.

The trail runs straight now, directly back to the furnace, on a berm of soil excavated when the canal was built. This upland section of the forest is a habitat distinct from the wetland swamp forest. It is dominated by loblolly pine; water, red, and white oak; holly; sweetgum; and dogwood. Many of the oaks have been damaged by gypsy moths. Among the more unusual flora, look for muscadine grape vines twining over branches and with stringlike aerial roots. Like many other life forms inhabiting the Nassawango watershed, they are at the northern edge of their distribution here. Greenbrier and poison ivy are other common vines that make trailblazing difficult in these areas. In May, pink lady's slipper orchids brighten the forest floor, especially under pine trees. Indeed, 15 species of orchids have been counted in the Pocomoke River watershed.

After about a mile, the trail returns to the furnace area, where your walk is concluded.

DIRECTIONS

From Baltimore or Washington, take Route 50 across the Bay Bridge to Salisbury. In the downtown area, turn right on Route 12. After about 15 miles, turn right on Old Furnace Road, where there is a sign for Furnace Town. Proceed about a mile to the park entrance. Furnace Town is open daily from 11 A.M. to 5 P.M. Access to the Paul Leifer Trail coincides with Furnace Town's hours of operation.

OTHER OUTDOOR RECREATIONAL OPPORTUNITIES NEARBY

Canoe access to Nassawango Creek is just a mile or so away, and the creek is a beautiful place to canoe. The Pocomoke River and Corkers Creek are just a bit farther away; see descriptions of all three in the canoeing section of this book.

Why Save Endangered Species?

Since the passage of the Endangered Species Act by the United States Congress in 1972, the general public has expressed great interest in rare and unusual organisms. This has been especially true of large, beautiful animals ("charismatic megafauna") like wolves and eagles. The immense majority of species considered endangered, however, are neither big nor especially attractive, and most are not even animals. For example, Maryland, which has assembled its own list of rare, endangered, and threatened species within the state, listed 121 animals and 497 plants in 1993. Among the animals, very few naturalists have even heard of, let alone seen, such unusual individuals as the green floater (a mollusc), Walker's tusked sprawler (an insect), the Cheat minnow (a fish), or the southern pygmy shrew (a mammal). The plants are even more obscure: twining bartonia, shaved sedge, anglepod, floating paspalum, and a host of others. Fungi, bacteria, and algae have never been investigated, let alone listed.

Why this interest in such obscure organisms? Three general reasons for preserving endangered species have been put forth.

First, such species may have an important use to humankind at some point in the future. In medical science, plant extracts are sometimes useful in therapies. In addition to being a source of drugs, plants are our primary source of food. Modern food plants are highly inbred strains whose ancestors and close relatives should be preserved as a source of genetic diversity for breeding in specialized traits that might be required in the future. Animals can also be useful. For example, the armadillo (although not endangered) is the best experimental model for the study of leprosy. In essence, preservation of all species ensures more options for the future.

Second, endangered species are biological indicators of the health of the ecological community in which they reside. Most species are endangered because of the action or activity of humans in that community, whether it be loss of habitat via human modification, pollution, or the introduction of nonnative species. As bioindicators, they report to us on the status of the natural world and what effect our activities have.

Third, rare species should be conserved for aesthetic reasons. Even though they are obscure, many of these organisms enrich our appreciation and enjoyment of the natural world. They may have no economic value, but they are nonetheless valuable.

Finally, as the dominant life form on our planet today, humans have a moral responsibility to other organisms. Extinctions are a commonplace occurrence in the natural world, but the pace of extinctions is far greater now than at any time in the past. The only reason for this high rate of extinction is our own shortsighted and careless attitude toward other living things.

These are all altruistic reasons, good for humankind as a group as well as for the organisms in question. But individuals may not be able or willing to practice such altruistic behavior. For example, developers who are prevented from building on a piece of land because it harbors an endangered species invariably feel that an exception should be made and development allowed, or that they should be duly compensated by society. The controversy over the spotted owl in the forests of the Pacific Northwest is a case in point.

In the past, concern for endangered species has led to a never-ending sequence of crises to be dealt with rather than a farsighted, carefully planned strategy for preservation. In addition, management by crisis has been expensive in terms of time, personnel, and money (especially legal fees). Most recovery programs deal with showy or charismatic species, but these are merely the most obvious representatives of a cast that includes thousands of supporting players that make up the foundation of the ecological community. Scientists and environmental activists believe that conservation now must go beyond merely a concern for species that are rare. Emphasis should now be placed on conservation of biological diversity, on the entire range of organisms in the context of their environment. The advantage of such an approach lies in its flexibility, timeliness, and cost effectiveness. If critical habitats and hotspots of biodiversity can be identified and preserved, other less critical parts of the landscape will be available for human activities. ✶

Calvert Cliffs State Park

County: Calvert

Distance: 3.6 miles

Difficulty: Mostly flat with a few small rises; sandy terrain

Highlights: View of Calvert Cliffs, bay beach, fossil-bearing gravels, coastal plain forest

More Information: Calvert Cliffs State Park, (410) 888-1622

THE STATE OF MARYLAND has many natural resources within its boundaries, but perhaps none is more famous (and justifiably so) than the paleontological site at Calvert Cliffs. For at least the last 150 years, fossils of scientific import have been extracted from the cliffs and have been studied at facilities as prestigious as the Smithsonian Institution. In addition, generations of young students have had their interest piqued and imaginations excited by the treasure trove of fossilized shark teeth found in the wave-washed gravel at the base of the cliffs.

The cliffs containing the fossil-bearing strata stretch almost 30 miles, from Fairhaven to Drum Point. Most of the coast is privately owned, and public access to the cliffs is not possible without the specific permission of the landowners. Only at a few places like Calvert Cliffs State Park can the public view the sandy bluffs. Unfortunately, the threat of excavation of the cliffs by visitors and the resultant increased rate of erosion, as well as the danger of cliff collapse, has caused the Department of Natural Resources to prohibit public access to the cliffs and adjacent shoreline. What remains for the visitor to the bayfront is a short, narrow stretch of beach about 100 yards long where you can pan the intertidal gravel or view the cliffs.

Calvert Cliffs State Park

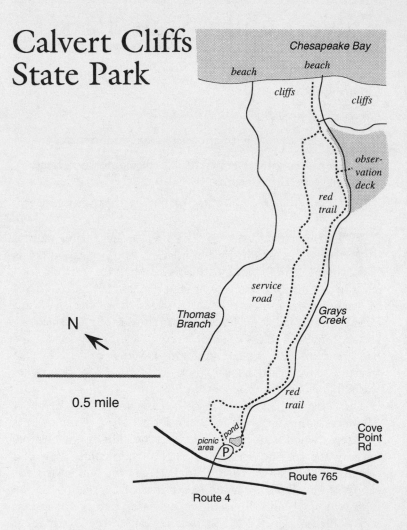

Chesapeake Bay

beach

beach

cliffs

cliffs

obser-
vation
deck

red
trail

service
road

Thomas
Branch

Grays
Creek

N

0.5 mile

red
trail

picnic
area

pond

P

Cove
Point
Rd

Route 765

Route 4

There are a number of trails winding through Calvert Cliffs State Park, but the most direct route to the water is on the red blazed trail. Fortunately, it is also a very scenic one, winding through a beautiful coastal plain forest rich with ferns and bird life. As such, it makes a nice destination for a family hike, a morning birdwalk, or an afternoon of botanizing. The walk described totals 3.6 miles round trip.

TRIP DESCRIPTION

Calvert Cliffs is a small park, and its developed area, just a few yards off Route 4, occupies only two or three acres. There are parking places for more than 100 cars, a wheelchair-accessible outhouse, a number of picnic tables, and a large playground for children. A small fishing pond is adjacent to the parking lot, and it is popular with local kids. All hiking trails depart from this area.

The most direct trail to the bayfront is the red trail, denoted by colored triangles attached to wooden posts or trees. Running alongside a small stream, Grays Creek, for its entire length, it is also the most interesting in terms of scenic beauty and wildlife. Leaving the parking lot at the uphill side of the pond, it skirts the water's edge, where croaking frogs can be heard and turtles and dragonflies seen. The trail then enters the woods. Although the trail has only slight dips and rises, the many roots crossing its path make for uneven footing. Also striking is the hilly nature of the land, unusual for a site in the coastal plain near the Bay. Although the hills are small (less than 50 feet in height), they give the land a dissected feel that also creates varying microhabitats, depending on the direction the hillside faces, its degree of shading, and its nearness to surface water.

As might be expected, the soil is a fine white sand enriched by organic matter only near the surface. Some parts of the trail are incised into the hill, and these exposures are a good place to examine the various layers of soil. Sandy soils are considered dry soils; if you were to pour a bucket of water onto sand, it would rapidly percolate through, draining from the interstices between the tiny, rock-hard grains. Thus, even in a well-watered climate, sandy soils are xeric in nature and support only those plant species that can exist in water- and nutrient-poor soil. For this reason, mountain laurel, blueberry, and spotted wintergreen are common in the shrub layer at Calvert Cliffs, and chestnut oak and Virginia pine are common trees. Drought-tolerant mosses hug the ground and help retain moisture for tiny insects and other forest floor inhabitants.

Because the trail follows the stream, however, water is more accessible to species living in its floodplain and diversifies the flora. Sweet gum, tulip poplar, American beech, white oak, and red maple are all commonly found here. Many specimens are quite tall, and the straight trunks and lack of low branches on tulip poplar and sweet gum trees give the forest an open feel. Cinnamon ferns, Christmas ferns, and interrupted ferns dot the forest floor near the stream.

After about three-quarters of a mile, the stream spreads out and meanders into a swamp. An earthen berm occupies the far end of the little valley, backing up the waters into an artificial nontidal wetland. Many of the trees in the swamp are doing poorly and appear to be dead except for a few branches of green leaves. Virtually every tree in this swamp is green ash, a hardy, water-tolerant tree that assumes this style of growth under hydric conditions. Note that not a single green ash can be found anywhere else in the forest; it is unable to compete with other species on upland, well-drained sites. The many dead snags make fine perches for birds like osprey, hawks, kingfishers, and herons, and birdwatching here can be rewarding, especially in the spring. A short boardwalk leads out to an observation deck, which offers a good platform for viewing both birds and the many turtles found here.

If you're observant, you'll note a beaver lodge near the middle of the swamp. These beavers often add sticks and branches to the water outlet in the berm, in an effort to raise water levels in the swamp. Park staff clear these branches periodically, managing the swamp not just for beaver but also for wood duck, who prefer a lower, muckier water level.

Within 200 yards of the berm, you arrive at Chesapeake Bay. There are fine views of the Calvert Cliffs to both the north and the south, although access to the base of the cliffs is blocked by hurricane fences. The cliffs undergo continual erosion, especially during winter storms, and can be dangerous where undercut. They are home to one of Maryland's endangered species, the puritan tiger beetle. This little beetle, less than an inch long, is known from about 10 sites in Calvert County and from one other site along the Connecticut River. Its larval stage lives in the cliffs; when adults emerge to mate in early summer, they use the narrow stretches of nearby beach.

The gravel intertidal at the Calvert Cliffs can be a good place to look for fossil shark teeth, especially after a storm event that erodes the cliffs. The occasional three-inch great white shark tooth is found, but the smaller teeth are by far the most common. First-timers often fail to realize that such teeth are *really* tiny—a quarter to a half inch long. Keep your eyes open! Your search can be made more efficient by use of a trowel and sieve.

No swimming is allowed at this beach. Behind the beach, under the shade of the forest trees, are six picnic tables and an outhouse. Return to your car by the same red trail, or choose one of the other trails if you prefer a different route. All lead back to the parking lot. The park is popular with mountain bikers; only the red trail described above is closed to them. Bicyclists intent only on reaching the Bay as quickly as possible may use the gravel service road (closed to public vehicles) that approximately parallels the red trail.

DIRECTIONS

From the Baltimore Beltway, take Route 3/301 south to Route 4, near Upper Marlboro. From Washington, take the Route 4 exit off the Capital Beltway. From the Route 4/Route 3 intersection at Upper Marlboro, continue south on Route 4 for about 30 miles. The entrance to Calvert Cliffs State Park is well marked and comes just after the entrance to Calvert Cliffs Nuclear Power Station.

OTHER OUTDOOR RECREATIONAL OPPORTUNITIES NEARBY

Flag Ponds Nature Park is located just a few miles to the north and has hiking trails and a mile of beachfront for swimming. It is described beginning on page 37 in this book. Baltimore Gas and Electric's Calvert Cliffs Nuclear Power Station, which connects Calvert Cliffs State Park with Flag Ponds Nature Park, has recently opened a nature trail to the public; ask at the entrance station.

Miocene Fossils

Although fossils may be found in several areas of Maryland, by far the best-known deposits are those at Calvert Cliffs and the adjacent Chesapeake Bay shoreline. Indeed, these eroded bluffs yielded the first American fossil (of the mollusc *Ecphora quadricostata*) to be described in the scientific literature, all the way back in 1685. Since then, generations of scientists, knowledgeable amateur collectors, and curious citizens have searched the cliffs and the wave-tossed gravels at their base for fossilized shells, shark teeth, and whatever else the action of wind and water might erode out.

The animals whose remains form these fossils lived long ago. Between 10 and 20 million years ago, during a geological epoch called the middle Miocene, a shallow ocean covered much of what is now southern Maryland. Its waters lapped gently against a shoreline located just east of present-day Washington, D.C. The climate was warmer than it is now, more similar to that of modern South Carolina, and forests of scrub oak, pine, and bald cypress dominated the dunes and marshes along the shore. Out in the fairly warm, calm waters of the ocean, a profusion of plants and animals lived and died, linked in a complex food chain. The shells, bones, and teeth of dead animals, resistant to bacterial and chemical degradation, settled gently to the bottom, where they were covered with mud and

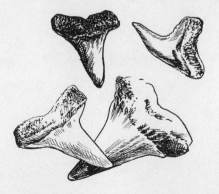

Shark teeth

fine sand. Over time, mineralization may have occurred, fossilizing the remains, but some shells and teeth remained unaltered. Sediments containing these fossils built up for millions of years into a 300-foot-thick band now known as the Chesapeake Group. More than 600 species of fossilized plants and animals have been classified from these sediments, including molluscs, arthropods, fish, reptiles, birds, and mammals.

Much of the fossil-containing cliffs in Calvert County are private land, and access to them requires permission. Even so, digging is never allowed, as this would hasten the rate of erosion. For these reasons, the fossils most commonly found are shark's teeth gleaned from the shoreline gravels at public beaches adjacent to the cliffs. They range in size from tiny teeth a few millimeters long to five-inch monsters from an extinct species of great white shark. Small teeth are plentiful and, once you develop an eye for them, easy to find. Indeed, it's hard to believe that this many sharks could have lived here! To explain this abundance, recent studies have shown that sharks replace their teeth as often as every eight days. Whatever the origin of this paleontological bounty, it represents a window into Maryland's past that never fails to excite the imaginations of young and old alike. 𝔨

Flag Ponds Nature Park

County: Calvert

Distance: About 2 miles

Difficulty: Gently rolling; sandy to muddy terrain

Highlights: Coastal plain forest, swamp, beach, fossil-bearing gravels

More Information: Flag Ponds Nature Park, (410) 535-5327

FLAG PONDS NATURE PARK is a little-known gem of a park just up the road from its better-known cousin, Calvert Cliffs State Park. Owned and operated by Calvert County, Flag Ponds is not just a conservation reserve and environmental education facility, as its name implies, but also an outdoor recreational park. With a mile of waterfront on Chesapeake Bay and a clean, wide swimming beach, Flag Ponds is a great place to take the family on a hot summer's day.

Flag Ponds is named for the three small ponds located just inland from the beach, where the wild iris (or flag) blooms in profusion each May. A trail system passes by the ponds and winds through the adjacent uplands. A fascinating historical display adds to the items of interest in the 327-acre park.

The Duncan's Pond Trail described here passes through a variety of habitats and gives an overview of natural communities in the rich, rolling hills of southern Maryland's western shore. Much of it is narrow and can be muddy after rains. Another section traverses a green ash-maple swamp via a boardwalk; bring along insect repellent in warm weather. The total distance is approximately two miles. Continuing on the

Flag Ponds Nature Park

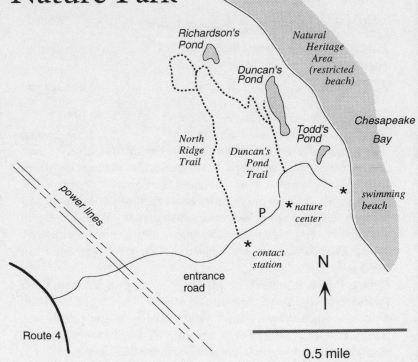

Richardson's Pond

Natural Heritage Area (restricted beach)

Duncan's Pond

North Ridge Trail

Duncan's Pond Trail

Todd's Pond

Chesapeake Bay

*swimming beach

P

* *nature center*

* *contact station*

power lines

entrance road

N

↑

Route 4

0.5 mile

beach adds about another half mile round trip, although the park will transport you via a shuttle bus in summer.

TRIP DESCRIPTION

All visitors to the park are met by staff at the contact station on the park's edge. They take the time to explain what is available at the park, a luxury not usually found in busier or less attentive parks. An entrance fee is charged. The main parking lot is a few hundred yards farther down the dirt and gravel road, near the nature center. Available here are bathrooms, water, a soda machine, shaded picnic tables, and, often, a naturalist on duty. On weekends in beach season, a shuttle bus picks up and drops off bathers intent only on reaching the beach. It's a shame that these sun worshipers don't take a few minutes to walk the trails, for the forest at Flag Ponds is a most cool and pleasant one.

Begin your walk at the nature center, and take the road downhill, through the gate, and past the first trail on your left. The second one on your left, marked as the Duncan's Pond Trail, leads off into a dense woods. If you have just come from Calvert Cliffs State Park, you'll immediately notice that Flag Ponds has a higher density of trees. This is especially true in the understory layer; the small trees are larger than shrubs but do not reach the sunlight at the treetop level. Although Flag Ponds is separated from Calvert Cliffs by only a few miles and possesses an identical geology, the availability of soil moisture at Flag Ponds makes all the difference. More water means more growth, and so the yearly loss of leaves provides more organic matter to enrich the soil. The resulting higher level of nutrients in the soil and increased ability to retain moisture in turn promote more growth. The species mix of trees is similar to that at Calvert Cliffs; it is just the density that is higher.

As you walk the Duncan's Pond Trail, you'll see one tree that's not common at Calvert Cliffs: the Eastern red cedar. Actually, most of the specimens here at Flag Ponds are dead, their dry wood giving off that peculiar incense so reminiscent of clothes closets and Victorian dressers. The reason for their presence, as well as their demise, is found in the past history of the area. Cedars are dry- to moderate-soil transgressives—small trees that colonize a site early, before a forest can develop. Old photographs available in park displays show that the land near the water was once more open, cleared by fishermen who used the shore for storage of their long pound net poles. Cedars occupied the back edge of this area. After abandonment, natural succession took over, and as larger trees were allowed to grow they shaded and crowded out the cedars. Today only splintered trunks and branches remain.

A side trail leads to an observation platform and blind on the edge of Duncan's Pond. The shores of this pond are filled with cattails and other marsh plants. Increasingly, the forest is encroaching into the pond, annually reducing its acreage by sedimentation. Without any inflow or outflow, Duncan's and several other ponds nearby become solar-powered incubators for duckweed in the summer. This most simple of the higher plants covers the ponds in a dense monolayer by late spring. Dragonflies patrol the pond's surface, and birds peculiar to the season haunt the reeds: red-winged blackbirds in late spring and summer, ducks in late fall.

The trail continues through the forest, eventually opening onto a boardwalk. This boardwalk traverses a few hundred yards of open swamp dominated by red maple and green ash. Only a few herbaceous plants grow from the shady, algae- and duckweed-covered mudflats and pools. The open nature of the forest here makes it easy to spot forest birds, and the junction of swamp and nearby wooded uplands augurs well for a diversity of species. Look for wood ducks, pileated woodpeckers, warblers, and owls.

The trail emerges from the swamp and soon heads uphill along an escarpment. A shortcut trail bears left; turn right instead for a slightly longer walk through a pleasant upland woods. Now called the North Ridge Trail, this path eventually returns you to the contact station.

Now is the time to retrace your steps past the nature center and down the road to the beach. There's an interesting display at a restored fisherman's shanty, documenting the history of the area. From 1915 to 1958, what is now Flag Ponds was the site of a commercial pound net fishery, where immense hauls of fish were taken from the bay and shipped to Baltimore, Washington, and other cities. The site was a popular one because of its wide beach sheltered on either end by the Calvert Cliffs and accessible to the deep water of Chesapeake Bay only a short distance offshore. This very efficient method of fishing diminished stocks so much that the fishery ceased being profitable by the 1950s.

The area around the fisherman's shanty resembles the secondary dunes of a barrier island like Assateague. Growing here are stunted loblolly pines, bayberry, and even a few prickly pear cacti. The trail quickly emerges from the trees onto the beach.

There's plenty of room for sunbathers to spread out on the beach and almost a mile of walking for the beachcomber. As at Calvert Cliffs, shark teeth can be found in the intertidal gravel, and they may be more common here since fewer visitors look for them. The beach at Flag Ponds is also home to an endangered species of tiger beetle, the northeastern beach tiger beetle. This small predaceous invertebrate spends its two-year larval stage in a burrow in the sandy beach, capturing small organisms that wander near. The adult "beetle" stage is shorter lived, being found on the beach in mid-summer. The beetle was once widespread up the coast as far north as Massachusetts, but there are now only about 10 populations, confined to Maryland and Virginia beaches. Human activity and development on beaches are the primary reason for this tiger beetle's decline; some portions of the beach at Flag Ponds may be fenced off for this reason.

The Calvert Cliffs rise at the far end of the beach in each direction, and the Calvert Cliffs Nuclear Power Station is visible to the south. The park also maintains a small fishing pier for anglers.

DIRECTIONS

From the Baltimore Beltway, take Route 3/301 south to Upper Marlboro. From the Capital Beltway, take the Route 50 exit to Upper Marlboro. From Upper Marlboro, follow Route 4 south for about 28 miles to the sign for Flag Ponds Nature Park. If you get to the entrance to the Calvert Cliffs Nuclear Power Station, you've gone too far.

OTHER OUTDOOR RECREATIONAL OPPORTUNITIES NEARBY

Calvert Cliffs State Park is located just a few miles to the south and is described beginning on page 29 in this book. Baltimore Gas and Electric's Calvert Cliffs Nuclear Power Station, which connects Calvert Cliffs State Park with Flag Ponds Nature Park, has recently opened a nature trail to the public; ask at the entrance station.

The Exuberance of Beetles

The eminent nineteenth-century evolutionary biologist Thomas H. Huxley was once asked by a clergyman what instruction might be taken from a study of natural history regarding God's plan for the universe. Huxley, tongue planted firmly in cheek, replied that God must have an inordinate fondness for beetles, given that there are so many of them. Indeed, there are more species of beetles in the order Coleoptera than there are species in any other order of plant or animal. This incredible diversification of a simple life form is one of the most striking and as yet unexplained patterns in nature.

Of the 1.5 million species of organisms now known to science, almost half are insects. There are more species of insects than of all other animals combined, and the total weight of all insects exceeds the weight of all other animals on earth, despite their diminutive size. Of the insect species, about half, or 300,000, are beetles. Scientists can only speculate on the reasons for this extensive diversification of the coleopterans. They probably evolved during the Mesozoic era about 200 million years ago; thus they are no more ancient than reptiles or amphibians. Beetles occupy virtually all terrestrial habitats; some are herbivores, some carnivores, and some detritivores.

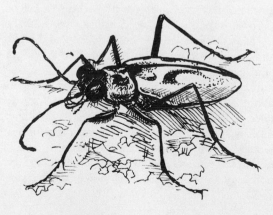

Northeastern beach tiger beetle

Beetles are characterized by horny or leathery forewings that meet in a straight line down the back. These forewings are sometimes brightly colored and iridescent, enhancing beetles' appeal to collectors. Hindwings are membranous and are used in flight. Mouthparts, wonderfully diversified, are modified for chewing. Here in Maryland, beetles are common, especially in forested ecosystems. Among the most rare is the endangered northeastern beach tiger beetle.

It is this large variety of beetles that has led, in large part, to a reassessment of our view of biological diversity and the role of taxonomy in science. The identification and classification of organisms preoccupied science from the time of Linnaeus through the early twentieth century. Since then, technology and advances in inferential disciplines like biochemistry and molecular biology have shifted the emphasis (and funding) for the biological sciences. Today there are so few taxonomists that expertise in some obscure groups may reside in only a single researcher. Since the mid-1980s, however, there has been increased recognition that we need to discover, identify, and preserve our planet's living heritage before the inexorable spread of human culture causes the extinction of species as yet unknown.

This recognition came about from the study of beetles associated with tropical trees. In 1982, a Smithsonian Institution scientist sprayed an insecticidal fog into the canopy of a huge tropical rain forest tree and collected whatever fell on plastic sheets. To his astonishment, he identified over 1,200 species of beetles, many of them species new to science, and 162 of which were obligately associated with this one tree species. Extrapolating the data using a few simple assumptions, he estimated the total number of species on earth at as many as 30 million. Since only about 1.5 million species have currently been described, and since much of this diversity resides in fast-disappearing tropical ecosystems, scientists realized that much of our biological heritage might become extinct before we even knew it existed. Thus the exuberance of beetles has been the catalyst for a reanalysis of the significance of biological diversity on our planet. ⚑

Elk Neck State Park

County: Cecil

Distance: 3.2 miles

Difficulty: Hilly; sandy terrain

Highlights: Views of Chesapeake Bay, forest

More Information: Elk Neck State Park, (410) 287-5333

WHEN MOST PEOPLE think of a Chesapeake Bay landscape, they visualize low flatlands gradually giving way to extensive marshes dappled with open water. Wide, sweeping vistas reminiscent of the western prairies are quintessential Chesapeake country. And so it is for a great deal of the more than 7,000 miles of Bay shoreline. In a few areas, however, dramatic cliffs rise directly from wave-pounded beaches, eroding steadily landward against the relentless assaults of water and time. Elk Neck is like that: a high triangular peninsula jutting southwest into the upper Bay, separating the Susquehanna Flats from the tidal Elk River. Much of the lower four miles of the peninsula is preserved as Elk Neck State Park, and there are several good hiking trails. Perhaps the best is the Turkey Point Trail detailed here. Traversing forest and field with fine views of the water, the trail eventually reaches the shores of Chesapeake Bay. It features the site of an old lighthouse, where traces of the past suggest to the imagination the trials and pleasures of rural life in the last century.

This is an easy, wide trail with a few gentle hills. It is well eroded in spots, however, and so is probably not suitable for strollers or wheelchairs. Round trip distance is 3.2 miles.

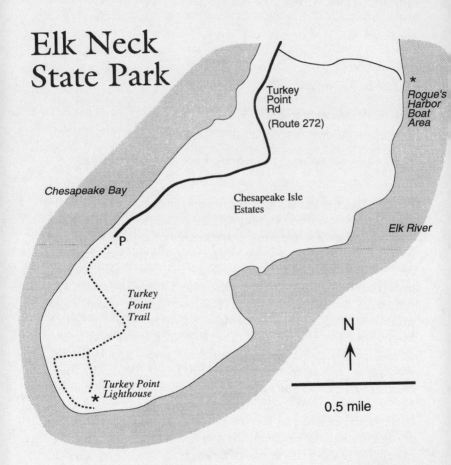

Elk Neck
State Park

Turkey
Point
Rd

(Route 272)

★
Rogue's
Harbor
Boat
Area

Chesapeake Bay

Chesapeake Isle
Estates

Elk River

P

Turkey
Point
Trail

N

↑

0.5 mile

Turkey Point
Lighthouse
★

TRIP DESCRIPTION

Begin your walk from the parking lot at the southernmost tip of Route 272. There is room for about 25 cars in this dirt and gravel lot, but no other facilities. (Bathrooms, drinking water, and telephones are available in the developed section of Elk Neck State Park, just off Route 272 before you reach the trailhead.) The trail is an old gravel, sand, and dirt road that is now gated; with the exception of the occasional patrolling park ranger, pedestrians are its sole traffic.

The first quarter mile leads slightly uphill through a sparsely wooded forest. The trail runs along the cliff edge; by walking only a few steps to the right, you can look down on the calm waters of the Chesapeake through gaps in the trees. When leaves fall in late autumn, the views across miles of open water toward Aberdeen Proving Ground are superb. Take care to keep small children in hand; not only are the cliffs almost vertical, but in some places erosion has significantly undercut them. Keep several feet away from the edge.

The road soon bears left, away from the cliffs, and leads across open fields bordered with shrubs and small trees of varying ages. These diverse habitats augur well for birding, and deer are commonly seen in the early morning and at dusk. Indeed, the deer population on Elk Neck is quite large, judging from the well-browsed understory. This poses a management dilemma for the park, since surplus animals have nowhere to go. With Bay waters on two sides and increasing human development on the third, the deer exist on what is essentially an island of habitat.

After just over a half mile of walking, you will come to a side trail posted with the symbol of a hiker. Take this branch to the left. Another quarter mile leads you to Turkey Point Light-house, now abandoned. It sits in the middle of a large field, for its builders had enough foresight to construct it well back from the edge of the eroding cliff. Stone fenceposts mark an old corral, and a few other crumbling ruins dot the land. The remains of abandoned garden plots are scattered about as well.

White-tailed deer

Views of the Bay are excellent, but once again be sure to stay away from the edge.

Return to the main road and turn left. The road leads downhill, dropping steadily to emerge at the Bay's shoreline. In order to curb erosion, the state has lined most of the bayfront with large, carefully constructed stone dikes. The service road put in during construction runs between the dike and the cliffs, allowing you to walk (to the left) along more than a half mile of bayfront. The rocks are popular with fishermen and picnickers.

The stone riprap eventually gives out, and further progress is no longer possible since the cliffs reach directly into the water. Return to your car by the same route.

DIRECTIONS

From Baltimore, take I-95 north. After crossing the Susquehanna River, take exit 100, Route 272 south. Proceed to the end of the road.

OTHER OUTDOOR RECREATIONAL
OPPORTUNITIES NEARBY

Elk Neck State Park features camping and picnic areas, a few other shorter walking trails, a swimming beach, and a boat ramp.

What Is Biodiversity?

There are few concepts in science today more fashionable—and more misunderstood—than biological diversity. Everyone is for biological diversity; like Mom, apple pie, rain forests, and whales, it is a modern cause célèbre. Yet most people have only a hazy understanding of what biological diversity (usually referred to as biodiversity) really is. Even among scientists there is sometimes disagreement.

One of the simplest yet most complete definitions of biodiversity is "the variety and variability among living organisms and the ecological complexes in which they occur." This definition implies that there are at least three components of biodiversity: variety of ecological communities within an ecosystem; numbers of species; and genetic variation among individuals.

Community diversity is perhaps the easiest to understand. It is merely the variety of habitats found within an ecosystem. For example, a barrier island ecosystem like Assateague Island contains several habitats: intertidal zone, beach, dunes, shrub zone, maritime forest, salt marsh, and freshwater pools. Different kinds of plants and animals live in each habitat. The more habitat types there are, the greater is the area's community diversity.

A second component of biodiversity is species diversity. This refers to the number of species present within a habitat. For example, the species diversity of a cornfield is rather low; there is only one plant species present (corn), and for this reason the number of species of insects, fungi, soil bacteria, birds, and small mammals is correspondingly low. By comparison, a similarly sized plot of abandoned farmland has a diverse collection of organisms. It will contain more species of every one of these groups of organisms, and it therefore harbors greater species diversity.

The most difficult to understand component of biodiversity is genetic diversity. This term applies to the variety of information coded for in the genes of different members of any one species. For example, wolves were once widely distributed throughout North America. Certain races or subspecies of wolves were specifically adapted to particular habitats; those found in the southern swamps were remarkably different from those of the northern tundra, in both physical appearance and behavior. Although these two races of wolves could interbreed, their individual genetic makeups were different enough that any blurring of them would impoverish the gene pool that serves as the basis for future natural selection and evolution. We have no idea what traits will be important for the future survival of a species, so conservation biology advises us to preserve all of the raw materials upon which natural selection acts. As Aldo Leopold said, "To keep every cog and wheel is the first precaution of intelligent tinkering."

Preservation of biodiversity therefore consists of more than merely saving rare or endangered species. On the largest scale, it encompasses preservation of landscapes and the habitats they contain. It applies to both rare and common species, valuing neither one over the other. And it implies that subtle genetic differences within a species over its entire geographic range have importance for evolution and should therefore be conserved. These principles are not trivial; they represent a paradigm shift in the way we look at and live with the natural world. ⸙

Susquehanna River Trail

County: Harford

Distance: 6.1 miles round trip

Difficulty: Flat; sandy to muddy terrain

Highlights: River valley forest, spring wildflowers

More Information: Philadelphia Electric Company, Conowingo Dam, (410) 879-2000. Susquehanna State Park,
(410) 939-0643

BIRDING AND BOTANIZING are two of the favorite activities of hikers who get out into natural
Maryland. The trail along the west bank of the Susquehanna River in the northeastern corner of the state is
among the best for both of these two hobbies, and it is largely
unknown outside the local community of diehard birders and
wildflower enthusiasts. Now the secret is out.

The hike described here traverses both public and private
land and represents an unusual cooperation between private
industry and state government. The winners, fortunately, are
all of us. Philadelphia Electric Company in particular is to be
congratulated for its preservation of the alluvial flats and steep,
rocky slopes that extend downriver from Conowingo Dam.
The site is known officially as the Shures Landing Wildflower
Viewing Area; Philadelphia Electric provides amenities and
comforts at the starting point, as well as protection of the
resource itself.

This hike is an easy one over flat terrain. After the first mile,
however, the trail is typically muddy in places, so wear appropriate footgear. There are plans to develop this trail into a

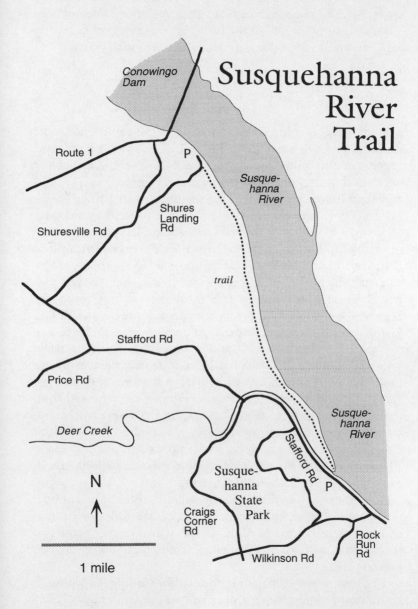

Susquehanna
River
Trail

Conowingo
Dam

Route 1

P

Susque-
hanna
River

Shures
Landing
Rd

Shuresville Rd

trail

Stafford Rd

Price Rd

Deer Creek

Susque-
hanna
River

Stafford Rd

P

N

↑

Susque-
hanna
State
Park

Craigs
Corner
Rd

Rock
Run
Rd

1 mile

Wilkinson Rd

wider, all-weather, packed sand path suitable for bicycles and strollers; call Susquehanna State Park for more information. The distance to the end of the little peninsula is three miles one way, but you can turn around whenever you wish.

TRIP DESCRIPTION

The hike begins from Shures Landing at the south end of the Conowingo Dam parking lot. Either before or after your walk, check out the public activity at the base of the dam, at the north end of the lot. Fishermen are everywhere, in all seasons and at all hours, taking advantage of the special artificial habitat. In winter, the water passing through the turbines creates an ice-free spot in even the coldest weather. In spring, anadromous fish migrating up the river to their spawning grounds in Pennsylvania and New York are blocked by the dam, providing an artificially high population density. In summer, the oxygen-rich, aerated water attracts fish from the upper Chesapeake Bay, where algal growth sometimes depletes the water of life-giving oxygen during hot spells. At peak times, fishermen jam the shoreline cheek by jowl and drop lines from the catwalk. You may also see Philadelphia Electric biologists at work on their fish lift project. In an effort to restore and increase anadromous fish spawning stocks, migrants are removed from the river, placed into aerated tanks, and trucked to the upstream side of the dam, where they are released. In the latest enhancement of this project, Philadelphia Electric will spend $12 million and have the capacity to transport 750,00 American shad and five million river herring.

Amenities in this area include picnic tables, a telephone, trash cans, a wheelchair-accessible portable toilet, soda machines, and a covered pavilion, housing a snack bar and bathrooms, that is occasionally open. There is space for about 200 cars to park.

The area around the dam is popular for birding. In winter, it is the best public place in Maryland to see bald eagles. They too are attracted by the large numbers of fish and the ice-free fishing opportunities. The colder the winter, the more birds you're likely to see. Most of these birds roost to the south on the Aberdeen Proving Grounds land, where they are free from human harassment. They seem unfazed by the noise of cannons, bombs, and other assorted tools of warfare. Since eagles nest as early as February, most breeding pairs will have dispersed by early spring. However, at least one pair nests in the area and can thus be seen at any time of the year. Juvenile bald eagles, who generally lack the white heads and tails of adults, can be found in the Conowingo Dam area year-round. A variety of gulls and herons invariably frequent the area below the dam as well.

A large sign identifying the wildflower preserve marks the start of the trail. The first half mile is over a gravel road. This gives way to a wide, hard-packed trail that becomes progressively narrower and muddier with distance from the parking lot. The scenery seems unspectacular at first glance; trees are rather short and scraggly, and honeysuckle threatens to cover anything within three feet of ground level if it doesn't move quickly enough. But the river is only a few feet away on your left, shielded from view by a thin screen of vegetation. Fishing trails frequently lead down to the water, providing access to a broader sweep of view. Large silver maples and sycamores line the shore itself, hardy survivors of high water events (although true floods have been moderated by the dam).

The right side of the trail is wetland, ranging from shallow water to merely soggy soil, populated by twisted box elder trees. Although it is hard to discern now, this area was once a barge canal, built in 1838 as part of an extensive network of such waterways connecting the tidewater to the fertile farmlands of central Pennsylvania. The canal owner's house, a large and gracious example of local architecture and stonework, may be seen in Susquehanna State Park.

The far side of the old canal abuts the steep rocky slopes of the Susquehanna River gorge. Rising 100 feet or so, these hillsides are entirely covered by spring wildflowers in mid- to late April. This may well be the best display of spring wildflowers in Maryland. Although it is not as diverse a collection

Trillium

as that along the Potomac River, the density of flowers is unparalleled.

The most common of these wildflowers is trillium, so called because its major parts are grouped in threes: three leaves, three creamy white recurved petals, and reproductive structures in clusters of three. Tens of thousands of these beautiful flowers occupy these hillsides for the entire length of this trip. This is an example of a locally common wildflower; trilliums, as well as all other species within its genus, are rare elsewhere in the state. Even within a few hundred yards of these productive colonies, none can be found. Apparently some unique combination of physical factors and lack of human disturbance has created the perfect habitat for these floral gems.

The petals of these trilliums are white, but they are apparently a rare form of the red trillium, *Trillium erectum.* Virtually every member of this population contains a mutation for pigment production that results in a colorless flower petal. This population of unusually pigmented wildflowers is an example of the genetic diversity that can exist in a species, and upon which future natural selection may act in the evolution of a new species. Red trillium is also known as stinking benjamin for its remarkably unpleasant scent.

Interspersed among the trilliums are Dutchman's-breeches, another uncommon wildflower found only in rich, well-developed woodland soils. These white flowers are aptly named; each looks like an inverted set of pantaloons, and several hang from an upright pole. Although Dutchman's-breeches are not as rare as trilliums in Maryland, they are still uncommon; there are probably as many here as at any other site in the state.

As the trail narrows to a footpath, an alluvial floodplain appears to the left between the trail and the river. This rich, sandy, well-drained soil is the perfect habitat for still another wildflower, Virginia bluebells. Clusters of sky blue, bell-shaped flowers hang downward; the leaves are succulent with smooth edges. Bluebells are common in the right habitat in Maryland: river alluvial floodplains like those along the Gunpowder and Potomac. However, they may be entirely absent from other areas of seemingly similar habitat. Some of the plants exhibit mutation in flower color; albino plants have white flowers, and a few are magenta in hue.

Virginia bluebells and Dutchman's-breeches are known as ephemerals, because they are visible to us for only about a month each spring. They grow rapidly in early April, taking advantage of the direct sunlight hitting the forest floor through the leafless trees. They flower, set seed, and die back by canopy closure in early May. The other 10 months of the year are spent as rhizomes or roots, quiescent beneath the forest floor. Other well-known springtime ephemerals of the forest include dogtooth violet, windflower, and spring beauty.

As the early spring flowers fade, this forest becomes popular with another group of naturalists: the birders. Early May is peak spring warbler migration, and many of these tiny and elusive birds follow river valleys in their northward journeys. Flying at night and resting during the day, warblers glean small insects from the sun-dappled treetops. Most birders identify warblers, as they flit rapidly from tree to tree, by their distinctive and usually complex calls.

Although spring migrants prompt the heaviest birdwatching activity, any time of year has its rewards. Ospreys return to the Susquehanna each spring; their distinctive, high-pitched mewing call often attracts attention to them as they soar over the river. Kingfishers are common along the banks in all seasons, as they seem to be along almost every watercourse in Maryland. Waterfowl, including wood ducks, geese, and mallards, can also be seen.

The trail proceeds south, and eventually the hillsides drop away. The trail occupies a narrow peninsula, with the Susquehanna on one side and Deer Creek on the other. Deer Creek approaches the Susquehanna, but instead of entering the parent river at a right angle it runs parallel for about a mile, creating this narrow strand of alluvial floodplain. The small riffles of Deer Creek were once home to the rarest fish in Maryland. The Maryland darter, a small minnowlike fish, was discovered here, but subsequent samplings have been successful only irregularly. The Maryland darter is probably now extinct.

An old railroad bridge spans the mouth of Deer Creek. It has been solidly planked in for foot travel, giving access to the parking lots of Susquehanna State Park. It is possible to leave a car here so that you need hike only one way.

DIRECTIONS

From Baltimore or Washington, take I-95 north. Exit at Route 543, taking it northwest. At the first light, turn right onto Route 136, and follow it to the intersection with Route 1. Turn right. As Route 1 drops down the hill toward Conowingo Dam, turn right on Shuresville Road. Make your first left on Shures Landing Road, and follow this to the Philadelphia Electric parking lot.

The Maryland Darter

The most recent animal extinction in Maryland has been the Maryland darter, *Etheostoma sellare,* a tiny fish found only in Deer Creek, Harford County. The Maryland darter was never a very common fish; first described by scientists in 1912, it was not seen again until 1962. A more intensive search in the 1960s led to repeated sightings, but only a few individuals were seen by the 1980s. The last observation was in 1988. After 1962, the fish were found only in a single riffle of Deer Creek about a mile from its confluence with the Susquehanna. The Maryland darter was officially listed as an endangered species by the federal government in 1967.

The Maryland darter is the kind of organism that critics of the Endangered Species Act use to vilify that law. Not big, fierce, or beautiful like the grizzly bear or the wolf (examples of "charismatic megafauna"), the darter is typical of the vast majority of species on the endangered or threatened list. Such species have no particular constituency of people who are willing to sacrifice time and energy to ensure their survival. They are so obscure that only a few aficionados have heard of them, even fewer have even seen them, and fewer still would have the skill to recognize them if they were seen. To critics, such species are unimportant and immaterial; that governments spend time, money, and human effort on the study and preservation of them is irksome. When the welfare of such a species clashes with plans for development, as with the snail darter and Tellico Dam, the critics get downright hostile.

However, there are many reasons why the preservation of rare species is important. The Maryland darter illustrates one such justification. Very often, endangered species are rare because they have narrow and very specific requirements for habitat: the place where they live. Any change to that habitat may drastically affect reproduction and survival of the species. As such, endangered species are our canaries in the coal mine; they tell us when environmental conditions have been adversely affected (almost invariably by our actions) and act as an early warning signal that continuation of the same trend may in time affect even such a numerous and adaptable species as humans. The Maryland darter is a canary for the Deer Creek watershed.

Much of the part of Harford County that drains into Deer Creek is rural. Farming dominates human activities, and the land is productive and lush. But even such seemingly benign land use patterns may reach a point at which their cumulative impact becomes significant. The Deer Creek watershed may have reached that critical point.

For example, a scientist sampling fish populations in Deer Creek found 45 individuals of 10 different species in 1990. In contrast, in 1986, 695 individuals of 24 species had been identified at the same spot with the same amount of effort. Scientists hypothesized that nutrient input from animal wastes and fertilizer runoff, and sedimentation from soil erosion, were affecting fish reproduction. The canaries of Deer Creek, including the Maryland darter, have alerted us to a problem; it remains only for us to decide what to do about it. ⋔

North Point State Park (Black Marsh)

County: Baltimore

Distance: 4.2 miles

Difficulty: Flat; generally well-drained terrain, with a few muddy spots

Highlights: Chesapeake Bay views, freshwater marsh, forest

More Information: North Point State Park, (410) 592-2897

BLACK MARSH IS AN anomaly: although it is perhaps the last large chunk of undeveloped, pristine upper Chesapeake Bay waterfront, it sits almost in the shadow of Bethlehem Steel, Maryland's largest smokestack industry. Owned by the state since 1987, this 1,310-acre tract has been designated North Point State Park, and it is scheduled to be developed as funds become available. In addition to being ecologically significant, the Black Marsh property has had a rich human history in ancient, colonial, and recent times. And this unique natural area is located within just a few miles of the Baltimore Beltway.

The area owes its informal name to the 232-acre Black Marsh, which with its surrounding 435-acre forested buffer forms a designated State Wildland and Natural Heritage Area. The marsh proper is considered to be among the best examples in the state of a tidal freshwater marsh; it harbors a wide diversity of birds, including a nesting pair of bald eagles, rare American bitterns, and elusive black rails. In temperate weather, the marsh is a refuge for wading birds such as herons

North Point State Park (Black Marsh)

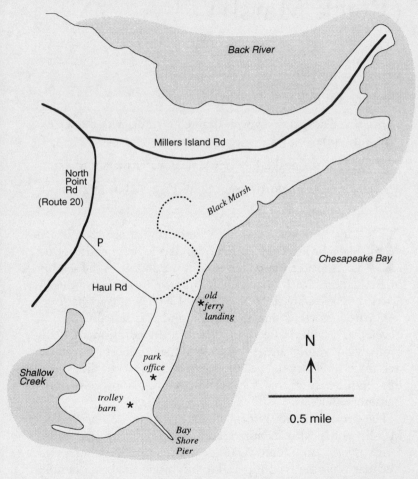

Back River

Millers Island Rd

North
Point
Rd
(Route 20)

Black Marsh

P

Chesapeake Bay

Haul Rd

old
*ferry
landing

N
↑

Shallow
Creek

park
office
*

0.5 mile

trolley
barn   *

Bay
Shore
Pier

and egrets, whose habitat around Bay waterfront is becoming increasingly stressed by encroaching civilization. In winter, waterfowl such as canvasback, goldeneye and ruddy ducks, mergansers, and scaup congregate here. Black Marsh is home to eight species of flowering plants that are considered endangered or rare and in need of conservation.

North Point State Park's human history dates back at least 8,000 years. Although generations of locals have discovered arrowheads and pottery sherds along eroded shorelines and in cultivated fields, a more formal but still preliminary archaeological survey yielded campsites, workshops, shell middens, and a village from the Late Woodland period.

Recorded history began when Maryland was settled in the 1600s. Todd's Inheritance, a plantation of several thousand acres on the North Point peninsula, included Black Marsh and was the first recorded residence in Baltimore County. The house was at least partially burned by the British in 1812, and today it is listed on the National Register of Historic Places. The area was in the British line of advance (and later retreat) in the campaign that culminated in the Battle of North Point.

More recently, a portion of the property south of the marsh proper was developed as the Bay Shore Amusement Park. Long a landmark for Baltimoreans, Bay Shore opened in 1906 and served several generations for 41 years. Today, all that remains are the old trolley barn, the central fountain, the 1,000-foot Bay Shore Pier, and much slag, rock, and cobble fill along the shore.

The Maryland Department of Natural Resources proposed a master plan for the development of North Point State Park in 1991. It quickly became the focus of much controversy, since the plan proposed making the old Bay Shore site into the park nucleus, complete with restored trolley barn and fountain, stabilized pier, boat slips with a dredged channel, amphitheater, and parking lots. Conservationists sought to restore and preserve the waterfront buffer by moving most development to less sensitive inland sites. As of this writing, the final disposition of these plans is uncertain, and funding is even more problematic. Check with the park to see if implementation of the master plan has begun, and if it has affected the trip description.

The walk described here totals about 4.2 miles over flat terrain. In warm weather, bring along insect repellent if you venture onto the trail leading through the swamp.

TRIP DESCRIPTION

Begin your walk at the parking lot found about 100 yards inside the gated entrance off North Point Road (Route 20). Although disabled visitors may drive about a mile down the entrance road (the Haul Road) to a small parking lot near the water, Department of Natural Resources staff ask all others to park on the periphery and walk in. Only a bulletin board greets you here.

Walk down the Haul Road. Long abandoned, it is in very bad shape, with chunks of broken asphalt, deep potholes, and scattered slag fill. The road passes between agricultural fields that are among the oldest in Maryland to be continuously farmed. Hedgerows of cherry, mulberry, multiflora rose, trumpet creeper, and poison ivy frame the view and make good habitat for mockingbirds, cardinals, sparrows, and finches. The road enters the forest after a quarter mile. Many large old trees dominate this part of the Black Marsh tract, including tulip poplar, walnut, sweet gum, willow oak, blackjack oak, and American holly. Understory vegetation is quite dense, and in summer it becomes all but impenetrable.

In another quarter mile, a gated road now reserved for hikers and bikers appears on the left. It leads into the marsh proper on the berm of the old trolley line, and it is in fact the only way (except by boat) to see Black Marsh itself. Since most people probably want to visit the waterfront, this trail is described below as part of the return circuit.

Another half mile of walking through shady woods brings you to the park nucleus. Portable toilets, a telephone, water, several picnic tables, a low observation tower, a small dock, and a modest but interesting visitor center are located here. Turn right, following the narrow beach, which is popular with fishermen. This was the site of the wading beach at Bay Shore Park; time, erosion, and forest encroachment have all conspired to make it much smaller than it was in the park's heyday. At the far end of the beach the old pier promenade juts 1,000 feet into Chesapeake Bay. Actually a jetty rather than a pier, it is composed of concrete bulkheads filled with slag from Bethlehem Steel. A few hardy stunted trees cling to a precarious existence on the thin soil, exposed to the prevailing winds and storm tides of Chesapeake Bay.

As you return off the pier, a dirt road cut through the bayfront vegetation leads back into the upland. Within 100 yards, the impressive weathered remains of the trolley barn, decorated in the Edwardian style, appear on the left. A bit farther on, a sidewalk leads to the central fountain, a major attraction at the old amusement park. The dirt road quickly returns you to the park nucleus.

For your best opportunity to view herons and other water birds, walk north along the shore from the park nucleus. The beach is merely a jumble of rocks and other junk that has been dumped to retard erosion, so the footing is precarious. After 100 yards or so, peek inland through the wall of vegetation that borders the shoreline. Here lies a small sheltered cove a few acres in size, partially filled with cattails and other marshland vegetation. Herons and other wading birds almost always frequent this little lagoon, sometimes loafing in the trees. In colder weather, dabbling ducks like the privacy and shelter here. Return to the park nucleus.

Returning a half mile up the Haul Road toward your car, don't miss the branch trail mentioned previously. Only 0.1 mile down this trail, another old road branches to the right, leading to the water and a concrete pier that was once the western terminus of an auto and passenger ferry serving the Eastern Shore. It is closed to public use but is a good place to look for resting gulls and other shorebirds. Return to the marsh trail and turn right. This road parallels the Bay for a short distance, giving views across the water. It soon reenters the rather scrubby forest and passes the concrete shell of what was once a generator station used to boost the electrical current to the trolleys. A half mile from the Haul Road, the trail enters Black Marsh Wildland. This marsh, dominated by narrow leaved cattail and three square, is alive with the snowy blossoms of swamp rose mallow in midsummer. Keep an eye peeled for muskrats, beaver, various marsh birds, and predators like Northern harriers, great horned owls, red-tailed hawks, and bald eagles. If you visit here in summer or early fall, expect harassment by mosquitoes and deerflies.

Within a few hundred yards, the trail enters a swamp forest unlike any other in Maryland. Short but ancient white oaks of wide girth dominate the nontidal wetland, but few other plants, either herbaceous or woody, grow here. The result is long views through an open understory, with only a few red maples and hollies interrupting the dominance by white oak. Finally, a mile from the Haul Road, the trail ends at an overlook. The wilds of Black Marsh surround you on all sides and give the impression of a setting far more remote than it really is.

Return to your car by retracing your steps.

DIRECTIONS

From the Baltimore Beltway, take exit 42, following the signs for Fort Howard Veterans Administration Medical Center. This will put you on Route 20 south (North Point Road). The park entrance is about four miles from the beltway on your left.

OTHER OUTDOOR RECREATIONAL OPPORTUNITIES NEARBY

Because North Point State Park is new, the master plan has not yet been implemented. Bicycling is not recommended at this time. All the trails are actually old roads, the surface of which is composed of rocks ranging from golf ball to tennis ball size. If and when the park's master plan is instituted, Black Marsh will be much more "user friendly" for cyclists. Almost four miles of crushed limestone hiker-biker trails are planned. Check with the park office regarding progress.

Black Rails

Black rails may not be the rarest species of bird in Maryland, but they are probably the least frequently seen. Only the most dedicated birders include a black rail on their life lists. Even scientists who study this elusive species are frustrated by the secretive nature of black rails, and there is much about the life history of black rails that is unknown.

A black rail is about the size of a house sparrow and is black to dark gray in plumage with white speckles on the back. Only the legs and large, strong toes exhibit any color, a yellowish green; they dangle awkwardly during flight. Like all rails, black rails have a narrow body that can be further compressed as needed, hence the expression "thin as a rail."

Black rails live in salty, brackish, or freshwater marshes. For this reason, the several species of rails are sometimes called "marsh hens" or "mud hens." The largest population of black rails in Maryland is probably on the lower Eastern Shore, in the extensive cordgrass marshes of southern Dorchester County around Elliott Island. Black rail populations are best censused by sound at the start of the breeding season, when males call

Black rail

just after sunset and before dawn. Their "kik" or "did-ee-dunk" note is distinctive, but so obscure was this bird that its call was not associated with the species until 1958. Fortunately for scientists and birders, males will respond to a tape-recorded call. In fact, black rails have been known to attack the speakers on a tape recorder! Black rails are so difficult to see that standard procedure is to avoid movement after playing the recording for fear of stepping on a bird. The typical sighting is a brief glimpse of a small, mouselike bird darting through the vegetation and disappearing in a blink. Compounding the difficulties of observing black rails is the fact that the best time to see them is at night in the lonely, bug-infested marshes of early summer.

Black rails nest in a cup of soft grasses that often arches overhead. These nests are next to impossible to find; one researcher, who spent an entire summer in the field, never discovered a nest! The first published photographs of a female black rail on a nest appeared in 1987, and the photographer noted that this was the first time in 30 years that a nest had been found. Six to eight eggs are usually laid, but little is known about the incubation time and the time to fledging. Insects, seeds, and marine crustaceans are common food items. By late October, black rails have migrated to their wintering grounds along the southern coast of the United States. Although reputedly weak fliers, black rails somehow complete this migration twice a year, in an anonymous fashion.

Our lack of knowledge about black rails precludes active management for their conservation. Right now, preservation of known black rail habitat, on both the breeding and the wintering grounds, is about all that can be done. The effects of marsh disturbances like ditching, burning, invasion by nonnative species, and insecticidal spraying on black rail populations are completely unknown. Black rails remind us that wildlife management is still an inexact science and warn us that hubris regarding our understanding of the natural world is largely unwarranted. ℵ

Great Falls Tavern Walk and Billy Goat Trail

County: Montgomery

Distance: Great Falls: Less than a half mile
Billy Goat Trail: About 3 miles

Difficulty: Great Falls: Flat; part sandy gravel, part
         boardwalk
Billy Goat Trail: Extremely rocky

Highlights: River gorge with waterfalls, bedrock terrace forest, historic canal

More Information: C & O Canal National Historical Park, (301) 299-3613

THE C & O CANAL towpath runs for 184 miles parallel to the Potomac River between Washington, D.C., and Cumberland, Maryland. Preserved and managed as a National Historical Park, it is a regional treasure for hiking and biking. Every mile of the towpath is worth walking, and indeed it is very popular, especially the stretch between Great Falls and Georgetown. Nevertheless, on weekdays the more rural parts of the trail can provide a sense of solitude. Campsites are located about every five miles, and backpackers contemplating a long trip in the wilderness can develop their skills and stamina on this flat trail with frequent resupply points.

A mile-by-mile description of the towpath would require an entire book, and in fact there are several on the market. In the hiking section of this book, two of the best segments are

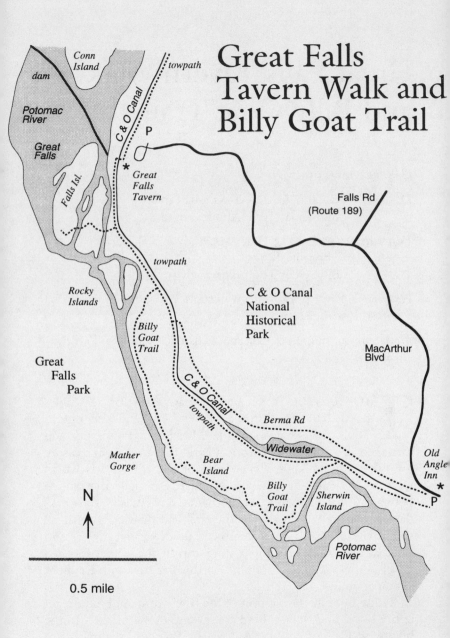

Great Falls Tavern Walk and Billy Goat Trail

Conn Island

dam

Potomac River

Great Falls

towpath

C & O Canal

P

*

Great Falls Tavern

Falls Isl.

Falls Rd
(Route 189)

towpath

Rocky Islands

C & O Canal
National
Historical
Park

Billy Goat Trail

MacArthur
Blvd

**Great
Falls
Park**

C & O Canal

towpath

Berma Rd

Widewater

Mather Gorge

Bear Island

Billy Goat Trail

Sherwin Island

Old
Angle
Inn

*

P

Potomac River

N

↑

0.5 mile

described: Great Falls Tavern Walk and Billy Goat Trail, and Harpers Ferry and the C & O Canal towpath (see page 141).

In the canoeing section of this book, beginning on page 466, three segments of the Potomac River adjacent to the towpath are described, but the towpath itself would make an equally fine destination for hiking or biking. These segments were selected for some outstanding natural or historic feature that is the focal point of the trip. They are Fort Frederick, Dam Number 4 Cave, and Paw Paw Bends and tunnel.

Also in the canoeing section, beginning on page 459, an overview of the physiography and natural history of the river valley can be found.

When you're looking for a quiet, easy getaway in a beautiful setting, the C & O Canal towpath is always a superb choice. Visit and enjoy!

The most dramatic landscape in Maryland is not some remote mountaintop view far to the west; instead it is found almost within sight of the Capital Beltway. Great Falls of the Potomac is a world-class scenic attraction within a 30-minute drive of more than a million people. Here the great river drops more than 60 feet over a series of waterfalls and steep rapids, carving a vertical-walled gorge through living rock. The wild landscape dwarfs the many visitors who scramble over rock fins and down steep chutes in pursuit of the ultimate view.

More than just scenery highlights the Great Falls area. It is a part of the C & O Canal National Historical Park, and mankind's mark on the land has been important. Several canal locks are clustered here, one of which is operational. The canal's towpath, parallel to the river, is very popular among joggers, cyclists, and walkers. For the naturalist, a large number of habitats cluster within a small area, making birding and botanizing superb. The Great Falls area has the highest density of rare plants and animals in Maryland. Taken together, the many points of interest and the extraordinary ecology and natural beauty make Great Falls a must to visit.

There are several access points to the Great Falls area, all of which are rewarding. Two hikes are described here. One is best for families with small children, for those in wheelchairs, or for those who want to see a great deal of scenery without walking far. The second is a true adventure hike that is probably the most challenging and beautiful in this book.

TRIP DESCRIPTION

Great Falls Tavern Walk

Begin this easy stroll from the Great Falls parking lot of the C & O Canal National Historical Park. There are hundreds of parking places here, but on prime spring weekends they may fill by 11 A.M. even though an entrance fee is charged. On such days, arrive early or late in the day; the rest of the year rarely sees such heavy usage, and space is almost always available. A snack bar with a few picnic tables borders the parking lot and is the first building you will encounter. A bit farther east is the restored Great Falls Tavern, a massive whitewashed structure dating from 1828 which houses a few basic displays; information is available from rangers inside. Wheelchair-accessible but aging and odorous bathrooms are in a separate building out back. Telephones and water are also available.

Great Falls Tavern faces a still-functioning lock that is very active in warm weather. The Park Service offers authentic mule-drawn canal barge rides from here, which pass through the lock and continue upstream. This is a very popular activity, and reservations are recommended. If you miss out on the canal barge rides, rangers frequently offer interpretive hikes from the tavern area; like such walks in every national park, they are invariably informative and worthwhile.

To explore the area on your own, cross the canal on the footbridge just outside the front door of the tavern and turn left. The narrow and busy towpath is wedged between the canal and the Fish Ladder, a narrow chute of the Potomac River where the rocks were long ago modified by engineers in an effort to aid the upstream migration of anadromous fish. Both sides have substantial dropoffs, so keep young children firmly in hand in this area. A sign notes that a number of deaths occur near here each year because of carelessness and poor judgment. The river in particular is very swift, accelerating rapidly toward its plunge over Great Falls.

Continue for about 100 yards, and then bear right toward the footbridge to Olmstead Island. Opened in 1992, this wheelchair-accessible bridge replaced a similar one destroyed by Hurricane Agnes in 1972. It first crosses the Fish Ladder. The incredible power of the river is displayed as it explodes in haystacks, recirculating holes, and rock sieves. But this represents only a tiny portion of the Potomac's flow, and even more dramatic views of Great Falls are ahead.

The bridge becomes a boardwalk trail that traverses Olmstead Island and the adjacent Falls Island for almost a quarter mile, passing through a unique natural habitat: a bedrock terrace forest. Dominated by the erosion-resistant rocks that form Great Falls, trees and other vegetation grow only in the cracks and depressions where floods have deposited silt and other alluvium. The same floodwaters that bring a new supply of soil and nutrients may also uproot and wash away trees and herbaceous plants. In fact, a flood of this magnitude occurs fairly frequently; there have been about 20 high-water incidents since 1936 that swept over at least parts of Olmstead Island, and three floods that covered the island entirely. Thus trees never get really big on Olmstead and Falls islands. Virginia pine, red oak, and post oak dominate the drier sites on the island, whereas pin oak, river birch, and swamp white oak can be found in depressions with poor drainage that makes the soil rather wet. This unique combination of habitats, coupled with the lack of human disturbance, makes these islands home to some of the most rare and unusual herbaceous plants in Maryland. For this reason, be sure to stay on the boardwalk.

The boardwalk terminates at a viewing platform where the Maryland chute of Great Falls is laid out in panorama. This spectacular series of waterfalls is undoubtedly the most striking scenery in Maryland. The falls have formed where the river flows over hard, erosion-resistant rocks and onto slightly softer, more erodable rocks downstream. Aiding in the erosion of these softer rocks is the fact that several faults, or zones of weakness in the rock, occcur in these strata. One such fracture zone is the dogleg linking the foot of Great Falls with the Mather Gorge about a quarter mile downstream.

Take your time and enjoy the view of the falls. There is good fall color along the far Virginia shore, and on occasion bald eagles may be spotted soaring overhead; in the last several years, a pair has nested on Conn Island just upstream of Great Falls. Kayakers are often seen surfing, ferrying, and playing in the Observation Deck Rapids just downstream from the foot of Great Falls. Surprisingly, every waterfall and chute of Great Falls has been kayaked, albeit only a few times, by teams of experts at summer low water. Return to the towpath; hiking both upstream and downstream is beautiful should you feel like more exercise.

Billy Goat Trail

The Billy Goat Trail, as its name implies, is a challenging hiking trail located just downstream of Great Falls. Families with small children, or those unaccustomed to difficult terrain, should consider carefully whether they want to tackle this difficult trail. But for groups of strong, experienced hikers, the Billy Goat Trail is not to be missed. Kids love the challenge of scrambling over rocks and along cliff edges, even if it makes their parents nervous. The trail is included in this book because it is a favorite of older children; yet I've seen kids as young as five hiking this trail every time I've been on it and they're invariably having a great time. So once again, take the Billy Goat Trail only if everyone in your party is strong and experienced.

Begin your walk at the Old Anglers Inn parking lot off MacArthur Boulevard. Arrive before 10 A.M. or after 3 P.M. in order to assure yourself a parking space, and obey all the posted signs. Latecomers often park illegally along the road shoulders of MacArthur Boulevard, and the sight of parking tickets fluttering in the breeze on a whole line of vehicle windshields is not uncommon; just because everyone else is illegally parked doesn't necessarily mean you can get away with it. When you park, close up the ranks so that more vehicles can fit in the available spaces, but do not block anyone else in.

Walk down the dirt road leading to the lower parking lot, favored by canoeists and kayakers, who must haul their boats several hundred yards to the river even from here. A pair of usually noisome portable toilets stand in a clearing just beyond the end of the lower parking lot. No water is available in this area; the restaurant across the road is a possiblity for refreshment, but it is definitely upscale. At a signboard, the trail leaves the parking lot, crosses the C & O Canal, and reaches the towpath. Turn right, heading upstream.

Large trees, dominated by oaks, line the towpath and make it a shady, cool place even on a hot day. Because these forests have not been disturbed for many decades, they harbor a wide variety of birds despite the narrowness of the river corridor within the miasma of suburbanization. Woodpeckers abound, and your chances of seeing the usually uncommon pileated woodpecker are excellent. These crow-sized birds with red crests and white underwings are more often seen than heard, their call louder than that of almost any other bird in the forest. Springtime brings a host of migrating warblers that rest during the day in the insect-rich woods, gleaning their prey from leaves and branches. Although warblers tend to stay near the tops of trees and flit around rapidly, experienced birders can usually locate a number of species. Warbler songs are species specific and are the best way to identify these tiny visitors.

Within a quarter mile upstream, the canal spreads out into the broad, rock-bounded expanse known as Widewater. At one time far back in geological history, this was the Potomac's riverbed, and the builders of the canal utilized this unusual feature. Because the shoreline is so rocky, and its borders are studded with pine trees, the view is reminiscent of a Minnesota northwoods lake rather than a canal just outside the nation's capital. Vultures, ducks, and geese nest on the few tiny islands and on the remote opposite shoreline.

Virginia bluebell

On the left a few hundred yards before the beginning of Widewater is a side trail prominently marked as the Billy Goat Trail. Note the light blue blazes on trees and rocks; these mark the trail for the next two miles. Since the area is honeycombed with side trails, it is easy to stray from the official trail; keep the blue blazes in sight.

In springtime, an incredible profusion of wildflowers grows just off the entrance to the trail. Hepatica, bloodroot, Virginia bluebell, trillium, Dame's rocket, spring beauty, and golden ragwort, to name just a few, flower brilliantly in April. The rich alluvial soils, built up after irregular floods, are mostly responsible for this spectacular vernal display. Wildflowers are common in the forest bordering the entire towpath, but in few other places are they so abundant or diverse. In fact, the Great Falls area is generally considered the place in Maryland to view the widest variety of spring wildflowers.

Within 50 yards, the trail drops precipitously down a rock face so steep that you will need to use your hands for balance. Remember the rock climber's rule: move only one hand or foot at a time, making sure the other three are firmly anchored. If this descent is too much for you, turn back now; the rest of the Billy Goat Trail is no easier.

A few more ups and downs will bring you to a rock promontory with a sweeping view of the Potomac River. Particularly wide at this point, the river splits around two islands and then bends sharply left. Great chunks of rock line the water's edge, and steep hillsides rise up to forested heights on the far (Virginia) side.

The Billy Goat Trail now winds back and forth between forest, scrub, and bare rock. Along the way, there are stream crossings, several beaver ponds, and lots more rock scrambling. Finally, after almost a mile of travel, the trail emerges onto flat, exposed rock with a spectacular and dramatic view of the Potomac and its gorge. For a section extending more than a half mile upstream, the river has carved its way downward through more than 60 feet of metagraywacke and mica schist, leaving vertical walls that are very popular with rock climbers. The river fills the entire channel, even at summertime low water; there is no floodplain. At high water, the river boils in whirlpools and reflection waves bounce off the walls, creating a chaos of churning, roiling water rushing madly on its way to the sea. This section is called the Mather Gorge; it is named after Stephen Mather, the first director of the United States National Park Service.

The trail leads upstream along the top of this barren rock ledge, and it is from this area that the trail gets its name. Hikers must jump from rock to rock and balance on thin fins of rock, much like a mountain goat. It's a challenging and exhilarating scramble!

All too soon the trail leads back into the forest, although views of the river and its rapids are still possible with a detour of only a few feet off the main trail. The undersized trees of this woods, stunted by the poor, rocky soil, are dominated by the scrubby-looking Virginia pine; its best trait is that it lends a pleasant green tint to the landscape in winter. After several hundred more yards of easy walking, the Billy Goat Trail returns to the C & O Canal towpath. You may turn right and return to your car or continue upriver to view Great Falls.

If you decide to continue, turn left on the towpath and pass Lock 16. A fence appears on the left and keeps small children and wobbly cyclists from falling more than 100 feet into the Potomac far below. The view from atop this cliff is spectacular. It looks out over a wide section of the Potomac where the river has carved a vertical-walled gorge. Farther along, the river is divided into three channels split by two huge islands, appropriately known as the Rocky Islands. At high water, usually in winter and spring, water fills all three channels, but by midsummer low water the two nearest channels are dry.

Continuing on the towpath, another 200 yards will bring you to the footbridge to Olmstead Island. This island is definitely worth a visit, as noted in the previous section. After seeing the Falls from Olmstead Island, return to your car at the Old Anglers Inn via the towpath. A much easier walk than the Billy Goat Trail, the towpath still passes through some pretty scenery, including several wetlands, and it is excellent for viewing birds and wildflowers. It is extremely popular, however, and you will probably never be out of sight of other people.

DIRECTIONS

From Washington, take the Capital Beltway west. The final exit in Maryland before crossing the Potomac on the Cabin John Bridge is exit 41, marked Carderock/Great Falls. Proceed 1.75 miles on the Clara Barton Parkway to its end. Turn left onto MacArthur Boulevard. The parking lots for the Old Anglers Inn are 1.1 miles farther on the left. To reach the Great Falls parking area, continue on MacArthur Boulevard to its terminus.

OTHER OUTDOOR RECREATIONAL OPPORTUNITIES NEARBY

Bicycling on the C & O Canal towpath in the Great Falls area is possible but not easy. The entire area is very crowded with tourists, dog walkers, and hikers, many of whom seem oblivious to other trail users. Use caution if you bike here. The towpath between the Old Anglers Inn and Great Falls has a 200-yard section that has eroded away and is passable only if you carry your bike over rocky terrain. To avoid this rough ground, the National Park Service encourages bicyclists to use the old Berma Road, found on the mainland side of the canal between the Old Anglers Inn and Lock 16. However, this road is not much better, being very rutted and rocky. Bicycling in the Great Falls area may be more trouble than it's worth.

Canoeing on the Potomac River between the top of Great Falls and the foot of Little Falls 11 miles downriver should be avoided by anyone who wishes to remain alive and healthy. In addition to the obvious dangers of the falls, other more subtle but equally hazardous situations abound, even in areas that may appear benign. Stay off this section of the river! That said, the C & O Canal from the Great Falls parking lot seven miles upriver to Violettes Lock makes an enjoyable trip. It is a pleasant, shady paddle on flatwater through an area rich in wildlife.

Why Preserve Biodiversity?

What is the importance of preserving biodiversity? Isn't it important only for the tropics, where most of the earth's species are found? Why should you care?

Preserving biodiversity in Maryland *is* important. At the most obvious practical level, our natural resources are the basis of much commerce, including timber harvesting and the outdoor recreation industry. A majority of our medicines come from plant extracts, but most of our plants have never been surveyed for such beneficial compounds. Biodiversity has intrinsic importance to the quality of our lives, because even the most insulated city dweller is still dependent on our air, land, and water. Biodiversity contributes to the integrity, stability, and resilience of the planet's life support systems, and this is as true at the local and regional levels as it is at the global level. Finally, and perhaps most important, biological diversity is the raw material for evolution, a process that ensures adaptation to changing physical environments and the continuance of life on earth.

Biodiversity in Maryland is under constant attack. Unlike the tropics, where several species may go extinct each day because of human activity, extinctions are not imminent here. However, a great many populations of all sorts of organisms are being negatively affected and stressed by our dominance of the world. The biologist Paul Ehrlich likens this insidious loss of biodiversity to an airplane that loses a rivet here and a screw there. Each loss is insignificant by itself, but eventually the individual losses add up and the airplane falls apart. Loss of local biodiversity is a warning signal that our natural support systems are under stress and that they may fail at some point in the future, with uncertain consequences. The challenge for us is to stem that tide.

What can citizens do to preserve biological diversity in Maryland? In general, everything we can do to hold down our impact on the natural world will be helpful and in the long run beneficial to us as well. Health and prosperity decline in a deteriorating environment; we should do what we can to preserve our air, land, and water. In the past, much conservation has been reactive, fixing things that are broken, rather than proactive. Thus we clean up pollution rather than reducing emissions from the pipe or smokestack; we institute growth management programs like the Critical Areas regulations in response to the degradation of Chesapeake Bay rather than managing growth before it gets out of hand; and we try to save endangered species instead of preserving the habitats and ecosystems of which they are a part. Our society needs to value our biological heritage just as we treasure our cultural heritage. Ultimately, we need to understand that the most significant evolutionary role we can play as the dominant species on earth today is that of an altruistic, careful, and conservative steward of our planet's riches, shepherding that natural heritage into an uncertain and unforeseeable future. ☚

Lake Roland Trail

County: Baltimore

Distance: Up to 6 miles, depending on route

Difficulty: Mostly flat; occasionally muddy terrain

Highlights: Forest, wetlands, serpentine barrens

More Information: Baltimore City Parks Department,
   (410) 396-7931

THE JONES FALLS is one of Maryland's most schizophrenic streams. Originating from upland springs in the patrician Greenspring Valley, its upper reaches drain the woods and pastures of the large horse farms for which the valley is so famous. The narrow little stream dances over gravelly riffles and through sandy flats, its water quality protected from the insults that irresistably accompany development. Trout lurk furtively in the pools, hiding in the shade of riverbank tree roots. Unfortunately, however, as the Jones Falls nears the Baltimore Beltway, it is joined by side streams that dump in sediment and storm sewer runoff. Interstate 83 occupies the river valley, in places elevated right over the creek. Farther south, in Baltimore City, pollution from industrial waste oozes in, and before long the Jones Falls has been relegated to an urban sewer, running forgotten through the backyards of Baltimore. As a final insult, the city has enclosed the river in a pipe, and its last two miles flow in stygian darkness under the city and into Baltimore Harbor.

Lake Roland occupies the middle portion of the Jones Falls, where water quality is still decent but will become degraded within a mile downstream. Owned by Baltimore City but

Lake Roland Trail

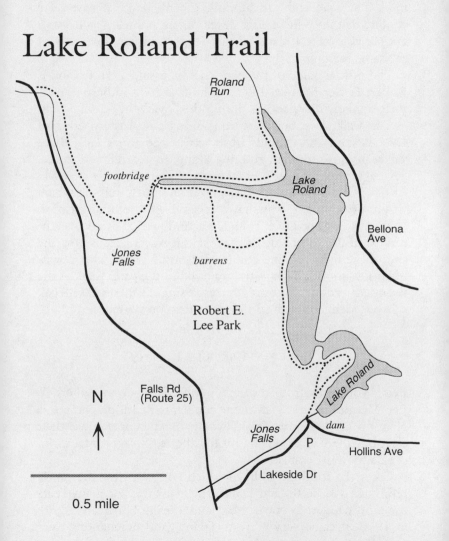

Roland
Run

footbridge

Lake
Roland

Bellona
Ave

Jones
Falls

barrens

Robert E.
Lee Park

Lake Roland

N

Falls Rd
(Route 25)

↑

Jones
Falls

dam

P

Hollins Ave

Lakeside Dr

0.5 mile

located in Baltimore County a short distance north of the city line, Lake Roland was once Baltimore's principal drinking water supply. The old stone dam backs up water for almost a mile. The lake and surrounding greenbelt are a haven for wildlife that finds increasing development reducing its habitat. People visit Lake Roland in surprising numbers, for many of the same reasons.

The official name of the park encompassing Lake Roland is Robert E. Lee Memorial Park. It hints at the southern sympathies of many Marylanders during the Civil War.

The walk described here runs along the western edge of Lake Roland and extends upstream in the Jones Falls River valley. It is mostly flat, running along an old railroad grade. Several spur trails make it possible to extend this five-mile walk. At this time, it is described as an out-and-back trail, on which you return the same way that you came. At one time, a circuit of the lake was possible, using an abandoned railroad track to return on the other side of the lake. However, this is now the site of the light rail line connecting Hunt Valley with downtown Baltimore, much as the train did in the early years of the twentieth century. Not only is trespassing on the tracks illegal, it is very dangerous given the electrification system.

TRIP DESCRIPTION

Begin your walk from the only public entrance to Robert E. Lee Memorial Park, just below the dam. Roadside parking is plentiful on Lakeside Drive, where most people leave their cars, but there is an official lot for about 50 cars upstream of the dam on the east side.

Cross the footbridge, from which you can view the newly refurbished Lake Roland Dam. This dam was for many years the most dangerous one in Maryland; during Hurricane Agnes in 1972, it came very close to failing, and evacuations were carried out downstream. It took twenty years for the money to be found to rehabilitate the old dam, despite the obvious danger; fortunately, it held in the interim, and it is now safe. At

Black-crowned night heron

dawn or dusk in summer, the bridge is a good place to observe black-crowned night herons fishing from the rocks below the dam.

The trail picks up on the far side of the footbridge as a long-neglected asphalt road. It is crumbling in many places, and passage by wheelchair or even stroller is problematic. Bathrooms with flush toilets are available here, as are picnic tables, trash cans, and drinking water. The developed areas of the park are somewhat frowsy, suffering mostly from neglect, which translates as a lack of money for repairs and upkeep.

Follow the old road along the edge of the lake. It passes through a parklike setting, with widely spaced trees and lots of grass. Upland sites are shaded by large old white oaks, whereas the flora along the border of the lake is more diverse. There are a number of places where fishermen can get down to the water's edge and cast without snagging lines on the back-stroke.

A quarter mile from the start, an unobvious trail branches off to the right, leading downhill. If the road appears to have looped back on itself and you're returning to your car, you've come a bit too far. This badly eroded trail leads down to the light rail line, which you should cross with care. From here, the trail borders the west side of the lake. It is flat, narrow in summer when vegetation impinges on it, and muddy in wet weather. It is always passable with care, however.

The upper end of Lake Roland is filled with cattails, willow, and other emergent marshland vegetation. This is largely because the lake is slowly filling with sediments, creating shallows where such vegetation can root and prosper. Sedimentation is a problem with every reservoir, but especially so with Lake Roland, since it is older than most. With continued upstream development, the size of these marshes will undoubtedly increase.

The variety of habitats at this upstream end of Lake Roland makes for good birding. Within a hundred yards or so are open water, marsh, swamp, river bottom forest, and upland forest. Ducks and geese like the open water in fall and winter; warblers frequent the river bottom forest on their May migrations. Year-round, look for kingfishers near water, woodpeckers in the forest, and great blue herons in the marshes.

After more than a half mile of walking adjacent to the lake, the trail bears left to run alongside the flowing waters of the Jones Falls. At mile 1.8, the trail crosses the stream on a narrow footbridge. At times of low rainfall, the Jones Falls flows clear and shallow here, but the extensive amount of sand in the riverbed speaks of the sediment load carried by the creek in times of flood. Many walkers stop at the footbridge and retrace their steps, but you have two choices for further exploration of the valley.

Continuing straight ahead from the footbridge allows you to remain on the railroad grade, which runs dead flat for another 0.7 mile. A few pretty rock outcrops are seen along this section, which follows the Jones Falls. The trail terminates at Falls Road.

Alternatively, you may turn right just after crossing the footbridge to explore the other side of the Jones Falls and the upper reaches of Lake Roland. This trail, too, ends at a road in a suburban neighborhood after 0.7 mile.

Both of these trails are narrower than the trail leading from the dam to the footbridge. Expect occasional briers across the path and to get your shoes soaked with dew during morning walks. Return the way you came.

About halfway between the footbridge and the light rail line on the return trip, a wide trail branches off to the right, leading uphill. It quickly leaves the floodplain and emerges into a strange landscape dominated by short, scrubby Virginia pine. Underfoot, sharp-edged, grayish tan rocks make for uneven walking. This is a serpentine barren, a smaller version of the extensive one at Soldiers Delight Natural Environmental Area. It is known locally as Bare Hills. Much of the previously dominant serpentine grassland habitat has been invaded by pine with an understory of thorny greenbrier. The otherwise sparse vegetation makes a distinct contrast with the rich habitats along Lake Roland and the Jones Falls just a stone's throw away. The trail occupies what was once an old rural lane and after about a half mile leads back to the main trail. Return through the barrens to the trail along Lake Roland, turn right, and retrace your steps to your car.

DIRECTIONS

From the Baltimore Beltway, take the Falls Road (Route 25) exit. This road heads north only. At the first stoplight, turn left onto Falls Road proper. Go 3.4 miles south, cross the new Falls Road Bridge, and make an immediate left onto Lakeside Drive. This road ends within a half mile at the park entrance.

Extinctions in Maryland

Maryland before the arrival of the white man almost 400 years ago was a remarkably different place than it is today. Even the best of our wild places, many of which are described in this book, have changed in appearance and in their biological diversity. Animals that roamed from the Chesapeake shores to the rocky wilds of the Appalachians are now missing, including some that were the biggest and most plentiful. New species, mostly invaders from other continents, brought here accidentally or on purpose by humans, have become established and have disproportional effects on native life forms. Even the kinds of trees that dominate Maryland's forested landscapes have changed.

Early white explorers and colonists were greatly impressed by the richness of Maryland. Animal life abounded, and hunters were rewarded with full larders. When the forests were cleared, the fertile soil responded with bumper crops of tobacco, grains, and vegetables. But as colonists spread to the far corners of what would later become Maryland, a number of species, mostly large mammals, were driven to extinction by overhunting. These included timber wolves, elk, wood bison, and cougars. Most were rare by the Revolution and extinct by 1850. Surprisingly, the white-tailed deer, so familiar to us now, was rare as well, surviving only in small populations in remote, tangled areas. Black bear were eradicated in the state, although strays from viable populations in nearby Pennsylvania and West Virginia were reported almost every year. With a ban on their hunting, black bears have recently become reestablished in western Maryland.

Bird life was rich as well. The river valleys of the southern Eastern Shore contained large numbers of Carolina parakeets, while the forested uplands harbored incredible densities of passenger pigeons during their migration. Both species are now extinct, not just in Maryland but worldwide.

The most significant extinction among the state's flora was more recent than most of the animal extinctions. Chestnut was the dominant tree species in the eastern forest, sometimes composing as much as 50 percent of the trees on a given site. Its annual production of mast (chestnuts) was an important food source for many forest-dwelling animals. Chestnut wood, hard and rot resistant, was prized by farmers and foresters. Sometime in the early years of the twentieth century, a fungal parasite known as chestnut blight arrived from Asia. Quickly establishing itself in the susceptible wild populations of chestnut trees, the fungus infected the inner bark of the tree. Death followed, although the hardy roots even today send up sprouts, more than 50 years later. Unfortunately, the fungus also still lives in the roots and reinfects the tree at the sapling stage. The only mature chestnuts left in the United States are in a spatially separated population in Michigan, to which the fungus has so far not spread.

Although these extinctions are the most famous, there have no doubt been many others, usually of obscure, poorly studied species like fish, insects, fungi, mosses, and bacteria. Even among the flowering plants, the Department of Natural Resources lists 139 species believed to have been extirpated from Maryland. Organisms that are rare to start with may never become known to science before going extinct. For example, the Maryland Natural Heritage Program discovered the state's first population of mountain sandwort, a small flower, in 1989. The site has now been protected from development.

Armchair naturalists like to speculate on how different the ecology of Maryland would be if we had with us the full complement of now-extinct species. Although such speculation is sheer guesswork, there is no doubt that Maryland is the poorer for the loss of its precious natural heritage. We can only dedicate ourselves to stopping future losses. ⚘

Oregon Ridge Park

County: Baltimore

Distance: 3.6 miles

Difficulty: Hilly; well-drained terrain

Highlights: Upland forest, stream valley

More Information: Oregon Ridge Park, (410) 887-1818

OREGON RIDGE IS A Baltimore County park best known as the summer home of the Baltimore Symphony Orchestra. The musicians play on an elevated stage while thousands of listeners picnic on the extensive lawns. Children play; teenagers wander. Not the best place for serious lovers of classical music, but a pleasant enough experience on a hot summer's night.

Oregon Ridge is also popular for swimming. An old quarry has been filled, sand trucked in to make a small beach, and picnic areas and playgrounds established nearby. A fee is charged.

So the majority of visitors to Oregon Ridge are casual tourists who occasionally take their recreation out of doors, where the temperature may not be perfect, where there may actually be a few bugs, and where the threat of rain becomes an important consideration. Most of them don't take advantage of the rest of Oregon Ridge's considerable charms: a modern nature center with interesting exhibits and a good library, and the miles of trails that wind over the hills and through the forest. Perhaps that's best, for it leaves the trails uncrowded and well maintained.

Oregon Ridge Park

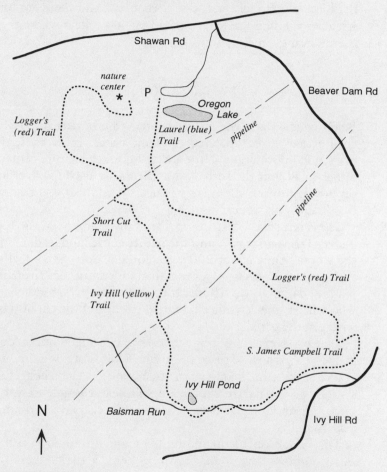

Shawan Rd

nature
center
∗

P

Oregon
Lake

Beaver Dam Rd

Logger's
(red) Trail

Laurel (blue)
Trail

pipeline

pipeline

Short Cut
Trail

Logger's (red) Trail

Ivy Hill (yellow)
Trail

S. James Campbell Trail

Ivy Hill Pond

N

Baisman Run

Ivy Hill Rd

0.5 mile

The walk described here traverses the most interesting parts of Oregon Ridge Park. In particular, the newly acquired (1990) Merryman Tract, which includes the valley of Baisman Run, is especially beautiful, and it is a forest habitat markedly different from the rest of the park. These trails are not flat, but the hills are gradual (with one exception), and there are long stretches running the length of ridges and valleys where there is little change in elevation.

TRIP DESCRIPTION

Begin your walk at the nature center, where there are wheel-chair-accessible bathrooms, drinking water, trash cans, displays, and information. The parking lot for the nature center is rather small, but the surrounding fields are used for overflow on hot days when the quarry is heavily used, so you too can park there if necessary; just obey the signs.

There is a paved "Handicap Trail" diverging from the road between the parking lot and the nature center and leading into the woods. Only about 200 yards long, it does give a feel for the forest and passes by several abandoned quarries (iron and marble) dating to the 1830s. If you have strollers, toddlers, or wheelchairs, this is your alternative to the soft dirt trails elsewhere in the park.

Leaving the nature center, cross the bridge over a deep ravine. This is a good place to do a little birdwatching, because you're at the same height as the tree branches, and the feeding stations at the nature center are still near enough to attract birds. Titmice, chickadees, and woodpeckers are common year-round.

The bridge opens up the trail system. Although you have many options, the walk described here is the longest one available. Turn right at the far end of the bridge; in a short distance, bear right again at the red-blazed Logger's Trail. The trail soon parallels a small stream, leading steadily but not steeply uphill. Christmas ferns line the stream's edge, lending a bit of color in winter. The hillsides on this north side of

Bird's-foot violet

Oregon Ridge have very dry soil, and undergrowth is sparse, limited mostly to shrubs like mountain laurel and huckleberry. Chestnut oak is the dominant tree. Few of the trees at Oregon Ridge are exceptionally large, indicating that a relatively short time has elapsed since its last timber harvest.

About halfway up the hill, a side trail branches off to the right. This leads to a more sheltered basin, where the soil is richer and tulip poplar dominates the slopes. The trail ends at a spring, where a trickle of water emerges from the base of a huge old tree. Continue on the red Logger's Trail to the top of the ridge, marked by a clearing for a gas pipeline. Surprisingly, this artificial habitat harbors some beautiful bird's-foot violets, an uncommon species of the genus *Viola*. With deeply dissected leaves and purple flowers, this spring bloomer is a good find. Violet seeds can persist in the soil for as long as 50 years before the right conditions allow germination; apparently the increased light along the pipeline cut was the stimulus for the growth of these violets. Turn right, follow the right-of-way for a short distance, and be alert for the trail to reenter the forest. Very soon, the Short Cut Trail, unblazed, branches to the right; follow it to the yellow Ivy Hill Trail, and turn right again.

The Ivy Hill Trail eventually drops steeply downhill to Baisman Run. On the left, Ivy Hill Pond is a beautiful woodland pool, sheltered by hemlocks and cool and damp even in midsummer. This makes a fine lunch spot; be sure to pack out all your own trash and pick up that of others as well.

From here, continue downstream along Baisman Run. Now known as the S. James Campbell Trail, the route is much narrower. The trail winds back and forth over the creek, which has incised a narrow valley. Water quality is excellent; the stream has one of the highest diversities of aquatic insect life found in central Maryland. Spring wildflowers are abundant here, in contrast to the drier slopes in the rest of the park, and include violets, trillium, bloodroot, and dwarf ginseng.

After more than a half mile, the trail approaches Ivy Hill Road. At this point, it climbs steeply out of the valley, a difficult climb. Once atop Oregon Ridge, however, it runs flat through the forest back to the pipeline right-of-way. Cross directly over and continue on the red Logger's Trail. Finally, turn right at the intersection with the blue-blazed Laurel Trail. This leads downhill off the ridge through a gully to finish near the parking lot.

Most of the trails in Oregon Ridge Park, except the S. James Campbell Trail along Baisman Run, are abandoned roads and are therefore quite wide. For this reason, they are especially suitable for cross-country skiing. Indeed, Oregon Ridge is very popular with the skinny ski set in winter. It's not for first-time skiers, however; the descent off Oregon Ridge, an easy one on foot, is considerably faster on skis.

DIRECTIONS

From the Baltimore Beltway, take I-83 north. The third exit is Shawan Road; take the cloverleaf west. Go one mile; turn left

at the first stoplight onto Beaver Dam Road. Make an immediate right into the park. The nature center is at the end of the
road.

OTHER OUTDOOR RECREATIONAL
OPPORTUNITIES NEARBY

The Northern Central Trail is located several miles due east of
Oregon Ridge Park, and it is excellent for both cycling and
walking. It is described beginning on page 299 in this book.
The upper Gunpowder River parallels part of the Northern
Central Trail, and it is a fine destination for canoeing. It is
described beginning on page 502 in this book.

Seeing the Forest for the Trees

When the first colonists landed in Maryland, much of the state was covered with mature forest. And Maryland's forests, in turn, were only a small part of the eastern forest that stretched over the entire continent westward to where the tallgrass prairie took over. Only in those few areas where the soil would not support trees were there significant natural breaks in this sea of chlorophyll. Native Americans also had an impact; by setting fires in the dry season, they created early successional habitats where hunting for game birds, rabbit, and deer was greatly improved.

Since the early 1600s, we humans have eradicated almost every acre of the original native forest in Maryland through clearing of land for agriculture, the harvesting of forest products, roads, housing, and industry. Of course, trees are a naturally renewable resource, and they have grown back over time. Today, the Maryland landscape is a patchwork of tree stands of varying ages that cover about 60 percent of the state. As positive as this statistic sounds, it belies two significant facts. First, the rate of forest land loss, mostly to development, is higher in Maryland than in any other state in the east. Second, the nature of today's forests, in terms of ecology and species diversity, is remarkably different than that of the virgin forest.

Trees are the ecological dominants in the forest. That is, they are large and conspicuous and play an important role in forest ecology. For this reason, there is a tendency to look at forests as assemblages of trees. For example, the forest products industry defines a tree as being mature when the rate at which it accumulates wood tissue reaches a maximum. Although this age varies from species to species, it is only a small fraction of the life span of the tree. The pejorative term "overmature" is applied to older trees and is used as the justification for making the decision to begin logging. In fact, the forest ecosystem, of which the tree is but one part, continues to change and mature for at least another century.

For example, different species of trees dominate a typical Maryland Piedmont mesophytic forest at 100 years than at

50 years. Ashes, elms, tulip poplars, locusts, red maples, and several types of oaks predominate at the earlier age; at a century, black and white oak are usually the most common species. Hickories reach the canopy even later.

Other changes occur that may be even more important. Among the leaves and branches, new species of insects appear. Although these species have been only poorly studied locally, an analogy to the biological diversity of tropical rain forest canopies may be instructive. When biologists first examined the insect life of those forests in the 1970s, they were astonished to find large numbers of species previously unknown to science, and a diversity and number that had never been even contemplated. Do such secrets remain hidden even today in Maryland forests?

Not all of a forest is above ground. Organisms important to the functioning of a forest ecosystem are found in the soil; without them, trees could not live. The top few inches of soil in a forest play an essential role in the nutrient cycles of the forest. Over time, the soil of a forest becomes increasingly enriched in organic matter as generations of leaves and insects decay. This process in turn conserves soil moisture and humidity, further improving soil conditions. Obscure organisms like bacteria, fungi, and tiny soil arthropods increase in number and diversity. They play a vital role as decomposers, recycling nutrients through the ecosystem.

Both on the surface and farther down in the soil, changes in the rhizosphere occur. Many plants have a mutually beneficial relationship between their roots and soil fungi. Typically the plant provides sugars for food, and possibly even some secreted protective chemicals, while the fungi assist the plant in the uptake of water and nutrients. In some cases, the association is so tight that the point where the plant ends and the fungus begins cannot be discerned even with the use of a microscope. Although the existence of these interactions is a known fact, the number and kinds of them and their role in the functioning of the forest ecosystem are as yet poorly understood.

The fungi associated with tree roots may be a bioindicator of the health of our forests. For example, if trees lose their associated fungi, they become less resistant to stress, including drought and cold. In Europe, where some forests have been dying since the late 1970s (probably because of air pollution), changes in forest fungi were noted even earlier. A rigorous survey of fungal species in marked, 1,000-square-meter plots in Holland showed a decline from 37 species in about 1970 to only 12 in 1990.

Thus a forest is more than just trees. It includes the herbaceous flora, a variety of birds, reptiles, amphibians, insects, and any number of tiny, obscure soil organisms. All are important to the proper functioning of the ecological commmunity. So when trees are cut down, more than just wood is harvested; the entire ecosystem is disrupted. Unable to exist in the sun-blasted, erosion-rutted, wind-scarred soil, most of the life forms migrate or die. Nutrients are lost; soil moisture evaporates. And although the trees will grow back in about 50 years, the forest will not mature (in terms of its biological diversity and ecological functioning) for at least a further century. 𝆏

Soldiers Delight Natural Environmental Area

County: Baltimore

Distance: About 3 miles

Difficulty: Hilly; rocky terrain

Highlights: Serpentine barrens with unique flora

More Information: Soldiers Delight Natural Environmental Area, (410) 922-3044

SOLDIERS DELIGHT is well known among botanists as one of the great natural areas in the mid-Atlantic states. A serpentine barrens, it harbors a variety of plant species that are rare, unusual, or endangered, including fringed gentian, fameflower, sandplain gerardia, and serpentine aster. But even for those not interested in the unique plant life, it is among the most beautiful and serene places in Maryland to visit. And it's not heavily used; even many Baltimore-area hikers are unaware of Soldiers Delight.

For many people, the charm of Soldiers Delight lies in its open, prairielike habitat, which gives long vistas over meadows of dry, tawny grasses. Copses of pines line swales in the terrain and stud the uplands, lending color and scent to the landscape. From high ground, the westering sun sets over distant rolling hills, setting a wide horizon afire. There is no other place in Maryland quite like Soldiers Delight.

The geology of Soldiers Delight is what makes the area unique and of special interest to naturalists. In few other places is the connection among underlying parent rock, soil, plant

Soldiers Delight Natural Environmental Area

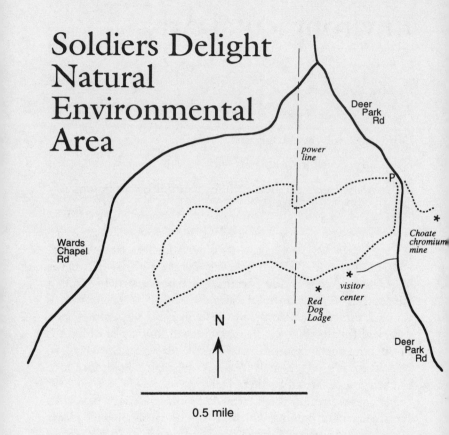

Deer Park Rd

power line

P

Wards Chapel Rd

Choate chromium mine

*

visitor center

*

Red Dog Lodge

*

N

Deer Park Rd

0.5 mile

life, and animal life so direct and easily understandable. The rock at Soldiers Delight is an uncommon one called serpentine. It is rich in magnesium, chromium, nickel, iron, and other heavy metals. The presence of these elements places stress on plants, very few species of which can tolerate these harsh conditions. Those plants that are found at Soldiers Delight tend to be those that cannot compete against more robust and common plants at sites where soil is richer and better developed. Because the number of plant species is so small, the number of animal species that this impoverished food chain can support is also reduced.

The land that Soldiers Delight comprises totals about 3,000 acres, and most of it is owned by the state of Maryland. It is administered by the Department of Natural Resources as a Natural Environmental Area. Until recently, development was limited to a small roadside gravel parking lot, a historical marker, and trails. In 1991, the state opened a visitor center; however, as of this writing, the visitor center is open on only a limited schedule owing to budgetary constraints.

Soldiers Delight is one of Maryland's most unusual place names. Explanations for the name date from the time of the French and Indian War, when Baltimore County was sparsely settled farmland. A contingent of local militia was stationed at Soldiers Delight, where the open nature of the landscape happily reduced the chance of ambush. In addition, legend has it that the militiamen were supplied with generous amounts of food by local families, adding further to their delight.

This hike of about three miles covers rolling, broken terrain but no large hills. The ground underfoot is frequently rocky, and those rocks have jagged edges. Thus care should be exercised when walking with small children. Older kids and those who hike with some regularity should have no problem.

TRIP DESCRIPTION

Although you could begin your walk at the visitor center (where there are wheelchair-accessible bathrooms, water, and information), the limited hours mean that the parking lot and facilities may not be open. It may be more convenient, therefore, to start from the gravel lot on Deer Park Road even though there are no facilities.

Deer Park Road marks a ridgeline separating watersheds: to the east, rain falls into Red Run, then Gwynns Falls, and finally into Baltimore Harbor; to the west, water drains into the nearby Liberty Reservoir, a dammed tributary of the Patapsco River. A rudimentary map adjacent to the parking lot shows loop trails on either side of the road. All are pleasant, but perhaps the most interesting is the three-mile, white-blazed loop. It is described here.

The trail begins on the west side of the parking lot, dropping steeply down a short hill. The path traverses loose rock of a fragile, easily broken nature that appears tan to white in color. Break off a piece of rock; the interior will be a greenish black. Upon oxidation during weathering, this serpentine-containing rock will return to its normal, dull appearance. This rock is of an unusual sort. It is rare on the east coast of the United States, and geologists believe that it represents a chunk of the earth's mantle, that semisolid region lying between the crustal plates and the molten core. During certain cataclysmic events like the collision of continental plates, portions of the mantle may have reached the planet's surface at widely spaced locations.

The trail rises and then dips again to a small stream, Chimney Branch. Only a giant step in width and a few inches deep, the little creek clearly has originated between here and the height of land at Deer Park Road, gathering its waters at imperceptible springs. Follow the trail through a small section of pine forest, through more scrubby trees, and down a rocky embankment to the stream, already a bit larger.

This enchanting little dell is a great place to stop, observe the local flora and fauna, and generally contemplate the universe. It is best known for its autumn blooming of fringed gentians, which flower profusely along the water's edge. This delicate herb is unusual not just for its late-season, October flowering, but also for its American-flag-blue coloration. The fringed petals open only at midday, folding up tightly from midafternoon to midmorning. Although the fringed gentian is not a rare species in the United States, this little stream in Soldiers Delight represents its only site in Maryland. And although it may be ephemeral elsewhere, blooming profusely one year and almost absent the next, the population at Soldiers Delight is typically constant in size and over time. Of course, don't dig up or pick the flowers; in addition to being unethical, it is illegal. Leave them for the next person to enjoy.

The trail continues alongside the stream through waist-high grasses. The rich earth tones of the many kinds of grasses found at Soldiers Delight have a special beauty evident only to those willing to stop and observe closely. Each seed head is actually a complex of many minuscule flowers that require a hand lens to truly appreciate. Botanists identify grasses, as they do other, more conspicuous flowering plants, by the structure of these tiny flowers. There may be more species of grasses at Soldiers Delight than on any other site in Maryland. Two species, tufted hairgrass and the vanilla-scented holy grass, have their only occurrence in Maryland here at Soldiers Delight.

The trail crosses Chimney Branch at least twice, but the creek is only an inch or two deep. Despite its modest flow, it boasts a surprisingly large and diverse aquatic fauna. The undersides of rocks in gravelly riffle areas will usually yield one or more aquatic insects. Caddis fly, mayfly, beetle, and dragonfly larvae all may be found during a search of a few minutes. Tiny salamanders are common, as are small fish in quiet pools. Some of these animals are grazers on live or dead vegetation; others are predators. Among the most notable, dobsonfly larvae, known to fishermen as hellgrammites, exhibit powerful hind pincers that can sharply pinch a finger. Taken together, these stream animals indicate a complex aquatic food web dependent on continued good water quality buffered by the surrounding undeveloped land.

As Chimney Branch passes under a set of high-tension lines, turn right (uphill) following the trail marker, a rather small, indistinct triangle of white. The area under the power lines is mowed frequently by the local utility company, and you may find anything from a short, crew-cut flora to large shrubs and small trees, depending primarily on the whim of the most recent trim crew. The soil under the power lines is deeper, richer, and better developed because of these prunings, which recycle aboveground biomass back into the ground on an irregular basis. After decomposition, the soil is that much richer for the next generation of plants. It shows; the kind of plants growing under the power lines are rather ordinary species characteristic of the better-developed soils of land adjacent to Soldiers Delight.

About halfway up the hill, the trail bears left into the surrounding oak woods, again at a trail marker. This is one of the few sites forested with hardwoods at Soldiers Delight; it is dominated by post oak and blackjack oak. In fact, only three species of trees grow in the upland portion of the barrens, the other one being Virginia pine. Note how dry the soil is, even under the shelter of the forest. Only those shrubs and small trees adapted to dry, thin soils can grow here. These forested areas are known as oak savannas and represent the oldest stage of plant succession at Soldiers Delight.

The trail soon breaks out into an upland portion of the barrens. Here the true harshness of the land is evident for the first time. Although thin stands of Virginia pine dot the landscape and clumps of grass grow here and there, there are substantial areas of barren rock. Only a few hardy lichens and weathered-looking, low-slung plants hang on in cracks and nooks in the sun-blasted rocks. For most of the next mile, the trail passes through this sere and harshly beautiful land; evening is especially striking. Stay alert for the white trail markers. At its westernmost point, the trail begins to bear left, crossing a wider but still equally shallow Chimney Branch again. More uplands follow. At an old dump, the trail makes a final, hard left, entering a woods of higher trees and tangled undergrowth.

At this point, the trail runs along the edge of the serpentine-containing soils of Soldiers Delight. Mixed with fertile soil derived from the surrounding metamorphic rocks of the Maryland piedmont, soils are more hospitable for plant growth, and the trees are signifcantly larger. Cherry, dogwood, and ash grow here, and a flourishing crop of poison ivy festoons the trees and ground. The trail follows this edge, or ecotone, eastward. By the time the power lines reappear, the trail leads back into the barrens.

Continuing uphill from the power lines, aim toward Red Dog Lodge, a handsome but abandoned hunting lodge built of native stone in the early years of the twentieth century. This area is another oak savanna, and deer in search of acorns are frequently seen here. Just beyond is a dirt road; follow it to the left, past the visitor center.

The area between the visitor center and Deer Park Road is one where experiments in grassland management are taking place. A number of scrub pines have been cut down, and their stumps are still visible. These stumps also show evidence of controlled burns, which have been used to promote the growth of grassland species. One such species, sandplain gerardia, flowers here in September, bearing small, pinkish blooms.

Just before the trail reaches Deer Park Road, another trail cuts off to the left. Paralleling the road but yards away from the traffic, it is a safe way to return to your car.

Before leaving Soldiers Delight, cross the road, pass the chained gate, and follow the trail for about a hundred yards to the long-abandoned Choate chromium mine. The largest and best preserved of the mines at Soldiers Delight, it was active in the first half of the nineteenth century. Much of the world's chromium supply at that time came from Maryland mines at Soldiers Delight and other sites in northeastern Maryland.

Return to your car after this walk of approximately three miles. Alternatively there are two marked trails and a number of abandoned roads to follow on the eastern side of Deer Park Road. Both horses and mountain bikes are prohibited on the trails at Soldiers Delight owing to the fragile nature of the soils and vegetation.

DIRECTIONS

From the Baltimore Beltway, take Route 26 (Liberty Road) west toward Randallstown. Go 4.9 miles. Turn right on Deer Park Road, and follow it for 2.3 miles to the gravel parking area. A historical marker and a sign indicate the lot.

OTHER OUTDOOR RECREATIONAL OPPORTUNITIES NEARBY

The hiking trails of the McKeldin area of Patapsco Valley State Park are about a 30-minute drive from Soldiers Delight. The McKeldin area is described beginning on page 110 in this book.

Sandplain Gerardia and the Conservation of Serpentine Grasslands

Soldiers Delight is home to dozens of rare and unusual species, but the sandplain gerardia is unique. This small annual herb, typically less than a foot tall, has pink flowers and blooms from August to October. A member of the snapdragon family, sandplain gerardia is known from less than ten sites in the world, and it is on the federal endangered species list. Soldiers Delight harbors the largest and best-protected population.

Sandplain gerardia is an annual plant. Thus only dormant seeds survive the winter season. Conditions for successful germination vary from year to year, and so the numbers of plants in a population may be equally variable. For example, in 1986 there were only 30 sandplain gerardia plants at Soldiers Delight. In 1987 there were about a thousand; the population declined to 150 or so the next year. But in 1989 there were over 10,000 plants, more than were found at all other sites combined!

Sandplain gerardia is always found in association with little bluestem; it may be parasitic on the roots of this prairie grass, or it may require some factor in the surrounding soil. This observation has allowed growth of the plant from seeds in greenhouses, providing an opportunity to study the factors affecting seed set, overwinter survivorship, and germination in a scientific fashion. Such research efforts are important, to be sure that management decisions made in natural areas are not detrimental to endangered species. Rare species are especially susceptible to local extinction by both naive management and random catastrophic events, resulting in a loss of genetic diversity in the species as a whole.

Although management of individual species is an important conservation tool, scientists now realize that the protection and proper management of the habitat as a whole are at least equally important. At Soldiers Delight, almost all of the unusual species are associated with the serpentine grasslands. Unfortunately, Virginia pines have slowly been edging into these open mead-

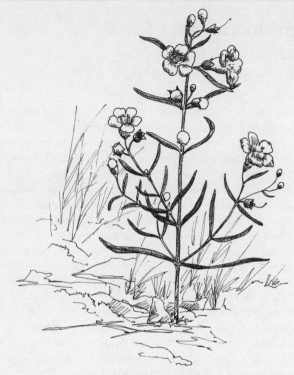

Sandplain gerardia

ows, reducing the total acreage of the prairie. The reasons for this change have to do with the historical landscape ecology of the area.

For thousands of years, native Americans set fire to grasslands, shrubby areas, and other early successionary stages in order to drive game toward waiting hunters. Such fires, in addition to improving habitat for game animals like whitetail deer, also prevented the growth of woody vegetation in serpentine grasslands. After colonists drove out native Americans in the eighteenth century, cattle were grazed on these poor soils. Only when these consumptive uses were phased out in the 1930s did Virginia pines begin to invade and spread.

In an effort to restore more grassland habitat and its unusual endemic species, scientists are conducting trial removals of pines and experimental controlled burns at Soldiers Delight. If successful, these management techniques may then be applied to more extensive tracts at one of Maryland's most valuable natural resources. *

Patapsco Valley State Park: McKeldin Area

County: Carroll

Distance: 2.8 miles

Difficulty: Hilly; rocky terrain

Highlights: River valley, forest

More Information: Patapsco Valley State Park,
  (410) 461-5005

A S A L I N E A R, river valley park, Patapsco Valley State Park stretches more than 40 miles from the river's upper reaches near Woodbine to tidewater at Baltimore Harbor. Never very wide, and interrupted by gaps where development reaches down to the water's edge, Patapsco Valley State Park still has some very pretty scenery in surprisingly pristine surroundings. One of the nicest sections of Patapsco is the McKeldin area, found near Marriottsville in Carroll County. Here, rolling hills and forested uplands lie in the fork of the river's north and south branches. Wildlife is abundant, trails are wide and well maintained, and visitor use is not heavy. All in all, it is a very pleasant place to walk at any time of the year.

The trail described here is almost three miles in length. There are two hills and two other places where the trail is rocky, irregular, and difficult underfoot, so it is not ideal for small children. In the last few years, the McKeldin area has become popular with mountain bikers, so stay alert while on the trail. When snow covers the trails in winter, cross-country

Patapsco Valley State Park: McKeldin Area

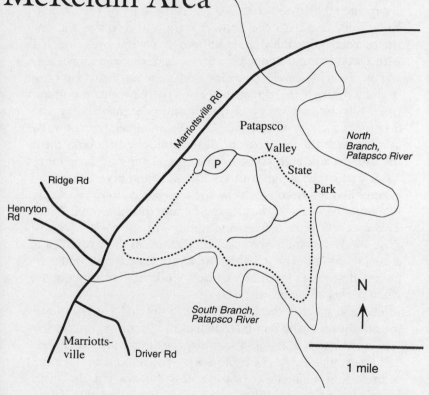

Marriottsville Rd

Patapsco

Valley

State

Park

North Branch, Patapsco River

Ridge Rd

Henryton Rd

P

South Branch, Patapsco River

Marriotts-ville

Driver Rd

N

1 mile

skiers test their skills against the curving, usually gentle down-hills.

TRIP DESCRIPTION

Begin your walk from the parking lot just beyond the contact station. A wheelchair-accessible bathroom is located here, as are picnic tables and water. To reach the start of the Switch-back Trail, return to the contact station and follow the entrance road downhill. The trailhead is prominently marked with a wooden trail sign within 50 yards of the contact station.

The Switchback Trail belies its name at first, running straight through the ridgetop forest. To the right, mountain laurel fills the understory of this dry hillside; in late May, the flowers create a profusion of blooms reminiscent of snow. In keeping with the xeric nature of the soil, chestnut oaks form the canopy, although several other species typical of the more mesic part of the soil moisture scale are found here as well.

After about a third of a mile, the trail begins to drop steeply in a series of sharp turns, incising its way through the hillside. This area was once a flagstone mine, and the spoil piles still exist. Note the chunks of rock; they glitter in the sun. Mica is a major component of this metamorphosed quartzite. In places, thin plates of mica can be found that are transparent when peeled away into sheets.

The trail reaches the bottom of the hill and emerges onto the floodplain of the South Branch of the Patapsco. Follow the trail left through grassy and shrubby openings in the sycamore and locust woods. As the trail rises off the floodplain, take the right fork at a junction, bearing downhill toward the river. Here, closer to water, silver maples dominate, but the feeling of openness still persists. Occasional floods rising onto this bottomland dump sediment around the roots of resident trees and shrubs, killing many of them and resetting the clock of succession. The trail runs along the edge of the slow-moving river; look here for beaver, ducks, woodpeckers, kingfishers, and even the occasional great blue heron.

The trail soon leads up the side of a hill, emerging on top at a paved park road. Turn right, and follow the road past picnic tables to its terminus. Continue downhill on the paved trail to the falls overlook. Here the South Branch of the Patapsco drops ten feet or so over a series of ledges into a wide pool, and the shaded dell forms a pretty scene.

At the downstream end of the falls viewing area, walk past an opening in the fence and scramble steeply downhill over exposed rocks. The gravel beach at the bottom is a popular sunbathing spot, but swimming is prohibited. The trail bears left, following a similar bend in the river. After 0.1 mile, the river makes another 90° turn, this time to the right. There is a trail intersection here; you should follow the river, again on a rocky trail, to a hillside of exposed rock. Scoured of vegetation by storms, the gneiss that forms this outcrop is among the oldest rock in the Maryland piedmont. Note how soil has accumulated in crevices and sheltered areas, allowing small plants to gain a foothold. Out on the bare rock, only mosses grow, low hardy cushions clinging to a precarious existence. The footing on these sloping rocks is usually slippery, especially if they are wet or icy; use care in crossing them.

The trail picks up on the far side of this rock outcrop, and the difficult parts are now behind you. Follow the narrow, sandy trail along the river for another 0.2 mile. Multiflora rose planted along here ensures birdlife in all seasons, and it is important as both food and shelter in the winter, when the south-facing slopes and sheltered river valley give protection to chickadees, titmice, cardinals, and other birds of brushy areas.

At the confluence of the North and South Branches, the trail bears left, ascending the North Branch of the Patapsco. Follow the trail paralleling the streambed. Water rarely flows in this arm of the Patapsco, since Liberty Dam is only about two miles upstream and releases no water. The result is a mostly dry slough. Nevertheless, pockets of rainwater persist into the summer, and this is a good place to surprise wood ducks and deer.

The trail traverses a fairly wide floodplain, with rich soils sponsoring a verdant undergrowth of shrubs and herbs. In

Wood duck

spring, violets, bloodroot, spring beauties, and jack-in-the-pulpits bloom along the trail's edge. By summer, the pace of blooming slows, but such lesser-known forest herbs as agrimony, avens, crowfoot, enchanter's nightshade, and galinsoga flower modestly. Asters and goldenrods replace them by late summer and into fall. Spicebush, with yellow flowers and red fruits, is the most common shrub.

About 0.7 mile from the junction of the two rivers, the trail reaches a fork. The right-hand trail is passable, but it eventually ascends a very steep hillside and is not recommended. Instead, take the left fork, which gradually ascends the same hill via an old road.

After a long uphill climb, the trail emerges from the woods in a dump and storage area. The forested area to the right, behind the dump, is a good site for spring wildflowers, but there are no trails through here. Instead, bear left and follow the road past a dense stand of white pine. Although these trees form a fine windbreak and shelter, an unthinned stand is a virtual biological desert. No light reaches the forest floor, and the decay of pine needles makes the soil more acidic than many organisms can tolerate.

The dirt road reaches the paved park road after 2.8 miles. Your car is just across the playing fields to your right.

DIRECTIONS

From the Baltimore Beltway, take I-70 west for 8 miles. Turn right (north) on Marriottsville Road. Continue for 4 miles to the park entrance on the right.

OTHER OUTDOOR RECREATIONAL OPPORTUNITIES NEARBY

Soldiers Delight Natural Environmental Area is located about a 30-minute drive from the McKeldin area of Patapsco Valley State Park. It is described beginning on page 99 in this book.

Wild Orchids

Among the most sought after and admired species that compose Maryland's natural heritage are several kinds of wild orchids. Although none is common and several are on the rare, endangered, or threatened list, pink lady's slipper and yellow lady's slipper are occasionally found by alert hikers. These slipper orchids are so named because their flower resembles a shoe; other common names include moccasin flower or, even more charmingly, whippoorwill's shoe. Both pink and yellow lady's slippers are woodland wildflowers. The pink variety prefers drier and more acidic soil and may be a bit more common on the coastal plain in pine forests. The yellow is more typical of piedmont forests with rich, deep, complex soils.

Orchids are uncommon in Maryland because of habitat loss and overharvesting. Conversion of mature forest into land for agriculture, development, and timber harvesting wipes out populations of woodland orchids. Indeed, the journals of naturalists in the eighteenth and early nineteenth centuries make it clear that orchids were common plants in then-undisturbed forests. Among those orchid colonies that have survived, collection by gardeners and commercial suppliers also takes a toll. This is unfortunate, because lady's slipper orchids never transplant successfully. Similarly, they cannot be grown from seed or by dividing rhizomes; any lady's slipper offered for sale has merely been dug up from a wild population.

Lady's slipper orchids are tightly adapted to their habitat. Specific conditions of microclimate, soil nutrient balance, soil pH, and microbial flora are required. A germinated seed does not emerge from its seed coat until the next year and usually takes three years to develop its first leaves. During this time, the embryo is nourished by specific strains of soil fungi. The fungal threads, or hyphae, invade the plant through a root tip and penetrate through several layers of cells to the cortex. The plant then extracts water and sugars from the fungus. Although most such mycorrhizal interactions are mutually beneficial, science has yet to learn what benefit the fungus derives from the orchid in this case. The plant-fungus relationship continues throughout the life span of the plant, which may be considerable; an orchid can take up to ten years to produce its first flower, and it will then continue flowering for many more seasons.

Yellow lady's slippers tend to be found in colonies. Some colonies are actually only a single individual plant, a complex net of rhizomes and roots studded with occasional above-ground shoots. This configuration explains the confusion of the great American botanist Asa Gray, who could not understand why colonies of yellow lady's slippers produced so few seeds.

The flower structure of lady's slipper orchids has evolved to ensure pollination. The most common pollinators are bumble-bees, which enter the flower by the large opening. Because the sides of the slipper are recurved, the bumblebee cannot climb back out. Instead, she eventually finds one of two smaller holes near the heel of the slipper. As she leaves, pollen packets cling-ing to her back are scraped off by barbs on the stigma of the flower, located just above the opening. A bit farther along, a stamen deposits a sticky pollen packet on the bee to transport to the next orchid. These specific interactions between orchid flowers and their pollinating insects were the topic of an entire (but obscure) book by Charles Darwin, written in 1862 to support his theory of natural selection.

There is little that can be done to conserve Maryland's wild orchids except to leave them alone. Some wildflower enthusi-asts will tell only their most trusted friends where a colony is located. Never pick or dig up an orchid! In addition, since orchids tend to be found in older forests, as much acreage as possible should be kept undisturbed to preserve suitable habitat. 🌾

Gunpowder South Trail

County: Baltimore

Distance: About 3 miles

Difficulty: Hilly; rocky terrain

Highlights: Narrow river valley

More Information: Gunpowder Falls State Park,
   (410) 592-2897

THE BIG GUNPOWDER river is one of the most beautiful natural areas in Maryland. By virtue of this scenic character, it is also one of the best outdoor recreational sites. Arising from many small springs and seeps in the farmlands of northern Baltimore and Carroll counties, the river flows though more than 40 miles of protected parkland on its way to tidewater. Developed paths and primitive trails follow most of its length. Several stretches of river, both tidal and flowing, are suitable for canoeing. As a greenway and corridor for wildlife, it skirts the development of Baltimore City and connects the Chesapeake Bay estuary with a variety of upland areas.

Much of the land bordering the Big Gunpowder River is preserved as Gunpowder Falls State Park. The park maintains a number of primitive trails for walking. One section, however, is so scenically outstanding as to warrant special mention, and it is described here. Running upstream from Falls Road to the base of Prettyboy Dam is a narrow trail through a constricted valley, rich in thick vegetation and rocky outcrops. Alongside the trail, the river sparkles over shallow riffles, dances through rocky chutes, and pours over steep drops into mysterious green pools. The overall impression is typical of a stream in far western Garrett County. In fact, this may well be the prettiest section of stream valley east of the mountains.

This walk of approximately three miles round trip has one steep hill and a section where scrambling over and among rocks is necessary. Although not an easy trail, it is well worthwhile, and older children will enjoy the challenges of the hike.

TRIP DESCRIPTION

Begin your walk from the tiny parking lot on Falls Road just uphill from the bridge. There is a trash can here and room for about nine cars, but no other facilities. (In the event that this lot is full, more parking is available at the top of the hill under the power lines. The Highland Trail links this parking area with the midway point of the Gunpowder South Trail.) No parking is allowed near Prettyboy Dam at the far end of the trail.

Leaving the parking lot, follow Falls Road downhill to the bridge. Now closed to vehicular traffic, the bridge affords lovely views of the river and its well-shaded valley. After enjoying the scenery, take the Gunpowder South Trail upstream, along the river's edge. The trail is clearly marked, usually with blue-painted jar tops nailed to trees. Within 100 yards, a cliff extends to the river's edge, forcing the trail up and over this obstacle. Climbing steeply over jumbled rocks for about 50 feet, the trail crests at a knife-edge ridge and then drops equally steeply back to river level. This rocky barrier is the most difficult section of the trail.

The Big Gunpowder River here flows through a very narrow, steep-sided valley. The hard, erosion-resistant mica schist rock has forced the river to wind its way through faults and cracks, creating a series of closely spaced, bouldery rapids. Small deep pools of flowing water are interspersed and invite a cooling dip on hot days. Since the water comes out of the depths of Prettyboy Reservoir just upstream, however, it is bone-chillingly cold, even in summer. The trail through this

Gunpowder South Trail

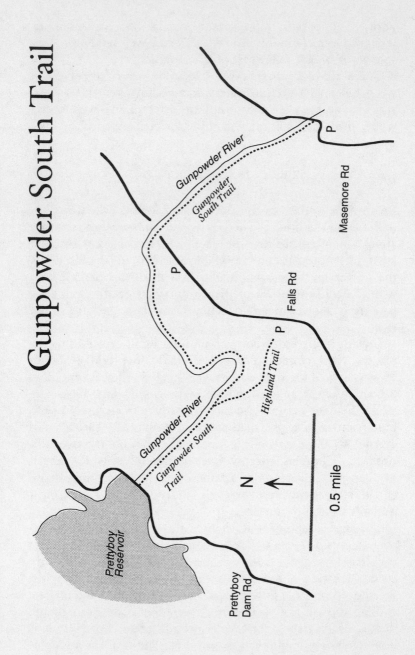

Gunpowder River

Gunpowder South Trail

P

Masemore Rd

P

Falls Rd

P

Highland Trail

Gunpowder River

Gunpowder South Trail

Prettyboy Reservoir

N

0.5 mile

Prettyboy Dam Rd

rocky section is very broken, winding atop and between boulders and over twisted roots. Take your time and use care in making your way over this stretch of trail.

The V-shaped gorge through which you are walking has no room for a floodplain, so the big old trees shading the river are those adapted to rocky, cool hillsides. There are river birch with peeling, patchy bark; cherries; a few tulip poplars growing in patches of richer soil; and the ubiquitous oaks scattered throughout. At the very steepest and rockiest sites, there are often a few hemlocks, trees typically found along streams and rivers in the western, colder parts of Maryland. This trail runs along the south bank of the Gunpowder, and so its northern exposure means that it gets much less sun in all seasons than the drier, exposed slopes on the opposite shore. An understory rich in mountain laurel, dogwood, spicebush, and witch hazel completes the list of important trees. Displays of early spring wildflowers like hepatica, bloodroot, spring beauty, and rue anemone are very fine in patches of rich woodland soil throughout the valley. By late summer and into fall, several species of petite woodland goldenrods and asters brighten the forest.

After about a third of a mile of walking, the river's gradient relents, and rapids give way to gravelly shallows. Between here and Prettyboy Dam, several large and well-constructed beaver dams span the river. Trees along the bank have been girdled and gnawed, and beaver tracks are usually evident in snow or mud. Beaver had been trapped out in Maryland for well over a hundred years when the Department of Natural Resources decided to reintroduce this charismatic fur-bearer in the 1950s. This stretch of the Gunpowder was the first place where beaver were reintroduced; they have since prospered and spread throughout the watershed. Today most stretches of river in Maryland have been recolonized by beaver.

The path soon heads uphill away from the water as the mountainside at river level becomes too steep for the trail; this point is marked by a blue wooden arrow labeled "Gunpowder South Trail." Although the path is narrow, there is good footing, and the higher elevation gives a nice view of the valley

Brown trout

where it makes a sharp bend. After a few hundred yards, this sidehill trail drops back to water level and runs straight for about a half mile. The imposing edifice of Prettyboy Dam soon dominates the narrow valley. On hot summer days, the little dell at the base of the dam may be the coolest place in Maryland, as the chill outflow air-conditions the gorge.

After enjoying a rest at trail's end, return via the same route. If you parked under the power lines at the top of the hill, you can reach this point by taking the pink-blazed Highland Trail that branches off from the halfway point of the Gunpowder South Trail.

Although there are superb scenery and hiking in this section of Gunpowder Falls State Park, most of the visitors you will see are anglers. Quite simply, this stretch of the Gunpowder River has some of the best trout fishing in Maryland, and indeed in the eastern United States. Surveys in the early 1990s yielded more than 100 pounds of trout per acre and more than 1,200 trout per mile. In large measure, this superb fishery is due to restoration of minimum flows from Prettyboy Dam, negoti-ated by the Maryland chapter of Trout Unlimited and the Maryland Department of Natural Resources. Before the mid-1980s, there was excellent habitat for a trout fishery, but lack of water prevented the trout population from reaching its full potential. It is amazing that a simple management step like maintaining minimum flows in the river could have such a remarkable effect on the ecological community. Fishing is catch and release only and of course requires a license.

DIRECTIONS

From the Baltimore Beltway, take I-83 north to Mt. Carmel Road, Route 137. Turn left. Continue on Route 137 to Evna Road; turn right. After several miles, turn right at a fork onto Falls Road and follow it to the end.

OTHER OUTDOOR RECREATIONAL OPPORTUNITIES NEARBY

The Gunpowder South Trail continues downstream from Falls Road for at least five more miles. A number of hiking trails surround Prettyboy Reservoir. Canoeing on the Big Gunpowder River downstream from this section is described beginning on page 502 of this book.

Trout and Beaver: A Conundrum in Natural Resource Management

The upper Gunpowder River below Prettyboy Dam is a beautiful and ecologically unique valley. Blessed with a regular minimum flow from the reservoir and a protected forested watershed, the little stream flows clear, cold, and clean year-round. These conditions have made the upper Gunpowder perfect for trout, and the river is one of the most productive in the east. Trout fishermen come from miles away to fish the Gunpowder.

What makes the upper Gunpowder able to support the state's best breeding population of trout is its reliable flow of cold water. Water temperature is the single most important factor affecting the persistence of trout populations. Because of deforestation for timbering and development, most free-flowing rivers in the mid-Atlantic states warm in summer, and trout are limited to small, endemic populations in remote, narrow upstream tributaries.

Three species of trout live and breed in the upper Gunpowder: brown, rainbow, and brook trout. Brook trout are the native species, whereas rainbows and brownies were introduced. Most fishermen are after brown trout, as they are the most numerous. A European species, brownies have flourished both in the Gunpowder and in other suitable streams throughout the United States because they are the least temperature-sensitive trout species. Brownies also grow larger and faster than brook trout, and for all these reasons they are the most popular species for Gunpowder fishermen.

Brown trout compete with native brook trout in the Gunpowder. Brookies have been partially displaced from the main river and are usually found in small tributaries. A number of other native fish species have probably been affected by the introduced brown trout as well.

Beaver also occupy the upper Gunpowder valley and use the river as habitat. Reintroduced in the 1950s after being trapped to extinction, beaver have flourished and spread throughout much of the state. Beaver build dams across flowing water, creating small pools; water in these pools tends to warm up more than does flowing water. In addition, beaver fell trees along the river, opening it to sunlight and further warming. Recently more beaver dams have appeared along the upper Gunpowder, and anglers are worried that increased water temperatures will affect the trout fishery. In response to their concerns, the Department of Natural Resources has begun a beaver trapping program. But killing charismatic animals like beavers is not popular with segments of the nonfishing public; they see native animals being sacrificed for the pleasures of a few sportsmen.

Beaver and their dams are an intrinsic part of our natural heritage. On the other hand, a blue ribbon trout stream is a rare commodity in Maryland today, and fishermen contribute to our economy by spending money on their sport. Such conflicts over natural resources are of increasing concern in our society; the resolution of this problem lies in the future. ☂

Little Bennett Regional Park

County: Montgomery

Distance: 3.2 miles

Difficulty: Gently rolling to hilly; well-drained terrain

Highlights: Upland forest

More Information: Little Bennett Regional Park,
   (301) 972-9222

FEW AREAS OF MARYLAND are growing as rapidly as the Washington, D.C., suburbs in Montgomery County. Perennially among the richest counties in America, Montgomery has had the finances and foresight to set aside a number of fine parks. Although many are intensive-use recreational parks, Little Bennett, set in the northwest corner of the county, is mostly just undeveloped, preserved land. A nature center and campground are located at the extreme southern edge of the park, where, in accordance with modern park design, they intrude little on the qualities of solitude and wildness that may be one of the rarest and most valuable commodities in our society today. The remainder of the 3,600-acre tract is crisscrossed by a variety of trails that make a fine destination for an active family outing.

Unlike the trail systems in many other parks, the one at Little Bennett is carefully cleared and maintained. Some of the trails follow old roads, and their width makes them ideal for cross-country skiing. Each trail intersection has a prominent sign directing you appropriately; it is difficult to get lost. The

Little Bennett
Regional Park

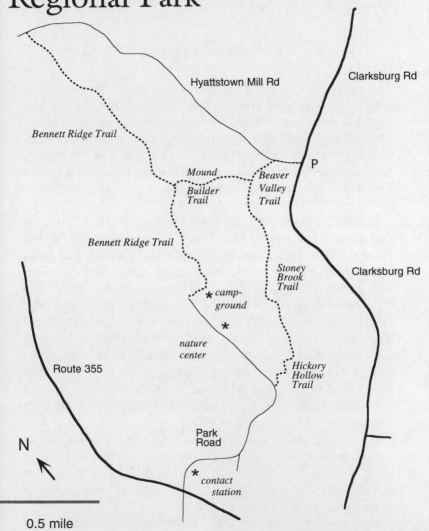

Hyattstown Mill Rd

Clarksburg Rd

Bennett Ridge Trail

P

Mound
Builder
Trail

Beaver
Valley
Trail

Bennett Ridge Trail

Stoney
Brook
Trail

* *camp-*
ground

*

nature
center

Route 355

* *Hickory*
Hollow
Trail

Park
Road

N

* *contact*
station

0.5 mile

terrain is not flat in Little Bennett Park, however. At least four streams, separated by low ridges, drain hilly uplands. The trail selected here maximizes the distance on relatively flat stretches, following a ridge and a small creek, and the two hills are gradual. This loop is 3.2 miles long.

TRIP DESCRIPTION

Begin your hike from a small parking lot at the intersection of Clarksburg Road and Hyattstown Mill Road near the heart of the park. Although it might seem more logical to begin at the nature center, parking is limited there, it is often closed (except on weekends), and an entrance fee is charged. The Clarksburg Road parking lot is actually more convenient, and it has room for about 16 cars. No other facilities are available here, however.

Carefully cross Clarksburg Road and walk 0.1 mile north on the gravel Hyattstown Mill Road. At the signpost for the Beaver Valley Trail, turn left. The wide, mowed trail leads across the Little Bennett Creek floodplain, rife with tall summer flowers like goldenrods, coneflowers, joe-pye weed, and New York ironweed. Occasional trees stud the valley, and briar tangles are common. All this is prime habitat for white-tailed deer, and if you move quietly, you'll be likely to see or hear our most numerous large mammal. Cross the creek on a footbridge, bear left, and continue left at two trail intersections to the Stoney Brook Trail. This trail soon narrows and enters a young forest of tulip poplar and red maple, with a complex understory of small trees and shrubs.

Winding generally uphill, the trail runs near Stoney Brook, a small woodland creek that dries up in arid weather. Be alert for the poison ivy that lines much of this trail. Since poison ivy is not typically found in the forest, these plants probably came in as seeds on the feet of horses or hikers.

One mile into your hike, turn right (uphill) on the Hickory Hollow Trail, the sign for which also indicates the direction of the nature center and the camping loops. Switchbacks leading

Maryland golden aster

up the hillside make the slope gradual; the trail passes through a forest now dominated by white oaks and tops out at the park road. Turn right.

The nature center is less than a half mile down the road. A pretty garden is planted with flowers that attract butterflies and hummingbirds. Soda machines, trash cans, and a bike rack are found here; if the nature center is open, its bathrooms will be accessible. If the nature center is closed, bathrooms in the camping loops could be used in an emergency.

Proceed along the road, walking the wrong way along a one-way camping loop. At the far end of the loop is a playground. Enter it past the gate, go 100 yards, and turn right to follow a wide gravel and dirt road leading into the woods. This is the Bennett Ridge Trail, although there is no sign here. This road was built when a sewer line was installed and follows the ridge for more than a mile. As with most ridges in the Piedmont, chestnut oak is the dominant tree, since the soil is poorly developed and drier than that on the adjacent slopes.

After about a half mile, turn right on the Mound Builder Trail, another wide path leading gently downhill.

The mystery of this trail's name is solved about halfway down the hill. As the trail breaks out of the forest into a clearing, a number of mixed soil and wood chip mounds are found. Some are quite large, ranging up to more than a yard in diameter and two feet high. They are home to Allegheny mound-building ants. The mounds are typically found in dry habitats and may serve to insulate the colony from heat and desiccation.

At the bottom of the hill, the Mound Builder Trail joins the Beaver Valley Trail. Turn left and retrace your steps across the Little Bennett Creek footbridge to Hyattstown Mill Road and back to your car.

ALTERNATIVE TRAILS

If you would prefer a longer trail without adding any more hills, continue on the Bennett Ridge Trail without turning down the Mound Builder Trail. Follow the Bennett Ridge Trail through fields and groves of small trees and then alongside Soper's Creek to its terminus at Hyattstown Mill Road. Turn right and follow this closed road, fording the creek at one point to the Earl's Park picnic area. Return to your car via the Hyattstown Mill Road, a park road that has only one house and is very lightly traveled. Total mileage for this longer loop is 4.9 miles. Other trails are available; consult the park map.

DIRECTIONS

From the Capital Beltway, take I-270 north toward Frederick. Take the Route 121/Clarksburg Road exit north. Proceed 2.5 miles to the parking lot at the intersection with Hyattstown Mill Road.

From the Baltimore Beltway, take I-70 west. At Mount Airy, take the Ridge Road exit and follow Route 27 south. Proceed

11.8 miles south, being careful to stay on Route 27 in "downtown" Damascus. Turn right on Brink Road, go 0.5 mile, and turn right on Route 355, Frederick Road. Go 2.6 miles north and turn right on Clarksburg Road. Proceed 2.1 miles to the parking lot at the intersection with Hyattstown Mill Road.

OTHER OUTDOOR RECREATIONAL OPPORTUNITIES NEARBY

Sugarloaf Mountain, with its network of hiking trails, is located about five miles due west of Little Bennett Regional Park. It is described beginning on page 134 in this book. The Monocacy River is also nearby, and it is a fine canoeing stream. It is described in this book beginning on page 493.

Deer Ticks and Lyme Disease

Of all the disagreeable pests that occasionally plague people in Maryland's outdoors, deer ticks are among the most unpleasant. Since the mid-1980s, an increasing percentage of deer ticks have been host to *Borrelia burgdorferi*, the infectious bacterial agent responsible for Lyme disease. Correspondingly, reported cases of Lyme disease have increased dramatically.

Lyme disease is a nasty illness characterized initially by swelling and pain in the joints, headache, fever, and especially fatigue. If the disease remains untreated, arthritislike symptoms often develop. In later stages, cardiac arrythmia, partial paralysis, meningitis, and permanent disability may occur. About 70 percent of cases exhibit a characteristic "bulls-eye" inflammation at the site of the tick bite, but the other one-third of patients have no such obvious marks. Furthermore, laboratory tests are not very conclusive, demonstrating up to 40 percent false negatives. Together, these characteristics sometimes make diagnosis difficult. Treatment with a course of antibiotics is effective early in the progression of the disease, but it cannot cure the infection and alleviate the symptoms if given later.

The intermediate vector between humans and bacteria is the deer tick. This modest tick is about the size of a sesame seed, significantly smaller than the more common dog tick. However, adult deer ticks rarely bite and transmit the disease to humans; it is the even tinier nymphal stage that is usually involved. Even a fully engorged nymphal deer tick is only about the size of the head of a pin. For this reason, people rarely notice the tick bite that transmits Lyme disease.

A female deer tick lays eggs in the spring. These later hatch into larvae, which most often feed on blood from the common deer mouse. In the spring of the second year, larvae molt into the nymphal stage. If the nymph is successful in obtaining a blood meal, usually from deer or humans, it molts into an adult in early fall. After it again attaches to a deer, mating occurs. The male deer tick dies, and the female overwinters, laying eggs in the spring to begin the two-year cycle again. Although mice, deer, and humans are the most typical hosts, ticks will bite almost any mammal from which they can get blood.

People who spend much time in brushy or grassy areas usually have several ticks on them by the end of the day. The most common tick is the dog tick, a species that does not carry the Lyme disease bacterium (it may, however, carry the causative agent of Rocky Mountain spotted fever). Dog ticks are larger; females have a large white dot on their backs, and males have white, wormlike markings. In addition to being less common, not all deer ticks are infected with the Lyme disease–causing bacterium. The state average is about 5 percent, although this figure varies from locality to locality. In 1992, 185 cases of Lyme disease were reported in Maryland, but the actual number may be well over 1,000 since private doctors are not required to report the cases they treat.

There are a few precautions that may lower your risk of getting bitten by a deer tick. Wear tightly woven, light-colored clothes so that you can easily see ticks, and tuck cuffs into your socks. Check your skin every time you return from the field. Nevertheless, the small size of nymphal ticks makes them easy to miss, so all of these measures are mostly of only psychological benefit. Stay out of woods, brushy areas, and tall grass, especially from midsummer through first frost. Spraying your shoes, socks, and pants with an insect repellent containing DEET may be helpful. The best advice is to be aware of Lyme disease symptoms and get immediate medical attention if such symptoms arise. 🦌

Sugarloaf Mountain

County: Frederick

Distance: About 1.3 miles

Difficulty: Gently rolling; rocky terrain

Highlights: Ridgetop forest, panoramic views of the countryside

More Information: Stronghold, Inc., P.O. Box 55, Dickerson, Maryland 20842

THE MARYLAND PIEDMONT, the area west of Baltimore and Washington and stretching to the Blue Ridge, is known for its gentle, ordered nature: scenic rolling hills, well-kept farms, peaceful shallow river valleys. Woodlots of old trees, preserved by longtime landowners, alternate in a patchwork with rich, deep-soiled agricultural fields. Wildlife is plentiful, even if it is the sort that has adapted to living in harmony with humans. The suburbs edge ever outward, year after year, but even today you can still go far enough "out" for it to seem rural. In the midst of this pastoral landscape, so much a product of the hand of humans, lies one incongruous mountain, towering wild and sentinel-like over the rolling countryside: Sugarloaf. Coming suddenly into view through your windshield, Sugarloaf Mountain, in southeastern Frederick County, is a surprise to all who travel here.

Sugarloaf is a monadnock: an isolated hill or mountain rising above an otherwise flat or gently rolling plain. The mountain itself is made of quartzite, a very hard and erosion-resistant sandstone distinct from the rock of the surrounding Piedmont. Thus it has been less susceptible to weathering, standing about

Sugarloaf Mountain

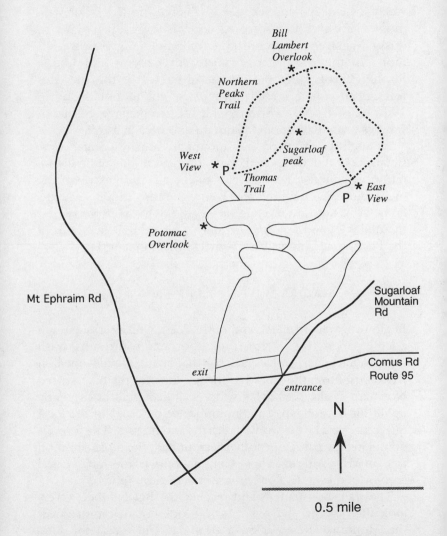

Bill
Lambert
Overlook
*

Northern
Peaks
Trail

West
View * P

Thomas
Trail

* Sugarloaf
peak

P * East
View

Potomac
Overlook
*

Mt Ephraim Rd

Sugarloaf
Mountain
Rd

exit

entrance

Comus Rd
Route 95

N

0.5 mile

700 feet above the rest of the countryside. The 570-million-year-old rock is similar to that found in the Blue Ridge a dozen miles or so to the west, but how the quartzite of Sugarloaf came to be here is not understood.

Unusual among parks and similar facilities, Sugarloaf is privately owned. No entrance fee is charged, no federal or state monies have ever been accepted, and it is always open (dawn to dusk). Managed by a nonprofit corporation, Sugarloaf is testimony to the vision and character of Gordon and Louise Strong. Recognizing the unique character of the site, this foresighted couple bought up most of the mountain and in 1946 transferred it to Stronghold, Inc., to manage. Sugarloaf was designated a National Natural Landmark in 1969.

As might be expected for a mountain, much of Sugarloaf is steep, rocky terrain. Indeed, many of the well-marked trails are rather strenuous. Fortunately, one trail circumscribes the mountain a few hundred feet below the top, and as such it is fairly flat. There are several fine views, the forest is pretty, and the trail is a good way to experience a typical upland woods of the Piedmont. This walk is about 1.3 miles in length.

TRIP DESCRIPTION

Begin your walk from the end of the road, which terminates in a large parking lot. Here are two portable bathrooms, trash cans, picnic tables, and a snack bar that is occasionally open on weekends. From the snack bar shelter, look for the blue-blazed Northern Peaks Trail. This wide, well-kept trail leads gently uphill for 0.2 mile, passing a number of outcrops of the local quartzite, heavily draped with lichens and mosses. The forest is dominated by oaks, especially chestnut oak, the most common tree on Maryland ridgetops. An understory of mountain laurel is colorful during its flowering season in early June.

The trail soon flattens and reaches the Bill Lambert Overlook after another 0.2 mile. As you look northwestward over the Monocacy River valley, a clear day will reveal the Blue Ridge in the distance. Continue on the blue trail, which is the smaller of two leaving the overlook. It leads downhill on a narrow course through a slightly more moist, and thus richer, woods. You'll see tulip poplar, red maples, and American beech trees here and some spring wildflowers, but no mountain laurel.

This trail soon intersects with a white-blazed trail; turn right. You're now traversing the north slope of Sugarloaf around to the east face. This trail is not wide, and in summer it may be draped with vegetation, since it gets less travel than other trails closer to the parking lots. At 0.72 mile, turn right at a white diamond branch trail and a sign saying "to East View." Within a few hundred yards, the East View looks out over a checkerboard of well-kept farmlands toward Washington, D.C. A parking lot with portable bathrooms, picnic tables, and trash cans is here. To continue, walk along the paved road shoulder to your starting point for a 1.25-mile loop of the mountain.

For those who want more exercise and are in shape, the summit (1,282 feet) may be reached via the Thomas Trail from the parking lot. Although steep, the trail has been improved with stone steps, and it is the most heavily traveled trail on the property. On top, there are jumbled piles of rocks, clusters of trees, and good views. On some days in autumn, it may be a good place to observe migrating hawks as they catch the updrafts generated by the isolated monadnock.

Stronghold, Inc., is an active participant in the American Chestnut Society, a nonprofit organization dedicated to research into and restoration of the American chestnut tree. This beautiful and useful tree species once flourished on Sugarloaf, until it was decimated by chestnut blight in the 1930s. Scientists are hopeful that new research techniques may provide a fresh insight into curing this poorly understood fungal disease.

DIRECTIONS

From Baltimore, take I-70 west. Turn south on Route 75. When this road ends at Route 355, turn left (south). At

Hyattstown, go right on Route 109, "Old Hundred" Pike. Pass under I-270. Go 3.0 miles to the crossroads hamlet of Comus, turn right on Route 95 (not the interstate!), and go 2.6 miles to the park entrance. Follow the only road to the end.

From the Capital Beltway, take I-270 northwest toward Frederick. Exit onto Route 109, and proceed as already indicated.

OTHER OUTDOOR RECREATIONAL OPPORTUNITIES NEARBY

The Monocacy River is just a few miles east of Sugarloaf and is a fine canoeing stream. It is described in the canoeing section of this book beginning on page 493.

Little Bennett Regional Park, with its network of trails, is located about five miles due east of Sugarloaf Mountain. It is described beginning on page 126 in this book.

Chestnut Trees and Chestnut Blight

The forests that cloaked most of Maryland at the time of John Smith's explorations were very different from the forests that exist today. Not only were there extensive tracts of huge old trees, shading the forest floor in a dim, filtered sunlight, but the kinds of trees in those forests were different. In particular, the stately American chestnut tree was an ecological dominant, representing about one out of every four trees on many upland sites. Colonists found it perhaps their most useful tree, for it grew fast and tall, split easily with a straight grain, was rot resistant, and was easily worked. Its wood was used for fence rails, siding, rough-cut boards, and furniture, and its meaty nut fed both people and animals. The chestnut is gone now from Maryland forests, eradicated by disease within living memory of our older citizens. Will we ever be able to restore the American chestnut to its former glory, the tree taking its rightful place in the canopy of our old forests?

American chestnut

The trouble began in 1904, when a scientist at the Bronx Zoo noticed several of the zoo's chestnut trees dying. The trees displayed cankers on the bark, abnormal growths with an orangish cast. The cause proved to be an infection caused by the chestnut blight fungus, *Cryphonectria parasitica*. The fungus enters the living part of a chestnut tree through a wound or minor damage and begins to grow. It sends out long threadlike filaments, known as hyphae, that grow, fuse, and eventually choke off nutrient distribution, killing the tree. Unfortunately, the chestnut blight spread steadily as fungal spores were carried on the wind and on the feet of birds; by the 1930s almost every chestnut in the Appalachians was infected and soon died.

Since then, the chestnut has been mourned by those who remember its grandeur, and it has not been forgotten. Hope for its reestablishment comes from several sources. First, there are a small number of native trees that are genetically resistant to chestnut blight; the fungus infects these trees, but is unable to kill them. Such trees will become important breeding stock, contributing their genetic heritage to a completely resistant strain in the future. Second, a virus that infects the chestnut blight fungus was discovered in Europe in the early 1950s. This virus causes the fungus to be less virulent, and such "hypo-virulent" strains typically allow the tree to survive. Unfortunately, the virus cannot "cure" every strain and variety of chestnut blight, and so it is currently of only limited usefulness. However, new techniques in molecular biology are being applied to improve the effectiveness of the virus, and scientists are hopeful that such advances will spell new hope in the restoration of one of our forest giants. 𝒦

Harpers Ferry and the C & O Canal Towpath

County: Washington

Distance: 5.6 miles

Difficulty: Flat; well-drained sand and gravel towpath

Highlights: River valley, water gap, mountains, historic town

More Information: Harpers Ferry National Historical Park, (304) 535-6371. C & O Canal National Historical Park, (301) 722-8226

T HE PASSAGE OF THE Patowmac through the Blue Ridge is perhaps one of the most stupendous scenes in Nature. . . . The scene is worth a voyage across the Atlantic." So Thomas Jefferson described the area around Harpers Ferry, where the three states of Maryland, Virginia, and West Virginia converge. High hills, steep cliffs, and tumbling whitewater make for beautiful scenery, and few places in the mid-Atlantic states have witnessed as many events of historical significance. Harpers Ferry is a fine destination for a day in the outdoors.

Much of the lower town of Harpers Ferry is a National Historical Park, restored and operated by the National Park Service. The U.S. Armory and Arsenal here was seized by abolitionist John Brown in 1859, in an incident widely considered the most important event presaging the Civil War. North and South exchanged control of the water gap many times between 1861 and 1865. Industry and commerce flourished both before and after the war, fueled by abundant water

Harpers Ferry and the C & O Canal Towpath

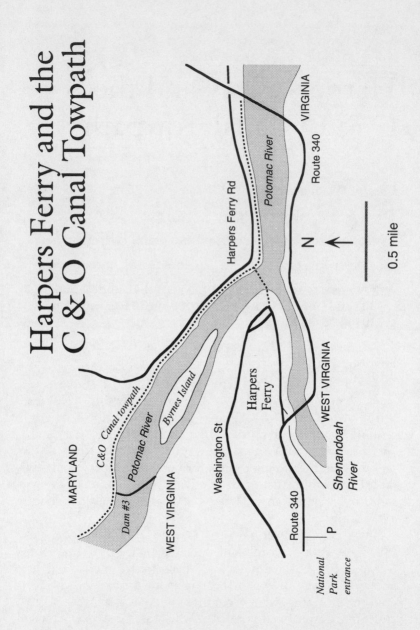

power, access to transportation systems (the C & O Canal and B & O Railroad) and surrounding rich farmland. Its location in the floodplain of both the Shenandoah and Potomac rivers, however, made the town subject to devastating floods, and by the Depression Harpers Ferry had become just another sleepy little mountain backwater. Tourism has now enlivened its fortunes, and the privately owned upper town is filled with curio shops, snack bars, and visitors.

The walk described here begins and ends in Harpers Ferry, West Virginia, but traverses the much more natural C & O Canal towpath across the Potomac in Maryland. The distance for this walk is almost six miles, but you can easily shorten or lengthen it. It is entirely flat, with a wide, well-drained path underfoot. The only impediment to strollers or wheelchairs is the stairway from the railroad footbridge to the towpath. You'll no doubt want to explore Harpers Ferry before or after your hike.

TRIP DESCRIPTION

Entry to the Harpers Ferry area depends on how early you arrive and the size of the tourist crowd. Parking in the town proper, mostly around the old railroad station on Potomac Street, is very, very limited. Chances are good that you will have to park at the new contact station and visitor center on Cavalier Heights about a mile west of town. Information, wheelchair-accessible bathrooms, water, trash cans, and telephones are available there. An entry fee is charged. From this point, a shuttle bus will take you into Harpers Ferry.

The shuttle drops you on Shenandoah Street, where much of the restoration has taken place. Most of the buildings have the same appearance as they had during the Civil War; a few may be entered, and others have window displays. One contains bathrooms (which are not wheelchair accessible); another is a bookstore with offerings on the Civil War and Harpers Ferry. An information desk is staffed here as well. Most weekends find volunteer Civil War reenactors wandering the lower town, and they give visitors a feel for what life was like here in the mid-nineteenth century.

The final block at the end of Shenandoah Street is Arsenal Square; small arms made in the U.S. Musket factory nearby were stored in the small arsenal building. John Brown's Fort, the old firehouse where Brown and his followers barricaded themselves after their ill-conceived raid on the arsenal, also stands here (although the original location was a short distance up Potomac Street on a site now occupied by the berm of the railroad).

At the intersection of Shenandoah and Potomac streets is an open space adjacent to Arsenal Square. Known as the Point, it overlooks the confluence of the two rivers. A footbridge leads across the Potomac from here, and it is the start of this hike.

Opened in 1985, this bridge gives safe, legal access to the C & O Canal towpath and Maryland Heights on the far side of the river. It was originally exclusively a railroad bridge, but a pedestrian walkway has now been built on one side, giving visitors an intimate view of the power and fury of a modern diesel as it roars by only yards away. On the way across, stop to look at the fine scenery. Below, the Potomac swirls deep and mysterious; upstream lie the rapids known as the Needles. Downriver, beautiful old stone bridge piers rise from the Potomac. These held the original railroad; the bridge was destroyed and rebuilt nine times during the Civil War. The flood of 1936 destroyed it for the final time, and the piers have stood alone in the river since then, a poignant reminder of the destructive powers of both man and nature. Ahead, the nearly vertical shale cliffs of Maryland Heights are decorated with a huge advertisement now weathered into obscurity. Painted in 1895 or 1896, it says "Mennen's Borate Talcum Toilet Powder." Rock climbers occasionally rappel down the face.

The footbridge is also part of the historic Appalachian Trail (AT). Winding its way for more than 2,000 miles between Springer Mountain, Georgia, and Mount Katahdin, Maine, the AT is probably the world's most famous foot trail. Re-routed in 1985 with the completion of this footbridge, the AT now includes about a mile of travel in West Virginia. Harpers

Ferry is the psychological if not the exact geographical halfway point, separating North from South. The town also houses the offices of the Appalachian Trail Conference, the primary source of maps, guidebooks, and other information for hikers.

At the Maryland end of the footbridge, a stairway leads down to the C & O Canal towpath. Turn right to follow the AT as it runs along the towpath. This section is very beautiful, lined by tall silver maples of great age and maturity. The Potomac runs fast through a series of rapids that extends downstream for about a mile. At high water, this stretch of river can be a killer, and even at summer low water the final rapids, White Horse, will flip most canoes. The interplay of water and rocks, however, makes a fascinating study from the safety of shore, and many hikers pause to relax with the sound of the river. On the opposite side of the towpath, spring rains often collect in the canal and provide breeding habitat for American toads and spring peepers. Orioles frequent the riverside maples in summer. Continue as far as the Route 340 bridge; below here the lands surrounding the towpath tend toward a boggy nature that makes the trail less attractive. Retrace your steps westward one mile to the Potomac footbridge, and then continue upstream on the towpath for a look at Lock 33. This lift lock was the way canal boats were floated uphill against the river's gradient. Also located here, on the other side of Harpers Ferry Road, are the ruins of the Salty Dog Saloon, reputedly one of the roughest places along the canal's 184-mile length.

The next mile of towpath is a fine area for birdwatching, as a variety of habitats closely abut each other. Over the river, look for the blue flash of a kingfisher making long, sweeping flights over the water and giving off a loud, rattlelike call. A smaller, drably colored bird fluttering out from an overhanging tree limb to pluck an insect out of the air and then quickly returning to perch may be a flycatcher. Trees lining the canal are home to species that may be found anywhere along its length: several woodpecker species, vireos, chickadees, and, in the spring, migrating warblers. Brushy areas harbor catbirds, towhees, and cardinals. The mulberry trees frequently found

Belted kingfisher

along this portion of the canal tempt the usually shy Northern oriole out of the treetops when fruits ripen in early summer. Its brilliant orange and black plumage makes it easy to spot. Equally resplendent are electrically colored indigo buntings, frequenting the top branches of small trees. The canal itself, overgrown here with herbaceous vegetation, is home to sparrows, and goldfinches flash yellow among the thistles. Over all, turkey vultures keep their silent watch, soaring on thermals and updrafts from the surrounding mountains.

About a mile from the footbridge, the Harpers Ferry Road that had been running on the opposite side of the canal from the towpath bears away, and nature closes in. This is a good chance to look at the rock that forms both Maryland Heights and the Potomac riverbed. It is known generically as Harpers shale; the term encompasses the actual mudstone itself as well as several metamorphosed related forms.

About 600 million years ago, shallow seas covered this area. Sediments accumulated slowly over time in regular layers to a depth of from hundreds to thousands of feet. Over time, pressure compacted the mud into shale, and the decaying remains of shelled marine organisms into limestone.

This geological calm and its accompanying period of deposition changed relatively rapidly about 230 million years ago. Collision of crustal plates to the east exerted tremendous forces in a westward direction that resulted in a period of mountain building known as the Appalachian orogeny. The mountains, now called the Blue Ridge, rose to immense heights, rivaling the Rockies of today. Pressure and heat generated during this time metamorphosed many of the rocks, creating quartzite, schist, and slate.

Since that time, erosion has been at work, and the Blue Ridge is today only a shadow of its former self. The Potomac has cut through the bones of the Blue Ridge at Harpers Ferry, giving rise to the dramatic scenery of today. The layering effect so common to sedimentary rocks is seen in places along the canal towpath, flat and level here, twisted and bent there. The more massive rock represents metamorphosed forms.

The towpath continues along in a very pleasant setting. The Potomac flows rapidly all along this section over small riffles at low water and in standing waves at higher flows. In several places, rock outcrops jut out into the channel from shore and make fine picnicking or sunbathing spots.

One and a half miles from the footbridge Dam Number 3, still recognizable although breached in many places, spans the Potomac. This dam was begun in 1799 to supply water to a millrace for Harpers Ferry. Improvements later allowed it to function as a water supply to the C & O Canal; thus the remains of Inlet Lock 3 are found here.

Just above Dam Number 3, the towpath bears sharply to the right. This land is the inner curve of a wide bend in the river and marks the farthest point on this walk. North of here the towpath passes through a rather scrubby and somewhat swampy forest of second growth trees that is less aesthetically pleasing. The river, backed up by the dam for more than four miles, is the playground of powerboats, bass fishermen, and water skiers. Return to Harpers Ferry via the towpath.

DIRECTIONS

From the Baltimore Beltway, take I-70 west. In Frederick, exit onto Route 340 south. Cross the Potomac River, then the Shenandoah River, and continue to the well-marked park entrance at the top of the mountain.

From Washington, take I-270 to I-70 in Frederick, and then exit onto Route 340.

Shorter routes through the countryside may be possible, especially for residents of northern Virginia.

OTHER OUTDOOR RECREATIONAL OPPORTUNITIES NEARBY

For the well-conditioned hiker, there are other trails in the area worth a visit. The orange-blazed Grant Conway Memorial Trail heads directly uphill from Harpers Ferry Road about a half mile west of the footbridge. It follows an old military road that eventually leads to the ridge of Maryland Heights and on to Crampton Gap eight miles away. A side trail, also orange blazed and actually more heavily traveled, leads across the grain of the ridge and down to the Harpers Ferry overlook. This entire area has many Civil War–era trenches, powder magazines, and stone ruins barely visible through the vegetation.

The Appalachian Trail rises out of the low point of Harpers Ferry via very steep climbs. In West Virginia, the trail is found a few feet from the south side of the Route 340 bridge over the Shenandoah River and leads up to Loudon Heights. In Maryland, the trail follows the canal towpath downriver for about two miles and then climbs steeply up Weverton Cliffs to the ridgetop of South Mountain. Fine views may be obtained from all these vantage points.

Canoeing on the Potomac River in the vicinity of Harpers Ferry is not recommended (except for groups of experienced whitewater paddlers) because of the heavy rapids.

Physiography of Maryland

Travelers through Maryland often remark how diverse in appearance the state is. Indeed, Maryland has been described as "America in Miniature" because it has coast, flatlands, rolling hills, and mountains, all of which can be visited within an easy day's drive. The study of different landforms is called physiography, and Maryland has five different physiographic provinces. They are, proceeding from east to west, the coastal plain, the piedmont, the Blue Ridge, the ridge and valley, and the Allegheny plateau. A knowledge of the location of these zones, how they formed during the past history of the planet, and what each one looks like allows the scientist, naturalist, or interested visitor to make sense of the landscape and understand why certain plants and animals exist there.

Imagine getting into your car in Ocean City, Maryland, the easternmost point in the state, along the Atlantic coast, and driving west. The appearance of the land changes little for a long part of your drive, as you pass through the agricultural regions of the Eastern Shore, cross the Bay Bridge, and weave your way through the endless traffic of Anne Arundel County. The land is mostly flat, although it may have a few very gentle hills, and if you took the time to get out of your car and feel the soil underfoot, it would invariably be sandy. This is the coastal plain, where the rocks that form the earth's crust are buried far underneath layers of sand, gravel, silt, and other unconsolidated sediments.

Somewhere west of a line extending from Washington to Baltimore, you'll notice that the land becomes more rolling. Hills are higher, and rivers cut more deeply into the landscape. You are now in the piedmont, named after an area in Italy with similarly rolling countryside. The transition from coastal plain to piedmont appears gradual to the eye, but in fact it is a rather sharp demarcation if you examine either the soil or the flow of rivers and streams. Soils of the piedmont are more complex. Sand plays a minimal role in such soils, and clays contribute much more. A spadeful of earth will be more difficult to obtain, since many small rocks will be present. Where rivers cut through the land, rock formations will be visible, and they create rapids where there is sufficient gradient. The final rapid on a river is called the fall line, and it often delineates the piedmont from the coastal plain.

An hour's drive west through the piedmont is a pleasant one, as the rolling hills get larger. Quite suddenly, just west of Frederick, a line of north-south–trending mountains appears, towering more than a thousand feet above the piedmont. This is the Blue Ridge province, which in Maryland is actually composed of two roughly parallel ridges, Catoctin Mountain and South Mountain. In between lies the Middletown Valley. These are very old mountains in geological terms, having been worn down over the millennia to mere nubs of their former grand stature. Although they may look similar to the mountains farther to the west, they have a very distinct origin and geology that make it worth our while to consider them as a unique physiographic province.

As you coast down the western side of the Blue Ridge, you soon enter the ridge and valley province. Here too are a series of north-south ridges, each pair separated by a small valley. However, the rock underlying the ridge and valley province is all sedimentary in nature, laid down in regular layers, and not at all like the massive blocks of metamorphic rock found in the Blue Ridge. The construction of I-68 through this region in the late 1980s and early 1990s has tended to even out the very dissected nature of the ridge and valley province for the automobile traveler; an alternate route on the Old National Pike (Scenic Route 40) gives a better flavor for the land.

Just west of Cumberland, you enter the final physiographic province of Maryland, the Allegheny plateau. The road leads uphill for 12 miles, gaining 1,000 feet in elevation. This is the most dramatic change in physiography in Maryland; the plateau is significantly higher, colder, wetter, and less populated than the rest of the state.

Six hours driving time from Ocean City brings you to the West Virginia border. Behind you are roughly 300 miles of asphalt road, almost a half mile of elevation change, and five distinct physiographic provinces. Maryland may be called America in Miniature, but it has its own special flavor and character, which make it unique. ⟁

Blue Ridge Duo

County: Frederick

Distance: Hog Rock Nature Trail: Less than 1 mile
Cunningham Falls Trail: About 1.5 miles

Difficulty: Hog Rock Nature Trail: Mostly flat; rocky terrain
Cunningham Falls Trail: Hilly; rocky terrain

Highlights: Hog Rock Nature Trail: Ridgetop forest, scenic
overlook
Cunningham Falls Trail: Hemlock forest, stream,
and waterfall

More Information: Catoctin Mountain Park (National Park
Service), (301) 663-9330. Cunningham Falls State Park,
(301) 271-7574

A S O N E D R I V E S W E S T on the interstate, the Blue
Ridge appears, hanging on the horizon like a dream.
The escarpment rises abruptly from the rolling country of the piedmont and marks the transition to western Maryland. There's not a lot of flat land in the Blue Ridge, so finding
an easy hike suitable for small children can be a bit of a
problem. The two hikes detailed here are the best solution to
that problem; both are short, together totaling less than three
miles. One is mostly flat, traversing a pleasant sugar maple
forest on a park nature trail. The other is hillier, but with the
reward of a waterfall at the end. They're located a short drive
apart, so you can break up the hiking with a stop at the visitor
center or a swimming lake. Taken together, these two hikes
make a great day trip in one of Maryland's most beautiful and
accessible natural areas.

Most of Maryland's Blue Ridge is preserved in parkland. South Mountain, Greenbrier, Gambrills, and Cunningham Falls state parks, the Frederick City Watershed, and Catoctin Mountain Park all occupy the ridgetops and slopes of our narrowest physiographic zone. All are scenic places to visit. But the best of the lot may be Catoctin and the parts of Cunningham Falls immediately adjacent to it. Here the mountains are higher, the buttresssed ridges more deeply incised, and the streams more plentiful. Visitation is greatest in the fall, and for good reason; the display of fall color is exceptional, primarily because the plentiful sugar maples are perhaps our prettiest autumn tree.

TRIP DESCRIPTION

Begin your trip to the Maryland mountains with a stop at the visitor center of Catoctin Mountain Park. Run by the National Park Service, it offers information, water, wheelchair-accessible bathrooms, and a small museum and bookstore. Walks or activities led by ranger-naturalists here (and at all national parks) are uniformly excellent, being both informative and fun, so check out the schedule before you wander off on your own.

Hog Rock Nature Trail

This short walk of less than a mile is splendid in autumn, when frost turns sugar maple leaves crimson. To reach the Hog Rock Nature Trail from the visitor center, drive 1.3 miles north on the Park Central Road. There are a paved parking lot for about 35 cars and wheelchair-accessible outhouses. The trail starts on the far side of the road, where trail guides are usually available in a wooden box.

This trail is relatively flat, with little change in elevation, but the ground underfoot is very uneven and studded with rocks. Indeed, much of the upper slopes of the Blue Ridge appears to be piles of rock with islands of soil built up in the crevices. Virtually all of the rock to be seen on the Hog Rock Nature

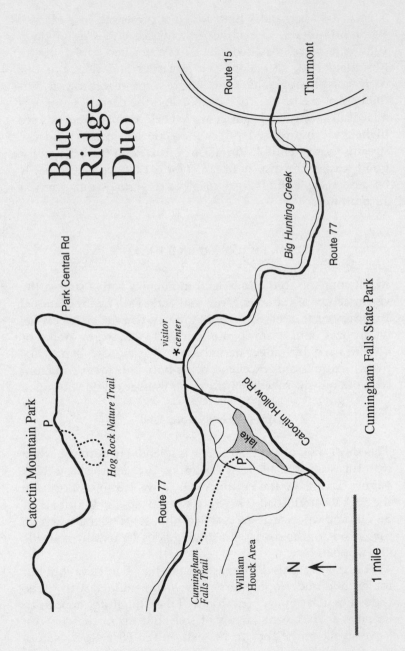

Blue Ridge Duo

Route 15

Thurmont

Big Hunting Creek

Route 77

Cunningham Falls State Park

Park Central Rd

visitor ★ center

Catoctin Hollow Rd

Catoctin Mountain Park

P

Hog Rock Nature Trail

Lake

P

Route 77

Cunningham Falls Trail

William Houck Area

N ←

1 mile

Trail is Catoctin greenstone, an aptly named metabasalt derived from ancient lava flows. Ridgetops in the park are often composed of quartzite, a very hard, erosion-resistant metamorphic rock. Almost 600 million years of age, these are among the oldest exposed rocks in Maryland. They are the remains of a much larger range of mountains. If you examine a topographic map of the Blue Ridge province, you will see that it is composed of two parallel ridges, the Catoctins, and, to the west, South Mountain. These once formed the slopes of a much larger mountain, the central part of which has been eroded away and is now the Middletown Valley.

The nature trail wanders slightly uphill and parallel to the park road for a short distance. At a fork, bear left. The forest is dominated by sugar maple, a graceful and stately tree that grows rarely east of here. In addition to their bright fall colors, sugar maples may be tapped each spring for their sweet sap, which is boiled to increase the sugar content of what then becomes maple syrup. The oldest trees date from the 1930s, when the land was last logged. Other trees share the canopy, including hickories, black gum, and several oaks, but sugar maples clearly constitute the majority of the trees found on these slopes. Because the soil is less well developed, the tulip poplars and American beeches so common at lower elevations of the park are missing. For this same reason, there are very few spring wildflowers along the Hog Rock Nature Trail.

After about a half mile, the trail reaches the Hog Rock overlook. At an elevation of about 1,600 feet, the view is between the arms of the Catoctins out onto the Piedmont farmland to the east. The overlook was named by local farmers who would bring their hogs to the base of the rock to fatten up on chestnuts and other mast that accumulated there.

From Hog Rock, the trail winds back on itself in a large circle through a very similar forest, returning you to the parking lot after a walk of almost a mile.

Cunningham Falls Trail

This short, 1.5-mile walk competes favorably for the distinction of being the most beautiful trail in the state. It traverses an unusually diverse forest where shafts of sunlight are filtered through the leaves of hemlocks, sugar maples, oaks, and beeches. Large outcrops of Catoctin greenstone litter the ground, giving the feel of a Bavarian landscape. This is not an easy trail, however. The first half is almost all uphill, and small children may get tired. Yet the scenic beauty of the trail, as well as the reward of a waterfall at the end, make this walk well worth the effort.

From the Catoctin Mountain Park visitor center, drive west on Route 77, going uphill, for about 0.2 mile. Turn left on Catoctin Hollow Road, noting the sign for Cunningham Falls State Park. Continue on this road for 1.2 miles, and then turn right at the entrance to the William Houck area. A park entrance fee is collected here during the summer. Park in the large lot servicing the beach area. When the beach is open, snacks, rowboat and canoe rentals, changing houses, and other amenities are available here; wheelchair-accessible bathrooms are open both before and after the beach season as well.

Walk across the grassy area toward the woods near the inlet side of the lake. A wooden sign indicating "Falls" here marks the entrance to the trail. The trail crosses a park road after about 150 yards of walking but then leaves civilization entirely. Winding uphill, you'll climb about 100 feet over the first third of a mile; the trail is a steady uphill pull, but never too steep. Once at the top, it will be almost flat to the trail's end.

This is a most scenic forest. Set on a north-facing slope, it receives little sunlight in the winter and is always chillier than the surrounding woods. Winter snows linger longest on such hillsides, and the microclimate is distinctly different, leading to a flora markedly distinct from that on south-facing slopes. Most notable is the preponderance of hemlocks, trees that are found mostly on rocky, shady, riverside slopes in Maryland. They are easily identified by their short, flat needles, dark green with two white stripes running longitudinally along the bottom. Hemlocks are uncommon in the eastern half of Maryland but dominate steep stream valleys in the cooler western part of the state. Sugar maples are also common in this forest, and their bright fall color set against the dark hunter green of the hemlocks makes for an enchanting autumn scene.

Near the end of this walk, hemlocks become almost the only tree in a dark, shady dell. Blackburnian and black-throated green warblers nest here. The trail terminates at Cunningham Falls, where a small stream cascades over a steep rock outcrop, dropping 75 feet over a run of 220 feet. It is a popular place, and at any given time the rocks will be populated with hikers taking in the scene. The falls is accessible by a short walk from a road, accounting for the number of visitors, but parking is very limited and roadside congestion is the rule. It's far better to reach Cunningham Falls by experiencing the best of the Blue Ridge forest on this trail! Return to your car via the same trail. If it is summer, everyone will enjoy a swim in the lake and a picnic lunch to conclude a wonderful day in the mountains.

DIRECTIONS

From Baltimore, take I-70 west to Frederick and exit on Route 15 north. From Washington, take I-270 to Frederick, where it becomes Route 15. Continue north to the Thurmont exit, Route 77, where there will be signs for Catoctin Mountain Park. Take Route 77 west. This narrow and scenic road winds uphill into the park along Big Hunting Creek, one of Maryland's premier trout streams. The Catoctin Mountain Park visitor center is on the right.

Forest Fragmentation

When Maryland was first colonized, almost all of the state was covered by mature forests. Chestnuts, oaks, hickories, and other species typical of Appalachian old-growth forests shaded rich, complex soils that harbored an abundance of wildflowers. Streams and rivers dissecting the forest flowed clear and clean, even after heavy rains. Animal life was abundant, although it tended toward insects, salamanders, and songbirds rather than species we tend to think of as "game." This primeval forest had evolved over thousands of years into a stable, diverse ecosystem, the likes of which we will never see again.

Today, only about 60 percent of Maryland is covered with forests, and most of that is in early or mid-successionary stages that in terms of structure, diversity, energy flow, and function bear only slight resemblance to a mature old-growth forest. Furthermore, most of the forests that do remain exist as patches distributed irregularly about the landscape, separated from each

Black-throated green warbler

other like islands in the sea. In this sense, the forest has been fragmented, and this fragmentation has major implications for the plants and animals that live there.

Scientists have long known that fragmentation reduces the diversity of organisms and renders populations more susceptible to extinctions. The number of species that a tract can hold relates to its size, but this species-area relationship is not linear or simple. The best example of this correlation is found among certain species of migratory songbirds. Many of our neotropical migrants nest in the interior of forests and thus require a rather large parcel of undisturbed, mature forest. Examples include ovenbirds, worm-eating warblers, veeries, and acadian flycatchers. In one study, red-eyed vireos were found in virtually 100 percent of woodlots between 50 and 75 acres in size but in only 10 percent of woodlots between 17 and 42 acres.

The degree of disturbance needed for "fragmentation" depends on the species affected; in some cases, even strip development, such as that for highways, power line cuts, or dirt logging roads, is sufficient to affect some animals. For example, it has been shown that female cowbirds use narrow strip corridors like dirt roads to provide access to the inside of large tracts of forest, where they parasitize the nests of forest interior–dwelling birds. Similarly, even small clearcuts where trees are logged from the interior of a large forest may have dramatic effects on relatively sessile species like salamanders. Salamanders rarely move more than a few hundred yards (and sometimes less) in their lifetimes. It is not unusual for a researcher who marks a woodland salamander to come back the next year and find it under the same rock! Most scientists believe that when salamander habitats are disturbed, many animals die rather than migrate.

Data such as these have prompted scientists and knowledgeable conservationists to call for the maintenance of our forests in large, unbroken tracts. In Maryland, such larger woodlands are mostly in public hands, on our state forests. Unfortunately, more than 50 percent of the acreage on these forests is managed for timber harvesting, and the most common harvest method, clearcutting, is carried out in a patchwork of small plots. Clearly, this process greatly fragments the forest, diluting the value of the forest acreage that remains. If logging has to occur on Maryland state forests (and many citizens feel that it need not), management decisions should be driven by consideration for the full spectrum of wildlife and multiple use values rather than merely harvesting trees for their economic value. Longer rotations between harvests, a ban on clearcutting, and wider use of peripheral cuts are all timber management techniques that reduce fragmentation and can be instituted on our state forests without significantly affecting the viability of the logging industry.

The Appalachian Trail

County: Frederick, Washington

Distance: Pen Mar to Wolfsville Road: 9.5 miles
               Wolfsville Road to Route 40: 7.7 miles
               Route 40 to Washington Monument
                  State Park: 3.2 miles
               Washington Monument State Park to Gapland
                  Road: 8.3 miles
               Gapland Road to the Potomac River: 10.3 miles

Difficulty: Steep climbs at passes, relatively flat along ridges; rocky terrain

Highlights: Scenic vistas, ridgetop forest

More Information: Appalachian Trail Conference, (304) 535-6331. South Mountain Recreation Area, (301) 791-4767

THE APPALACHIAN TRAIL (AT) is the most famous walking trail in the world, and we are fortunate that a section of it traverses Maryland. Thirty-nine miles of the AT follow the crest of the Blue Ridge between Pen Mar and Harpers Ferry, providing the opportunity to hike or backpack through some fine mountain scenery punctuated by several dramatic overlooks. In addition, the trail passes through the site of a small but significant Civil War battle, South Mountain.

The AT runs more than 2,000 continuous miles between Springer Mountain, Georgia, and Mount Katahdin, Maine. It was the brainchild of Benton MacKaye, who in 1921 proposed linking a series of currently existing trails into a continuous network. It was an idea whose time had come; it was im-

The Appalachian Trail

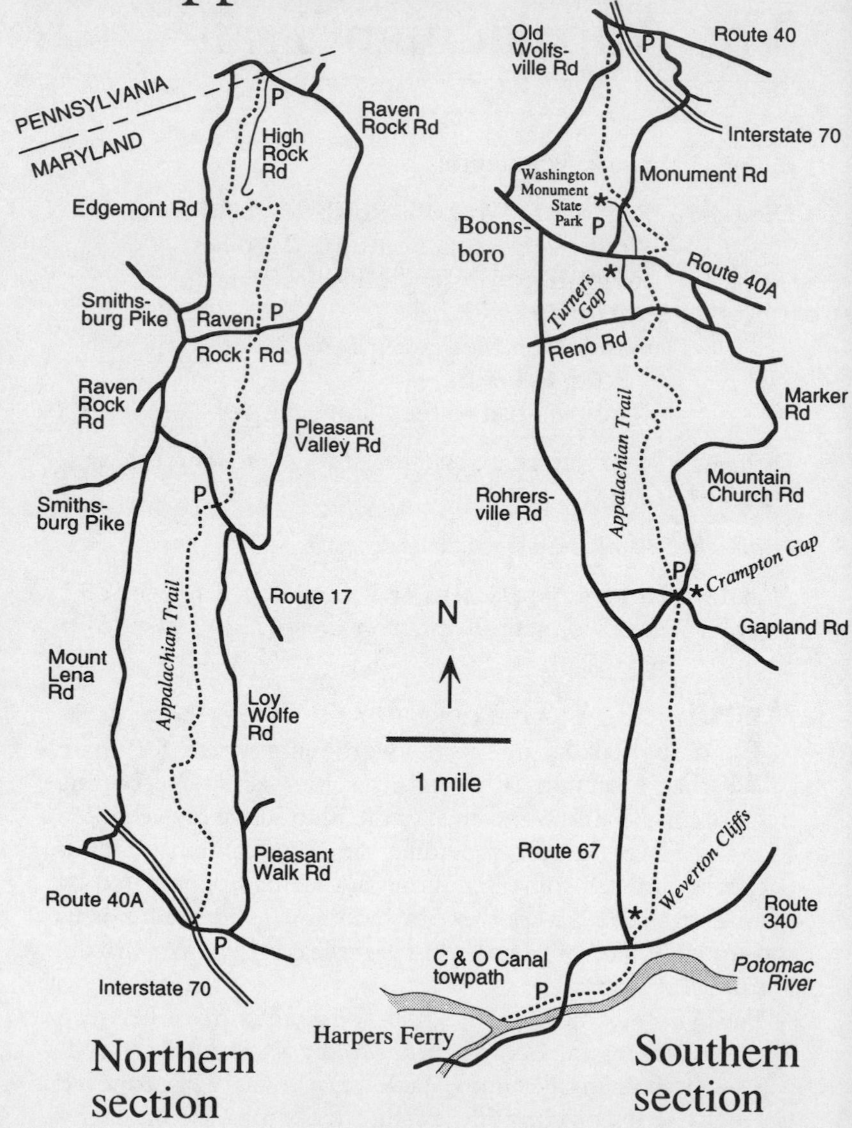

PENNSYLVANIA
MARYLAND

P

High Rock Rd

Raven Rock Rd

Edgemont Rd

Smithsburg Pike

Raven Rock Rd

P

Raven Rock Rd

Pleasant Valley Rd

Smithsburg Pike

P

Route 17

Appalachian Trail

Mount Lena Rd

Loy Wolfe Rd

N

1 mile

Route 40A

Pleasant Walk Rd

Interstate 70

Old Wolfsville Rd

P

Route 40

Interstate 70

Monument Rd

Washington Monument State Park

P

Boonsboro

Turners Gap

Route 40A

Reno Rd

Marker Rd

Appalachian Trail

Rohrersville Rd

Mountain Church Rd

P

Crampton Gap

Gapland Rd

Route 67

Weverton Cliffs

Route 340

C & O Canal towpath

P

Potomac River

Harpers Ferry

Northern section

Southern section

mediately accepted, and thousands of volunteers and Civilian Conservation Corps crews laid out and built the trail. Completed in 1937, the AT was named the nation's first "National Scenic Trail" in 1968. Federal and state money has since been appropriated to buy the trail corridor and surrounding buffer lands, ensuring permanent protection for this national treasure.

Hiking the AT affords one the chance to connect with a much larger community of outdoorspeople, past and present, who have enjoyed and even been changed by their experiences on the trail. Each year, at least 100 people set out to hike the entire trail, an adventure that takes a minimum of three months. Despite the hardships of cold and heat, biting insects, rain and mud, too little water and food, and the physical deterioration of the body that occurs after endless days of physical exertion, many "through hikers" report their experience to be the most significant period of personal growth of their lives. Many mention that friendships formed with other hikers along the way are deep and intense in a way that more casual relationships in the outside world can never be. The largest pulse of through hikers reach Maryland between Memorial Day and Father's Day; a conversation with one of them is always interesting.

Although the AT is definitely a mountain trail, much of it is not excessively difficult hiking. Large segments run for several miles along the crest of the Blue Ridge with little change in elevation. Significant uphills and downhills tend to be clustered at the trailheads, where roads cross the escarpment at gaps and hollows. Judicious use of this guide or the excellent topographic map published by the Potomac Appalachian Trail Club will allow selection of a trail segment appropriate for the experience and fitness level of your group.

TRIP DESCRIPTION

For the following trip descriptions, the AT has been divided into convenient sections for long day hikes or short overnight backpackers. The segments correspond to those road crossings where parking is readily available. For backpackers, be forewarned that cars left overnight are an obvious target for vandals and thieves; arrange for a drop-off and pick-up if possible. Mileages are given relative to where the AT enters Maryland at Pen Mar (mile 0.0). The entire trail is marked by white blazes, 2 × 6-inch rectangles painted at eye level on trees adjacent to the trail. A pair of blazes alerts hikers to a change in direction.

Pen Mar to Wolfsville Road

This most northerly section of the AT in Maryland is perhaps the hilliest in the state. The trail crosses the Pennsylvania border into Maryland at the little town of Pen Mar. Once a vacation community for city dwellers who wanted to take the mountain air, Pen Mar features some beautifully kept, very large old houses. The trail runs fairly flat for 2.5 miles but then climbs steeply for more than 500 feet to High Rock. A dramatic rock outcrop with fine views of the Hagerstown Valley to the southwest, High Rock is the premier hang glider launch site in Maryland. On any weekend with a decent breeze from the appropriate direction, a number of pilots will launch themselves off the cliff in what is truly a leap of faith. Spiraling on thermals rising from the heating valleys, they can stay aloft for up to several hours and look down on miles of Maryland landscape.

To avoid the drudgery of the uphill slog to High Rock, day hikers can consider driving up High Rock Road and parking at the top (there is no overnight parking). The AT is accessed from here by a short, blue-blazed branch trail. From this point, the AT rises a further 250 feet in elevation to its highest point in Maryland, at just over 2,000 feet atop Quirauk Mountain. Over the next 2.5 miles, the trail dips almost 1,000 feet into pretty Raven Rock Hollow. Like many such coves in the Appalachian Mountains, richer, deeper soils accumulate here, and springheads and headwater streams make water available for plant growth. Trees grow taller, there is more diversity, and understory growth is more luxurious. After crossing Raven

Rock Road, the trail climbs over Buzzard Knob and into Warner Gap, a narrow, shady dell where hemlocks are common. The last two and half miles in this section cover shallow hills.

Wolfsville Road to Route 40

This section of the AT in Maryland is one of the easiest and has two striking overlooks that are a favorite day hike destination. It is also quite popular as an easy backpack trip, with a designated backcountry campsite about halfway along the route.

The parking lot at Wolfsville Road is small but situated in a nice hemlock forest. The trail rises several hundred feet out of this shallow gap but then runs along the ridge with only small changes in elevation for the next six miles. This narrow ridge, known as South Mountain, is capped by quartzite, a hard, erosion-resistant rock. Together with Catoctin Mountain to the east, South Mountain was once the middle slopes of a much larger and higher peak. Over time, the action of water and wind eroded the softer rock that composed the bulk of this mountain, so that what was once its center now lies at a lower elevation and forms the Middletown Valley.

Ridgetops are very dry habitats for plant life, since springs and seeps typically emerge at lower elevations. Soils are thin and poor in nutrients. Under these harsh conditions, fewer plants can survive and thrive. Thus this ridge is dominated by chestnut oak, a tree so well adapted to dry, poor soils that in places it may be the only tree species present. Chestnut oaks are easy to recognize, with thick, furrowed bark and a wavy-edged leaf. Gypsy moths prefer oak, and so in the 1980s they made their first penetrations southward into Maryland along these ridges. Although some trees died from several consecutive years of defoliation, most are healthy, and gypsy moths have probably not had any long-term effects on this forest.

Near the old Black Rock Hotel site at mile 13.4 is the Pogo Campground. It is one of the few places on the trail where springs emerge close to the ridgeline. Within another mile and after a short climb, a marked side trail leads to Black Rock.

This striking outcrop of quartzite gives a panoramic view of the valley below. It often catches the breeze, and so it is a cool place to rest on a hot day. Interstate 70 passes far below; Black Rock is the boulder pile visible from the highway. A surprising amount of noise reaches Black Rock from the highway, testament to mankind's all-pervasive influence on the natural environment. About one mile farther south on the AT is another lookout, Annapolis Rocks. Overlooking an amphitheater of forest, Annapolis Rocks is more sheltered and quieter than Black Rock.

The trail south from Annapolis Rocks runs flat for a short distance and then drops steeply downhill to Route 40 at mile 17.2. The most popular day hike on the Maryland section of the AT begins at Route 40 and runs northward to the overlooks at Annapolis Rocks and Black Rock; the first part of the trail is fairly steep, however.

Route 40 to Washington Monument State Park

This short segment is described separately because the state park is often a destination in itself, and it is a relatively safe place to leave vehicles.

The AT leaves Route 40 and crosses Interstate 70 by a footbridge. Over the next 2.5 miles, a rolling but generally uphill hike leads to the base of Monument Knob. Here the trail rise steeply for 250 feet to a little pinnacle topped by the nation's first monument to George Washington. It's an ugly, jug-shaped structure of native stone, but there are nice views of the surrounding countryside from its top.

The monument is also Maryland's premier site for watching the annual fall migrations of hawks. As the days shorten, hawks and other predatory birds like ospreys and eagles begin drifting south for the winter. They congregate over several major flyways, one of which leads down the spine of mountains that includes the Blue Ridge. As prevailing winds strike these isolated ridges, updrafts are created that the birds can use to gain altitude. Spiraling upward on these invisible wind currents, hawks can conserve energy by gliding rather than having to

Sharp-shinned hawk

flap. Once the updraft gives out, the birds drift southward to the next rising air current.

Two species of hawks dominate the autumn migrations. Broad-winged hawks are moderate-sized, soaring hawks characteristic of woodlands. On occasion, proper winds at peak migration will give rise to dramatic "boiling kettles" of several dozen birds soaring in tight circles within an updraft. Broadwing migration usually peaks in about the middle of September. During the first week in October, sharp-shinned hawks dominate. These small accipiters, not much larger than a blue jay, have pointed wings, a squared-off tail, and bright coloration around the head and chest. Sharpies are among the "fighter planes" of the bird world; feeding almost exclusively on songbirds taken on the wing, they are fast and highly maneuverable. Although broad-wings and sharpies are the two species most frequently seen from the monument, birders delight in spotting the rarities: merlins, goshawks, peregrines, and eagles.

A side trail connects the AT to the parking lots at the state park.

Washington Monument State Park to Gapland Road

This section of the AT is another hilly one, with a number of climbs and descents. It is perhaps of greatest interest to those who enjoy visiting Civil War battle sites; they can traverse the land where the Battle of South Mountain was fought.

The AT drops steeply southward from the Washington monument, rises a bit, and then begins a mile-long, shallow descent to Turners Gap. At less than 1,000 feet elevation, Turners Gap is the lowest Blue Ridge crossing, and it is about two miles in width.

In mid-September 1862, the Army of Northern Virginia under General Robert E. Lee had advanced north into Maryland. It split into several groups and became dispersed over much of central Maryland. About half of Lee's troops laid siege to Harpers Ferry in hopes of capturing that important Union garrison, with its abundant munitions and supplies. The rest were near Hagerstown, their flank guarded by the Blue Ridge and a light garrison of troops in Turners Gap and Crampton Gap.

The Union Army, under General George B. McClellan, was east of the mountains and searching for the Confederates. By September 14, McClellan knew where Lee was, and he began marching up old Route 40 toward Turners Gap. Although the rebel army held the high ground, they were badly outnumbered, and the width of the gap made their position susceptible to a flanking maneuver. Fighting was fierce for most of the day, although the Union army got only a small portion of its troops into action. Confederate reinforcements arrived just in time, and by nightfall they still held their ground. After dark, the rebels withdrew, having achieved their strategic goal of slowing the Federal army. Harpers Ferry would soon fall, and both armies would gather at the nearby hamlet of Sharpsburg on September 17 for a battle that would change the course of American history: Antietam.

Only a series of roadside plaques marks the battle at Turners Gap. With the exception of the AT corridor, much of the site is privately owned, slipping quietly into history.

South of old Route 40 (now Route 40A), the AT continues mostly flat for two miles. It then climbs unrelentingly upward for more than a mile to Lambs Knoll and then drops slowly to Crampton Gap and Gapland Road at mile 28.7.

Gapland Road to the Potomac River

Crampton Gap is another of the low passes through the Blue Ridge. Like Turners Gap to the north, it was the site of a Civil War battle on September 14, 1862. However, because this is a narrower defile, the fight was smaller and of less significance. A few roadside markers commemorate the battle.

Also at the Gapland Road trail crossing is a very unusual monument. A large castlelike arch of stone was erected by Civil War correspondent Alfred Gath in the years after the war. It is the only known monument to war correspondents. The arch and the nearby graveyard lend an eerie presence to the old battlefield.

This section of trail is probably the easiest for hikers who want to get on the AT but are not sure of their capabilities. The trail rises very gently out of Crampton Gap and then runs fairly flat for almost five miles. The only difficulty is the footing; the entire AT is very rocky, and care must be taken to avoid tripping or sliding.

At mile 33.5, the trail begins a long downhill stretch leading to the Potomac River. There are fine views of the river and the water gap at Harpers Ferry from Weverton Cliffs, the final overlook before the trail drops very steeply to the river. Finally, the trail runs west for almost three miles along the C & O Canal towpath. Just opposite Harpers Ferry, a footbridge spans the river and the trail leaves Maryland.

Gypsy Moths

The forests of Maryland have faced a variety of insults and threats since European colonization more than 350 years ago. Trees have been burned down; ripped up; sawed through; infected by fungi and bacteria; subjected to acid rain, ozone, and air pollution; and generally treated badly. Unfortunately, the 1980s added injury to insult with the arrival of gypsy moths. These small forest lepidopterans are exotics, a Eurasian species brought to the United States in 1869. They quickly escaped, and they have been munching their way through the eastern forest for more than a century.

The life cycle of gypsy moths is now familiar to most Marylanders; citizens have become intimately acquainted with this insect to a degree they never would have thought possible. Tiny caterpillars hatch out of tannish egg masses in mid-April and climb upward onto tree limbs. Leaves have just appeared, and the larvae eat the tender young foliage. As these larvae grow, they shed their outer skin, going through five molts for males and six for females. At maturity, the hairy caterpillars may be up to 2.5 inches long, and they are recognized by five pairs of dark blue spots followed by six pairs of brick red spots on the back. By mid-June, the larvae spin a cocoon and pupate for about two weeks. Adult moths hatch out; males are gray to brown, whereas females are off-white and flightless. Mating occurs within a few days of emergence, and after the eggs are laid the moths die quickly.

Heavy infestations of gypsy moths can defoliate an entire forest. Fortunately, such acute damage usually occurs only at the leading edge of the expanding gypsy moth range; once gypsy moths have been established for a few years, the population crashes dramatically. As of this writing, most of Maryland has experienced the worst of these infestations, and gypsy moths are already becoming less troublesome than they were previously. Nevertheless, we can expect to live with gypsy moths in the future, with more severe outbreaks occurring every seven to nine years.

In response to public pressure, Maryland's Department of Agriculture instituted an aerial spraying program to control gypsy moth outbreaks. At present, the insecticide of choice is Dimilin, an effective chemical that interferes with the ability of a gypsy moth larva to molt. Dimilin has low toxicity to humans and other mammals and does not accumulate in the food chain. However, studies have shown that Dimilin persists in the environment for many months and has a wide spectrum of action on nontarget organisms. For these reasons, many forest ecologists and environmental advocates oppose its use. The Nature Conservancy, for example, has a policy that brands Dimilin unacceptable for use on or near its preserves.

Because Dimilin's spectrum of action includes aquatic insects and crustaceans, it is never used near streams, rivers, or lakes. Instead, riparian forests are sprayed with *Bacillus thuringiensis* (Bt), a bacterium that produces a protein toxic to moths and butterflies. Although Bt has a more specific host range, its window of activity is smaller; it must be ingested at the second or third caterpillar growth stage, or instar. Many people now feel that Bt exclusively should be used if spraying is necessary, but that the negative impacts of both Dimilin and Bt are significant enough that not spraying at all is the best approach over the long term.

The long-term implications of gypsy moths for our forests are unknown. Gypsy moths prefer oak leaves, and oak is the dominant forest tree throughout much of Maryland. Large patches of gypsy moth–killed trees are visible in several places in the state; it is conceivable that less palatable trees like tulip poplar may assume a more dominant role in the canopy. Less obviously, repeated spraying reduces populations of forest insects, especially butterflies and moths, with unknown effects on the ecology of the forest. What is certain is that gypsy moths will be with us for the forseeable future, and that we will have to learn to accept some background level of damage to trees in forests and around our homes. ⸙

Rocky Gap State Park

County: Allegany

Distance: 2.1 miles

Difficulty: Gently rolling; rocky terrain

Highlights: Dry second-growth forest

More Information: Rocky Gap State Park, (301) 777-2138

THE MOUNTAINS OF western Maryland must have been an imposing barrier to eighteenth-century colonists moving westward in search of new land. A series of ridges running generally north and south defines the region between Hagerstown and Cumberland, blocking easy westward progress. Today, Interstate 68 cuts directly across the grain of these mountains, and even with the extensive amount of filling and cutting that was done, trucks labor up the long slopes.

A few gaps pierce these ridges, and early travelers made good use of them. The most significant is the water gap created by the Potomac River, but there are others. Rocky Gap was the site of a wagon road, the Old Hancock Road, developed even before the National Pike, linking the Potomac River town of Hancock with Fort Cumberland. Today Rocky Gap has been developed into a most accessible, family-oriented state park. It is perhaps best known for hosting a country music festival each summer.

The focal point of Rocky Gap is the 243-acre artificial Lake Habeeb, around which most activities occur. There are two sandy bathing beaches, staffed by lifeguards and served by bathhouses, washrooms, and food concessions. Canoes, row-

Rocky Gap
State Park

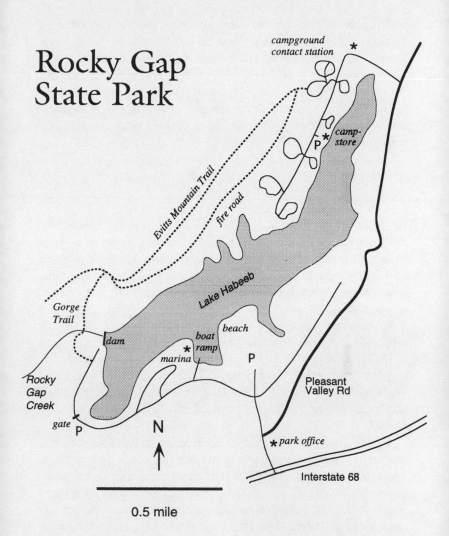

campground
contact station

*

camp-
store

P *

Evitts Mountain Trail

fire road

Gorge
Trail

Lake Habeeb

dam

beach

boat
ramp

marina *

P

Rocky
Gap
Creek

gate
P

N

Pleasant
Valley Rd

* park office

Interstate 68

0.5 mile

boats, and pontoon boats can be rented at a marina, and there is a boat launch ramp for electrically powered motor boats. The 278-acre campground is modern and well laid out, with vegetation screening most sites. At some point in the future, a championship golf course may be developed at Rocky Gap. Despite all these conveniences, much of the acreage at Rocky Gap is completely undeveloped, and several forest trails provide a most pleasant hike. The route described here traverses some very easy, mostly flat terrain; optional extensions are much more difficult and are suitable for older, well-conditioned hikers.

TRIP DESCRIPTION

Begin your hike from the campstore-beach parking area within the campground complex. In order to park here, you must have a hang tag permit, obtained at the contact station at the entrance to the campground. Just explain that you would like to hike the Evitts Mountain Trail from the "D" loop in the campground.

Wheelchair-accessible bathrooms, drinking water, and picnic tables are available near the campstore parking lot.

Walk uphill to the parking lot entrance, cross the road, and climb a short set of wooden steps. These lead within a hundred yards to the paved "D" loop road. Continue walking uphill; the Evitts Mountain Trail is marked and branches from campsite 92.

The first part of this trail is an abandoned and eroded fire road that leads up the shallow slopes of the lower part of Evitts Mountain. After a few hundred yards, the fire road turns abruptly left while the hiking trail narrows and continues uphill. The trail then follows a shallow arc left so that it too runs southwestward along the side of the hill, with little elevation change.

This entire hillside was once clearcut of all timber, since all the trees now present are about the same size. With boles less than a foot in diameter, this is a young forest. Chestnut oak is

Mountain laurel

the dominant tree, indicating a dry, thin soil poor in nutrients. There is much mountain laurel and blueberry present in the shrub layer, similarly indicating a soil type near the xeric end of the soil moisture spectrum.

White-tailed deer are common on these lower slopes of the forest, browsing on herbaceous plants and twigs and the tender greenery of woody plants. The forest also provides shelter during the day, but it is accessible to the brushy and open habitats of the park and nearby farmland. Under the relative safety of darkness, deer move out into the open to feed at dawn and dusk.

Much less common and very rarely seen are black bears. Requiring large expanses of forest land or somewhat smaller tracts linked by corridors of suitable habitat, black bears have been increasing in numbers since the 1970s. Although the largest population is in Garrett County on the higher, colder Allegheny Plateau, there are bears living in Allegany County in large, lightly populated areas like those around Rocky Gap.

The trail underfoot is rocky, with large patches of a fine, firm, cushionlike moss. During periods of dry weather, these mosses become much desiccated and assume a pale green color. Rain restores them to active growth, and they become much greener and softer. Mosses do not have a vascular system to move water internally, so they are very dependent on surface water, trapping and conserving rain in their dense cushions.

After traversing the side of the hill for almost a mile, the trail bears right and uphill. This new south-facing exposure allows pines to take their place in the forest; look for white pine, with needles in bunches of five; scrub pine, with needles in groups of two; and pitch pine, with needles in groups of three. At mile 1.1, the trail emerges onto the fire road, and hikers have several options.

If you're tired or have young children, you can return directly to the campground via the fire road. It parallels and is wider than the Evitts Mountain Trail, is less rocky underfoot, and has similar scenery. Round trip distance for this option is 2.1 miles.

For very strong hikers, consider continuing on the Evitts Mountain Trail. It climbs steeply more than 500 feet to the top of Evitts Mountain in a tough uphill slog. When the leaves are off the trees in cold weather, there are excellent views across the valley. The trail ends at an old homesite, reputed to be that of Mr. Evitts (or Evarts), a pioneer in Allegany County. Rebuffed in an affair of the heart, Mr. Evitts decided to contemplate his bachelorhood from this isolated mountaintop, far from the comforts of society. Returning by the same route, hiking distance for this option is about 3.5 miles.

Finally, birders, botanists, or anyone interested in downright pretty scenery should continue on to the Gorge Trail, whose entrance is a few hundred feet farther along the fire road. This narrow trail over rocky, broken ground leads steeply downhill into the gorge of Rocky Gap Run. A narrow defile choked with big trees, especially hemlocks, it is always shady and cool.

Rhododendron tangles form a claustrophobic understory along the tiny creek. Bird life is abundant here, including cedar waxwings, chickadees, titmice, and black-throated green and blackburnian warblers. With sunlight filtering through the dense canopy and reaching the ground only in isolated sun-flecks, this is an enchanting place. Return to the campground for a round trip of about 2.8 miles. It is also possible to start your hike from the south end of the lake, parking at the Nature Trail lot and visiting the gorge first.

DIRECTIONS

From Baltimore or Washington, take I-70 west. Just beyond Hancock, exit onto I-68. Continue for about 28 miles; the state park exit is prominently marked. Go 100 feet; the park office and entrance are just ahead. To reach the campground, turn right on Pleasant Valley Road, go 1.5 miles, and turn left at the campground sign.

Poisonous Snakes

Snakes, especially poisonous ones, are viewed by a great many people with a curious combination of repulsion and perverse fascination. Our ambivalent attitude toward these tubular reptiles seems to be deep seated but inexplicable. You may still not want to handle a snake, but a little knowledge and understanding of the life histories of snakes goes a long way toward building an appreciation of their role in the natural world.

There are only two species of poisonous snakes in Maryland: the copperhead and the timber rattlesnake. Copperheads are found throughout much of the state, typically along mountain ridges, in rocky places, on stone walls, on debris piles, and in swamps on the coastal plain. Timber rattlesnakes are much less common and are confined to rocky mountains in the western part of the state and possibly a few isolated sites elsewhere.

Both of these species are pit vipers, considered the most evolutionarily advanced group of snakes. Their pits, located halfway between the eyes and the mouth, are actually infrared heat sensors that can pick up temperature differences as small as 0.002° between an object and its background. These pits are an important sensory organ aiding in nocturnal hunts. Although they are diagnostic in identifying a poisonous snake, they may be difficult to see from a safe distance. Pit vipers have an elliptical pupil; in nonpoisonous snakes the pupil is round. The tongue of snakes is not just an organ of taste; it picks up chemical cues in the air. The tongue is then retracted and placed into Jacobson's organ in the roof of the mouth, where these chemical signals are analyzed and from which the results are sent to the brain. These snakes give birth to live young in late summer.

Copperheads average about two feet long with a stout body, a broad triangular head, and hourglass-shaped bands of reddish-brown along the body. The top of the head is coppery in color, as their name implies. A copperhead hunts on the forest floor, frequently camouflaging itself under dry leaves as it waits for prey to wander past. Food includes small rodents, birds, frogs, grasshoppers, and other large insects. Copperheads are not as aggressive as rattlesnakes, and they will almost always try to escape if challenged.

Timber rattlers are much larger, measuring from three to as much as six feet in length. Their bodies are very thick, with a markedly triangular head. Rattlers are tan to yellow in color with dark, wavy bands over the body, although there is a dark phase of the species as well as considerable variation in coloration. Rattles on the tail act as a warning to predators; one rattle is added each time the snake sheds its skin, an event that occurs about twice a year. Rattlesnakes prey on birds and small rodents, especially deer mice. Rattlers are preyed upon in turn by raccoons, red-tailed hawks, black racer snakes, and probably foxes, mostly when the snakes are young. Humans are a major source of mortality; in addition to road kills, den sites have in the past been dynamited. There is no faster way to decimate a population of rattlesnakes than to kill them in their winter den. Rattlesnakes exhibit a strict den site fidelity; many such hibernacula have probably been used for thousands of years. A snake caught out of its den in cold weather will die.

Venom from poisonous snakes like copperheads and rattlers is injected from a set of hollow, recurved, retractable fangs in the upper jaw. It is a mixture of more than 100 proteins that dissolve tissues and nerves; a number of them have been isolated and are used by modern medical science. Not all bites from a poisonous snake include injection of venom, and the amount of venom injected is highly variable. Nevertheless, any venomous bite is painful, and a severe one can be life threatening. Although about 8,000 poisonous snake bites are reported annually in the United States, only about 8 to 15 are fatal.

Snakes play an important role in maintaining the balance of nature, especially in controlling populations of small rodents. There is no reason to fear, harass, or kill them; snakes are happy to be left alone. Coexistence with snakes is mostly a matter of adapting our attitudes and keeping out of each other's way. 𝕂

Swallow Falls State Park

County: Garrett

Distance: Just over 1 mile

Difficulty: Hilly; rocky terrain

Highlights: Virgin hemlock forest, whitewater river gorge, waterfalls

More Information: Swallow Falls State Park, (301) 334-9180

S WALLOW FALLS STATE PARK, at 257 acres, is one of Maryland's smallest state parks, but it packs an incredible amount of beautiful scenery into that tiny parcel. It contains the highest waterfall in Maryland, a significant tract of virgin forest, and the deep whitewater gorge of the Youghiogheny River. Swallow Falls State Park is a wonderful destination for a weekend of camping, sightseeing, and hiking.

The walk described here covers the most scenic parts of Swallow Falls. The trail forms a loop and is short; the total distance is only about 1.25 miles. Nevertheless, you should allot at least two hours and make your walk a leisurely one. Although the trail is entirely paved with loose gravel, a few steep spots, steps, and wooden water diversion bars make it unsuitable for strollers or wheelchairs.

TRIP DESCRIPTION

The day-use parking lot, with about 80 spaces, is located about a quarter mile from the park entrance. There is a comfort

Swallow Falls State Park

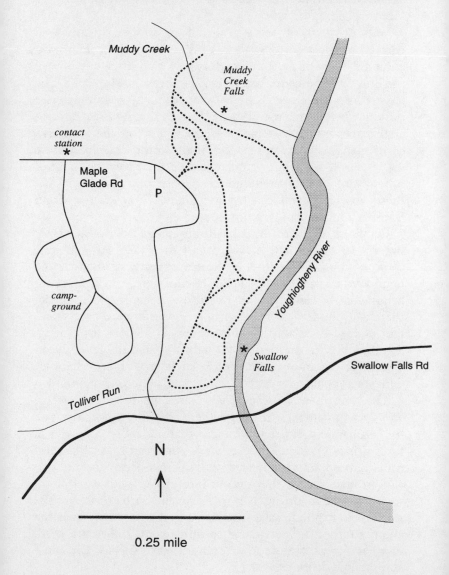

Muddy Creek

Muddy
Creek
Falls
*

contact
station
*

Maple
Glade Rd

P

camp-
ground

Youghiogheny River

*
Swallow
Falls

Swallow Falls Rd

Tolliver Run

N

0.25 mile

station here with wheelchair-accessible bathrooms, drinking water, and a soda machine. Begin your walk on the opposite side of the park road at the bulletin board. You'll find maps of the trail system here as well as at a number of other strategic locations along the way.

Walk downhill on the gravel trail for about 50 yards, and then turn right toward Swallow Falls at the signpost. Here you enter a 37-acre virgin hemlock forest (with a few white pines), the only such never-timbered stand of forest in Maryland. The largest trees are more than 300 years old, and thus they were standing before the arrival of the European colonists. But not all the trees are that old and large; the forest contains hemlocks of all ages and sizes. In the deep shade and rocky, thin, acidic soil, the only seedlings that can survive and grow are those of other hemlocks. As the large forest patriarchs eventually die, these younger hemlocks replace them. Thus even a virgin forest is a mixed-age stand of trees.

Continue on the main trail. Although a number of side trails branch off to the left, they shortcut the main trail and miss some of the best scenery. Notice how shady it is under the hemlocks. Summers are deliciously cool here, and winters are brightened by reflections off the snow. Because of the shade, there is no undergrowth of shrubs or wildflowers, except in a few places. Invariably, this is where a hemlock has fallen, leaving a hole in the canopy for light to reach the forest floor. The most common wildflower in such spots is wood sorrel, with shamrocklike leaves and white petals lined with pink.

The trail passes by several wet places where springs, seeps, and streams dampen the earth. These are superb places to look for salamanders, small amphibians that are more common in forests than is generally appreciated. Turn over rocks, logs, and other debris in muddy areas to find salamanders. Most are two to four inches long; they do not bite. A fast hand is required, since exposed salamanders burrow quickly into crevices in the soil. Avoid handling salamanders for long, since they have the ability to discard their tails when threatened, and return them to their site of capture after examination. Replace the rocks and organic debris as well.

After about a quarter mile, the trail drops toward a small stream. It then turns left alongside Tolliver Run. The tiny stream has carved a minigorge for itself through the underlying rock. The creek jumps over a five-foot waterfall into a pool surrounded by a rocky amphitheater and overhung with hemlocks. The sandy beach at this sylvan scene invites a dip in the mountain pool, but the water is ice cold even in August and keeps out all but the hardiest souls.

Notice the rocks surrounding this pool; they form flat plates in horizontal layers. The rock here is a form of sandstone, a sedimentary rock composed of relatively coarse particles cemented together. As the name implies, the layers of sand formed atop one another at the calm edge of an immense inland sea, layer upon layer being deposited over time. This regular accumulation gives the rock its characteristic appearance as stacks of flat plates.

The rock strata here give a clue as to why all of extreme western Maryland is part of the physiographic province known as the Allegheny Plateau. It's hard to believe that this area is a plateau, given the high mountains and incised river gorges. But the flat layers of rock demonstrate that this whole upland was lifted as a unit, not tilted and folded like the ridges and valleys to the east in Allegany County, or compressed by heat and pressure like the Blue Ridge Mountains. Indeed, if you find a vantage point on a high ridge from which you can look out over a large section of Garrett County, you will see that the tops of all the mountains are at about the same elevation and that all are fairly flat.

The steep, rocky banks along Tolliver Run sponsor a lush growth of rhododendron. This woody shrub with leathery, evergreen leaves blooms in late June and early July. Its big, white, fragrant flowers lend a festive atmosphere to the trail.

The trail bears left as Tolliver Run tumbles into the Youghiogheny River. Within 100 yards, the river reaches the lip of Swallow Falls, a sloping, 25-foot-high waterfall that is a focal point for hikers and one of the best-known landmarks in Maryland. In the summer, the flat rocks in the riverbed above and below the falls are filled with sunbathers, and if the river is low there is good wading in the deeper pools. Wintertime makes the falls a fairyland, as spray builds ever-higher fountains of ice over the rocks. And the fall color here is among the best in Maryland, as the reds and yellows of the sugar maples contrast sharply with the dark green of the hemlocks.

Just downstream from Swallow Falls is a large sandstone plinth with vertical sides, called Swallow Rock. In colonial times, large numbers of swallows nested on the protected cliffs, giving the area its name.

The trail follows the river downstream. Now called the Canyon Trail, it is narrower and more broken underfoot. In places, giant slabs of sandstone overhang the trail, as hikers scramble nervously to get out from under them. A few trailside boulders feature fossil tree trunks.

After about a half mile of such outstanding scenery, the trail almost imperceptibly leaves the Youghiogheny River. But the sound of water music is never far away, as the trail heads uphill alongside Muddy Creek, a tributary of the river. The trail soon opens to give a view of Muddy Creek Falls, the largest waterfall in Maryland. A stairway leads up the cliff face alongside the falls through gardens of wildflowers bathed in eternal mist. The top of the falls is a broad, flat rock where most visitors are tempted to see how close they can come to the edge. What is most mysterious is that such a wide, white curtain of water can come from such a tiny volume of water in the streambed.

From the top of the falls, turn left into a broad, grassy area marking the site of a camp where Henry Ford, Thomas Edison, Harvey Firestone, and the writer-naturalist John Burroughs met in August 1918 and again in July 1921. Western Maryland was a popular summer tourist destination even then, and many of the famous personalities of the day escaped the heat and humidity of Washington, D.C., to visit inns and summer homes near Oakland.

The trail returns uphill to the parking lot, less than a quarter mile away, passing through more fine hemlocks.

DIRECTIONS

From Baltimore or Washington, drive to Deep Creek Lake in Garrett County. From Deep Creek Lake, continue south on Route 219. After losing sight of the lake, the first major road on your right will be Mayhew Inn Road. Turn right and go 4.2 miles. At the stop sign, turn left on the Oakland–Sang Run Road. Go 0.4 mile and turn right on Swallow Falls Road. Continue 1.2 miles to the park entrance.

OTHER OUTDOOR RECREATIONAL OPPORTUNITIES NEARBY

A five-mile hiking trail connects Swallow Falls State Park with Herrington Manor State Park, where there are a swimming beach and canoe and rowboat rentals. Cranesville Swamp Preserve is only a 10-minute drive from Swallow Falls and is well worth the trip; it is described beginning on page 189 in this book.

Black Bears in Maryland

For the typical Maryland resident, there is probably no wildlife sighting more treasured than that of a black bear. At the same time, there are very few Marylanders who have actually observed a black bear in its native habitat. Many people who hike, camp, or work in the forest have never seen a free-roaming black bear in our state. In part, the reason for this is historical; in the mid-1950s, there were fewer than a dozen bears living in Maryland. But for the most part these intelligent and adaptive mammals are rarely seen because they don't want to be; naturally shy and elusive, they have learned that interaction with humans can be stressful, harmful, or even deadly.

Black bear

Black bears, the only species of bear native to Maryland, were fairly common throughout the state before its settlement. The extensive tracts of mature forest that covered most of the state constituted prime habitat, providing a plentiful supply of tender grasses and herbs in spring; roots, fruits, and insect grubs in summer; and mast in the fall. With no significant predators, bear populations were limited only by the food supply. With the coming of the colonists, however, bears were quickly hunted to the brink of extinction. The state legislature voted to approve bounties, and hunters like the legendary Meshach Browning prowled the woods secure in the knowledge that they were not only doing their civic duty but also making the land safe for settlement. Only a few of the most wary and elusive bears hung on, in deep, impassable swamps or on large tracts of forest in Garrett County.

Hunting was banned in 1949, and the black bear was listed as a state endangered species in 1972. As a result of these actions, as well as efforts to restock bears in the surrounding states of West Virginia and Pennsylvania, numbers of bears slowly began to rise. A resident, breeding population was established by the mid-1970s. Human-bear interactions, including road kills, nuisance complaints by farmers and beekeepers, and reported sightings have increased almost every year since. Bears were removed from the endangered species list in 1980, and in 1985 they were made a forest game species with a closed hunting season. Department of Natural Resources biologists estimated the black bear population in Maryland in 1992 at about 150 to 170 animals. Most are found in Garrett and western Allegany counties, on the high, forested Appalachian Plateau. There is a smaller, more fragmented population in Washington and Frederick counties, and every few years a juvenile male wanders eastward to the fringes of suburbia and into the local news.

Female black bears breed in midsummer and give birth while in the winter den in January or February. Three cubs per sow is typical for Maryland bears; at birth the cubs weigh only about eight ounces. Their eyes open after 30 to 40 days. When they leave the den by early April, cubs weigh five pounds. Throughout the spring and summer, the family wanders across a home range of several square miles, the cubs gradually learning to feed themselves and find food. They are weaned by eight months and shortly thereafter spend their first full winter with their mother and siblings in the den. By their second summer, cubs are on their own, although sexual maturity takes three years. Bears' life span in the wild is probably about 12 to 15 years, although zoo specimens may live up to 25 years.

Bears are not true hibernators; their pulse and respiration are almost normal in winter, and they will respond (groggily) if disturbed. However, their digestive system shrivels in winter and is blocked by a hard anal plug. During the rest of the year, bears avoid human contact by being mostly nocturnal; bears in true wilderness are much more active during the day.

As the population of both bears and humans in Maryland increases, contact is more and more unavoidable. Although some people welcome an increased opportunity to view wild bears in their native habitat, many others have concerns for public safety. Currently, problem bears are typically captured and relocated, although state law allows their destruction in extreme cases. In addition, sportsmen would welcome a hunting season on bear whenever the population can withstand the harvest pressure. Whatever its eventual fate, interest and controversy will no doubt continue to follow this forest animal of almost mythic proportions. 𝑟

Cranesville Swamp Preserve

County: Garrett

Distance: About 1 mile

Difficulty: Flat; boardwalk underfoot

Highlights: Frost pocket bog, unique flora

More Information: The Nature Conservancy (West Virginia Field Office), (304) 345-4350

FAR OUT ON THE extreme western edge of Maryland, where the winters are long and the people few, lies one of the most interesting and unique natural places in the state. Cranesville bog, owned by The Nature Conservancy, harbors dozens of species that are rare or threatened or that exist nowhere else in Maryland. A visit to Cranesville bog elicits the feeling of the great north woods of Maine or Canada, with spruce trees outlined against the sky and tundralike vegetation underfoot. The hike described here is not a long one, but it should not be missed if you're vacationing at Deep Creek Lake or visiting state parks in Garrett County.

Cranesville Swamp occupies a low, bowl-shaped depression in the highlands of the surrounding Allegheny Plateau. Streams drain off the hills, and their waters accumulate in the valley because the underlying substrate is impermeable. Since the water has nowhere to go, the soil remains saturated year-round, promoting the growth of only those species that can exist in perennially moist, nontidal wetlands. Furthermore, the low average yearly temperature prevents the growth of wetland

Cranesville Swamp Preserve

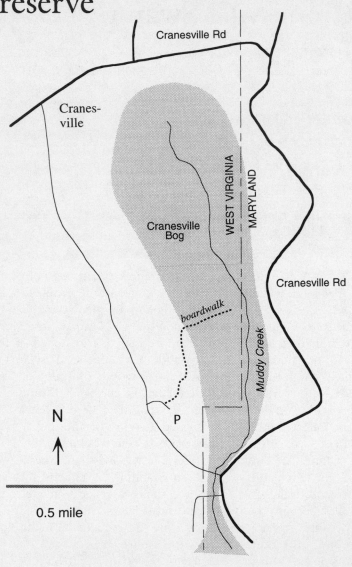

Cranesville Rd

Cranes-
ville

WEST VIRGINIA

MARYLAND

Cranesville
Bog

Cranesville Rd

boardwalk

Muddy Creek

N

P

0.5 mile

plant species characteristic of other parts of Maryland. For this reason, Cranesville and a few other smaller bogs in Garrett County are referred to as "frost pocket" bogs.

When the last ice age ended about 12,000 years ago, the climate of Maryland was considerably cooler than it is now. Boreal forest dominated the land, including such trees as spruce, fir, and tamarack. As the ice cap receded, temperatures warmed, and vegetation better adapted to this more benign climate replaced the boreal forest in most of Maryland. Only in such high, cold places as the river valleys and frost pockets of Garrett County could remnants of the boreal forest hang on. For this reason, the vegetation of Cranesville resembles that of more northerly latitudes.

The walk described here is only about a mile in length. Nevertheless, allow at least two hours to observe the plants and enjoy the solitude. A 1,500-foot boardwalk makes the bog accessible and holds down human impact on the fragile flora. Cranesville Swamp was declared a National Natural Landmark in 1965.

TRIP DESCRIPTION

Park your car in the small lot established for visitors. There are no facilities here at all, so arrive prepared. The trail to the bog is initially an old access road, now closed by a locked gate. It winds through a forest of white pine planted a number of years ago. The trail soon bears left, cutting across and then underneath the power lines. The Nature Conservancy cuts the vegetation every few years, so it is never more than waist high; there are several kinds of sweet-smelling ferns growing here, including bracken, a weedy species that grows in disturbed areas of the north woods. It is easily recognized as a coarse, upright fern up to two feet high with three regularly arranged horizontal leaves. The trail reenters the woods on the far side of the power line cut and passes through a pleasant but unremarkable forest. Finally, the trail drops down a slight hill and emerges into the open bog, about a quarter mile from the parking lot.

As you enter the swamp, scan the area for wildlife. You may surprise wary resident animals like a white-tailed deer, great blue heron, hawk, or owl. Once you leave the shelter of the surrounding forest, you're much more likely to be spotted by these and other such shy animals. Among the breeding birds found in Cranesville that are officially designated as "rare" are the Nashville warbler, alder flycatcher, and saw-whet owl. Among mammals, black bear and bobcat frequent the swamp, although your chances of seeing one of them are slim. More diminutive but equally rare is the northern water shrew, a tiny but ferocious carnivore that feeds voraciously on insects and amphibians.

As you enter the swamp, a squarish pit with tannin-stained, open water marks the site at which peat was mined from the bog at some time in the past. Virtually all boreal bogs like Cranesville are underlain by thousands of years of the accumulated, compressed vegetation known as peat. Mostly sphagnum moss, the dominant plant of the open portions of the bog, peat is formed when each year's growth dies back. The extreme acidity of the water in a bog, however, prevents the microbial growth that causes decay, and peat accumulates to a depth of many feet. The pit is a good place to look for frogs and salamanders, as well as aquatic insects like whirligig beetles and water striders.

About 50 feet out from the woods, the boardwalk forms a square enclosing a 12 × 12-foot section of the bog. This is a fine place to get down on hands and knees and examine the surface of the bog. Sphagnum moss occupies most of the surface in a dense mat; in wet areas, it is possible to push down on one section with a hand or foot and see the ripple spread out over the surface, similar to the effect when a pebble is tossed into a lake. Although a bog may look solid, it definitely is not! The boardwalk was installed, therefore, to provide dryshod access to the center of the bog.

In addition to sphagnum moss, another common plant is the wild cranberry, a trailing vine with half-inch-long, elongate leaves spaced alternately. Their fruit becomes ripe in October, when visitation to Cranesville bog increases dramatically. Cran-

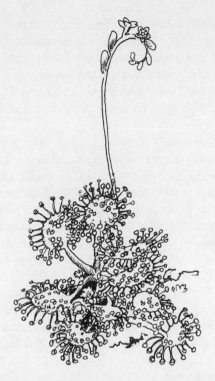

Sundew

berries host one of the rarest insects in Maryland, the bog copper. Females of this little orange and black butterfly lay eggs on cranberry leaves; the larvae that hatch out feed on the juices of the leaf.

A common but minuscule plant can be found here as well. Look for tiny sundews on muddy, clear spots on the bog surface. These "carnivorous" (actually insectivorous) plants are much smaller than most people expect; many of them are less than an inch in diameter, so you will need to look closely. Leaves are circular and covered with glandular hairs that secrete a sticky substance capable of entrapping small insects. The leaves then secrete enzymes that digest the animal in place. The sundew derives nutrients, especially nitrogen, from the decomposition of the insect.

Patches of shrubs and even small trees form islands in the open parts of the bog. These represent areas where soil has collected around hammocks of vegetation, and the micro-habitat is a bit drier than that on the surface of the bog. The buildup of higher, drier areas becomes a self-perpetuating occurrence and can lead to a gradual reduction of open bog over time.

The boardwalk leads into a central part of Cranesville Swamp where trees have established themselves. It is from this wooded portion of the preserve that Cranesville gets its official name of "swamp." The term *swamp* applies to any wooded wetland; a bog is more limited, referring to a peat-filled wet-land with acidic water. Hemlock, black spruce, and red maple dominate the swamp, but the rarest tree is the tamarack (also known as larch). One of the few deciduous cone-bearing trees, it has short, yellow-green needles that are found in clusters of twenty or so. The easiest time to locate a tamarack is in late autumn, when its needles turn yellow before falling. Only a single tamarack is easily observed from the boardwalk; it is found to the right about 30 feet off the boardwalk as it enters the tree zone.

The boardwalk ends as of this writing in a beautiful, sun-dappled meadow of grasses, sedges, and cinnamon fern under several pines. The Nature Conservancy plans to extend the boardwalk even farther as time and money allow, until it eventually reaches the open water of Muddy Creek.

Return on the boardwalk to the point where it enters the uplands. Make an immediate left turn; a narrow trail runs along the border of the bog. The crabapple trees that screen your view of the bog are an indication that the upland area was once farmland with mixed usage. The trail passes under the power lines again, right at the edge of the bog. A few old railroad ties are visible here and there; when the power line was put in, heavy equipment crossed the bog on this "corduroy" road. Fortunately, most of the scars from this insult have healed.

The trail turns right, uphill, a few yards beyond the power line cut. The pine plantation on the left has white and red pine growing in dense rows and some stands of Norway spruce. The trail returns you to the parking lot within 200 yards. Total distance on this walk is about a mile.

Biting insects are surprisingly few at Cranesville. A few mosquitoes or deerflies may be present in the early summer, but in general you will not need insect repellent.

DIRECTIONS

From Swallow Falls State Park, turn right on Swallow Falls Road. Go 1.35 miles, and turn right on Cranesville Road. Go 4.25 miles. Turn left on Lake Ford Road, which soon turns to gravel. Go 0.35 mile; bear right at the fork. Continue for about 200 yards, cross a small creek, and make an immediate right under the power lines. The parking lot is about 100 feet ahead. All these turns are marked with signs directing visitors to the "swamp" or "nature preserve." This parking lot is actually in West Virginia, as is the boardwalk; the border runs through the middle of Cranesville Swamp.

OTHER OUTDOOR RECREATIONAL OPPORTUNITIES NEARBY

Swallow Falls State Park is just a few miles from Cranesville, and it offers a beautiful hike through different scenery. Herrington Manor State Park is also nearby, and it has hiking trails, a swimming lake, and rowboat and canoe rentals.

"Carnivorous" Plants

Bogs like Cranesville are some of the most unusual and interesting habitats in Maryland. To many people, however, a bog conjures up a variety of unpleasant images: clouds of pernicious, biting insects, disguised patches of sucking, quicksandlike mud, and malevolent carnivorous plants that reach out to kill unsuspecting animals. All of these misconceptions, however, have scant basis in fact. Take, for example, the so-called carnivorous plants. Although this name has stuck in the public imagination for such organisms, "insectivorous plants" might be a better one. These plants obtain some of their nutrients by the capture and digestion of small insects; their prey does not include any of the vertebrates.

The most common of the carnivorous plants in North America are sundews, bladderworts, pitcher plants, and Venus flytraps. Only the latter is not found in Maryland, being confined to the Carolinas. The other species are rare, however, and are found only in specialized habitats like bogs.

Sundews, pitcher plants, and bladderworts all share certain characteristics. Each of them captures insects, primarily as a way to obtain nitrogen for the manufacture of protein. Nitrogen is usually a limiting factor in bogs; it is present in soils at levels insufficient for the proper growth of many plants. Sundews, pitcher plants, and bladderworts all attract insects to a chamber from which escape is difficult. Once an insect is captured, digestion is accomplished by the release of enzymes that break down its soft parts (although digestion by bacteria also plays a role in decomposition of the animal).

Sundews are the most common insectivorous plant in Maryland. They are found in most bogs, whether those bogs are in the extreme western part of the state as at Cranesville or on the coastal plain of the Eastern Shore or southern Maryland. The plants are tiny, in some cases less than an inch across, and require observation on hands and knees (sometimes not an easy thing to do in a bog!). The insects are captured on the surface of modified leaves, which are arranged on short stalks in a basal rosette. Each leaf has a number of hairs, and each one is tipped with a sticky substance that sparkles in the sun. When an insect lands on the leaf pad, it becomes entangled in the goo and eventually dies. The sundew flowers in June, although, in keeping with its inconspicuous nature, a hand lens is required to see any detail.

Bladderworts are less well known than the other insectivorous plants, but in some places they are more common. They tend to be found near open water because they capture swimming rather than flying prey. A small bladder is found on the surface or just under the water. When an insect touches the trigger hairs, a trapdoor on the bladder swings open, water rushes in, and the insect is swept along. The trapdoor closes behind, and the insect is eventually digested.

Finally, pitcher plants are the largest of our insectivorous plants. Their leaves are modified and fused to form a series of upright tubes with an attractive, mottled appearance. The interior of the tube is very slick, with downward-pointing hairs. Insects may fly or crawl in, but many cannot get out. Eventually they fall into the mix of rainwater, bacterial sludge, and enzymes in the bottom and die. The pitcher plant flowers in June, putting up a large, conspicuous, liver-colored flower.

The best place to see these insectivorous plants is the Pine Barrens of southern New Jersey. Although suitable wetland areas in Maryland tend to be small and disjunct, the Pine Barrens contains thousands of acres of bog habitat. A canoe trip down the Oswego or Wading rivers passes many bogs where all three of these families of insectivorous plants are common. Together, these plants compose a fascinating and unique addition to our natural heritage. ☈

CYCLING

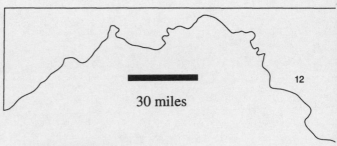

30 miles

12

1. Assateague Island Bike Trail
2. Blackwater National Wildlife Refuge
3. Point Lookout State Park
4. Quiet Waters Park
5. Baltimore and Annapolis Trail
6. Patuxent Environmental Science Center
7. Rock Creek Trail
8. Capital Crescent Trail
9. National Arboretum
10. Patapsco Valley State Park: Avalon-Orange Grove Area
11. Northern Central Trail
12. Antietam National Battlefield
13. Chincoteague National Wildlife Refuge
14. Mount Vernon Trail
15. Gettysburg National Military Park

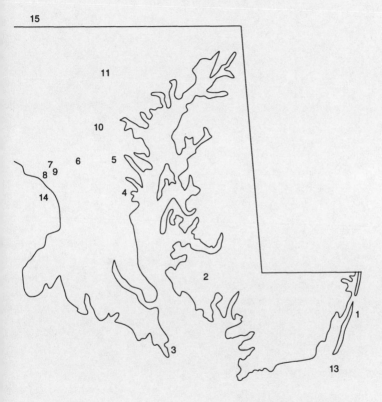

CYCLING WITH KIDS

KIDS LOVE TO GO CYCLING. Bikes represent freedom and independence to them, the chance to explore the far reaches of the neighborhood, the opportunity to do new and different things, and the experience of covering ground quickly and cleanly. In many ways, a bike is to a ten-year-old what a first car is to a teenager.

Twenty years ago, most people abandoned their bicycles when they earned their driver's licenses. Not anymore. A high percentage of adults now have bicycles and ride them with some regularity. Bicycling is a healthy, noncompetitive, nonpolluting form of exercise. It has also become a family activity, enjoyed not just by kids and parents but by grandparents as well. The popularity of cycling has been due, in large measure, to two factors: the creation of safe, off-road bike trails and the invention of sturdy, reliable, and comfortable mountain bikes. Together, these advances give a family the opportunity to spend an enjoyable day in the outdoors bicycling together.

Because older children are so familiar with bicycles and bicycling, Mom and Dad are sometimes the novices on family bike trips. Nevertheless, with younger children, parents will have to assume their usual roles as leaders, teachers, and guardians. A few simple preparations and precautions will help ensure a safe, satisfying bike ride.

The purpose of this chapter is to address those aspects of bicycling that are specifically different because children are along. It is not a comprehensive treatment of bicycling in general. A number of good books can supply you with more information regarding the sport of bicycling; consult your public library or bookstore.

EQUIPMENT

More so than walking or canoeing, bicycling depends on good equipment to be fully enjoyed. For kids, that means a sturdy, reliable bike and a carefully fitted helmet. Bicycles should be made of good-quality materials and components and should have an efficient, easy-to-pedal design. Choose a reputable, brand-name bike, even if it is more expensive than a generic one. Such bikes will usually hold up longer and retain more of their value upon resale. Most important, the bike should fit the child properly. Never buy a bike for a child to "grow into." This means that you will have to buy several bicycles for a child between the time that he or she learns to ride and maturity. Bicycles that are outgrown can always be resold or passed on to a younger child. Purchase children's bikes from a reputable bike shop, where an experienced salesperson can determine the correct frame size for the child. If the proper frame size is not in stock, have the shop order it or look elsewhere; do not settle for the next closest size.

Helmets are the single most important safety feature for bicycling. All children's helmets must be approved by the American National Standards Institute or the Snell Memorial Foundation; notice of such approval is found on the helmet itself or the box in which it is sold. Helmets with a hard plastic shell are sturdier than those made of foam with a fabric cover. Young children riding in child seats require helmets with fuller coverage. As for the bicycle itself, a professional salesperson (or an experienced rider) is the best source of advice. To provide effective protection in a crash, a helmet must fit properly. Heads come in all shapes and sizes, but helmets do not. Most helmets come with foam strips that can be glued into the helmet in order to provide a more customized fit, but achieving such a fit may take more foam than is supplied. A properly fitted helmet should not wiggle around loosely on the head. Wear the helmet forward so that it covers the temples and upper forehead; these are the areas most likely to take a blow in a crash. Finally, insist that children wear their helmets at all times when riding—and set an example by wearing yours.

Adults should carry standard repair and emergency equipment. A spare tube for each size tire, a pump, and a small tool kit are important components of a repair kit. One should also bring along duct tape, lubricant, and a cloth with which to wipe off grease. Emergency equipment includes identification, money, toilet paper and a plastic shovel, a knife, and a small first aid kit. Unless the area to be covered is close to home or very familiar, an up-to-date map is also a must.

CARRYING SMALLER CHILDREN

Children learn to ride a bike on their own at varying ages, but most are usually on training wheels by age six or seven. Younger children can ride with an adult. In the past, kids typically rode behind the cyclist in specially designed chairs that bolted onto the bicycle frame. However, these child carriers had some major drawbacks. Some were cheaply constructed or poorly designed. The child was usually strapped in by a single seatbelt, an arrangement that was insecure at best. Most significant, the child's presence raised the center of gravity of the bike; a sudden movement could upset the balance of the rider, and executing emergency maneuvers safely was almost impossible.

A far safer alternative is to carry a child (or even two) in a bike trailer. These sturdily constructed trailers attach to the bike at the seatpost and are stable and comfortable for both the cyclist and the child. Pedaling is only slightly more difficult. Two kinds are currently on the market: one in which the child faces the rear and another in which the child faces forward. Consult your local bike shop for more detailed information.

ON THE ROAD OR TRAIL

In some ways, bicycling with kids is easier than walking with them, because the activity of biking is satisfying to children in and of itself. Most kids will not need encouragement to keep up; if anything, they may tend to get out too far ahead. Keep your group together as much as possible. Stop frequently to rest and for play; this is especially important for small children riding in trailers, who get restless after a half hour or so of inactivity. Feed children often and have high-energy snacks available. It's easy to get dehydrated when pedaling, so be sure that children drink regularly. Bring along spare jackets for everyone; nylon shells are excellent windbreakers, and pile and fleece linings add warmth. You probably do not need rain gear except on longer rides with older children; bicycling in the rain is so miserable that it's best just to stay home or do something else. Most important, teach your kids the rules of the road and their responsibilities as cyclists, and insist that they be safe and courteous riders.

There's a wonderful world out there to explore, and bicycling is a great way to see some of the most interesting parts of Maryland. So saddle up the family and roll on out. Good cycling!

Assateague Island
Bike Trail

Section: State Park day-use parking lot to terminus and return

County: Worcester

Distance: 9.5 miles

Type: Designated roadside bike trail

Surface: Asphalt

Difficulty: Flat

Hazards: Traffic on adjacent road, biting bugs

Highlights: Barrier island, salt marsh

More Information: Assateague Island State Park, (410) 641-2120. Assateague Island National Seashore, (410) 641-3030

THE BARRIER ISLANDS on Maryland's Atlantic coast are some of the most beautiful and appealing places in the state. Fenwick Island, on which Ocean City is located, becomes the second largest city in Maryland on prime weekends like Memorial Day, July Fourth, and Labor Day. Just to the south, separated by a narrow inlet, is Assateague Island, considerably less populated but only slightly less popular. The conjunction of land and sea at places like these attracts us and has a calming, restorative effect on the human psyche.

In large measure, it is the ocean beach that draws people. But on a natural barrier island like Assateague, the beach is just one of a number of distinct habitat types, each with its own

Assateague Island Bike Trail

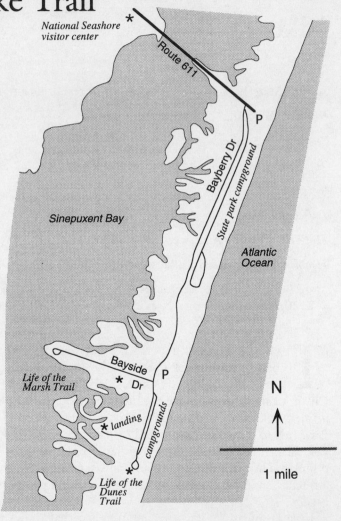

National Seashore visitor center

Route 611

P

Bayberry Dr

State park campground

Sinepuxent Bay

Atlantic Ocean

Bayside

P

Life of the Marsh Trail

Dr

* landing

campgrounds

Life of the Dunes Trail

N

1 mile

characteristic flora and fauna. The dunes, shrub zone, maritime forest, and hypersaline marshes are all equally interesting, although conditions may make them less accessible. Fortunately, the National Park Service has helped by establishing interpretive walking trails through each life zone on Assateague, linked by a very pleasant paved bike path. Cyclists will find this trip to be a fine opportunity to explore the "other" Assateague: the land behind the dunes.

This bike trail is 9.5 miles in length when ridden as described. It is a separate, paved lane that runs adjacent to the park road and is separated from it by a few feet of gravel. The bike path is only wide enough for a single bicycle, so it must be ridden in single file. It is suitable for children of all ages, although adults should supervise them closely at the few road crossings and should ensure that they don't stray from the bike lane.

TRIP DESCRIPTION

Begin your bicycle tour from the day-use parking lot of Assateague Island State Park, located a short distance east of the bridge from the mainland. Operated by Maryland's Department of Natural Resources, this is the primary parking area on the island for beachgoers. There is parking here for hundreds of cars, usually sufficient if you arrive before 11 A.M. or after 4 P.M. in beach season and always ample at other times of the year. An entrance fee is charged. Changing houses with cold-water showers, flush toilets, drinking water, and a snack bar are available.

To reach the bike path, ride out of the parking lot via the road on which you entered, being careful of vehicle traffic. Pass the entrance kiosk and turn left onto Bayberry Drive, the island's only paved road. Use care at this busy intersection. At this point, join the separate, marked bike lane.

The bike path traverses the shrub zone of Assateague Island. Thus a dense hedge of vegetation dominated by fragrant bayberry, wax myrtle, common reed, cattail, loblolly pine, and poison ivy encroaches on the bayward (western) side. Bird life is abundant, including catbirds, various sparrows, and yellow warblers in the woody vegetation and red-winged blackbirds in the reeds. Insect life abounds as well; if the day is without a breeze, don't dawdle or the mosquitoes will attack in droves!

Pass the campgrounds of Assateague State Park, which occupy the area on the ocean side of the road and bike path. After two miles, management of the land passes to the National Park Service and you are actually in Assateague Island National Seashore. Go another half mile and turn right onto Bayside Drive. Although this road has no official bike path and no shoulders, it is lightly traveled, and all but the youngest riders should not mind the traffic. A short distance down Bayside Drive is the parking lot for the Life of the Marsh nature trail. This is a fine opportunity to see some of the prettiest natural habitats on Assateague, so lock your bike and walk to the trail entrance.

A boardwalk leads through the wall of vegetation and out onto the salt marsh. This enables visitors to see the life of this most interesting habitat without the difficulties normally involved: slippery, smelly mud underfoot and clouds of mosquitoes rising to your epidermis for a prospective blood meal.

A salt marsh is a place of transition, where land and sea meet, yet it is different from either. Washed by high tides twice a day, the plants and animals that live here are exposed to hours of inundation by salty water that pulls precious fresh water from living tissues. At low tide, sun and wind cook and desiccate, imposing a whole new set of stresses. In spite of these extreme conditions, a number of organisms have adapted to this harsh and beautiful environment. Indeed, salt marshes are the most productive natural habitat found on earth today.

The marsh at Assateague is dominated by salt marsh cordgrass, *Spartina alterniflora*. This tough, resilient grass covers many acres surrounding the boardwalk and gives the first impression of a neatly kept lawn. It is one of only a very few species of higher plant that can tolerate the twice-daily tidal cycle of flooding and desiccation and, therefore, much of the low marsh is a monoculture of cordgrass. Cordgrass exhibits several adaptations that allow it to live in salty water. Like dunegrass, cordgrass can secrete salt through special cells along the blade. In the early morning light, these crystals of salt may glitter like jewels scattered across the marsh. The roots of cordgrass can filter out fresh water from the salty bay water.

Despite the stresses with which they must deal, plants living in a salt marsh enjoy certain advantages. Each high tide brings a fresh supply of nutrients and oxygen to the cordgrass, and light and competition from other plant species are never limiting factors. Cordgrass spreads aggressively by means of underground rhizomes that form a thick, dense mass. This root system filters out sediments from seawater and thus builds up the marsh. In fact plantings of cordgrass have been successful in controlling erosion along some shorelines in Chesapeake Bay.

Cordgrass plays a dominant role in the ecology of Sinepuxent Bay, the hypersaline embayment behind Assateague Island. Dead plant material is broken down into detritus by the actions of bacteria, waves, and microscopic grazing animals. About half of this detritus stays in the marsh and acts as a food source for marshland inhabitants, while the other half is washed into the bay. Here it forms the basis for an aquatic food chain, being consumed by mussels, clams, oysters, molluscs, and other creatures. Cordgrass also provides shelter and protection to immature and small adult fish, shrimp, crabs, and snails.

The area traversed by this boardwalk was dredged and drained in the 1950s to be made into a marina as part of the grandiose development schemes for Assateague Island. The devastating storm of 1962 dashed these hopes, however, and the island was purchased by the federal government in 1965. Thirty years later, evidence of ditching for mosquito control, spoil banks where fill dirt was dumped during construction, and dredging for boat slips still mars the landscape.

An arm of the boardwalk leads to an observation platform. From this slight but significant elevation, the wide expanse of Sinepuxent Bay and surrounding marshes spreads for miles. This is a good place to look for birds; laughing gulls and common terns are frequently seen diving for fish in warm weather. Overhead, snowy egrets, glossy ibis, and various gulls glide by. Willets feed in the marshes, their wings flashing a black and white pattern as they fly.

The boardwalk trail leads down to the water's edge and a tiny white sand beach. Windrows of eelgrass have been tossed up to the high tide line, where beach fleas, flies, and other insects forage through the decaying vegetation. Eelgrass is a submerged aquatic flowering plant that covers extensive areas of the floor of Sinepuxent Bay. Like dunegrass on the beach and cordgrass in the marsh, eelgrass is a keystone species for the aquatic community, providing a protected habitat for a large number of animal species and stabilizing bottom sediments and dampening wave action. It contributes to the food chain both indirectly by acting as a substrate for algal growth and directly when it dies back each winter. Small patches of eelgrass growing on the bottom may be seen in the shallow water just offshore; more extensive seagrass meadows lie farther out in deeper water.

Many visitors to the Life of the Marsh trail are content merely to observe from the boardwalk. However, there is no better way to really appreciate the marshes and back bays of Assateague than to wade right in and become a part of them. So roll up your pants legs, kick off your shoes, and step into the water! This little semienclosed bay of a few hundred yards' diameter is ideal for a fluvial walk because it is very shallow and not too muddy.

Taste the water of Sinepuxent Bay. Seawater is very salty to the taste and measures about 33 parts salt per thousand parts water, with very little variation. Here in the back bays, however, a series of sunny, calm days may evaporate so much water (leaving the salt molecules behind) that salinity rises to as high as 40 parts per thousand. Because the whole bay is so shallow (typically less than four feet deep at low tide) and connections to the ocean are so few, bay water does not get mixed with ocean water, and it becomes so hypersaline that one can taste the difference.

As you slosh along the shore, all sorts of small aquatic animals will scurry away. These creatures can be easily captured and examined by running a seine net, available from stores that sell fishing equipment. In such shallow waters, a typical pass along 50 feet of shoreline will yield hundreds of animals. Most common will be small fish, especially members of the minnow family like killifish and mummichogs. Grass shrimp, transparent crustaceans about an inch long, will be equally plentiful. Immature blue crabs sheltering in patches of eelgrass sometimes show up, but most are too quick to be trapped by the seine.

A visit in late May or early June will most likely yield a few horseshoe crabs cruising the shallows. These primitive arthropods evolved more than 200 million years ago in shallow warm seas and have flourished unchanged ever since. With a hard brown carapace averaging about a foot in diameter and a nasty-looking (but harmless) spike protruding from the rear, horseshoe crabs patrol the bay and ocean bottoms for clams and worms. In late May, horseshoe crabs migrate to the beaches of lower Delaware Bay to breed, resulting in one of the truly impressive wildlife spectacles in North America. Although Delaware Bay is the epicenter of breeding activity, some also occurs on more distant beaches, such as those at Assateague.

Explore as much of this little bay as you care to, and then return to the boardwalk. The path passes through another screen of dense vegetation at the edge of the marsh and ends at the parking lot.

Remounting your bike, continue west on Bayside Drive. The road ends at a picnic area on an exposed peninsula of land that is almost always windy. For this reason, it is a popular area for windsurfers, and their colorful sailboards are frequently seen darting back and forth across Sinepuxent Bay. Clamming is allowed here, although beds near the shore become depleted rather early in the season.

Pedal back up Bayside Drive to Bayberry Drive, turning right to continue your ride south on the island. Within 100 yards, the bike path leaves Bayberry Drive by bearing left into the even more lightly traveled campground access road. If you like wildflowers, check the grassy wet swales in the campground itself; blue-eyed grass and blue toadflax abound in spring, and summer brings on meadow beauties and ladies' tresses orchids. Purple gerardias are common in the fall. The bike trail terminates 0.6 mile farther on at the Life of the Dunes nature trail. Once again, park and lock your bike.

This trail is a short loop through the secondary dune and shrub habitats. Although it is interesting, be forewarned: unless there is a strong breeze, the mosquitoes could well be intolerable between May and October. A number of factors interact to determine how bad the level of mosquitoes will be on Assateague, including time of year, wind speed and direction, and rainfall. If the island has undergone a long dry period, the mosquito population may not be too large, but wet weather usually results in an unpleasant experience with Assateague's most numerous species.

The trail winds through the secondary dunes, where expanses of bare sand alternate with hillocks of vegetation. Plants that colonize bare sand are true pioneers, which are especially adapted to life in a hot, dry, nutrient-poor environment. Most of them have deep-delving, extensive root systems, a dense, bushlike structure, and leaves modified by waxy cuticles, scales, or dense hairs. The most common of these plants is beach heather, a low, spreading shrubby plant with scalelike leaves. In dry periods, it may appear dead, but a good rain will restore it to green health. Beach heather is quite beautiful in May, when it bears many tiny yellow flowers.

As plants like beach heather and dunegrass grow and expand, they modify the habitat by building soil, preserving soil moisture, serving as wind-breaks, and increasing local humidity. This modification in turn allows other plants to colonize, including shrubs like bayberry, wax myrtle, and winged sumac, and vines like posion ivy and muscadine grape.

As the trail winds farther back into the secondary dunes, vegetation becomes more lush, and most of the bare sand is covered. Small trees, such as beach plum, black cherry, sassafrass, and a few oaks appear; these provide food for island animals. Most of these trees are short because the salt spray kills the tender growing buds at the crowns of trees. Instead of growing vertically, these trees tend to spread outward as they grow.

This scrubby habitat is excellent for birding, and catbirds, quail, towhees, cardinals, and robins are common. Raccoons and foxes are surprisingly plentiful on Assateague, and this is the best habitat in which to encounter them (usually at dawn or dusk, when you're alone and very quiet). The diversity of insects of all types increases dramatically in the denser vegetation.

The Life of the Dunes trail eventually loops back to the start after a walk of less than half a mile. Return to your car via the bike path.

DIRECTIONS

From Baltimore or Washington, cross the Bay Bridge and continue south on Route 50 through Easton, Cambridge, and Salisbury. Just before the bridge to Ocean City, turn right on Route 611 at the prominent sign marking Assateague Island National Seashore. Follow Route 611 for 5.8 miles, crossing the bridge onto Assateague Island. Continue straight ahead to the entrance kiosk for Assateague Island State Park. A fee is charged. Park in the bathing beach parking lot straight ahead.

OTHER OUTDOOR RECREATIONAL OPPORTUNITIES NEARBY

Camping facilities are available at both the state park and the national seashore. The state park has hot-water showers and flush toilets; it is so popular that reservations are a must. The national seashore sites have only portable toilets and cold-water showers. In hot weather, a screen house is a virtual necessity at both campgrounds, providing refuge from the sun and bugs. Because of the physical discomfort of camping on the beach, consider camping at the Shad Landing area of Pocomoke River State Park, about a 45-minute commute away.

The beach at Assateague is a great place to walk. For a description of the best beach hike, see the chapter on North Beach in this book.

Canoeing at Assateague is not recommended, despite official park literature that mentions it. The prevailing breeze from the south almost always keeps Sinepuxent Bay choppy, and wind affects even the relatively sheltered tidal guts leading through the salt marshes.

Eelgrass, Submerged Aquatic Vegetation, and Water Quality

Eelgrass (*Zostera maritima*) is one of the most important life forms to the ecology and biological diversity of Chesapeake Bay. Yet relatively few people have actually seen this flowering plant living in its natural habitat, because eelgrass grows underwater in the shallows of the Bay estuary. If people can recognize this plant at all, it is as the long, slender blackish-green dead leaves that wash up in windrows along the shore or serve as a common packaging material for soft crabs.

Eelgrass community

Eelgrass grows on sandy to somewhat muddy bottom sediments in the saline waters of the lower Chesapeake Bay at depths of up to nine feet. It requires good water quality, so that sunlight can penetrate through the water to reach the photosynthetic apparatus in the ribbonlike leaf. Once established, eelgrass forms extensive, dense stands known as seagrass meadows. The protection and food provided by these underwater "forests" make them home to an incredible diversity of animals, a unique assemblage of life found nowhere else in Chesapeake Bay.

Few animals directly eat the leaves of eelgrass. However, their surface is colonized by algae, protozoans, and bacteria in very high densities. These microscopic plants and animals are grazed upon by worms, sea slugs, and snails; in fact, a typical eelgrass leaf may be covered with so much life that the plant itself may not be visible. The sediments around the bases of eelgrass provide protected homes for more worms, amphipods, clams, and scallops. Developing larval stages of many aquatic animals, as well as fish and crabs, shelter in the waving strands. Indeed, blue crabs in the process of shedding their shells typically make for these safe havens. The leaves, seeds, and roots of eelgrass are eaten by almost two dozen species of waterfowl. Thus, eelgrass is what ecologists call a keystone species: like the keystone of an arch, it has an importance to the whole community greater than its mere size or abundance would indicate.

Eelgrass and several other species of underwater plants more common in low-salinity portions of Chesapeake Bay are together known as submerged aquatic vegetation, or SAVs—and SAVs are in trouble in the Bay. Massive die-offs of SAVs were noted in the 1970s; by 1984 they grew over only 37,000 acres of bay bottom out of a historic coverage of about 600,000 acres. All the other life dependent on seagrass beds declined correspondingly.

What caused these die-offs of eelgrass and other SAVs? It took scientists several years to unravel the mystery. It is now believed that steadily increasing inputs of nitrogen and phosphorus from sewage treatment plant effluents, agricultural runoff, and atmospheric deposition of automobile exhaust fumes are responsible. These nutrients fertilize the Bay waters, stimulating excess growth of microscopic algae, thereby clouding the water and sheathing the leaves of SAVs so heavily that they cannot conduct photosynthesis. Sediment pollution from eroding construction sites and agricultural lands further exacerbates the problem.

Recognition of what caused the decline of SAVs gave scientists and managers the knowledge with which to design a program to restore Chesapeake Bay. Since 1984 significant and expensive efforts to control the input of nitrogen and phosphorus have been undertaken. The handling of phosphorus has been a success story, in part because it is easier to control and remove than nitrogen, and not inconsequentially because of a ban on phosphate-containing detergents. Nitrogen removal has proven more intractable, but efforts continue.

Eelgrass and other SAVs are bioindicators of how succesful programs to control nutrient inputs have been. The total acreage covered with SAVs has almost doubled since 1984, and the health of seagrass meadows is generally (but not rapidly) improving. With any luck, we may yet see a resurgence of these important underwater grasses and the community of animals that they support. ๕

Blackwater National Wildlife Refuge

Section: Refuge loop

County: Dorchester

Distance: 7.5 miles

Type: Refuge roads and lightly traveled public roads

Surface: Asphalt

Difficulty: Flat

Hazards: Light vehicular traffic

Highlights: Salt marsh, waterfowl, bald eagles, and other birds

More Information: Blackwater National Wildlife Refuge,
  (410) 228-2677

MORE MARYLANDERS have been introduced to birdwatching at Blackwater National Wildlife Refuge than at any other single location. No matter whom you talk to in Washington or Baltimore, he or she has probably visited Blackwater, or at least heard of it. On any given weekend in fall and winter, cars full of casual birdwatchers and hard-core birders circle Wildlife Drive, awed by the teeming flocks of Canada geese, pleased at the glimpse of a great blue heron, and hopeful of sighting a bald eagle. Birding can be spectacularly good at Blackwater, especially for novices, and crowds don't seem to affect the birds any more than a single vehicle does. In the past few years, the refuge has opened the drive to bicycle traffic, allowing the more energetic

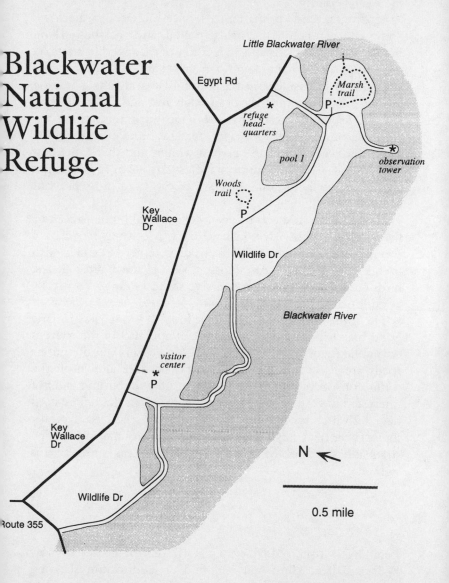

Blackwater
National
Wildlife
Refuge

Little Blackwater River

Egypt Rd

Marsh
trail

P

refuge
head-
quarters

*

pool 1

observation
tower

*

Woods
trail

P

Key
Wallace
Dr

Wildlife Dr

Blackwater River

visitor
center

*

P

Key
Wallace
Dr

Wildlife Dr

Route 355

N ←

0.5 mile

a chance to stretch cramped legs after the two-hour drive from the western shore.

Blackwater exists primarily to service migratory waterfowl. Some overwinter on the fields, ponds, and marshes, taking advantage of the seeds and vegetation of managed habitats on the refuge or traveling out to nearby farms to glean waste agricultural grains. Other birds use Blackwater as a staging ground—a place where they can safely rest and fatten up for a few weeks before resuming the southward migration. For these reasons, Blackwater has its greatest abundance and diversity of birds in late fall and earliest winter, and that is the best time to visit. Choose a sunny, windless day when the thin light warms the chilly air, and Blackwater can be a most pleasant place.

Finally, make sure you bring along a pair of binoculars and a field guide to birds. If you have one, a spotting scope on a tripod is also useful and will make you very popular with friends and strangers. At almost all sites in the United States, birds are wary and keep just outside shotgun range, so a really good look requires magnification.

The route described is a 7.5-mile loop. It is not a particularly good bike trip for children because almost half of the route is on public roads with no shoulders. However, even the public roads are fairly safe for adult riders, because almost all the traffic consists of refuge visitors intent only on birding and not interested in getting somewhere fast. Roads in the refuge itself have a 25-mph speed limit and are very safe; bicyclists typically move faster than cars. Just be alert for vehicles making sudden stops and starts, oblivious to your presence, as a new bird is sighted.

TRIP DESCRIPTION

Begin your visit to Blackwater at the visitor center on Key Wallace Drive. Here you will find an auditorium showing movies, mounted birds (so you can brush up on your field marks), a census of avian inhabitants updated weekly, and a notebook of rarities and oddities observed by recent hard-core birders. The refuge staff on duty can answer most of your questions. Immediately upon arrival, take a glance out the back window and check out the dead trees standing far out in the marsh. These perches are frequented by bald eagles. If something is occupying a tree, scope it by leaving the building and walking around to the back fence; the window glass in the visitor center will distort the image you see through binoculars. The visitor center has wheelchair-accessible bathrooms, drinking water, trash cans, a few picnic tables, and 22 parking spaces.

From the visitor center, cycle down the driveway to Key Wallace Drive. After the geese arrive, typically in mid-October, the adjacent fields will be full of the big honkers. Canada geese are the most common birds at Blackwater, where counts of 50,000 are not uncommon. However, these numbers have been decreasing in recent years. The reasons for this decline are controversial. Most biologists cite poor reproduction at arctic and subarctic nesting sites. Some hunters believe that the declines are not significant and that the census techniques of biologists are inaccurate, perhaps even biased. There can be no doubt that hunting takes its toll as well, especially when the birds must run a gauntlet of flying steel shot along the length of their flyway. On a regional level, more and more geese are stopping their migration farther north; censuses from Harford and Cecil counties and southern Pennsylvania have been increasing each year. For the present, however, there are times at Blackwater when geese darken the sky in immense flights, and the world seems young and immortal.

Among the brown and black Canadas, some snow geese are usually found. These smaller birds come in two color phases: the "blue goose," with a white head and otherwise overall muddy blue coloration, and the prettier white phase, with black wing tips. There are few sights more spectacular than a flight of snows wheeling over a salt marsh, sunlight glinting off their wings, turning in unison and settling to the earth like autumn frost.

Turn right on Key Wallace Drive. There are no shoulders, so keep to the right and use care. After 1.7 miles, turn right just past the refuge headquarters onto Wildlife Drive. An entry fee is charged, even for cyclists.

Just beyond some large storage sheds, Pool 1 to your right is often filled with loafing Canada geese and a nice variety of ducks. Mallards are typically the most common, but you can almost always see pintails here as well. Key identification marks for the pintail are a conspicuous white line running from the white neck into the side of the dark head and a long needle-pointed tail. Other ducks might include the nondescript black duck, gadwall, and blue-winged teal. All of these ducks are "dabbling ducks," so named for their habit of feeding. They require shallow water, and merely invert themselves so that their rear ends point skyward as they glean seeds, grains, and insects from the pond bottom. During spring and summer, this freshwater pool is drained, and a variety of high-quality wetland plants grow to maturity. The pool is then flooded in the fall to a depth of less than a foot, killing the plants and making their seeds and stems available to ducks.

The road forks near the far end of Pool 1. Turn left and pedal to the parking lot for foot trails. Dismount and take a stroll through the loblolly pine forest. Between the evergreen loblolly pines, holly, and greenbrier, it's a colorful place on a winter's day. Look for typical winter residents like chickadees, titmice, nuthatches, and various woodpeckers. At the far end of the trail, a boardwalk traverses the salt marsh to a viewing platform, where you can scan the Little Blackwater River for herons, eagles, and dabbling ducks.

Return to your bike and pedal farther out this spur road to the observation tower. Dismantled in 1992, it is scheduled to be rebuilt as soon as funds become available. Views from the top are spectacular, looking out over thousands of acres of mud and water populated by flocks of birds. This exposed site is always windy, and thus cold, so dress warmly if you plan to stay for more than a few minutes.

Cycle back to the fork and bear left onto Wildlife Drive. The road follows the south side of Pool 1, but views over the marsh are broken by a screen of vegetation. In early fall, American egrets can sometimes be seen here, before they migrate.

The road enters a mixed hardwood–loblolly pine forest and continues in this habitat for about three-quarters of a mile. Here is your best chance to sight a Delmarva fox squirrel. An endangered subspecies, Delmarvas are almost twice as big as common gray squirrels and have a lighter pelage and more erect, foxlike ears. They prefer mature woods with an open understory, habitat conducive to their habit of running across the forest floor rather than climbing the nearest tree. At the end of this straightaway are another parking lot and trail—pleasant enough, but not too different from the rest of the forest through which you have just cycled.

The road emerges from the woods and runs westerly, built on a spoil bank dredged from the inside of the road. Thus the ditch adjacent to the road is a permanent freshwater pool, and wet agricultural lands and freshwater marsh lie beyond. More geese and ducks may be found here, and great blue herons stand sentinel at regular intervals. Northern harriers (formerly called marsh hawks) are frequently seen coursing over the land in search of prey.

On the opposite side of the road and about a mile farther along, a nesting platform stands above the marsh. This platform and others like it in more remote places in the refuge were erected for use by osprey. Thirty years ago, these fish hawks were rare in the Chesapeake Bay region, their numbers having been decimated primarily by DDT and other pesticides. Once these chemicals were banned, osprey made a dramatic comeback that was speeded by their acceptance of artificial nesting platforms. Today osprey are very common throughout the Bay. In winter, when ospreys have migrated, this platform is favored by resting bald eagles.

Wildlife Drive continues through similar habitat, with wide vistas across the marsh, for several miles. There is one fork in the road in this stretch; turn left here unless you're in a hurry to get back to the visitor center. Wildlife Drive ends at Route 335. Turn right, go 200 yards, and turn right again onto Key Wallace Drive. Return to the visitor center.

Most visitors to Blackwater leave home in the morning, arriving at the refuge before noon and leaving a few hours later. But if you can arrange your schedule accordingly, there is no more dramatic time at Blackwater than dusk. By late fall, many of the geese go out to feed in nearby fields, returning in wave after wave at day's end. Goose music fills the air in a cacophony so loud as to render conversation impossible. Outlined against a red sunset sky, chevrons of geese make such moments unforgettable.

DIRECTIONS

From Baltimore or Washington, take Route 50 over the Bay Bridge. As you leave Cambridge, look for Woods Road, then turn right. Go 0.9 mile and turn right onto Route 16. Proceed 6.3 miles to the little crossroads of Church Creek. Turn left onto Route 335. Go 3.9 miles to Key Wallace Drive. Turn left; the visitor center driveway is 1.0 mile ahead on your right.

Bald Eagles

Few sights in Maryland are more stirring than a bald eagle in flight. As it soars high overhead on a seven-foot wingspan, its size, white head, and white tail make it unmistakable. We are fortunate that our national bird is found in many parts of Maryland throughout the year. Although bald eagles are not common, your chances of seeing one are fairly good—if you know where to go.

Bald eagles

Bald eagles are birds of the water. Their primary food is fish, snatched from near the water's surface by powerful talons, although they will feed on carrion, waterfowl, and even turtles. For this reason, they are most common along the 5,620 miles of Chesapeake Bay shoreline. The population before the start of colonization in the seventeenth century has been estimated at 600 breeding pairs (plus a fair number of nonbreeding juveniles).

Bald eagle populations declined dramatically in the 1950s. By 1962 there were only about 65 pairs in Maryland. Worse still, those eagles that were left were experiencing severe reproductive failure. Of 37 nests observed, only 5 produced seven young that year. Clearly the bald eagle was threatened with extinction in Maryland.

That same year, Rachel Carson published *Silent Spring,* documenting the extent of related problems with many bird species and proposing that pesticides like DDT were responsible for these declines. In the subsequent decade, she was proven correct; studies conclusively demonstrated that eggshell thinning was correlated with levels of pesticide residues, especially those of DDT and its metabolites. In the Chesapeake region, DDE levels exceeded five parts per million in eggshells, and these same shells decreased in thickness by 13 percent. This thinning weakened the eggs so much that incubating mothers often broke them. In 1967 the bald eagle was listed by the U.S. Fish and Wildlife Service as an endangered species, both in Maryland and throughout the nation.

In an unusual example of science driving public policy, the Environmental Protection Agency banned organochlorine pesticides, including DDT, in 1972. Within a few years, eggshells became thicker, and more young eagles were fledged. For example, in 1977 41 pairs fledged 45 eaglets, an average of 1.1 per pair per year. In 1991 128 pairs fledged 169 young; not only had the breeding population size tripled, but reproductive success was up to 1.3. With similar positive reports coming in from most of the bald eagle's breeding range throughout the United States, the U.S. Fish and Wildlife Service in 1994 changed the status of the bald eagle from endangered to threatened. Although this downlisting does not affect the protection afforded the bald eagle, the change in status is an indication that populations of endangered species can be restored by careful management.

Although all this is good news for bald eagles in Maryland, their future is not all rosy. Further expansion of the population is dependent on the availability of suitable nesting habitat, and the amount of such habitat is declining rapidly as development takes away more and more waterfront land. Bald eagles are very susceptible to human disturbance (unlike ospreys), and so require large tracts of undeveloped land. For example, by far the largest roost site in the Chesapeake region is Aberdeen Proving Grounds, where artillery testing provides large tracts of land where humans do not venture. The birds are willing to put up with the noise in exchange for the privacy. The second largest roost site is the protected lands of Blackwater National Wildlife Refuge.

Still, bald eagles in Maryland are doing well. We are all the richer for living in a state where we might look up to see the majestic beauty of one of these birds, wheeling overhead, sunlit against an azure sky, the symbol of a free America. ♣

Point Lookout State Park

Section: Park office to the end of the peninsula and return

County: St. Mary's

Distance: 5.4 miles

Type: Public road

Surface: Asphalt

Difficulty: Flat

Hazards: Traffic

Highlights: Chesapeake Bay and Potomac River views

More Information: Point Lookout State Park,
(301) 872-5688

POINT LOOKOUT IS known as the southernmost tip of land on Maryland's western shore; the site of a Civil War prisoner camp; a popular state park; and a premier site for watching birds during spring and fall migration. It is a great place to take the kids because it sponsors such a large number of human activities in a small piece of real estate; if they get bored, just try something else. For example, the point itself is very popular for fishing and crabbing. When the kids get tired of this, you can take them over to the swimming beach for some splash time. After that, a visit to a small Civil War museum? Or perhaps renting a canoe for a cruise around Lake Conoy? Finish up the day by toasting marshmallows over the campfire and listening to a ghostly tale spun by the local ranger. There's lots to do at Point Lookout.

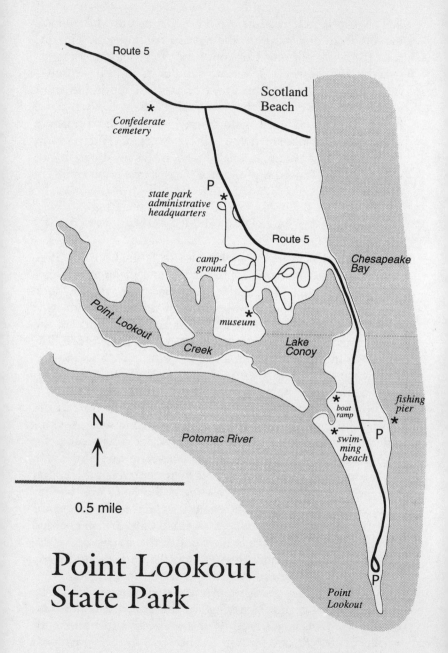

Route 5

Scotland
Beach

*
*Confederate
cemetery*

P

*state park
administrative
headquarters*

Route 5

*camp-
ground*

Chesapeake
Bay

*
museum

Lake
Conoy

Point Lookout

Creek

N

↑

Potomac River

*
*boat
ramp*

*fishing
pier*
*

*
*swim-
ming
beach*

P

P

0.5 mile

Point Lookout
State Park

*Point
Lookout*

This trip is described as a bicycle trip because bikes make moving from one venue to the next so fast and easy. The one road to the tip of Point Lookout is not for young or inexperienced riders, however. It has no shoulders, and on weekends traffic can get heavy. The speed limit is 30 mph, and most vehicles go slower than that, so older riders will often travel faster than cars. Use care and discretion and you won't have any problems, especially if you visit on a weekday. Alternatively, this route could be just as easily hiked, or (as most people do) toured by car. Round trip distance for this ride is 5.4 miles.

TRIP DESCRIPTION

Begin your ride from the parking lot of Point Lookout State Park's administrative offices; this is the first parking area after you enter the state park. There are no facilities available here, but there are bathrooms and water just down the road. Ride south on Route 5 for about 100 yards and turn right into the campground. Pass the contact station and gate and follow signs for the visitor center and museum. This building has wheelchair-accessible bathrooms, water, trash cans, information, displays, sale items, and a small museum.

The museum records the history of the Point Lookout site during the Civil War. This isolated spot, within sight of Confederate territory in Virginia, was a prisoner of war camp for tens of thousands of rebel soldiers between 1862 and 1865. Since it is surrounded on two sides by water (which the Union Navy controlled completely), United States troops had to maintain security only at a bottleneck of land along the peninsula. Confederate prisoners were jammed onto a small guarded site, about half of which is now under the waters of Chesapeake Bay. Living conditions were terrible, but still not nearly as bad as those at the worst prisons of the era; at Point Lookout, prisoners could supplement their meager rations by fishing, crabbing, and oystering. In the crowded conditions, disease was especially feared. With no effective treatments for smallpox, cholera, and even simple bacterial diseases, men died by the hundreds; in fact, more men succumbed to disease in the Civil War than were killed in battle. The little museum contains a number of artifacts recovered from the Point Lookout site.

Just outside the visitor center is a short dock leading across a narrow marsh and out into Lake Conoy, a shallow impoundment with a small opening at the far end into the Potomac River. Fiddler crabs scurry over the muddy intertidal flats of the pond, and mud-colored snails (marsh periwinkles) graze on the algae covering salt marsh cordgrass. In cold weather, the sheltered waters of the lake are home to a wide variety of ducks and geese, including some less common species like canvasbacks, scaup, and buffleheads.

Returning through the campground to Route 5, turn right. Within a quarter mile, the road passes over a causeway lined with large boulders to prevent erosion. To the left is Chesapeake Bay, here at its widest point. To the right is Lake Conoy, a shallow tidal pond connected to the Potomac by a narrow dredged channel. Parking is allowed on broad paved shoulders along each side of the road, and on weekends humanity jams in cheek by jowl, fishing and dipnetting. After a half mile of such congestion, the land widens, and loblolly pines appear on either side. A pair of rusty generator wheels and a marker denote this spot (to the Bay side) as the site of the Confederate POW camp. If you visit on a blazingly hot summer day or a windy, stormy afternoon late in the season, it's easy to imagine the privations endured on this site so long ago.

The area near the site of the POW camp is the widest in the two miles of peninsula and has lots of loblolly pine and smaller, dense vegetation. Although birding in this area can be rewarding in all seasons, there are occasions (admittedly rare) during spring and fall migrations when it can be spectacular. Like the better-known peninsula tips at Cape May, New Jersey, and Cape Charles, Virginia, Point Lookout is at the end of a south-pointing funnel of land that concentrates migrating birds in autumn, especially hawks and warblers. These birds prefer to fly over land; as they move southward, they tend to stop at places like Point Lookout to rest up for the over-water crossing, especially if the wind is out of the south. Alternatively, look for lots of birds on the move after a period of stormy weather passes. The two most common hawks, broad-winged and sharp-shinned, peak in numbers about two weeks into September and one week into October, respectively. Warblers have less discrete peaks and can be present anytime during this period. Check loblolly pines just off the road, protected from the wind.

Similarly, look for migrating monarch butterflies in August and September. These conspicuous orange and black butterflies migrate south as well and congregate at Point Lookout for the same reason as the birds.

Another quarter mile brings you to a large parking lot on the right. There is a campstore, boats may be rented, and headboat charters are available. The next parking lot, only 100 yards farther along, is at the boat launch ramp, where a fee is charged. Just down Route 5 is the road to the fishing pier, on the left. This pier provides an unusual opportunity, even for nonanglers, to get far enough offshore to obtain a perspective on the broad sweep of the peninsula. It's also a fine place from which to view the more pelagic species of birds that typically loaf a hundred yards or so offshore in winter. These include oldsquaw, scoters, horned grebes, and red-breasted mergansers. There are wheelchair-accessible bathrooms, trash cans, and parking for about 70 cars near the fishing pier.

Returning to the main road, continue southward. Pass the picnic area and the swimming beach, which requires a fee for use. The road emerges from the trees onto the point itself. Only a few trees provide shelter in this most exposed portion of Point Lookout. Both the Chesapeake and Potomac shores are now lined with boulders to prevent erosion, and they are popular sites for surf casting with the heavy rigging that it takes to fish these waters successfully. Bluefish are often taken here in late summer, feeding voraciously before the onset of cooler weather. In summer, look for double-crested cormorants, gulls, and terns loafing on the offshore pilings on the Potomac side. Cormorants, large birds with long necks but short legs, can often be seen with their wings outstretched, drying them in the sun. There are wheelchair-accessible bathrooms here at the point.

Bluefish

Finally, the extreme end of Point Lookout is occupied by the Point Lookout Tracking Station, Chesapeake Test Range, Patuxent Naval Air Test Station. Bloodsworth Island, due east across the Bay, is used for target practice by aircraft based at Patuxent in Lexington Park. Obviously, access is strictly prohibited, even along the beach.

Return to your car at your leisure by the same route, stopping wherever you like.

DIRECTIONS

From Baltimore take Route 3/301 south. In Upper Marlboro, turn east on Route 4. From the Capital Beltway, take Route 4 east. Follow Route 4 south to the end of Calvert County, cross the bridge at Solomons, and continue for 3 miles. Turn left (south) on Route 235; this will join with Route 5 within a few miles of Point Lookout.

OTHER OUTDOOR RECREATIONAL OPPORTUNITIES NEARBY

The hiking trails of Calvert Cliffs State Park and Flag Ponds Nature Park are located within about a 45-minute drive of Point Lookout State Park; they are described beginning on page 29 in this book.

Monarch Butterflies

Insects as a group are often looked upon with distaste; many have unusual or bizarre bodies, and others are associated with disease, pestilence, or filth. The exception to this generalization is the lepidopteran order, which includes butterflies and moths. Among the butterflies, perhaps none is more familiar than the beautiful orange and black monarch. A numerous and wide-spread species, monarchs nevertheless pose a dilemma for modern science. Researchers still do not understand how such neurologically simple organisms can migrate thousands of miles each fall to wintering sites none of them has ever before seen.

Monarch butterfly eggs are laid on milkweed plants. The pale green eggs hatch, and the boldly striped yellow, black, and white caterpillars feed on the juices of their host plant. They molt four times and then transform into a quiescent pupal stage. Over a period of several days, the body structure is completely rearranged, and eventually a butterfly emerges. Two or three generations occur each summer, so that the butterflies that migrate south in August are not the same ones that arrived in late spring.

In late summer, the last generation of the year begins to drift slowly southward. Butterflies cluster at the south ends of peninsulas like Cape May, Cape Charles, and Point Lookout, awaiting favorable winds that will aid them in their flight over open water. By November, monarchs from the east coast arrive in the mountains of south central Mexico to spend the winter in discrete roost sites that are only a few acres in size. By one estimate about 100 million butterflies arrive, clustering in sheltered places where the temperature and humidity are just right. They cover entire trees in a spectacular display but are very torpid and may die if disturbed in any way. In fact, only about 1 percent survive the winter to fly north in the spring. Surprisingly, these winter roost sites were discovered by scientists only in the mid-1970s. Since then, efforts to protect the sensitive butterflies and their roost sites have been underway.

If the unusual migratory behavior of monarchs is still puzzling, their feeding behavior is much better understood, and its consequences are important evidence for the theory of evolution by natural selection. Monarch larvae feed exclusively on milkweed juices, which in turn contain high concentrations of cardiac glycosides. These chemicals accumulate in the bodies of monarch caterpillars and butterflies, making them highly distasteful to birds and other vertebrates. Naive blue jays fed monarchs exhibit symptoms of discomfort, usually vomit up the meal, and thereafter will recognize and avoid monarchs. For this reason, most predators leave monarchs alone; their bright coloration is thought to be an "advertisement" of their distastefulness. Taking advantage of this warning coloration, a completely unrelated butterfly, the viceroy, has evolved a very similar coloration. The viceroy benefits from its visual similarity to monarchs and is also rarely preyed upon. 🚲

Quiet Waters Park

Section: Park circuit

County: Anne Arundel

Distance: 4.5 miles

Type: Off-road bike trail

Surface: Asphalt

Difficulty: Generally flat, with a few rolling hills

Hazards: None

Highlights: River views, forest

More Information: Quiet Waters Park, (410) 222-1777

THE SCENIC, HISTORIC port town of Annapolis is the capital of Maryland and the seat of legislative power for the state. Thus everyone who is anyone in Free State politics spends at least part of the year in residence on the banks of the Severn. It is only fitting, then, that Annapolis should have what is undoubtedly the Rolls Royce of parks in Maryland. Quiet Waters Park, managed by the Anne Arundel County Department of Recreation and Parks, opened in 1992 and has every comfort and convenience imaginable. As of this writing, everything is spanking new, and the grounds are superbly landscaped and maintained.

For the family interested in cycling on a hard-surfaced route free of motor vehicles, Quiet Waters has a beautiful winding bike path over four miles in length. Traversing forests and open fields that occasionally open to views of the South River, this is tidewater Maryland at its best.

Quiet Waters Park

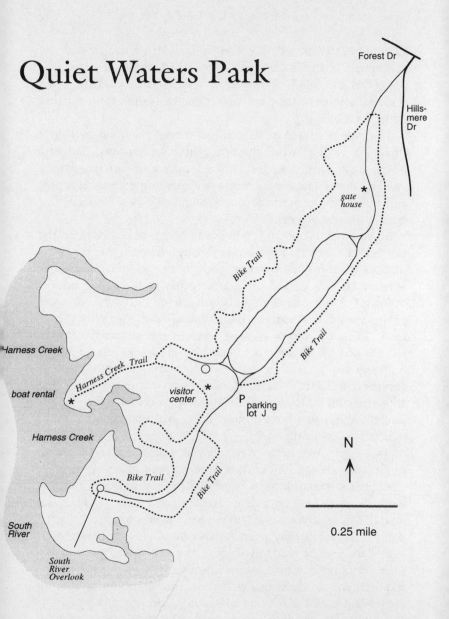

Forest Dr

Hills-
mere
Dr

*gate
house*

Bike Trail

Bike Trail

Harness Creek

Harness Creek Trail

boat rental

visitor
center

P
parking
lot J

Harness Creek

Bike Trail

Bike Trail

N

South
River

South
River
Overlook

0.25 mile

TRIP DESCRIPTION

Enter Quiet Waters Park off Hillsmere Drive and stop at the gatehouse, where a user fee is collected. Proceed down the park road and follow the signs for visitor center parking. Lot J is the largest lot in the park, and it makes a convenient starting point for a bike trip.

The visitor center is located just across the road and up a small hill. It has wheelchair-accessible bathrooms, drinking water, trash cans, telephones, warming rooms for ice skaters, vending machines, a small restaurant that is open on weekends, and information. Staff members even leave out a water-filled bucket for dogs to drink from!

Begin your ride at lot J, where the bike trail begins from the north end. The first mile winds through fields and small tracts of woods but is limited on one side by the park boundary and adjacent neighborhood and on the other by the park road.

After 0.7 mile, as the gatehouse comes into view, the trail passes a small wetland filled with cattails and edged by willow trees. Even this newly created wetland has attracted wildlife: red-winged blackbirds and mallards nest in the marsh, while bullfrogs and green frogs bellow their mating choruses. All the common frogs in Maryland have very distinctive calls that allow easy identification. Bullfrogs have a well-known, deeply pitched roar, like a bowed bass fiddle; green frogs sound like a plucked banjo string.

As a sign notes, this wetland was artificially created as a mitigation project. Under Maryland law, construction projects that destroy wetlands must be mitigated by the creation of new wetlands elsewhere on at least an acre-for-acre basis. Thus the goal of this legislation is a "no net loss" policy for wetlands. To date, it has been only partially successful. Developers are allowed to destroy wetlands before the mitigation project begins, resulting in a time lag in fulfillment of the "no net loss" requirement. In addition, environmentalists note that not all wetlands are of equal value to wildlife and in providing valuable ecosystem services. For example, this little marsh at Quiet Waters Park is not part of any series of wetlands that might provide corridors for obligate wetland species, is subject to local species extinctions because of its small size, and probably plays no role in filtering runoff of nutrients and sediments into local creeks and bays.

The bike path crosses the entrance road at mile 1.0; use caution at this intersection. The path enters a large tract of pleasant forest with some tall trees and an attractive scattering of holly in the understory. Several kinds of ferns adorn the herbaceous layer close to the ground, and there are even a few woodland wildflowers. Especially common along this section of the trail is partridgeberry, a low, trailing plant with roundish dark evergreen leaves. For most of the year, a small red berry adorns the plant and lends an air of Christmas to the forest. As the name implies, the fruit is commonly eaten by a variety of birds. The flower, found for only a week or two in early June, is distinctive. It is white in color and trumpet shaped, has four petals, and is always found in pairs. In fact, it is the only known plant on which two flowers share a single ovary.

The trail continues through the forest for more than a mile. Even though Quiet Waters is on the coastal plain, the trail is not flat; although long stretches are an easy coast, a few small, short hills may require a low gear. Even so, small children should have to walk on only one or two occasions. The 10-foot-wide blacktop path also has a few sharp turns, but most are wide enough to be handled at full speed. Together, the hills and turns make the bike path interesting as it traverses varied terrain.

At mile 2.5, a short branch trail leads to the right. The Wildwood Trail is for foot traffic only and features a composting display. A bit farther on, the Harness Creek Trail leads down to the marina, where rowboats, sailboats, and canoes may be rented on weekends from a concessionaire. Once again, no bikes are allowed. Extensive stands of mountain laurel, blooming in early June, make this short walk a worthwhile diversion.

The bike trail now runs behind the visitor center, where official vehicles use it on rare occasions as an access road. A stop here to visit the adjacent formal gardens is well worth-

Lesser scaup

while. Just beyond the visitor center, the bike path turns right to parallel the park road. A sign admonishes bikers to control their speed on a short but steep downhill. Just beyond, at mile 3.1, an overlook of Harness Creek provides an inviting look at the shallow cove.

As you leave this overlook, the trail passes into a striking forest composed almost exclusively of tulip poplar trees. Tall, arrow-straight trunks uncluttered by branches for 30 or 40 feet give a cathedral-like appearance to the forest as sunlight filters through the leaves. The tulip poplar is a fast-growing tree; a specimen a foot in diameter may be 40 years old, whereas an oak of similar size will be at least twice that age.

A sign marks the entrance to the South River Promenade. A formal overlook here gives a wide view of the river that forms the southern border of Annapolis. Chesapeake Bay is visible in the distance, and on weekends sailboats will densely populate the horizon. The open, sunny promenade is a fine place to enjoy a picnic lunch. In winter, birding for waterfowl may be profitable; look for goldeneyes, scaup, and buffleheads nearer to shore and oldsquaw, mergansers, and loons in more open water.

Leave the promenade and return to the bike path, continuing to the right. The trail, lined by maples and dogwoods that are beautiful in autumn, leads gently downhill through fields and scattered picnic tables. Where the bike path intersects the park road, turn right. An uphill pedal of 0.1 mile brings you back to parking lot J. Total distance is 4.5 miles.

DIRECTIONS

From Washington, take Route 50 east from the beltway. From Baltimore, take Route 3/301 south from the beltway. Branch onto Route 97 and follow it until its junction with Route 50 east. Immediately exit onto Route 665. Continue for 4.6 miles; the road name changes to Forest Drive. Turn right on Hillsmere Drive, go 100 yards, and enter the park.

OTHER OUTDOOR RECREATIONAL OPPORTUNITIES NEARBY

The southern terminus of the Baltimore and Annapolis Trail is located about five miles from Quiet Waters Park. It is described beginning on page 246 in this book.

Jellyfish

Chesapeake Bay is the most prominent geological feature of Maryland, bisecting the state from south to north. It is greatly loved by citizens, but its waters have one major drawback: the Chesapeake is unswimmable most of the time. This remarkable misfortune is due to the ubiquitous presence of *Chrysaora quinquecirrha,* the stinging sea nettle. These jellyfish sting immediately upon even a brushing contact, producing a painful, fiery, itching rash that persists for 20 minutes or so. Neither big nor fierce, jellyfish are nevertheless among the most feared animals in Maryland.

What the jellyfish lacks in size it makes up for in numbers. Stand on a dock in mid-Bay in August and it seems that every square foot of water has its own jellyfish, pulsing and throbbing in mindless menace. Yet jellyfish are not present every year; their spread is highly dependent on salinity. In wet years, when freshwater inflow from the Susquehanna and other tributaries measurably dilutes salty water from the ocean, jellyfish stay in the saline waters of the lower Bay. Even in dry years, beaches of the northern Bay are usually free of sea nettles.

Sea nettles are rather simple organisms, but the cells that sting, called nematocysts, are fairly sophisticated. Thousands of these cells coat each tentacle. Each nematocyst has a trigger attached to a capsule, inside of which the stinging filament is coiled. When the trigger brushes against something, it opens the capsule's trapdoor, and the coiled stinging filament is propelled outward. The filament is coated with venom and is also barbed so that the venom will remain in contact with the victim. The result is pure pain.

Sea nettles have a complex life cycle of which most people are unaware. Adult male jellyfish release sperm into the water; females pump that water past their eggs and fertilization occurs. Tiny larvae called planulae develop; these are released to float freely with the other plankton of Chesapeake Bay. After a short time, the planulae settle to the bottom and attach to a solid substrate much as do oyster and barnacle larvae. They soon develop into the polyp stage, tiny vaselike structures. Polyps overwinter in this stage of their life cycle, forming cysts if the weather gets too cold or if they are subjected to other environmental insults. In spring, the polyps begin to grow again and mature to bud off a floating stage. Called ephyra, these tiny discs resume a planktonic existence. They eventually grow tentacles and begin to look like mature jellyfish.

Adult jellyfish are free-floating, although they can propel themselves with contractions of the body. They feed on small fish and other animals that they encounter, immobilizing the prey by stinging. The prey is then taken into the transparent bell, where digestion occurs. Having evolved more than 250 milion years ago and thrived in estuarine waters ever since, sea nettles are eminently succesful, well-adapted creatures. If only they weren't such a pain! ᕗ

The Baltimore and Annapolis Trail

Section: Glen Burnie to Boulter's Way near Annapolis

County: Anne Arundel

Distance: 13.3 miles

Type: Off-road bike trail

Surface: Asphalt

Difficulty: Flat

Hazards: Road crossings

Highlights: Suburban backyards, with some natural forests

More Information: Anne Arundel County Department of Recreation and Parks, (410) 222-6244

THERE ARE FEW PLACES in Maryland more thoroughly suburban than the strip development lining both sides of Ritchie Highway (Route 2) in Anne Arundel County between Glen Burnie and Annapolis. Until 1989, this was the only good road between Baltimore and the Bay Bridge, and weekends found interminable lines of cars creeping along in stop-and-go fashion between innumerable red lights. Businesses sprang up adjacent to the highway in an effort to strip-mine frustrated tourists from the lines of traffic. Yet running along the rear of the shopping centers, parallel to Route 2, is another world. The Baltimore and Annapolis (B & A) Trail, a paved thread of asphalt laid on the old railroad

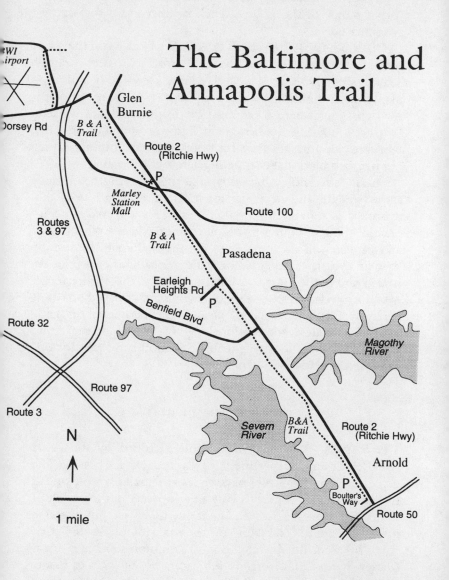

The Baltimore and Annapolis Trail

BWI Airport

Dorsey Rd

Glen Burnie

B & A Trail

Route 2 (Ritchie Hwy)

P

Marley Station Mall

Routes 3 & 97

B & A Trail

Route 100

Pasadena

Earleigh Heights Rd

Benfield Blvd

P

Route 32

Magothy River

Route 97

Route 3

Severn River

B&A Trail

Route 2 (Ritchie Hwy)

Arnold

N

P

Boulter's Way

Route 50

1 mile

grade, runs for over 13 miles past pocket wetlands and under large trees. Considering that more than 140,000 people live within a mile of the B & A Trail, it maintains a surprisingly sylvan nature.

That's not to say that the B & A Trail will give you the same sort of experience as, say, the more rural Northern Central Trail; it won't. On weekends, that same accessibility and popularity make the B & A excessively crowded. There are many road crossings where bikes must be dismounted and walked. In places, housing developments line the trail. But an early morning ride can still reveal a woodpecker drumming on an old tree or a blacksnake slithering across the pavement.

The B & A Trail is currently 13.3 miles in length, running arrow straight and dead flat for most of its length. For this reason, it is suitable for cyclists of all ages and makes a fine practice road for young riders on training wheels. Wheelchairs and strollers will also be able to use the trail easily. Be sure to keep an eye on younger riders at the many road crossings. At some point in the future, as funding permits, the northern end will be extended westward to join with another paved bike trail currently being constructed around the perimeter of Baltimore-Washington International Airport. Contact the Anne Arundel County Department of Recreation and Parks for updates on the status of this project.

TRIP DESCRIPTION

The B & A Trail is managed and patrolled by the Anne Arundel County Department of Recreation and Parks. The department provides two parking lots for trail patrons, one at the south end off Boulter's Way and the other in the middle at Earleigh Heights Road. In addition, there are innumerable private shopping center lots on the east side of Route 2 that could be used. But by far the most common starting point is Marley Station Mall, at mile 2.8, near the junction of Route 100 and Route 2. This access point provides unlimited parking and is a well-known landmark. Bathrooms are available in the

Tulip poplar

mall, as is the usual assortment of fast food restaurants. Bike racks are found at trail's edge.

From Marley Station, the trail stretches 2.8 miles to the north, traversing the backyards of suburban Glen Burnie. This portion of the trail is a bit less enjoyable because of the developed nature of the neighborhood, and most trail users choose to pedal southward.

As the trail leaves the rear of Marley Station Mall and crosses over Route 100, it passes through dry, sandy woods. The twisted and irregular branches of Virginia pine dominate the overstory, and on hot days the pungent odor of pine wafts over the trail. Long, tawny grasses sweep back and forth in the breeze. Check these woods in May for the beautiful flower of the pink lady's slipper orchid.

The Earleigh Heights ranger station is located at mile 6.8, a renovated 1890s-era grocery store. Information, a few exhibits, water, picnic tables, wheelchair-accessible bathrooms, and parking for 14 vehicles may be found here. The station also marks the approximate halfway point on the 13.3-mile trail.

The trail continues through a landscape that alternates between suburbia and small pockets of natural habitat. The southernmost three miles of the trail are the most pleasant. Trailside development is more sparse, and where it is found it tends toward large, pleasant-looking houses on shady lots. Several stretches of mature forest border the trail, featuring fine, tall stands of tulip poplar. A few streams dissect the land, creating small hillsides where the undergrowth is dense and green.

The trail ends abruptly at Boulter's Way, as it reaches the end of the peninsula on which it is located. Annapolis and the United States Naval Academy lie just across the Severn River. Return to your car by the same route.

DIRECTIONS

To reach Marley Station Mall from Baltimore, take the Route 2 south exit from the Baltimore Beltway. The mall is about four miles south, on the right.

From Washington, it may be more convenient to park near the southern terminus of the trail. From the Capital Beltway, take Route 50 east. Cross the Severn River Bridge. The first exit will be Route 2 north. Park in any lot on the left (west) side of the highway. You'll find the trail to the rear of these buildings.

OTHER OUTDOOR RECREATIONAL OPPORTUNITIES NEARBY

Quiet Waters Park is located about five miles south of the southern terminus of the Baltimore and Annapolis Trail. It is described beginning on page 238 in this book.

Fireflies

Evening settles slowly over the lawns and forest edges of Maryland in June; dew gathers on the grass in the thick, humid air. It's a sweet, magical time, when adults gather to chat while children romp for the last time before bed. In the gloaming, lights appear, blinking on and off, silent and mysterious as the dark watches of night. What child has not watched and wondered at the lightning bug, perhaps our most familiar and engaging insect?

Lightning bugs are beetles, insects with leathery, veinless wings that meet in a straight line down the back. These fireflies are the only group of insects that can make controlled flashes of light; they do so to attract and find mates. In Maryland, there are at least six species of firefly within the genus *Photinus,* the most common group; *Photinus pyralis* is the most numerous species of suburban lawns.

Fireflies overwinter as larvae, buried in the soil, and emerge in spring to feed, usually in wet or swampy areas. The larvae are predatory, feeding on snails and small insects, but little is known about this portion of the lightning bug life cycle. By late May, the larvae form pupae, emerging as the familiar fireflies just over two weeks later. By mid- to late June, fireflies are on the wing at dusk.

Actually, only male lightning bugs fly. Females, which in some species lack wings altogether, remain near the ground, climbing grass blades or other low vegetation. When ready to mate, a female responds to the light signals from a flying male with a brief flash of her own, orienting her abdominal lamp toward the male. The responding male flies closer and repeats his signal, and the process is reiterated until the two beetles find each other. After mating, the female lays eggs in the soil; these develop into the larval stage, completing the life cycle.

The several species of firefly that live in our area avoid one another by means of behavioral adaptations. Each species has its own characteristic flash duration and response time, to which other species will not respond. Firefly species also segregate by habitat and by time of night for flashing. Our common local firefly, *Photinus pyralis,* begins flashing as early as 20 minutes before sunset and remains active for about 45 minutes.

The flight path of a male *Pyralis* firefly is a J-shaped hop. The firefly sinks a little, flashes on as he approaches the bottom of the signature, begins to rise, and then flashes off early in the rise phase. The remainder of the upstroke of the J is completed in darkness. He then flies on to another prospective flash location, sinking as he does so, and repeats the signature. The whole flash pattern lasts for about 6 seconds at 70° Fahrenheit, and the flash itself lasts about half a second. Females respond about 2.5 seconds later, with a flash duration of half a second.

By imitating the "call" of a female firefly with a covered flashlight, you can attract males. Place a penlight or other small flashlight over your hand so that just a dim glow emerges through the tissue. When a male flashes nearby, signal as if you are a female. With some practice, you should be able to get male fireflies to land on your hand within a few flash sequences. ⚲

Patuxent Environmental Science Center

Section: Visitor center to terminus and return

County: Anne Arundel

Distance: 17.0 miles

Type: Very lightly traveled park road

Surface: Asphalt, but cracked and broken

Difficulty: Rolling

Hazards: Uneven pavement, unexploded ordnance if you leave the road

Highlights: Second-growth forest, land recovering from abuse

More Information: Patuxent Environmental Science Center, (410) 674-3304

T HE BALTIMORE-WASHINGTON corridor has been one of the fastest-growing areas in the United States for at least half a century. Each year, development takes woods, fallow lands, once productive farms, and privately owned open space, converting them into housing tracts, strip malls, and superhighways. The density of people increases each year, and commuters become ever more frustrated with jammed roads and gridlock. The suburbs of Washington now overlap with the suburbs of Baltimore, and no end to the process seems to be in sight. Yet in the exact middle of this crowded metropolis lies the largest contiguous tract of forest in central Maryland, held in the public domain and

Patuxent Environmental Science Center

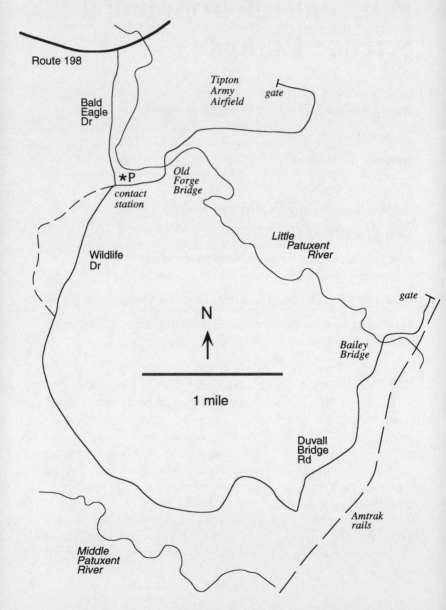

protected from development. Largely unknown to most citizens, portions of the Patuxent National Wildlife Refuge opened for public visitation in 1991.

Known as the Patuxent Environmental Science Center, this 7,600-acre tract once housed Fort Meade, a training center for the army. Much of the land was kept in its natural state for years, although it was heavily used by vehicles (including tanks) and soldiers on foot. As the Department of Defense budget was reduced in the late 1980s and early 1990s, Fort Meade was deemed superfluous. After much debate, the adjacent Patuxent Wildlife Research Center was named the supervisory agency. The land is to be managed for the conservation research and educational activities of the center, but also to maintain biological diversity for the protection of native and migratory species. Finally, the new property is to be open to the public for compatible recreational uses.

More than eight miles of paved roads traverse the North Tract and make a fine bike trail. Although this road is open to cars, it is sparsely used, mostly by hunters and fishermen, and the speed limit is 25 mph. Although the route is not flat, hills are mostly minor. Years of use and abuse have rutted this road, and there are many patched potholes, but these only make for a bumpy rather than a dangerous ride. Given the very few options for safe, traffic-free bicycling in Maryland, most of us are willing to put up with an uneven pavement!

TRIP DESCRIPTION

Begin your visit with a required stop at the contact station on Bald Eagle Drive. Obtain a written permit for your use of the area; it must be carried with you at all times. The staff is friendly and enthusiastic and will explain your options and give advice. There are wheelchair-accessible bathrooms here, as well as drinking water, trash cans, and a few picnic tables.

As of this writing, there is one critically important rule for the use of the Patuxent Environmental Science Center. Do not, under any circumstances, leave the paved road! The surrounding forests and fields contain unexploded ammunition of various sorts and sizes that could detonate if handled or stepped on. Decontamination of the property is scheduled to be finished by about 1995, but there is no guarantee that every shell will be found. Although hiking trails will probably be established after this date, carefully obey all rules for off-road travel and report—but do not touch—any unexploded ordnance you might find.

Mounting your bike, leave the parking lot at the contact station and turn left on Wildlife Drive. To the left, the road passes through the typical local forest of mixed hardwoods and pines. Few of these trees are very old or large, indicating that the land was once more open than it is now. After 0.4 mile, a bridge crosses the Little Patuxent River. This coastal plain riparian habitat is the nicest natural area on this ride. From the bridge, look for great blue herons, mallards, wood ducks, and kingfishers on the water in all seasons. The streamside silver maples, box elders, and sycamores are fine large trees and host a variety of tropical migrant songbirds in early May. Attracted by this expanse of unbroken forest, these tiny warblers rest and feed in areas like this before resuming their migration at sundown.

After crossing the bridge, the road leads up a shallow hill, paralleling the Tipton Army Airfield. Finally, it inscribes a loop, passes the Fort Meade stables, and ends at a gate. Return the way you came, passing the contact station after 4.5 miles of pedaling.

The road continues in a rolling fashion past open fields and forests. None of the hills is particularly steep, but neither is the road flat, and you'll have to exert some energy to get up them. After a few miles, the land to the right slopes down into the floodplain of the main stem of the Patuxent River, where holly, American beech, tupelo, and river birch are found. Indeed, one of the joys of this trip is the number of big, gray-barked beeches that have no initials or dates carved in them! Even in our protected parks, vandals continue to deface these beautiful trees.

Multiflora rosa

The old Fort Meade property is rich in wildlife, and if you sit quietly by the roadside before too many visitors have arrived you may see some. Deer are especially plentiful, thriving in the early successional stages and at the edges of fields. In order to control this population and to provide recreational hunting opportunities, the Fish and Wildlife Service permits bow, black powder, and shotgun hunting in November, December, and January. Indeed, the Patuxent Environmental Science Center is closed to visitors for most of December for this reason; it would be wise to call ahead between Thanksgiving and New Year's for information on hours. Other mammals present include beaver, mink, raccoon, muskrat, otter, mice, shrews, voles, and rabbits. A pair of bald eagles have nested on the center property recently, successfully fledging a number of young.

As you near the end of Wildlife Drive, recross the Little Patuxent River at Bailey Bridge. Emerging from the heart of the Patuxent Environmental Science Center, the river looks pastoral and inviting. The floodplain, where the rich alluvial soil accumulates, has a fine collection of wildflowers, but, once again, for safety's sake view them with binoculars from the bridge! Just beyond Bailey Bridge is a pretty little marsh filled with cattails and a dense collection of wooden duck boxes. All too soon the road ends at a gate; return the way you came. The distance from the contact station to this gate and back is 12.5 miles.

DIRECTIONS

From Washington or Baltimore, take I-295, the Baltimore-Washington Parkway. Exit at Route 198, turning east. Go 1.8 miles and turn right onto Bald Eagle Drive. Continue 0.9 mile on this dirt road to the contact station.

Silent Spring Revisited:
The Decline of Forest Songbirds

More than thirty years ago, Rachel Carson's landmark book *Silent Spring* ushered in a new age of environmental awareness, exposing the dangers of DDT to wildlife and human health. Its influential message was a clarion call to action, and the public clamor it created resulted in a ban on DDT and its poisonous relatives. Since then, many of the most severely affected bird species, like bald eagles and peregrine falcons, have made dramatic recoveries.

Today, however, a new threat to birdlife has appeared, and scientists are just beginning to realize the magnitude of the problem and its implications. Many of the species of songbirds that form our most beautiful avifauna are rapidly declining in numbers. In particular, species that nest in the deciduous forests of North America and winter in Mexico, Central and South America, and the Caribbean are affected the most severely. Called neotropical migrants, most of the warblers—as well as many thrushes, orioles, and tanagers—are in trouble throughout their range. Overall, the total number of individuals of these species is declining at the rate of about 1 percent per year.

The plight of forest songbirds here in Maryland is no better, and is perhaps worse, than that in other states throughout the eastern half of the nation. Anecdotal evidence for reduced numbers of neotropical migrants abounds; just ask any long-time birder. More rigorous proof, evidence from scientific studies analyzed statistically, is harder to come by. Nevertheless, some good records exist, in cases in which sites with mature, undisturbed vegetation have been monitored by dedicated groups of volunteers for more than 40 years. The best records are from sites in downtown Washington, D.C.: Rock Creek Park and Cabin John Island in the C & O Canal National Historical Park.

Both of these sites, less than 10 miles apart, are on federally owned land preserved forever from development. Cabin John Island is a mature floodplain forest of 18 acres; the Rock Creek site is much larger, consisting of 66 acres of upland deciduous forest. Experienced birders visited these sites between mid-May and mid-June, the peak nesting season, and sought to identify every breeding pair of birds on the tracts.

The data are unequivocal. For the Cabin John Island site, the density of breeding pairs (expressed per 250 acres) averaged about 260 in the 1940s, 1950s, and 1960s, with little variation between decades. By the early 1980s, the average was 130, exactly half. In Rock Creek Park, the statistics are even more grim: about 85 pairs per 250 acres in the 1940s, 1950s, and 1960s declined to 35 in the early 1980s. Most important, the decline was almost exclusively among neotropical migrants; year-round local residents and short-distance migrants like robins and blue jays held their own. In the early years of the census, neotropical migrants formed 60 to 80 percent of the breeding pairs; recently, they composed less than 40 percent. Hooded warblers, Kentucky warblers, black-and-white warblers, and yellow-throated vireos are extinct at these places. Several other species are present in some years but not others, or are present at extremely low densities relative to the past. Clearly, these forest-dwelling species are in trouble; their conservation is a test of our resolve to coexist peaceably with the full spectrum of organisms that share Maryland, our nation, and our planet. ⚲

Rock Creek Trail

Section: Section 1: Lake Needwood to Candy Cane City,
near the D.C. border
Section 2: Beach Drive
Section 3: Pierce Mill to the Potomac River

County: Section 1: Montgomery
Section 2: Washington, D.C.
Section 3: Washington, D.C.

Distance: Section 1: 12 miles
Section 2: 4.7 miles
Section 3: 4.3 miles

Type: Sections 1 and 3: Off-road bike trail
Section 2: Park road closed to most traffic on
weekends

Surface: Asphalt

Difficulty: Sections 1 and 2: Rolling terrain
Section 3: Flat

Hazards: Section 1: Some sharp turns, road crossings
Section 2: Occasional cars
Section 3: Narrow, crowded trail with some
adjacent heavy traffic

Highlights: Forested river valley

More Information: Rock Creek Park, (202) 426-6832.
National Capital Parks and Planning Commission,
(301) 495-2525

Upper Rock Creek Trail

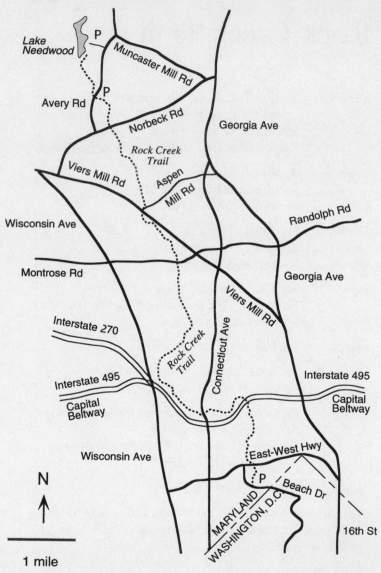

Lake Needwood

P

Muncaster Mill Rd

P

Avery Rd

Norbeck Rd

Georgia Ave

Rock Creek Trail

Aspen

Mill Rd

Viers Mill Rd

Randolph Rd

Wisconsin Ave

Montrose Rd

Georgia Ave

Viers Mill Rd

Interstate 270

Rock Creek Trail

Connecticut Ave

Interstate 495

Interstate 495

Capital Beltway

Capital Beltway

Wisconsin Ave

East-West Hwy

N

P

Beach Dr

MARYLAND

WASHINGTON, D.C.

16th St

1 mile

Rock Creek Trail: Beach Drive

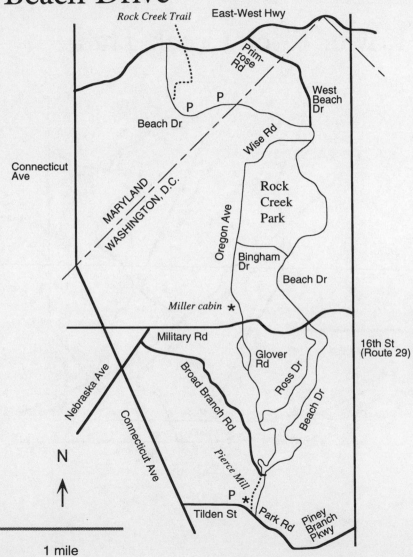

Rock Creek Trail

East-West Hwy

Prim-rose Rd

West Beach Dr

Beach Dr

P P

Wise Rd

Connecticut Ave

Rock Creek Park

MARYLAND

WASHINGTON, D.C.

Oregon Ave

Bingham Dr

Beach Dr

Miller cabin ✶

Military Rd

Glover Rd

16th St (Route 29)

Nebraska Ave

Broad Branch Rd

Ross Dr

Beach Dr

Connecticut Ave

N

↑

Pierce Mill

P ✶

Tilden St

Park Rd

Piney Branch Pkwy

1 mile

Lower Rock Creek Trail

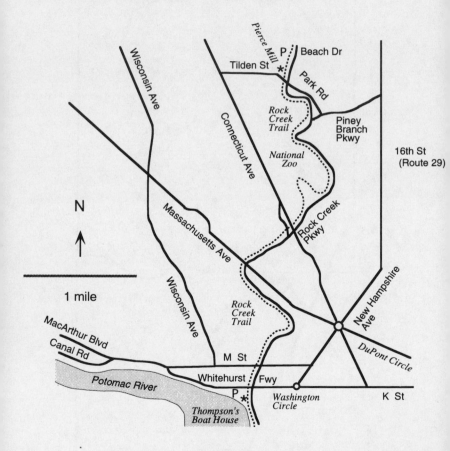

THE DISTRICT OF COLUMBIA and surrounding counties boast a complex of off-road, mostly paved bicycle trails that is the envy of other metropolitan areas. It is possible, for example, to park your car in the distant suburb of Rockville, Maryland, mount your bike, and pedal downtown to visit such world-class attractions as the National Zoo, the Lincoln Memorial, and the Kennedy Center. By crossing the Potomac River, you can cycle south to visit Mount Vernon, George Washington's home. Or you can pick up the C & O Canal towpath in Georgetown and pedal 184 miles west to Cumberland. And with all this mileage, you will not have to share a single yard with automobiles (although, unavoidably, there are a number of intersections to be crossed). In addition, the Metro, Washington's subway system, provides access to these trails at several points. (Bicycles are allowed on the Metro only on weekends and holidays.)

The Rock Creek Trail is one of the best of these paths. Originating north of the city in the rapidly expanding Gaithersburg-Rockville biotech corridor, the Rock Creek Trail follows its namesake stream for 21 miles, winding through a leafy, cool greenway. Furthermore, it provides access to downtown without the hassles of driving through city and tourist traffic. To the first-time visiting cyclist, it is nothing less than amazing to emerge from a fastness of tall trees and flowing water to see the Washington Monument in the distance and the Kennedy Center just down the road.

The Rock Creek Trail is best divided into three sections. The upper trail runs from Rockville to just inside the city line and is the least crowded. At this point, the official bike trail leaves the valley and is rarely used. Instead, Beach Drive, which parallels the creek and is closed to traffic on weekends, constitutes the second section of the trail. Finally, the off-road bike trail picks up again at the terminus of Beach Drive near Pierce Mill and runs downtown to the Potomac River near Foggy Bottom and Georgetown. Each of these sections has its own charm, and each is well worth a visit.

TRIP DESCRIPTION

Lake Needwood to Candy Cane City

The upper Rock Creek Trail follows the Rock Creek stream valley for a distance of 12 miles. This portion of the Rock Creek Trail is paved, shaded by a canopy of large trees, and follows a greenbelt of small recreational and picnicking parks. Unlike Washington's part of the trail, it is less manicured and generally somewhat wider and frequently has suburban houses in sight. Despite the more civilized feel of the upper Rock Creek Trail, however, it is a valuable resource, for in few places has there been enough foresight to set aside so many miles of undeveloped corridor for recreation and re-creation.

The upper Rock Creek Trail is heavily used by the local community, especially on weekends and in the evening. Expect to see lots of kids, strolling couples and families, and a scattering of joggers. As with virtually all trails, visit on a weekday for a more solitary experience.

This trail is not flat. It winds over small hills that on occasion are steep and require standing on the pedals. In addition, the trail has a number of sharp turns, some located on hills, that make proper control of the bicycle a must. Be courteous to fellow cyclists and pedestrians, and yield the right-of-way whenever possible.

This trip begins at the northernmost end of the Rock Creek Trail, at Lake Needwood, a unit of the Rock Creek Regional Park. Administered by the National Capital Parks and Planning Commission, it is a popular picnic site and can be crowded during the summer. Fishing is allowed (with the proper Maryland license) in the lake, although swimming and boating are not. The Rock Creek Trail begins at the south end of the lake, where parking for 100 cars, water, trash cans, and bathrooms are available.

For the first few hundred yards, the path occupies a narrow, artificial valley. Although the bottom of this valley is grass, the sides are not mowed, and a variety of wild plants have established themselves on the slopes. In summer, look for edible

blackberries on thorny bushes; by early fall, goldenrods dominate the slope.

The trail soon enters the woods and proceeds steeply downhill, rejoining Rock Creek at mile 0.35. This area, chosen as
the damsite for Lake Needwood, is a narrow point in the Rock
Creek valley and therefore has both river forest and upland
forest trees within a short distance of one another. Contrast
the sycamores, birches, ashes, and maples that are found near
the creek with the oaks and hickories that dominate the upland
regions.

At mile 0.9, the trail crosses Avery Road. This is a good trail
access point for those who wish to avoid the entrance fee
charged at Lake Needwood. There is gravel parking for about
20 cars, but no facilities at all.

At mile 3.7, the path leaves designated parkland and runs on
residential streets for a few hundred yards. Follow the bike trail
signs. Carefully cross the busy Viers Mill Road intersection at
mile 4.0. No further travel off the bike path is necessary
between here and the D.C. line (although there are some
major roads to cross that require dismounting).

The Rock Creek valley in Montgomery County is a shallow
one. Few dramatic outcrops of rocks or cliffsides are seen, in
contrast to the fall line gorge below Military Road in the
District. The bike trail passes through several forested habitats.
River bottom forest is more common in the upper reaches of
the trail, where low riverbanks allow floodwaters to spread out
among the tree boles. Most of the lower sections of the trail
pass through a mixed mesophytic forest of modest proportions. These are mature but not really large trees on a soil of
moderate moisture content—sort of the "silent majority" of
forest habitats in the Maryland piedmont. Finally, significant
portions of the trail border or dissect recreational lands, complete with tot lots, tennis courts, soccer fields, and the like.

The trail ends at Meadowbrook Park, just north of the city
line. Public stables operated by the National Capital Parks and
Planning Commission are found here and offer riding lessons
to children. Just beyond are a picnic area (with shelters), trash
cans, a telephone, bathrooms, playing fields, and an extensive

playground known as Candy Cane City. Parking space for 70 cars is available.

From here, the designated bike trail leaves the Rock Creek valley and is not recommended for families with children. Parts of it run through residential streets, which, although not crowded, are quite steep. When the trail finally returns to an off-road character, it is isolated, narrow, very winding, still hilly, and encroached upon by vegetation. On weekends, however, Beach Drive near Candy Cane City is closed to vehicles, and this route is described as the second section of the Rock Creek Trail.

Beach Drive

On weekends and holidays, a remarkable transformation overcomes Beach Drive, a busy artery that normally funnels traffic into downtown D.C. The National Park Service closes 4.7 miles of Beach Drive to motorized traffic from 7 A.M. to 7 P.M., so that walkers, joggers, cyclists, and, most recently, in-line skaters can have unhindered use of both lanes. Such an unusual and insightful decision has been a real boon to cyclists of all ages and abilities, and the public has responded by making Beach Drive a very popular weekend destination. Fortunately, there is plenty of room for all because the road is so much wider than a typical bike path. If you're slow, or merely busy looking at the scenery, just keep to the right.

This trip begins at the point where Beach Drive is gated to vehicles, just inside the city line. Several parking lots line Beach Drive north of here; just pick any one that has available space. All are associated with tall trees shading picnic tables and grassy play areas.

The upper reaches of Rock Creek Park are downright beautiful. The park is almost a mile wide, not just a mere greenbelt (as it is in much of its upper and lower sections). The rolling hills feature well-developed soils that harbor all sorts of mature trees. Birdlife is more common and diverse, since there is space enough for a viable population. Spring wildflower displays are at their best here.

If this first gate is mile 0, a break in the sylvan peace comes quickly, at mile 0.6. Vehicular traffic is allowed between here and Wise Drive, a few hundred yards south. Use care in this short stretch, although drivers are usually courteous to cyclists. The next three miles are a pure delight, as the road winds through the shady coolness, always within the sound of flowing water in Rock Creek. In summer, this is a most pleasant place, as the temperature is frequently 10° cooler than in the surrounding city streets; this is the place to go for an early morning ride on those steamy, humid summer days.

At mile 2.4, the Miller Cabin appears on the west side. Home to Joaquin Miller, a prominent poet who lived here in the 1880s, it is the site of summertime poetry readings. Just south of here, the path crosses busy Military Road. During the Civil War it was an important supply route to the ring of forts protecting the nation's capital.

At Military Road, Rock Creek crosses the fall line, the last set of rapids before the river enters the gravels and sands of the coastal plain. Extending downriver for the next half mile, the creek drops dramatically over boulders and through tight chutes. Because the flow of Rock Creek is normally so small, the water will be almost imperceptible, and you can cross the creek by jumping from rock to rock. But when a summer thunderstorm hits Washington, rainwater from a thousand storm sewers dumps into Rock Creek, and the river becomes a roaring, cascading torrent of mud, logs, and other debris. An impressive sight.

The rapids cease by the time Beach Drive crosses the river on the aptly named Boulder Bridge. The walls of the bridge are composed of large rounded boulders from Rock Creek. You won't find another bridge like this one anywhere.

At mile 4.4, Glover Road converges with Beach Drive. This marks the end of the closed section of Beach Drive, as the bike path has returned to the valley. Join the bike path for a short 0.3-mile jog to Pierce Mill.

Although Beach Drive is officially closed to traffic, you will encounter the occasional car. A number of reservable picnic areas line most of Beach Drive, and vehicles with permits are allowed access to them.

Pierce Mill to the Potomac River

This 4.3-mile section of the Rock Creek Trail is most notable for its surprising character. As the trail slices through the heart of the city, few cyclists would ever imagine the pulse of urban life going on just beyond the trees that top the valley rim. This would be a very pretty trail even if it were not in the city; its urban nature merely adds utility to its other, not inconsiderable, charms.

There are a few drawbacks to this lower portion of the trail, however. Care must be taken, especially with children, at a number of road crossings. At rush hour, these intersections may be next to impossible to cross; D.C. drivers are not notable for their courtesy. The path is heavily used, as you might expect, and not just by bicyclists; it is a favorite place for city-dwelling joggers who have few other options. Finally, the path is a narrow one, ranging between four and eight feet wide. That's just enough room for two bikes to pass, assuming they're both in control. All of these problems can be avoided by visiting at less popular times, especially on weekdays.

Begin your ride on the lower Rock Creek Trail at Pierce Mill, a restored 1820s-era gristmill. Operated by the National Park Service, which administers Rock Creek Park, the mill uses water power to convert whole grain into finely ground flour. Cornmeal and buckwheat flour are available for sale when the mill is open. Adjacent to the mill is the Art Barn, where local artists display their efforts and conduct classes. Picnic tables, trash cans, a telephone, outhouses, and parking for about 50 cars may be found at Pierce Mill.

Leave Pierce Mill, heading southward. The trail continues to follow Rock Creek, a small tributary that has been subjected to most of the many insults that an urban stream faces. High-density development of a large portion of the watershed means that any significant rainstorm will bring flash flooding, scouring the riverbed and piling up debris. This runoff contains a witches' brew of nasties, including lawn and industrial chemicals; street pollution like oil, antifreeze, and dog feces; sediment; and just plain junk. Rock Creek is a seriously and chronically wounded stream, but the protection afforded by its adjacent greenbelt assures its continuing, albeit sickly, survival.

The initial mile of the trail passes through a forest of large trees that indicate that logging has not occurred in some time. Indeed, Rock Creek Park was created by an act of Congress in 1890, setting aside about 1,800 acres. Since then, it has been a popular retreat for Washingtonians weary of the summer heat but without the time or means to leave town.

At mile 1.0, the trail begins to border the National Zoo. A large fence keeps trail users out and residents in. The point at which the fence intertwines with a stand of evergreen bamboo marks the location of some exhibits, judging by the exotic odors that waft past your nose. An entrance to the zoo is next, and, although bicycles are not allowed in the zoo, you can lock your bike to a fence and walk through the zoo grounds.

Below here, the park reaches its narrowest point, appearing on maps as a thin green line among the grid of roads. The vegetation shows the stress of city living. Gone are the large, graceful trees of the upper, wider portions of the park; only the hardiest, like ailanthus, hold on. Also known as Tree of Heaven, these oriental exotics thrive in many of our cities, growing in trampled, sun-blasted soil and even through cracks in concrete. Ailanthus is almost impossible to eradicate, and a tree cut back grows all the more vigorously, up to twelve feet in one growing season. In addition to ailanthus, a number of nonnative shrubs and vines choke out the native vegetation along the creek where sunlight penetrates. At least all of this is green!

At mile 3.2, the trail passes Oak Hill Cemetery. Predating the Civil War, a number of ornate monuments speak of a time when the dead received more honor than they do today. The dead are well protected: razor wire tops the low stone cemetery wall. Just beyond the cemetery, the trail passes under a beautiful old pink sandstone bridge. Dozens of gargoyles in the persona of a war-bonneted Indian chief grace the bridge;

they are one of the mostly forgotten treasures of this capital city.

The frequency of bridges and intersections on this portion of the trail indicates that the terminus is near. The trail runs as a sidewalk adjacent to busy Rock Creek Parkway for a portion of its last mile, and care must be taken here on the narrow path, with heavy traffic just inches away.

A brick pathway overhung with willow trees at mile 4.1 marks the origin of the C & O Canal towpath. The canal is thoroughly urban in its first few miles, and its worldly character in Georgetown belies the remote rural nature of the rest of the 184-mile towpath.

The Rock Creek Trail ends at the parking lot for Thompson's Boat House. From here, the Watergate Hotel is to your left, with the Kennedy Center just beyond. The Washington Monument peeks over the buildings lining Virginia Avenue, also to your left. Thompson's has parking for 65 cars and rents bikes, canoes, rowboats, small sailboats, and rowing shells. Water and sodas are available; bathrooms are not wheelchair-accessible, being located on the second floor of the boathouse.

From Thompson's, you may want to visit the Mall and the monuments of downtown Washington, D.C., or you may return to Pierce Mill via the Rock Creek Trail.

DIRECTIONS

Because of the length of the Rock Creek Trail and the complexity of the roads reaching and crossing it, refer to the maps for access points.

OTHER OUTDOOR RECREATIONAL OPPORTUNITIES NEARBY

The C & O Canal towpath originates from the Rock Creek Trail in Georgetown, just a few yards from the trail's end. It is possible to explore the Mall and monuments of downtown Washington, D.C., on designated bike paths. Canoes may be rented from Thompson's Boat House to explore the Potomac River and Theodore Roosevelt Island.

The Decline of Forest Songbirds II: Causes

That forest songbirds, especially those that migrate each autumn to the neotropics, are in a precipitous decline is now undisputed. The causes of this thorny problem in conservation biology, however, are still hotly debated by amateur birders and professional ornithologists alike. Until all the contributing factors are better understood, it could be that we will be powerless to improve the situation. What are some of the best hunches scientists have about the decline of eastern forest songbirds?

One of the difficulties in sorting out this problem is that neotropical migrants live in not one but three habitats separated in space and time: their breeding grounds, their wintering grounds, and their migration route. These birds spend about half the year in the tropics, scattered throughout Mexico, Central and South America, and the Caribbean. Development, especially conversion of large tracts of tropical old-growth forests to slash-and-burn agriculture, may contribute to the prob-

Hooded warbler

lem. However, recent investigations have shown that many species of neotropical migrants can use a variety of agricultural, scrub, and second-growth habitats on the wintering grounds. For this reason, researchers now believe that, with the exception of certain species with narrow winter habitat requirements, factors associated with the summer breeding grounds in North America constitute the most significant threats to neotropical bird populations.

Loss of habitat here at home is undoubtedly a major culprit. Everyone knows a favorite woods or birding spot that has fallen to development. That means that wildlife residents of that plot of land have to move on and find other suitable habitat or they will perish. Birds, at least, are mobile and can search a large area rather quickly for new habitat, but such islands of suitable habitat become smaller and more distant from each other every year.

Related to habitat loss is fragmentation: the constant encroachment of development on remaining tracts of forest, splitting them into ever smaller chunks. Most species of forest songbirds are "area sensitive"; fledging of young is far more successful in large tracts of unbroken, mature forest than in smaller parcels split by roads or power lines and surrounded by a sea of agricultural lands. This is because small tracts have a higher ratio of "edge" to "interior" relative to large tracts. Such "edge" habitat, as well as artificial corridors leading to the interior of an otherwise unfragmented parcel of forest, provides access for predators like raccoons, jays, crows, foxes, and domestic animals. To examine the effect of such predators on bird eggs and nestlings, scientists placed artificial nests stocked with quail eggs in forests of varying sizes. Small suburban woodlots showed almost 100 percent predation of nests, whereas the largest forest tracts had almost none. In addition to predation, brood parasitism by brown-headed cowbirds is also a major problem, especially in smaller woodlands.

Finally, neotropical migrants may be affected by at least two threats that are only now just beginning to be appreciated. As the gypsy moth arrived in Maryland in the 1980s, the state responded aggressively with spraying campaigns in many Maryland forests. The two most common insecticides, Dimilin and

Bacillus thuringiensis, affect the caterpillar stage of woodland insects, which form the primary food of many forest songbirds. Still another potential threat to those birds that nest on the ground may be the state's burgeoning populations of white-tailed deer. In areas with lots of deer, vegetative cover can be eaten to the ground, exposing nests to higher levels of predation. Studies in which deer are excluded by fencing are underway in Shenandoah National Park to test how vegetative defoliation affects the nesting success of birds.

What can be done to save our avian natural heritage? First, preservation of critical wintering habitat in its natural state will be important. Scientists have only very recently identified such habitats, and work continues on this project in the tropics. Second, critical stopover areas during migration must also be preserved. The value of such stopover points has been well established for migrating shorebirds, but the locations of similar stopovers for songbirds have not been carefully cataloged, primarily because they are more disperse in time and space. Finally, in Maryland and surrounding mid-Atlantic states, we should preserve our public forests in large unbroken tracts. In order to do so, these forests must begin to be managed for the full diversity of plants and animals present rather than merely for game animals and lumber production. ⬲

The Capital Crescent Trail

Section: Bethesda Road to Georgetown

County: Montgomery and Washington, D.C.

Distance: About 7 miles

Type: Off-road bike path

Surface: Asphalt

Hazards: Traffic at road crossings

Highlights: Wetlands, riparian forest

More Information: National Capital Parks and Planning
Commission, (301) 495-2525

TRANSPORTATION planners long ago realized the
value of a beltway that circumnavigates a metropolitan
area, arcing through the suburbs to connect one outlying district with another. Now bicyclists have their own beltway, or at least a portion of one, on the west side of Washington,
D.C. The Capital Crescent Trail links Bethesda with Georgetown, running through the diverse suburbs west of the city
line and then following the Potomac River into downtown.

The Capital Crescent Trail is yet another old railroad bed
that has been converted to recreational use. Originally the
Georgetown Branch of the B & O Railroad, it has now
achieved a higher calling. Construction of the Capital Crescent
Trail is just beginning as this is written, so a detailed trip
description is impossible. Check with the National Capital
Parks and Planning Commission before riding for an update
on trail conditions and completion dates.

The Capital Crescent Trail

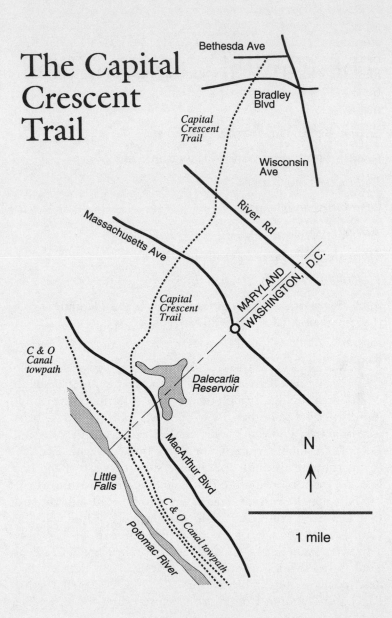

Bethesda Ave

Bradley Blvd

Capital Crescent Trail

Wisconsin Ave

River Rd

Massachusetts Ave

MARYLAND

WASHINGTON, D.C.

Capital Crescent Trail

C & O Canal towpath

Dalecarlia Reservoir

MacArthur Blvd

Little Falls

C & O Canal towpath

Potomac River

N

1 mile

Plans for the Capital Crescent Trail call for a 10-foot-wide asphalt lane bordered where possible by a 4-foot-wide crushed stone footpath. This ideal is achievable over about 60 percent of the route; in other places, various constraints prevent full implementation. There are few changes in elevation, turns will be gradual, and at-grade road crossings will be minimized. A major bridge will carry the trail over busy River Road. A significant feature of the trail will be the MacArthur Boulevard Tunnel, 300 feet long and 20 feet high with attractive brick facings. Vegetational buffers will be planted along the trail to screen out the heavily suburban and sometimes industrialized setting. All in all, this should be another fine Washington-area bike path that will nicely complement the existing network.

TRIP DESCRIPTION

There are three segments of the Capital Crescent Trail, although they may not be evident upon completion. The National Capital Parks and Planning Commission is responsible for the 3.6-mile segment between the trail's origin at Bethesda Road and the District line near the Potomac River. Sections of this trail will be built in a southward direction as funds allow. The National Park Service is in charge of the segment within District of Columbia borders, much of which runs parallel to the heavily used, soft-surfaced C & O Canal towpath. Finally, a segment running north and east from Bethesda Road to the Silver Spring Metro station may in fact never be built, since planners have reserved this corridor for possible service as the right-of-way for a light rail line.

The segment of the Capital Crescent Trail paralleling the C & O Canal towpath was finished in 1994. Because the towpath is narrow, eroded, and heavily used inside the District border, completion of a parallel, hard-surface path for bicycle use is especially valuable. The trail is densely shaded by mature trees, and so it is a cool place to cycle in the summer heat. A surprising amount of bird life inhabits this forest despite its urban character, attesting to the value of riparian habitat for wildlife. A number of small wetlands exist far above the level of the Potomac River, fed by leaks from the C & O Canal. There are excellent views of the Potomac and the church spires of Georgetown when the leaves have fallen.

The Capital Crescent Trail terminates in Georgetown at the quaint facilities of the Washington Canoe Club. Victorian accents to the sagging clubhouse speak of more prosperous days, when flatwater canoeing was among the most popular of pastimes.

DIRECTIONS

As of this writing, the completed segment of the Capital Crescent Trail within Washington, D.C., is not accessible by car. Instead, cycle to it via the C & O Canal towpath.

OTHER OUTDOOR RECREATIONAL OPPORTUNITES NEARBY

The C & O Canal towpath runs parallel to the Capital Crescent Trail for several miles. The towpath continues through Georgetown to its eastern terminus at the Rock Creek Trail. To the west, it stretches for 184 miles to Cumberland, Maryland. Running almost dead flat and wide enough for several cyclists to ride abreast, it is one of the premier venues in Maryland for a bike ride.

Virtually any section of the towpath provides an enjoyable ride. The only difficult segment is found between Great Falls and the Old Anglers Inn, just outside Washington D.C., where the trail is unsuitable for bicycles. Several hundred yards of towpath require you to shoulder your bike and hop from rock to rock in muddy terrain. This dramatic section of the towpath should not be missed, but it is best explored on foot.

The rest of the towpath is suitable for all but thin-tired racing bikes. Mountain bikes and hybrid bikes are probably best suited for riding on the towpath because they are more rugged, and most children's bicycles are acceptable as well. Substrate ranges from sandy soil to gravel with a few muddy spots, and rocks and roots often protrude from the ground, so the towpath is not a high-speed ride. In some places, the bank drops off steeply into the adjacent canal, so good bike control is a necessity. Despite these considerations, a ride on our longest bike path is well worthwhile for a family outing.

Mayflies

Evening on the Potomac: the sun has set and the sweet humid dusk of summer settles over the river. Rocks still radiate the heat of the day, but the air is now cool, and the Potomac is calm and mirror-flat in the gloaming. Dimples appear on the river's surface, tiny concentric circles expanding outward. Just above the water, small dun-colored insects mill about; occasionally one drops her abdomen to the water's surface for a moment, creating the dimple, and then flies back upward. Soon more insects appear, and within minutes a living blizzard of mayflies whirls over the river. The early summer swarm is underway, a synchronous frenzy of breeding and egg-laying that will ensure continuation of the species into another year.

The adult mayflies that appear in these breeding swarms make their presence briefly known by their sheer numbers, but for most of their life mayflies are rather anonymous animals. In fact, adult mayflies live for only a few hours to a few days; because of their short adult life, their taxonomic classification has been given the order name Ephemeroptera. There are about 575 species of mayfly in North America, and they are widespread in all sorts of freshwater aquatic habitats where water quality is reasonably good.

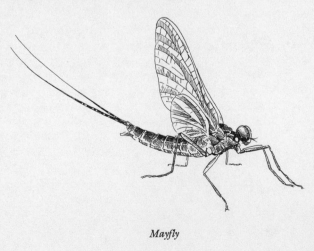

Mayfly

Adult mayflies are beautiful creatures. Two pairs of nearly transparent wings are held vertically, and forelegs and tail filaments extend a great distance from the body. Adult mayflies have one purpose only: to breed. They do not feed; in fact, their mouthparts are not functional. Mayflies rely on stored body tissue to supply energy for their brief adult life. After mating, female mayflies lay their eggs singly or in clumps on the surface of the water. The eggs quickly sink to the river bottom and attach to a rock. They grow and develop, eventually hatching out into the larval stage known as the nymph.

A nymph has three distinct body segments: head, thorax and abdomen, with a pair of external gills found on the middle abdominal segment. It has three pairs of legs and three tails and grows by shedding its exoskeleton. Nymphs are either herbivores or detritivores, grazing on algae or dead vegetable material, respectively. Mayfly larvae are fed upon by fish and by predatory aquatic insects like the larval forms of dragonflies, damselflies, dobsonflies, and stoneflies. As such, mayflies form an important part of the aquatic food chain.

Mayfly nymphs typically spend about a year in the larval form. After their final molt, the body begins to rearrange itself into an adult and eventually floats to the surface. There the adult hatches out, dries its wings, and flies off. Mayflies are very vulnerable to predation in this form, and fish feed voraciously during a mayfly hatch.

Perhaps the most unusual aspect of mayfly hatching is its synchrony. When a hatch occurs, almost all members of a population hatch together, within a few minutes to an hour of each other. Scientists believe this synchronous hatching holds predation to a minimum by saturating the environment with hatching mayflies. Although predators take a heavy toll, only so many mayflies can be eaten in such a short period of time; the rest survive to continue the species by breeding. ✦

The National Arboretum

Section: Park loop

County: Washington, D.C.

Distance: Variable, depending on route

Type: Lightly traveled roads within the grounds

Surface: Asphalt

Difficulty: Rolling to hilly

Hazards: Traffic

Highlights: Flowers, shrubs, trees, National Capitol Columns

More Information: The National Arboretum, (202) 475-4815

WASHINGTON, D.C., is a city of contrasts: The capital of the most powerful country in the world, it is home to hundreds of thousands of people, some of whom live in opulent houses in enchanting neighborhoods and others who live in crime-ridden poverty as bad as that in any urban center in America. Its trash-filled streets lie close to fine old parks filled with large trees and a sense of wildness. Finally, it is a magnet for visitors and tourists, who hit all of the must-see museums and monuments while ignoring a number of fine facilities and national treasures. The National Arboretum is one such underappreciated place. Located near the outskirts of the city proper, far from any other tourist meccas, the 444-acre arboretum is visited mostly by metropolitan D.C. residents as a refuge for relaxation from the bustle and stress of urban life. In most seasons, it is usually uncrowded, and even in winter there are always some beautiful plantings to delight

The National Arboretum

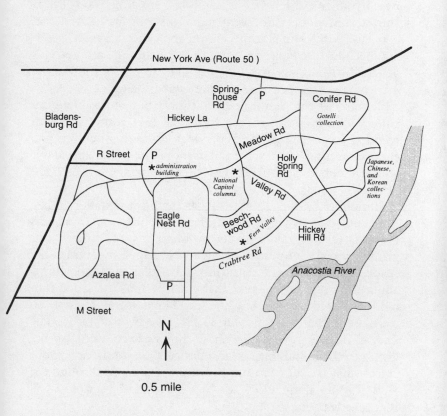

New York Ave (Route 50)

Springhouse Rd

P

Conifer Rd

Gotelli collection

Bladensburg Rd

Hickey La

Meadow Rd

R Street

P

★administration building

Holly Spring Rd

Japanese, Chinese, and Korean collections

★

National Capitol columns

Valley Rd

Eagle Nest Rd

Beech-wood Rd

Fern Valley

Hickey Hill Rd

★

Azalea Rd

Crabtree Rd

Anacostia River

P

M Street

N

↑

0.5 mile

the eye. Over nine miles of paved roads wind gracefully through the gently rolling property, and bicycling these lightly traveled paths is a true delight.

TRIP DESCRIPTION

Begin your ride from the parking lots just within the R Street entrance. An information center and gift shop are located near here, and bathroom facilities, water, and candy and soda vending machines are available. Be sure to pick up the arboretum's general brochure; its map provides a key to the location of the many kinds of gardens and vegetational displays.

Because of the aesthetically pleasing but almost random pattern of arboretum roads, no formal bike route is recommended here. Instead, use the map to ride wherever you choose, visiting whatever exhibits hold the most appeal for you. Described here are a few of my favorite gardens and plantings.

Undoubtedly, the arboretum gets the most visitation in late April and May when its justly famous collection of azaleas blooms. Over 70,000 plants in hundreds of varieties are planted mostly informally along forest edges and under the shade of native trees. It is a truly spectacular sight, and this is about the only time of year that you will find the arboretum roads crowded. Fortunately, the speed limit is only 15 mph, so cyclists are frequently moving as fast as vehicular traffic. The azaleas occupy rolling terrain in the western third of the grounds; the uphills may be too difficult for young riders, but at least they are short. A number of foot trails lead through the woods; bring along a lock for your bike, and be sure to stroll these shady paths.

The central third of the arboretum is flatter and more open, with dozens of acres of grassy lawns. The roads in this portion of the park are more suitable for younger riders who might have trouble on the uphills elsewhere. Two sites here are especially worth visiting. Dominating the area are the National Capitol Columns. These historic sandstone columns graced

Azalea

the east central portico of the United States Capitol from 1826 to 1958, when an addition was built. The 22 columns are a testament to the artistry and skill of stonecarvers and other craftsmen in the early years of our country. Not far away is Fern Valley, also worth a stroll on foot. In addition to a number of ferns, the deeply shaded site along a tiny trickle of a stream displays a number of native woodland wildflowers. Spring is the best time to visit here for the most diversity. In the meadow just outside Fern Valley are many varieties of native wildflowers adapted to the high light and heat of open land.

The eastern third of the Arboretum grounds is dominated by conifers. On a hot day, the smell of their resins wafts through the air and lends a delightful scent to the landscape. The Gotelli collection of dwarf conifers is carefully landscaped, as are the formal gardens of the Japanese, Korean, and Chinese collections overlooking the Anacostia River.

Finally, don't miss the exotic Bonsai displays near the administration building and the parking lots. If you're an aficionado of almost any other kind of plant, you're very likely to find displays of it elsewhere on the arboretum grounds. Enjoy!

DIRECTIONS

From the Capital Beltway, take the Baltimore-Washington Parkway, I-295, in toward the city. Exit at New York Avenue, Route 50. At the first stoplight, Bladensburg Road, turn left. Go three blocks, turn left on R Street, and proceed to the arboretum entrance.

OTHER OUTDOOR RECREATIONAL OPPORTUNITIES NEARBY

Washington, D.C., and its surrounding suburbs have a number of surprisingly pleasant bike paths, including the Rock Creek Trail, the Mount Vernon Trail, and the Capital Crescent Trail. These three trails are described elsewhere in this book.

Medicinal Plants and the Value of Biological Diversity

In the 1970s, far up in the remote mountains of central Mexico, a college student found a very different-looking variety of wild maize. This significant discovery turned out to be a previously unknown species of corn, *Zea diploperennis*. This newly discovered species proved to be resistant to several diseases, and more important, it is the only variety of corn that is perennial rather than annual. *Zea diploperennis* could be worth billions of dollars, because it provides a potential source of genetic information that can be transferred into domesticated varieties both by standard breeding methods and by new techniques in molecular biology. The little patch of corn covered less than 25 acres and was slated to be destroyed within a week when it was discovered.

In addition to being the basis for a significant part of our diet, plants have been the source of most of our medicines. About 80 percent of these medicines were originally plant based, and even today about 30 percent include plant products. Aboriginal cultures have long used plants as remedies for health problems, but even in the United States only a fraction have been scientifically investigated.

The reason for this has as much to do with the prejudices of science and scientists as with anything else. In colonial times, much of medical practice was quackery, practiced by rascals with no training or scruples. Plant extracts were often prescribed as remedies and cures, but the few kernels of truth in herbalism were often obscured by much nonsense. The doctrine of signatures, a holdover from medieval times, is one such quaint example. The doctrine held that God had put plants on earth for mankind's use and had left on each plant a physical clue as to how it might best be used. For example, the woodland wildflower hepatica, with its purplish color and three lobes, resembles the human liver and was thus thought to be useful for liver-related ailments. Although a few of these signatures were fortuitously correct, most were not. As scientific medicine evolved in the mid-nineteenth century, doctors understandably ignored herbalism as mere folklore. Today, we are reexamining plants for their usefulness in medicine.

Among the flora of Maryland are several medically useful species:

- The common woodland plant mayapple contains podophyllin, an anticancer drug.
- Extracts of bloodroot also have antitumor activity.
- Paw paw trees contain biologically active compounds called acetogenins that are under investigation for their effectiveness in cancer therapy.
- The active ingredient in aspirin was originally isolated from willow twigs.
- The heart drug digitalis comes from foxglove, a forest wildflower that has now been naturalized.
- Indian tobacco yields lobeline, a muscle relaxant, and extracts of the plant are also useful in respiratory disorders.
- Jimsonweed and other members of the tomato family produce hallucinogenic alkaloids.

The list goes on, and it will probably never be complete.

The wild plants of our world, therefore, have an economic value in addition to an aesthetic one. When members of the public question the value of a snail darter or spotted owl, or of a tract of wetland or old-growth forest, it is usually from a position of naiveté. Most of our biological heritage remains unexplored for its utility and must be preserved until such time as it can be. Most bacteria, algae, fungi, lower plants, and obscure classes of animals have never been investigated in this regard. There is general agreement among scientists that a wealth of useful compounds exists in plants and other organisms. For this reason alone, preservation of biodiversity is not a luxury but a necessity that our society cannot afford to ignore. ᨞

Patapsco Valley State Park: Avalon–Orange Grove Area

Section: Avalon–Orange Grove circuit

County: Howard, Baltimore

Distance: 5.5 miles

Type: Lightly traveled park road, off-road bike trail

Surface: Asphalt

Difficulty: Flat with one hill

Hazards: None

Highlights: River valley, footbridge

More Information: Patapsco Valley State Park, (410) 461-5005

PATAPSCO VALLEY State Park is another of Maryland's linear greenways, flanking both sides of the Patapsco River from where it flows, tiny and narrow, through the rich farmland of Carroll County to tidewater in the industrial backyards of Baltimore. It is known locally as the "River of History": Lafayette's soldiers camped along its shores on their way to join Washington's forces at Yorktown; Benjamin Banneker, our country's first black man of science, lived and died near the Patapsco; and the valley was the site of the first commercial railroad line in the United States. Along

Patapsco Valley State Park: Avalon–Orange Grove Area

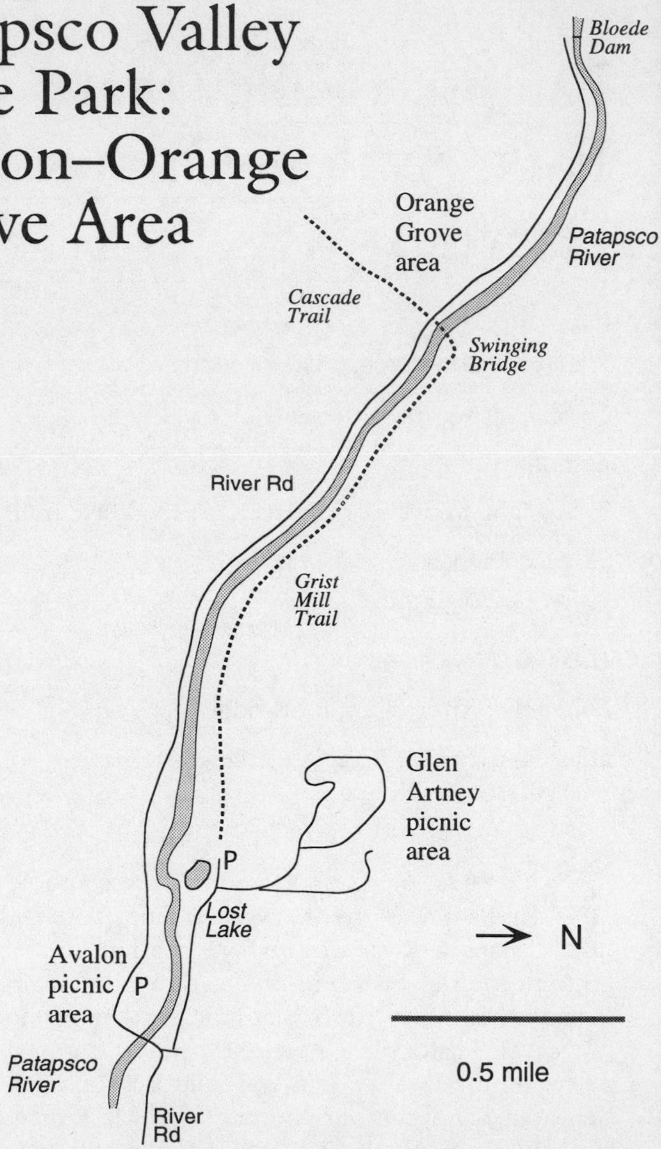

Bloede Dam

Orange Grove area

Patapsco River

Cascade Trail

Swinging Bridge

River Rd

Grist Mill Trail

Glen Artney picnic area

Lost Lake

Avalon picnic area

Patapsco River

River Rd

→ N

0.5 mile

its course, the Patapsco encounters sewage treatment plants, rampant development, active and abandoned industrial works, and several dams. Despite these insults, the land preserved by the state park is quiet, beautiful, and well worth a visit. Several sections of the park are suitable for hiking with small children, because the trails follow the river valley and therefore have few hills. Located within easy reach of millions of Marylanders, "Patapsico" (as the locals pronounce it) is one of the state's most familiar parks.

The Avalon section of Patapsco Valley State Park is a very scenic and pleasant site for a bike ride. It is often shady and cool, even in midsummer, with big, old trees overhanging the road and trail. In winter, the north-facing River Road lies entirely within the shadow of the steep hillsides and will not see sunlight for months. Wildflowers abound, especially in spring and fall, and the riparian habitat makes birding a rewarding pastime.

The bicycle trip described here is a 5.5-mile loop ride in the Avalon–Orange Grove section of the park. The circuit was made possible only recently (1992) by the paving of what was once a muddy service road. This 1.3-mile portion, known as the Grist Mill Recreational Trail, was specifically designed to be accessible to the disabled. An eight-foot-wide blacktop lane is bordered by a three-foot-wide strip of gravel, providing a contrast in texture underfoot. Sturdy metal railings line the trail wherever there is a dropoff. The rest of the ride is on roads open to park traffic, but vehicle use is typically light, being limited to those willing to pay the entrance fee.

TRIP DESCRIPTION

Enter this portion of Patapsco Valley State Park from Route 1. An entrance fee is charged seven days a week except in winter. Pass under the Thomas Viaduct, the first multiple-stone-arch bridge built in the United States; more than 150 years after its construction, it still carries a major railroad line south to Washington, D.C. Follow the road to a T junction, turn left to cross the river, and park in the large lot near the picnic pavilions at Avalon. Trash cans, water, telephones, and wheelchair-accessible bathrooms are available here. Athletic fields and a playground are located nearby.

Begin your ride by recrossing the Patapsco River into Baltimore County over the bridge on which you drove in. Instead of turning right toward the contact station, continue straight for 50 yards and then turn left. Within a quarter mile, this narrow road ends at Lost Lake. An artificial pond rebuilt after the ravages of Hurricane Agnes in 1972, it is very popular with fishermen, especially after early spring stockings. Several mulberry trees line the upland edge of the parking lot, and their fruiting in late spring attracts many songbirds.

The far end of the Lost Lake parking lot is gated and marked as the Grist Mill Recreational Trail. Enter the trail, located on a narrow bench of land bordered by the railroad and a seasonally flooded wooded wetland. Spring peepers and American toads are the most common amphibians in this swamp, using the puddles for vernal breeding. This is good birding habitat as well, especially in early morning; you may want to walk the obscure footpaths that wind through here to the riverbank for the best chance of seeing pileated woodpeckers, warblers, ospreys, and ducks.

The trail continues upstream, although it is separated from views of the river in most places. The alluvial floodplain, scoured in 1972, has few big trees, but it is dominated by a dense tangle of box elder and small maples. In winter, the southern exposure keeps this part of the trail pleasantly warm and sunny, in contrast to the icebound River Road on the shaded opposite bank of the Patapsco.

After a little more than a mile, the paved trail reaches the ruins of the Orange Grove Flour Mill, built in 1856 and burned to the ground in 1905. Only a few foundation walls are left of the six-story building in which flour was ground using dammed-up river water to power three large millstones.

Prominently marking the site of the mill is the Swinging Bridge, a landmark familiar to generations of Marylanders. For more than a century, kids have visited this bridge in its various incarnations. Constructed of steel cables with wooden plank-ing, the entire bridge sways from side to side in response to a hiker's footfall or a tug on the support wires. It's great fun, and even adults are allowed to let down their hair and join in.

Crossing the Swinging Bridge brings you to a flat open area known as Orange Grove (named after the osage orange trees that grew here). Once the site of eight mill workers' houses, it is now a parking lot, and has a water fountain and wheelchair-accessible bathrooms. At the upstream end of the Orange Grove parking lot lies a sheltered forest whose rich soil pro-motes an incredibly dense profusion of wildflowers in early spring (typically April). Trout lily, Dutchman's-breeches, and several species of violets carpet the forest floor in such density that it is impossible to walk without crushing them underfoot. Look but don't trample, and above all don't dig them up! Leave them intact so that you can bring your children back to this same spot, year after year.

Continue riding upstream on River Road. The pavement ends after 0.7 mile with a nice view of Bloede Dam, recently stabilized by the Park Service. One of the first private hydoelectric dams in America, it had long been abandoned and was not only a hazard of crumbling concrete but a block to the migration of anadromous fish to their spawning grounds on upstream tributaries of the Patapsco. A fish ladder was built around the dam in 1992 as part of an effort to reestablish these populations. After viewing the dam and fish ladder, return to Orange Grove.

A short hike originating from Orange Grove is well worth-while. Park and lock your bike in the rack provided and walk about 200 yards up the blue-blazed Cascade Trail, the en-trance to which is located between the comfort station and the large parking lot. The trail is very steep at first but then flattens out and becomes merely rocky. After about 150 yards, the trail reaches an enchanting little dell overhung with hemlocks and birch. An eight-foot-high waterfall tumbles over a rocky ledge into a clear, frigid pool and makes a pleasant picnic spot on a hot day. Most people retrace their steps back to the parking lot, but continuing onward opens up the steeper and more difficult upland trail system of the park. If you're interested in this sort of hiking, ask at the fee station for their map of the area.

Returning to your bike, leave the parking area, heading downstream on River Road. It is usually open to vehicular traffic but is rarely busy; nevertheless, watch for cars, especially if you have small children. Pedal up a hill (the only one on this circuit) for a nice view of the valley. The road continues on, bordered by steep, heavily forested hillsides occasionally split by sparkling creeks in steep ravines. Displays of spring wildflowers are excellent all along here, and in autumn the foliage is beautiful.

About a mile downstream of Orange Grove, the road emerges from the forest at a rocky outcrop to give a good view of the valley and Lost Lake. Note how the far shore of the Patapsco has been reinforced with baskets (called gabions) containing large rocks to ensure that floodwaters do not erode the berm separating Lost Lake from the river. Coast down the hill to your car at the Avalon parking lot.

DIRECTIONS

From the Capital Beltway, take I-95 north to I-195, the exit for BWI airport. From the Baltimore Beltway, take I-95 south one exit to I-195. Follow the I-195 exit east, toward BWI airport. At the first exit off I-195, turn south on Route 1. As the exit ramp dumps you onto Route 1, go only 50 yards and turn right on South Street. The entrance to Patapsco Valley State Park, called River Road, is on your left.

Springtime Ephemeral Woodland Wildflowers

Among the most eagerly awaited and avidly enjoyed phenomena of the natural year in Maryland is the appearance of wildflowers each April on the forest floor. Confined to mature woodlands with rich, well-developed soils, a number of native plant species sprout, flower, set seed, and die back in the short space of two months or so. These ephemeral harbingers of spring share some common life history characteristics that link them to the ecology of their habitat.

The most common springtime ephemeral wildflowers in Maryland are trout lily, spring beauty, marsh marigold, Dutchman's-breeches, rue anemone, bluebells, and trillium.

Spring beauty

Some other species that flower at the same time and in the same habitat but whose leaves persist for a longer period of time include bloodroot, mayapple, and hepatica. All are perennial; most of the year is spent as a quiescent rootstalk.

All of these plants flower, but most do not release a large number of seeds. In fact, a flower like trout lily may put out fewer than 10 viable seeds each year. In contrast, many annuals release thousands or tens of thousands of seeds. In large measure, this is because annuals live in a variable, uncertain environment where the best strategy for success over time is to spread lots of progeny over lots of space in the hopes that a few will survive. Conversely, in a stable habitat like a mature forest, conditions are suitable and unchanging over time, so the best strategy is to devote most energy and resources to vegetative growth of the perennial rhizome. Only a few seeds are produced, mostly as a counterbalance against the possibility of a disturbance to the habitat.

For this reason, springtime ephemeral wildflowers often spread asexually. Trout lily rootstalks (known as corms) will put out a long shoot called a "dropper" that penetrates the soil for several inches. The end of the dropper forms a bulbous swelling that later develops into a new corm and can be the source of new roots and shoots. Thus, a colony of these plants may actually be genetically identical individuals linked by a network of underground roots and droppers. This life history strategy often explains why such plants are frequently found in clusters.

Woodland wildflowers play an essential role in forest ecology. Pollen and nectar associated with flowers act as an important food source for a number of insects, especially bees and ants, at a time early in the season when other food sources are scarce. Springtime ephemerals also play an important role in the cycling of nutrients, especially the element phosphorus. Early spring rains dissolve nutrients in the forest floor litter and carry them downward through the soil, where they will eventually become less available to plants for growth. These vernal wildflowers, growing rapidly at a time when other plant life is still dormant, rescue nutrients for their own development. As they die back in late spring through summer, the released nutrients become available to other plants. ♣

The Northern Central Trail

Section: Ashland to the Pennsylvania border

County: Baltimore

Distance: 19.7 miles

Type: Off-road bike trail

Surface: Crushed limestone

Difficulty: Flat, with some slight steady uphill gradient

Hazards: A few road crossings

Highlights: River valley, rolling farmlands

More Information: Gunpowder Falls State Park,
(410) 592-2897

O F ALL THE GOOD ideas that have ever been proposed to benefit the public good, one of the best has been the conversion of abandoned railroad right-of-ways into recreational trails. Such linear greenways are often among the few remaining tracts of land available for purchase in suburban regions and connect population centers with more sparsely settled rural areas. They provide corridors for wildlife, too, and often are surprisingly natural in setting. Rail trails have proven immensely popular with almost everyone. In Maryland, the most notable are the Baltimore and Annapolis Trail, the Capital Crescent Trail, and the Northern Central Trail. The Northern Central Trail may well be the best of its kind.

The Northern Central Trail extends due northward from the suburbs of Baltimore for 19.7 miles. Originating at Ash-

The Northern Central Trail

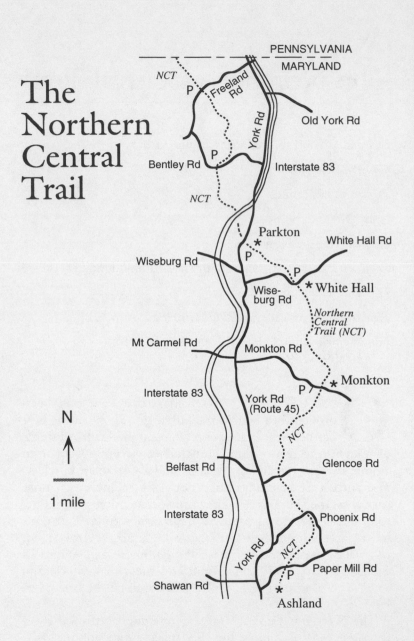

land, the trail follows the Gunpowder River, Little Falls, and then Bee Tree Run upstream to the Pennsylvania border. The Keystone State has just begun (as of this writing) to extend the recreational trail as far as York. The Maryland portion of the Northern Central Trail is administered by Gunpowder Falls State Park.

Since its opening in 1984, the Northern Central Trail has been one of the most popular outdoor recreational facilities in Maryland. Walkers, joggers, cyclists, cross-country skiers, birdwatchers, fishermen, and equestrians all flock to this unique resource. Although it's not a place to find solitude, the linear nature of the trail ensures you of some space of your own. Nature lovers will find an unexpected diversity of plants and animals, owing in large part to the adjacent river corridor.

The trail itself is a generous 11 feet wide in most places, ample space for a biker to pass a strolling couple. It is composed of a type of crushed rock that is about the consistency of heavy sand and makes a firm surface for bicycling. The trail drains well, even after a heavy rain, and most puddles have disappeared within 24 hours. The Northern Central Trail has no hills, but its northern half rises steadily in elevation. It is a great place for even the youngest riders, as well as strollers and wheelchairs. Access is generally good, although parking lots and road crossings near Baltimore are often full on weekends. Park somewhere north of Monkton and you'll be rewarded with fewer trail users.

TRIP DESCRIPTION

You may begin your ride on the Northern Central Trail at any of the road crossings, but only two have enough parking to accommodate a large number of cars. If you arrive late on a pleasant weekend day, plan on parking along Paper Mill Road near the southern terminus of the trail, or at Monkton, near the halfway point. There are no facilities at all at Paper Mill Road, and the parking is along a road shoulder. In contrast,

Monkton has bathrooms, water, telephones, trash cans, a few picnic tables, a ranger station (open only on weekends), and a store that sells snacks (again open only on weekends). Because most cyclists approach the trail from the south, the ride is described from south to north.

The Northern Central Trail originates in Ashland, an old mill community that time and development seemed to have forgotten—until the 1980s. The old mill houses have now been rehabilitated and sell for a price previous tenants would have thought a king's ransom. New townhouses have sprung up, and suburbanites barbecue on decks overlooking the trail's origin. Fortunately, creeping upscale development is left behind after the first few hundred yards. On the other side of the trail are the upper reaches of Loch Raven Reservoir. Sedimentation has created extensive marshes of cattail and common reed; red-winged backbirds and great blue herons are frequently seen.

Shortly, the trail crosses Paper Mill Road, the busiest by far of the road crossings. Use particular caution here, and walk bikes across the intersection. Fortunately, at this point the worst of the Northern Central Trail lies behind you, and you can look forward to more pastoral scenery between here and Pennsylvania.

The trail now becomes mostly shaded, with medium-sized trees overhanging the path. In some places, private property reaches to the edge of the trail and a scattering of houses lie adjacent to it, mostly from the era when the railroad connected outlying towns with the commerce of Baltimore. These dwellings are never intrusive, however, and the older houses lend a rustic simplicity to the scene.

The sound of flowing water is never far away from the Northern Central Trail. The southernmost half borders Big Gunpowder Falls, a narrow river that alternately sparkles over rocky riffles and flows through deep green pools. Water quality is excellent; indeed, a resident population of trout lives in the cool, shaded waters. There are occasional floodplains with beautiful stands of summer wildflowers, although the trail is always at a higher elevation.

To build this level roadway, the railroad made liberal use of cuts and fills. Today, only the cuts are obvious, and there are many along the Northern Central Trail. Here, rock out-croppings are exposed, and their dark color and the deep shade contribute to a sense of foreboding as the path winds between rock walls. Many ferns poke out of crevices or spray across slopes where soil has accumulated, and their appearance is striking. Most are hay-scented ferns, but cinnamon and Christ-mas ferns are common, and a few royal and New York ferns may be found. Curiously, in many of the northern cuts pure stands of ferns are sheltered exclusively by red maple. A sunny fall afternoon makes these places vibrant with rich colors.

Perhaps the most scenic section of the trail is that between the junction of Little Falls with the Gunpowder River and the tiny community of Parkton, between miles 9 and 13. Little Falls is a lively small stream here, flowing noisily over large boulders and through water-worn chutes. The sound of water music and the close proximity of the trail are most pleasant and invite tired cyclists to rest in the cool shade and dip hot, tired feet into the soothing waters.

Another interesting area lies between miles 17 and 18, south of Freeland. Here, a beautiful little wetland is situated adjacent to the west side of the trail. Unlike river floodplains, a wetland such as this one has a constant high water table throughout the year. Standing water is found here; it is sometimes obvious and sometimes not, lurking under hammocks of vegetation where an unwary step can result in a wet, muddy foot. These nontidal wetlands are fairly common along the Maryland-Pennsylvania border and harbor their own unique flora and fauna. Red maples and alders dominate the shrub layer, while water-loving species like cinnamon fern, sensitive fern, skunk cabbage, steeplebush, and joe-pye weed are found covering the mud. Many kinds of bacteria and algae grow on and in the mud. Oxygen penetrates poorly into this substrate, resulting in the "rotten egg" odor of hydrogen sulfide being given off when the mud is disturbed. These wetlands have a distinctive appear-ance to even the casual observer because of their unusual flora. More reclusive is the fauna of these wetlands, the most interesting member of which may be the bog turtle. These small turtles, identified by a slash of color along the side of the head, remain buried in the weeds of nontidal wetlands and are almost impossible to find.

This northern section of the trail rises almost imperceptibly uphill, but walkers or cyclists will not get winded. As the change is gradual, it is not very noticeable as you pedal north-ward. The return trip for the most northerly three miles takes about half as much time as the outbound trip.

The Pennsylvania line is reached without fanfare and is marked only by a gate. Turn your bike around and note that, wherever you started from, you're now halfway home. But the downhill nature of the trail makes for smooth sailing, and the return trip is always faster. The Northern Central Trail is the finest bike path in Maryland; would that we had more recrea-tional trails like it!

DIRECTIONS

The Northern Central Trail approximately parallels I-83 north of Baltimore, and the latter road provides easy access. From the Baltimore Beltway, take I-83 north. To reach Paper Mill Road, take the Shawan Road exit east from I-83. Go 0.8 mile and turn right on York Road, Route 45. Proceed 0.3 mile and turn left on Ashland Road. This soon becomes Paper Mill Road; continue until you cross the Northern Central Trail and park along the road shoulder.

To reach Monkton, take I-83 north to the Mt. Carmel Road exit. Go right (east) for 0.5 mile, and turn right on York Road, Route 45. Proceed only about 200 yards, and then turn left on the obscurely marked Monkton Road, Route 138. Cross the river, continue for 0.2 mile, and park in the lot next to the old train station. In the event that this lot is full, return the way you came, cross to the west side of the river, and make an immediate left onto Old Monkton Road, where there is road-side parking.

OTHER OUTDOOR RECREATIONAL OPPORTUNITIES NEARBY

A beautiful section of the Big Gunpowder River suitable for canoeing is described beginning on page 502 of this book. An exceptionally pretty hike in the upper watershed is described beginning on page 118.

Bog Turtles

Few animals in Maryland are as obscure in the public mind as the bog turtle. Confined to a series of wet meadows along the Pennsylvania border in Carroll, Baltimore, and Harford counties, bog turtles occupy a habitat where we humans rarely venture. Even if you decide to wade into the mixture of mud, water, dense vegetation, and insects that forms these nontidal wetlands, you're unlikely to come across a specimen of *Clemmys muhlenbergii*. Scientists working with the species say that locating a bog turtle requires almost a sixth sense—a feeling that one clump of grass looks "turtley" while the next one over does not.

Bog turtles are small (three to five inches in length), brown, and inconspicuous. They are easily identified by a yellow, orange, or reddish blotch on each side of the head. Like most turtles, they are omnivorous, eating insects, some plant mate-

Bog turtle

rial, and carrion. Bog turtles move around very little; radio-tagged turtles are frequently found within a few yards of their previous location. In part, this sedentary nature may be due to the limited size of their habitat, since most of the Maryland bogs and wet meadows in which they are found are quite small. Sexual maturity is reached after five to eight years. Mating occurs in the spring, and nesting may be delayed for several months. Females dig a rough depression in elevated ground, especially mossy or grassy tussocks. Three to five eggs are typically laid, and these hatch in early September.

Maryland is at the southern edge of the distribution of the largest population of bog turtles (although there is a disjunct group in the North Carolina mountains). For this reason, and because of its reputation as a rare species, Maryland placed the bog turtle on its endangered species list in 1976. That action stimulated research on the species, and it was subsequently found at over 170 sites. In 1978, it was delisted, although it remains on a watch list. The greatest threat to bog turtles in Maryland is habitat loss; farmers and developers may drain wet meadows or change the drainage pattern that supplies water to the wetland. Strong nontidal wetlands legislation will ensure the continued existence of this harmless and obscure reptile. ⚲

Antietam National Battlefield

Section: Battlefield circuit

County: Washington

Distance: 8.3 miles

Type: Mostly lightly traveled park roads; a short section on public roads

Surface: Asphalt

Difficulty: Hilly

Hazards: Traffic, especially in Sharpsburg

Highlights: Rolling farmland, battlefield site

More Information: Antietam National Battlefield, (301) 432-5124

NESTLED IN THE RICH farmlands of central Maryland, out where life is quiet and peaceful, lies the site of the most violent day in American history. Antietam National Battlefield exists today much as it did in September 1862. Corn ripens slowly in the summer sun; leaves wither, yellow, and drift sparsely down from autumn-tinged trees. Over one hundred and thirty years after fate brought together opposing armies, pastoral scenes still surround the battlefield, and the nearby town of Sharpsburg drowses quietly. No fast food restaurants, no wax museums, no motels blight Antietam, unlike so many of our other Civil War battle-

Antietam National Battlefield

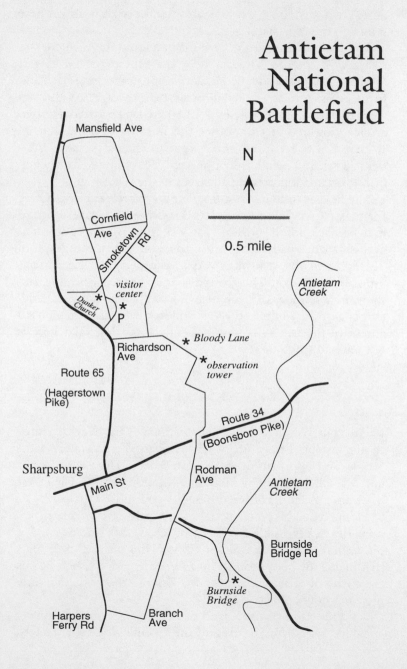

N
↑

0.5 mile

Mansfield Ave

Cornfield Ave

Smoketown Rd

Antietam Creek

visitor center

*
Dunker Church

*
P

* Bloody Lane

* observation tower

Richardson Ave

Route 65
(Hagerstown Pike)

Route 34
(Boonsboro Pike)

Sharpsburg

Rodman Ave

Antietam Creek

Main St

Burnside Bridge Rd

*
Burnside Bridge

Harpers Ferry Rd

Branch Ave

fields. It is a national treasure not just for what went on here long ago but for what it is today.

The Union Army of the Potomac attacked the Confederate Army of Northern Virginia here on September 17, 1862. Fighting was desperate, fierce, and bloody, sweeping back and forth across a relatively small piece of landscape. As the sun went down, casualties totaled 23,110 men. Exhausted, the two armies glowered at each other the next day before General Robert E. Lee retreated into Virginia. The battle gave President Abraham Lincoln the opportunity to issue the Emancipation Proclamation, freeing all slaves in the rebel states.

The field at Antietam is a fine one for bicycle touring. Of all the major Civil War battlefields, this is the least developed, so it is perhaps not surprising that visitation is light. Although cyclists share roads with auto tourists, the speed limit of 25 mph and the lack of crowds make pedaling the narrow, intimate roads a joy. The ground is quite broken, however, and there are a number of steep but short hills. Bicycling at Antietam is best for adults and older children who are experienced and have the necessary stamina. The loop described here is 8.3 miles in length.

TRIP DESCRIPTION

Begin your bicycle tour at the National Park Service visitor center just off Route 65 north of Sharpsburg. Water, bathrooms, and information are available here. The visitor center has a small museum, a film presentation, and a Civil War bookstore. A fee is collected here for your use of the park.

Mount your bike and pedal in a northward direction, toward the clearly visible Dunker Church. Just 0.1 mile north of the visitor center, the Dunker Church is a plain stone edifice that marks the high ground on the battlefield. As such, it was the focus of repeated attacks by Union troops in the early morning hours of September 17.

Continuing north, the road passes through and eventually encircles the North Woods and the Cornfield. Unfortunately, these landmarks of American history no longer exist as they were in 1862; the North Woods is now agricultural fields, and the Cornfield is in pasture. The National Park Service recently announced plans to purchase some inholdings of private land and to revegetate the area in a manner consistent with its appearance at the time of the battle. Monuments abound in this area, as so many men of both sides fought and died over these few acres.

At mile 2.0, the designated auto tour bears right onto Cornfield Avenue; instead, continue straight on the Smoketown Road. After 0.2 mile, turn left toward Mumma's Farm. At mile 2.8, turn left on Richardson Avenue. Paralleling this park road is an old sunken road known in military annals as the Bloody Lane. This salient in the Confederate defenses was the focus of over four hours of intense fighting around midday on September 17. An observation tower at mile 3.1 provides a panoramic view of this portion of the field.

From the tower, the hilly, rural nature of the Antietam landscape is evident. There are a large number of rock outcrops poking through the earth in agricultural fields, and many fencelots are so rocky as to be suitable only for pasturage. The area around Antietam is underlain by limestone, a hard but erodable rock. In places where cracks or faults in the limestone develop, soil water can slowly dissolve the rock. Sinkholes, caves, and small but steep undulations in the terrain can result; this karst topography, as geologists call it, is best typified in Maryland by the Antietam area.

Soils derived from these limestone strata have high concentrations of calcium carbonate, leached from the rock by rainwater. Calcium carbonate acts as a buffer and maintains the soil pH in the neutral to slightly alkaline range. Such soils allow plants to take up nutrients more easily than many other soil types; thus such land is especially rich and valuable as farmland.

South of the observation tower, the road passes through an area that saw little fighting, separating the northern and southern phases of the battlefield. Cross Route 34, the Boonsboro Pike, at mile 3.8 and continue south for 0.6 mile to a T intersection. Turn left and take the road downhill for 0.4 mile to Burnside Bridge, the most famous landmark on the battle-field. Here 400 Georgia riflemen held off thousands of Union troops for hours, preventing these forces from cutting off Lee's line of retreat across the Potomac. This is a pleasant area for a picnic, and a foot trail leads downstream along Antietam Creek.

Return uphill on the same road, cutting across the top of the T intersection, now called Branch Avenue. This area was the site of the final fighting of the battle of Antietam, occurring late in the day. Having finally crossed Burnside Bridge and routed the Georgians, Union troops were ready to fall on Lee's flank and cut off his escape. The Confederate Army was saved by the timely arrival of A. P. Hill's division, which had just completed a forced march of 17 miles from Harpers Ferry.

At mile 6.3 of this bike tour, turn right onto Harpers Ferry Road, a public road with no shoulders. However, the speed limit here is still only 25 mph, and traffic is not heavy. As you enter Sharpsburg, turn right on Main Street, Route 34, being careful of traffic. After one block, turn left on Route 65, South Church Street, also known as the Hagerstown Pike. As this is the main intersection in town, it might be prudent to walk bikes across it. Route 65 is less heavily traveled and has good shoulders; it will return you to the visitor center at mile 8.3. Should you desire not to ride on public roads, it would be possible to retrace your route from Burnside Bridge, thus ensuring that all travel is within the national battlefield.

Much of the Antietam battlefield is prime habitat for blue-birds. These beautiful but shy birds prefer open, agricultural land bordered by hedgerows with tree cavities for nesting. Since bluebirds will also use artificial nesting boxes, the Park Service has placed a large number of them on fenceposts around the battlefield. Look for a flash of blue and an undulating flight pattern as you ride.

DIRECTIONS

From Washington or Baltimore, take I-70 west. Exit south onto Route 65 and proceed about nine miles. The visitor center is just off the main road and is well marked by signs.

OTHER OUTDOOR RECREATIONAL OPPORTUNITIES NEARBY

The National Park Service maintains a walking trail through the Antietam battlefield that is distinct from the paved roads. Ask for a map at the visitor center. In addition, the C & O Canal towpath is only a few miles away, and it is very beautiful and peaceful in this area. A very nice canoe trip on the Potomac River ends near Sharpsburg and is described in the canoeing section of this book, beginning on page 466. Antietam Creek is a pleasant, easy canoe trip as well, when it has sufficient water (typically in winter and spring, and within 48 hours of a hard rain in summer and fall).

Bluebirds

Few birds in the eastern United States are more beloved than bluebirds. Fabled in song and folklore, they are a companionable species that adapts fairly well to human activity. Shy and unaggressive, bluebirds appeal to both the eye and the ear. In the last twenty years or so, bluebirds have made a comeback, due in large measure to human intervention. Their conservation is a good example of how successful the science of wildlife management can be.

Bluebirds are unmistakable denizens of farms, fields, and open country. Just a bit larger than a sparrow, males are bright blue on the back with a rusty chest; females are somewhat duller

Bluebird

all over. In Maryland, many birds overwinter in small flocks, occupying areas with sufficient winter food supplies (mostly berries and other fruits). By March, the birds spread over the landscape, investigating nesting cavities in trees, fenceposts, or bluebird boxes. Eventually, a male will set up a territory around a suitable cavity and defend it against all comers while trying to attract a female. If he is successful, the female will build a cup-shaped nest of rootlets, weed stems, grass, and small twigs. After mating, four or five pale blue eggs will usually be laid and incubated by the female for about two weeks. The blind, helpless chicks develop rapidly and leave the nest after another two weeks. The male bluebird will often tend these fledglings for several more weeks as they learn to gather their own food (now mostly insects). Meanwhile, the female may lay another clutch of eggs; no sooner is the first brood independent than the process begins again for the exhausted parents! Juveniles of the first brood frequently help feed subsequent broods, an altruistic behavior that is not common among bird species. In some cases, a third clutch may occur, so that family duties extend well into August.

A little-known fact about bluebird mating habits is that monogamy is not always the rule, despite the appearance of domestic bliss in bluebird families. In one study, up to 25 percent of broods were fathered by more than one male. Either sex may be polygamous if given the opportunity.

By 1970, bluebirds were a declining species in Maryland and in most of their breeding range throughout the eastern United States; one estimate was that populations had declined by 90 percent in this century. Bluebirds were no doubt affected by the use of pesticides in the period between 1945 and 1972. However, the single most significant factor was loss of suitable nesting cavities. There were two causes. First, widespread use of metal fenceposts, more intensive management of woodlots that included removal of dead trees, and loss of hedgerows and edges from agricultural lands all decreased the number of available nest sites. Second, house sparrows and starlings, both alien species that expanded their range in this century, aggressively competed with bluebirds for the nesting cavities that were left. Starlings are larger birds, and they will almost always displace bluebirds. House sparrows are a more even match, but aggressive individuals sometimes kill bluebirds, usually pecking through the front of the skull.

Fortunately, we humans have helped by saturating the landscape with bluebird houses and increasing the public's awareness of the plight of bluebirds. The species readily accepts these boxes, and probably 90 percent of all bluebirds nest in these artifical cavities. It is probably impossible to have too many bluebirds, however, given the enjoyment they impart to us. So help out by setting out bluebird houses in areas of suitable habitat. ⬚

Chincoteague National Wildlife Refuge

Section: Refuge tour

County: Accomack, Virginia

Distance: 8.1 miles

Type: Off-road bike path, road shoulders

Surface: Asphalt, sandy shoulders

Difficulty: Flat

Hazards: Traffic, biting insects

Highlights: Birds, salt marsh, brackish pools, ocean beach

More Information: Chincoteague National Wildlife Refuge, (804) 336-6122. Assateague Island National Seashore (for information about beach recreation and naturalist programs), (804) 336-6577

CHINCOTEAGUE National Wlidlife Refuge occupies the southern portion of Assateague Island, along the Atlantic coast just south of the Maryland-Virginia border. Established in 1943, the refuge is a wintering ground for many species of waterfowl and a stopover site for a host of long-distance migrating birds. Still other species live year-round at Chincoteague, nesting in the marshes, dunes, and forests. In addition to birds, exotic mammals like the Sika deer, Delmarva fox squirrel, and feral horse call Chincoteague home. Indeed, the ponies of Chincoteague are probably the

Chincoteague National Wildlife Refuge

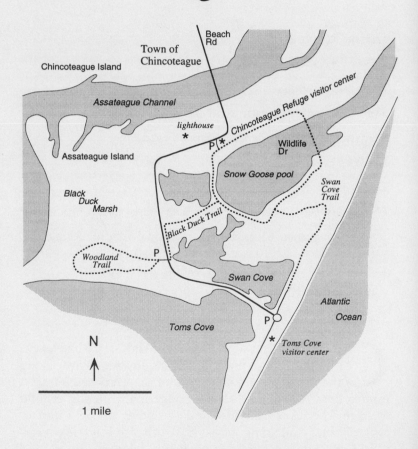

Beach Rd

Town of Chincoteague

Chincoteague Island

Assateague Channel

lighthouse
*

Chincoteague Refuge visitor center

P *

Wildlife Dr

Snow Goose pool

Assateague Island

Swan Cove Trail

Black Duck Marsh

Black Duck Trail

Woodland Trail

P

P

Swan Cove

Atlantic Ocean

Toms Cove

P

* Toms Cove visitor center

N

↑

1 mile

best-known residents, made famous by both the children's book *Misty of Chincoteague* and the annual roundup and sale, which make the evening news reports each summer.

Chincoteague National Wildlife Refuge is not in Maryland. However, it is included in this book (along with the Mount Vernon Trail and Gettysburg National Military Park) because opportunities for cycling on hard-surfaced bike paths are relatively uncommon. Chincoteague is just a few miles from the Maryland border, and it is easily accessible from the Maryland oceanfront resorts.

Although every season at Chincoteague holds its own special charms, autumn is probably the best. Gone are the hordes of mosquitoes, green-headed flies, and other assorted life forms consisting mostly of wings and jaws and possessed of a predilection for human blood. Gone, too, are the hordes of tourists who each summer clog the only road in their single-minded migration to the ocean beach. Waterfowl have arrived, and the still-warm ocean moderates the climate considerably. Opportunities for bird- and wildlife-watching are superb. There are about eight miles of paved roads for cycling and virtually unlimited hiking on the beach. The trip described here is all on hard-surfaced roads. Because some sections of road are open to vehicular traffic, the entire tour is not suitable for small children on bicycles or for strollers or wheelchairs. However, those portions where cars are prohibited are indicated, and they constitute a sizable part of the route.

TRIP DESCRIPTION

Begin your trip at the Chincoteague Refuge visitor center just a few hundred yards from the contact station at the refuge entrance, where an entrance fee is charged (but is good for seven days). There is parking for about 70 cars here, along with wheelchair-accessible bathrooms, drinking water, telephones, trash receptacles, and bike racks. The visitor center itself is staffed by knowledgeable individuals who can provide information on which species of birds currently reside on the refuge. Books are for sale, and programs are offered in the adjoining auditorium.

At the opposite end of the parking lot, the entrance to Wildlife Drive is guarded by a gate. Vehicles are allowed on this 3.3-mile loop only after 3 P.M., but even then it is rarely crowded and never dangerous. The road begins in a loblolly pine forest where wax myrtle, an evergreen shrub, forms a dense understory. Take a moment to crush the leathery, dark green leaves; they exude a pleasant, spicy fragrance. If the scent is familiar, it's because wax myrtle is a close relative of bayberry. In fact, the two species hybridize, making unambiguous identification difficult.

Follow the one-way sign to the right as the road emerges from the trees. This area is a good place to see Sika deer grazing on shrubs and herbaceous plants. These small mammals are actually more closely related to elk; they were introduced to Chincoteague in the mid 1920s. They are generally quite tame, and you can approach close enough to get good photographs. As with all animals, keep the "wild" in wildlife by not feeding them.

Wildlife Drive encircles Snow Goose Pool on your left. In summer, the pool is drained and plants grow abundantly in the wet soil. By early fall, the only open water is in the deeper canal adjacent to the roadway. The pool is progressively flooded as winter comes on, the now-submerged plants and their seeds becoming a food source for dabbling ducks, swans, and geese.

Vistas across the refuge are at their widest here on Wildlife Drive. Birds are everywhere, in all seasons. The most common year-round residents include mute swans, mallards, gadwalls, great blue herons, a few Canada geese, and an assortment of gulls. White-tailed deer frequently graze the vegetation, especially near dawn and dusk.

Within a third of a mile, the Black Duck Trail, also paved, branches to the right. With small trees, shrubs, and much vegetational diversity on both sides, this intimate half-mile path is a good place to see swallows, kingfishers, woodpeckers, nuthatches, and wood ducks. The latter, North America's most colorful duck, is a cavity nester. Because hollows in trees are rare and in great demand by a number of species, refuge staff have helped out by placing nesting boxes atop short poles in flooded swamps for the wood duck. Most have a conical piece of sheet metal on the pole to discourage predators like fox and raccoon. Several of these nesting boxes are visible from the trail, but of course they are not occupied in the fall.

The bike path now converges with the main park road but runs parallel and separate for a quarter mile or so. On your left is a narrow, permanently flooded canal that is a favorite fishing and loafing site for herons and egrets. Indeed, it is almost inconceivable that you would not see a great blue heron here in fall, winter, and spring. These tall, awkward-looking birds stand up to four feet tall; have long, thin legs and a compact, slate-blue body; and sport a long neck whose white underside is lined with vertical rows of dark feather tracts. Great blue herons eat minnows and other small fish, insects and other invertebrates, frogs, snakes, and virtually anything else that swims past. There is even a documented report of a great blue swallowing a muskrat, a feat of gluttony almost beyond the realm of anatomical possibility! Typically, great blues stand quietly in the shallows and wait for fish to come to them, but occasionally one will stalk with slow-motion, stop-and-go strides reminiscent of a cross-country skier. A heron in flight resembles the popular impression of a pterodactyl. The long neck is tucked into an S-shaped curve, and the long legs dangle awkwardly behind. If startled, the bird may give out a loud, croaking call upon taking flight.

Most visitors are content to view great blue herons and other birds of Chincoteague for a few minutes and then move on, but investing a bit more time is often rewarding, revealing details of feeding behavior, and even interactions with other birds. For example, most species of herons, egrets, and bitterns exhibit the habit of "sky pointing" in an attempt to camouflage themselves. The neck is extended fully and the beak points skyward as the head tilts back. The vertical lines on a great blue's neck disrupt the outline of the bird and cause him to blend with the upright stalks of many kinds of marsh vegetation. This characteristic behavior is also exhibited during territorial squabbles between birds. However, its purpose then is probably to impress other birds with as large a silhouette as possible.

The bike path ends after paralleling the road for about a quarter mile. Cross the main road with care onto the Woodland Trail. This 1.6-mile paved loop is closed to vehicles and passes through a loblolly pine forest. The winding path is a delight to ride on, the pungent scent of pine accompanying you the whole way. Low spots in this woods are tangles of greenbrier, but the drier, slightly higher places have little vegetation in the understory. Look here for the Delmarva fox squirrel, an endangered subspecies characterized by large size (Delmarvas are almost twice as big as the familiar gray squirrels), light gray fur, and erect ears. When startled, Delmarvas run across the forest floor rather than up the nearest tree, one reason why they favor these open woods. The thirty or so numbered boxes nailed to trees along this route are to encourage nesting by these squirrels. The Delmarva fox squirrel is not native to Chincoteague, but was introduced as part of the recovery plan for this endangered species. The squirrels have flourished in this protected, suitable habitat, and the surplus population is transplanted to other sites on the Delmarva peninsula. As a result of this work, the populations of Delmarva fox squirrels are no longer as endangered as they were 30 years ago.

The Woodland Trail is a loop, returning to the parking lot. As you leave the Woodland Trail, turn right on the main park road, pedaling with care along the shoulder of this busy avenue. For the next mile, you will share the road with motor vehicles, some of whose drivers may be so intent on looking for wildlife that they fail to notice bicyclists. Ride defensively, wear a helmet, and use the dirt pullouts when possible. Fortunately, most cars move slowly, so that it is possible for you to move as fast (or faster) than traffic. Nevertheless, this is no place for children on bicycles. If you have kids in your group, you can walk the bikes on the road shoulder, facing traffic. This berm is quite wide, with space for roadside parking and for birders to set up spotting scopes, so there is plenty of room for walking your bikes beachward. An alternative route that avoids all roads with vehicular traffic is outlined later in this chapter.

Birdwatchers will want to risk the traffic and continue east on the main park road, as the stretch ahead offers some of the best birding in America. Within a quarter mile, dry land narrows into a causeway leading east toward the beach. On the left is a large, shallow, fresh to slightly brackish impoundment, Swan Cove. On the right is the much larger Toms Cove, connected to the ocean and thus tidal and salty.

Swan Cove typically has the highest concentration and greatest diversity of birds of any place on the refuge. As its name implies, swans are commonly found here. These large, graceful white birds are conspicuous in all seasons, the introduced mute swan nesting at Chincoteague. Our native swan, the tundra swan, overwinters here and may be seen in cold weather. Smaller white birds are snow geese, which rise and land in clouds. This species has a "blue" phase, during which the birds exhibit a muddy, bluish coloration, but birds of both colors belong to the same species. You are likely to see Canada geese here, too, flying in their familiar chevron formation. Occasionally, a smaller goose with similar coloration will be spotted: brant. Together, these four species comprise all the large waterfowl likely to be seen in the eastern United States.

A variety of ducks populate Swan Cove. Some species are more tolerant of the crowds of humans lining the causeway than others. Among those easily spotted and identified with binoculars will be mallards, black ducks, pintails, Northern shovelers, scaup, and ruddy ducks.

Because they are large and conspicuously colorful, ducks are perhaps the easiest of birds to identify. In contrast, shorebirds pose some of the thorniest problems in bird identification for newcomers to the hobby. Even so, their quick-stepping gait and precision flight maneuvers make them fun to watch. Look for them on the exposed mudflats. Swan Cove also harbors several species of gulls and terns.

On the Toms Cove side of the causeway, wave action and exposure to the prevailing southerly breezes reduce the numbers of birds. It is, however, worthwhile to check the choppy waters for loons or cormorants. They have longer necks than ducks; longer, saw-toothed bills; and bodies that ride lower in the water, giving them a characteristic silhouette. A cormorant that catches a fish may put on quite a show. Swimming underwater, the fish is speared by the bird's bill and brought to the surface. The cormorant must then remove the fish from its bill without losing it and orient it so that the fish's head faces down the bird's gullet. This process may take several minutes, much maneuvering, and occasional fumbles.

The main park road to the beach reaches its most easterly point at a traffic circle. To the right is the Toms Cove visitor center, which has a fine saltwater aquarium, books for sale, information, displays, telephones, drinking water, and bike racks. Wheelchair-accessible bathrooms and a bathhouse are nearby. Ranger-led beach walks originate from the visitor center and are the best way to learn about the natural history of this beautiful area. The road continues parallel to the beach for a short distance south before ending at a point beyond which the refuge can no longer fund the continual rebuilding that storm washovers cause.

At the northern end of the visitor center parking lot, the Swan Cove trail begins. This 1.2-mile paved trail connects with the Wildlife Loop. The first part of the trail runs parallel to but behind the primary dune, passing in and out of the shrub zone. Several pools of fresh water punctuate the sand near the trail, creating islands of wetland vegetation among the dunes. These freshwater ponds are very important to the animals living on Chincoteague, enabling them to exist in this dry, harsh environment, and they act as a magnet for wildlife. Evidence of this role litters the asphalt, alternatively and colloquially known as the Pony Poop Trail. After about 0.7 mile, the trail turns landward, cutting through a ghostly forest of dead upright snags. Most of the trees here were killed by the intrusion of salt water during a series of storms in 1992. Under the relentless pounding of ocean waves, the primary dunes eroded away and the sea overwashed the low-lying swamp to landward. The dunes have since been bulldozed back into place and stabilized with plantings of dune grass, but the damage to the vegetation of this swamp is permanent. The Swan Cove Trail soon joins the Wildlife Loop; turn right.

As you pedal down this cool, shady, pine-scented road, be sure to stop at the trail to Snow Goose Overlook. An elevated wooden deck gives fine views over the marsh, which in fall and winter will harbor thousands of waterfowl engaged in feeding, preening, and loafing.

Continuing north, Wildlife Drive emerges from the maritime forest and turns westward. The road occupies a berm bisecting the marsh, and more opportunities for observing geese and ducks exist here. Finally, the road turns left at the edge of the forest, completing its encirclement of Snow Goose Pool. At this junction, a gated dirt road leads north for about seven miles through the dunes and washover flats of the little-visited north end of the refuge. This road is open to vehicles (but not bikes) during Thanksgiving week only, and it is well worth the visit.

As Wildlife Drive returns toward the visitor center, stop at a foot trail leading out to another elevated deck overlooking Snow Goose Pool. At the overlook, the trail bears right (south) on a sandy berm winding through several diverse habitats. There are small pools here where waterfowl shelter on windy days; there are also trees and shrubs in which small birds and mammals can occasionally be seen. The foot trail soon leads back to the paved road, where you can remount your bike. Within 200 yards, Wildlife Drive returns you to the visitor center.

HELPFUL HINTS ON BIKING AT CHINCOTEAGUE

It is possible to reach the beach from the Chincoteague Refuge visitor center without biking on roads traveled by cars. To do so, merely take Wildlife Drive to Swan Cove Trail to the Toms Cove visitor center.

In the event that the small parking lot at the Chincoteague Refuge visitor center is full, as it often is by 11 A.M. in autumn, drive to the Toms Cove visitor center, where there is always plenty of parking (except in summer beach season). You can begin your lap of Chincoteague Refuge from here as well.

Bicycles are available for rent at several places along Maddox Boulevard in the town of Chincoteague. However, these bikes tend to be old and worn out, and the chances of finding one that is sized properly are slim. In addition, demand is greater than availability, so plan to rent early in the day or you may be shut out. Bring your own bicycle from home if you can. Cycling from town onto the refuge is possible but risky; road shoulders are minimal. The only reassurance is that many people do it, so that motorists are usually on the lookout and traffic is typically slow moving.

DIRECTIONS

From Baltimore or Washington, take Route 50 across the Bay Bridge onto the Eastern Shore. In Salisbury, take Route 13 south. After entering Virginia, turn left on Route 175. Pass Wallops Island Flight Center (whose museum makes a fine rainy-day destination) and drive over the causeway to the town of Chincoteague. As the road crosses a drawbridge and dead ends at a stoplight in town, turn left onto Main Street. After several blocks, turn right onto Maddox Boulevard. After passing the shop and motel district, the road crosses another bridge onto Assateague Island proper and the Chincoteague National Wildlife Refuge. The contact station is just ahead. The Chincoteague Refuge visitor center is a further quarter mile ahead on your left.

OTHER OUTDOOR RECREATIONAL OPPORTUNITIES NEARBY

The bike route described here may be covered on foot as well; the slower pace may reveal more intimate or concealed details of life on the refuge. Other paths are open only to hikers. From the Toms Cove visitor center, 10 miles of unspoiled beach extend northward to the Maryland line. Oversand vehicles are not allowed here, so this area provides a true wilderness experience. The beach also extends to the south, but oversand vehicles are allowed by permit. The southern tip of Assateague Island, Toms Cove Hook, is closed to all visitation between March 15 and August 31 in order to protect the sensitive nesting sites of shorebirds.

The Lighthouse Trail, only a quarter mile in length, begins at a parking lot along the main park road a short distance from the contact station. It leads to the Chincoteague Lighthouse, located on the highest ridge on the island. On the walk back to your car, note the exceptionally old and large loblolly pines growing in the shelter of the ridge. In summer, pine warblers nest here, and in the evening the plaintive call of chuck-will's-widow echoes through the forest.

Piping Plovers

A casual visitor to Chincoteague might find it disappointing that a large and most attractive section of beach, the Toms Cove Hook, is closed to visitation between mid-March and Labor Day. However, Chincoteague is a National Wildlife Refuge, and here the welfare of animals comes before the recreational enjoyment of people. Toms Cove Hook is closed primarily because it is the nesting area of piping plovers, migratory shorebirds that are on the federal endangered species list. Indeed, the Atlantic coast population consists of only 742 breeding pairs (as of 1991), and the species itself numbers less than 4,500 individuals. Although considerable effort has been exerted to monitor and increase the size of populations of piping plovers, the species has so far responded only minimally to these conservation efforts.

Piping plovers are small, rather nondescript shorebirds that resemble a number of sandpiper species referred to by frustrated beginning birders as "peeps." Piping plovers are very pale in color, with feathers similar in color to dry beach sand. They have yellow-orange legs, a yellow bill with a black tip, a white rump, and a black partial collar. Piping plovers migrate, overwintering most typically in the southern United States.

Piping plover

The nesting habits of piping plovers have been the single most significant factor contributing to their decline. They nest on the open beach, typically on sand or washover gravel with shells, pebbbles, wrack, or beachgrass nearby. Three to five eggs are laid in late April, May, or June and are incubated for 27 days. The young are precocial, running about actively soon after hatching. Fledging takes about 25 days. At Chincoteague, about 40 pairs nest at three sites: Toms Cove Hook, the Wild Beach several miles north of the swimming beach, and the Wash Flats behind the primary dune inland from the Wild Beach. To the north, on Assateague Island in Maryland, more piping plovers nest near the northerly tip of the island within sight of Ocean City.

As we have developed our beaches for recreation, the extent of nesting habitat suitable for piping plovers has declined. Today, these birds nest almost exclusively on protected beaches where visitation by humans is minimal. Among the threats to breeding success are off-road vehicles (ORVs). These can take a heavy toll on nestlings, who wander widely and spend much time at the water's edge feeding. At Chincoteague, ORV use is prohibited at all the known nesting sites, but even official vehicles used in research may have an impact. Severe weather and predation by foxes, raccoons, crows, and even ghost crabs are the major causes of egg and nestling loss at Chincoteague. In an effort to reduce predation, scientists have placed exclosures (fences of mesh wire with a ceiling of monofilament fishing line) over many of the nests at Chincoteague. Although such structures keep out foxes and raccoons, they also attract the attention of these animals; in the time it takes for a predator to explore the boundaries of the exclosure and decide that he can't get in, adult plovers will sometimes abandon the nest. Furthermore, exclosures reduce predation on eggs, but not on hatchlings, which quickly leave the nest area and disperse widely outside the fence. In an effort to reduce predation, foxes and raccoons are routinely trapped and then removed or killed. However, it has proven impossible to trap all the predators on the island, and they still affect piping plover populations.

The outlook for piping plovers at Chincoteague and along the Atlantic coast is guardedly optimistic. Despite the expenditure of much time and money, recovery of the population has been very slow. In large measure, this outcome has been due to the low natural rate of reproduction and certain aspects of the behavior of these unusual birds, factors that are not easy for wildlife managers to manipulate. Nevertheless, the downward trend has been halted, and it seems likely that the size of populations of piping plovers will continue to increase slowly for the foreseeable future. ⚲

The Mount Vernon Trail

Section: Section 1: Theodore Roosevelt Island to
Alexandria
Section 2: Belle Haven Park to Mount Vernon

County: Section 1: Arlington County, Virginia, and the
City of Alexandria
Section 2: Fairfax County, Virgina

Distance: Section 1: 7.4 miles
Section 2: 7.7 miles

Type: Off-road bike path

Surface: Asphalt

Difficulty: Flat to gently rolling with one hill

Hazards: Sharp turns, road crossings

Highlights: Historic mansion and grounds, river views, freshwater marsh, airport views

More Information: George Washington Memorial Parkway, (703) 285-2598. Mount Vernon, (703) 780-2000

GEORGE WASHINGTON had an eye for land. As a surveyor, he traveled widely in the colonies, accumulating properties both before and after the Revolution. As commander-in-chief, he chose his battlefields wisely. And he sited his home, Mount Vernon, on a beautiful bluff overlooking the Potomac River.

Today, Mount Vernon is a popular tourist destination for visitors to the nation's capital. It is only eight miles from the Capital Beltway, and its pastoral setting, once so rural, has

The Mount Vernon Trail: southern section

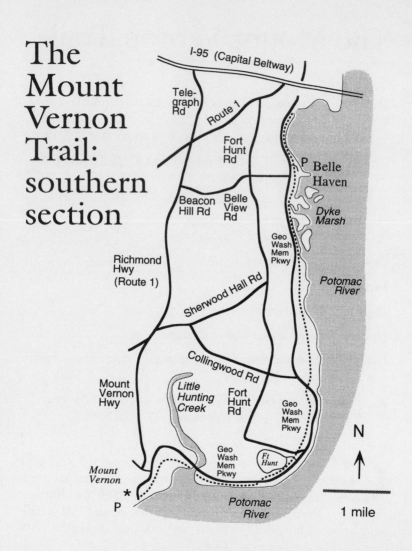

I-95 (Capital Beltway)

Telegraph Rd

Route 1

Fort Hunt Rd

P Belle Haven

Beacon Hill Rd

Belle View Rd

Dyke Marsh

Geo Wash Mem Pkwy

Richmond Hwy (Route 1)

Potomac River

Sherwood Hall Rd

Collingwood Rd

Mount Vernon Hwy

Little Hunting Creek

Fort Hunt Rd

Geo Wash Mem Pkwy

Geo Wash Mem Pkwy

Ft Hunt

Mount Vernon

P *

Potomac River

N

1 mile

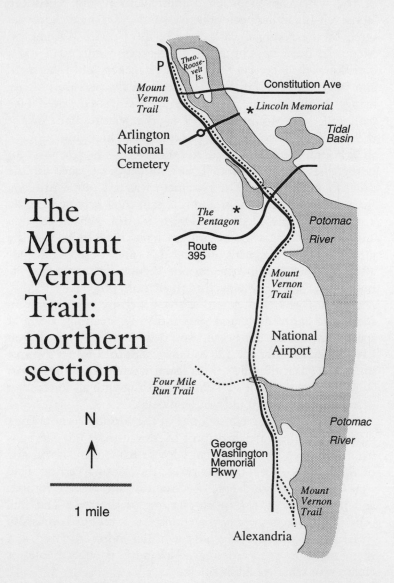

P

Theo. Roose-velt Is.

Constitution Ave

Mount Vernon Trail

* Lincoln Memorial

Arlington National Cemetery

Tidal Basin

The Mount Vernon Trail: northern section

The Pentagon

*

Potomac River

Route 395

Mount Vernon Trail

National Airport

Four Mile Run Trail

N

↑

Potomac River

George Washington Memorial Pkwy

1 mile

Mount Vernon Trail

Alexandria

been overcome by creeping development. Fortunately, much of the waterfront between Mount Vernon and Theodore Roosevelt Island has been preserved and maintained. Administered by the National Park Service, the George Washington Memorial Parkway is both a limited-access scenic road and a corridor park. Here tall trees shade picnickers and fishermen, and jaded suburbanites seek respite from the pressures of city living. Paralleling the parkway is a heavily used paved bike path, called the Mount Vernon Trail, that features fine views of the river and grassy, shady slopes that invite lounging.

Although the path is devoted exclusively to bicycle and foot traffic, the Mount Vernon Trail is not a great place for the timid or novice rider. The pavement was laid out with many sharp turns, some on hills, and it is flanked closely by trees, so a premium is placed on good bike control. Where the trail crosses wetlands, wooden bridges have been built, but the junction between asphalt and wood is often bumpy and may affect steering. Finally, the Mount Vernon Trail seems to attract more hard-core bicyclists than most other paved trails. Attired in flashy clothes and riding expensive bikes, some of them ride aggressively and pass suddenly, steaming along at speeds faster than the posted speed limit of 15 mph. If you have children under age 12, you may want to consider some of the more "user-friendly" trails listed elsewhere in this book. But for adult riders, it's a beautiful setting with an interesting destination and so should not be missed.

There are two discrete sections of the Mount Vernon Trail, separated by the waterfront port of Alexandria. One part runs from Theodore Roosevelt Island downstream to the north side of Alexandria. A second section of the Mount Vernon Trail runs between the south side of Alexandria and Mount Vernon, and it is probably the more pleasant of the two. The trail officially connects these two sections, but it requires cyclists to share the narrow streets of old town Alexandria with cars, and there are many road crossings. Alexandria is not suitable for children or tentative adult riders.

This trail is technically in Virginia rather than Maryland. But Maryland owns all of the Potomac River, right up to the

Virginia shoreline, so the Mount Vernon Trail is always within a stone's throw of the Free State. With off-road bike trails such an uncommon and valuable resource, that's close enough to Maryland!

TRIP DESCRIPTION

Theodore Roosevelt Island to Alexandria

Begin your ride on the upper Mount Vernon Trail from the parking lot at Theodore Roosevelt Island. There are no bathrooms here, but there is one on the island footpath. A walk over the island's quiet trails is a very worthwhile diversion either before or after your ride. No bikes are allowed on the island's trails.

The hard-surfaced Mount Vernon Trail parallels the lesser arm of the Potomac, known as Little River. It immediately leads onto a boardwalk that spans some small wetlands featuring cattails and other herbaceous vegetation. Swamp rose mallow, with showy white petals and a crimson throat, brightens the shoreline in midsummer. The slower current and shallow water of Little River make it a popular loafing place for waterfowl in late autumn. Mudflats are likely to contain snowy egrets in summer and a few migratory shorebirds in spring and fall.

The trail now continues south, flanked by a busy maze of roads on one side and the Potomac on the other. Well-tended lawns with strategically placed shade trees border the trail. At mile 1.8, within sight of the Pentagon and Arlington National Cemetery, the Navy and Marine Memorial pays tribute to all those Americans who have been lost at sea. This striking monument depicts several waterbirds flying in the lee of a foaming ocean wave and evokes the loneliness of the sea even in the midst of this busy metropolis.

At mile 2.9, the trail bears right at the edge of National Airport. This is an extraordinary aircraft viewing area, and it is the highlight of this section of the Mount Vernon Trail. Separated from it by only a small body of water, cyclists can look right down the throat of the main runway at National. Planes that are landing glide just overhead with a deafening roar; there is always a lineup for takeoff. There may be no better public place to view the power and glory of flight.

Over the next mile, the trail runs on the landward side of National Airport. There are several road crossings, where care should be taken by both adults and children. The most prominent feature of the trail here is the palisade of office buildings that form Pentagon City and Crystal City.

At mile 4.8, the trail forks. Bear right over a bridge to stay on the Mount Vernon Trail; the other trail is the Four Mile Run Trail, which leads westward into Virginia. More lawns and civilized countryside follow. The trail forks again at mile 6.1; the left fork is more interesting, leading along the Potomac for almost another mile. Finally, the trail ends at mile 7.4, continuing on Alexandria city streets as a designated but on-road bike route. Old town Alexandria is a charming historical waterfront, and it can easily be explored on foot after locking up your bike.

Belle Haven Park to Mount Vernon

This trip begins at Belle Haven Park, less than a mile downriver from the Woodrow Wilson Bridge on I-95. There is plenty of parking here, and water, bathrooms, trash cans, telephones, and picnic tables are also available. The marina nearby has snacks, sodas, and ice.

Before you begin on the Mount Vernon Trail proper, pedal or walk out to Dyke Marsh, a very popular spot among D.C.-area birders. Almost 300 species of birds have been seen here, with several distinct habitats clustered into a small area. A causeway, part of an old dike system supplemented with rubble fill in the 1960s, leads out into the river. The first half mile, heavily forested, is almost entirely covered with wild grape, its vines tangling over everything that doesn't move. The extreme end of the causeway, subjected to harsher environmental conditions, has only small specimens of fast-growing trees like

Chestnut oak

willow and sycamore and much herbaceous vegetation, including some pretty late-summer wildflowers. Look for spring and fall migrants, including Tennessee, northern parula, magnolia, blackpoll, and black-and-white warblers, among the trees. In late fall, a wide selection of ducks raft up on the sheltered waters, including ruddy ducks, buffleheads, both greater and lesser scaup, and pintails.

Returning to the Belle Haven parking lot, mount up and ride south. The asphalt is about eight feet wide, enough for one lane of traffic in each direction. Stay near the right-hand side so that cyclists passing you will have enough room. Between mile 0.6 and mile 0.8, the path is a wooden bridge across Dyke Marsh; although the marsh vegetation consists mostly of cattails, there are some good stands of wild rice that should be ripe in August if the birds don't beat you to it.

These first two miles of the lower Mount Vernon Trail are relatively flat, straight, and open, running alongside the parkway through mostly manicured lawns and forest. Crossing over the parkway, the second two miles of trail traverse a buffer between the road and a residential neighborhood. There are three stop signs where the trail crosses public roads; use care in crossing, especially with small children. At Fort Hunt, the trail joins a lightly traveled park road for a few yards, where caution is in order as you cycle through a short tunnel. Picnic tables, bathrooms, water, trash cans, telephones, parking, and recreational fields are available at Fort Hunt.

The next two miles or so are the best of the Mount Vernon Trail. The path runs close to the Potomac, now skirting the water, now bending away into the trees. Wooden bridges are numerous, fording small wetlands and streams. The trail becomes increasingly winding and is great fun where clean sight lines reveal no oncoming traffic. Finally, the trail leaves the river after crossing Little Hunting Creek and heads steadily uphill through a dry forest dominated by chestnut oak. The parking lots of Mount Vernon appear at the top of the hill after 7.7 miles of pedaling.

For thirsty or hungry cyclists, there is a snack bar at Mount Vernon as well as a gift shop. Admission to the grounds and a tour of the mansion requires a fee. Leave your bike locked at the bike racks; bicycles are not allowed on the grounds. After rest and refreshment, return via the same route. The steep downhill out of Mount Vernon is considerably more exhilarating than the uphill slog!

DIRECTIONS

Theodore Roosevelt Island, the start of the northern part of the trip, may be reached only from the northbound lane of the George Washington Memorial Parkway in Virginia. From the Capital Beltway, I-495, take the Baltimore-Washington Parkway, I-295 south. In downtown Washington, exit onto I-395. The George Washington Memorial Parkway will be the first exit after crossing the Potomac; head north.

To reach Belle Haven Park, from which the southern half of the trip commences, cross the Potomac on the Capital Beltway into Virginia over the Woodrow Wilson Bridge. Take the first exit south; it is listed variously as Route 1, the Jefferson Davis

Highway, or the Richmond Highway. Go 2.3 miles and turn left on Beacon Hill Road. A landmark for this turn is the Beacon Hill Shopping Center on one side and the colorfully named Dixie Pig restaurant on the other. Follow Beacon Hill Road, which becomes Belleview Road, for 1.7 miles. Turn left on the George Washington Memorial Parkway, go 0.2 mile, and enter Belle Haven Park.

OTHER OUTDOOR RECREATIONAL OPPORTUNITIES NEARBY

Theodore Roosevelt Island is found at the northern terminus of the Mount Vernon Trail and is a beautiful short walk in a shady setting. The Mount Vernon Trail connects directly with the Arlington Memorial Bridge and the George Mason Memorial Bridge, both of which carry bicyclists in dedicated lanes across the Potomac to Washington, D.C. It is then possible to link up with the Rock Creek Trail and the C & O Canal towpath.

The Brown-Headed Cowbird: Brood Parasite Extraordinaire

A winter's day at dusk: the setting sun's rays flare off the bottoms of clouds, setting them ablaze with color. The reflected light suffuses the landscape, lending it a warm glow that belies the season. Across the sky, a column of birds appears, on its way to a nightly roost. The birds pass overhead in a seemingly endless parade, thousands of birds for minutes on end.

These winter flocks are mixed groups of Icteridae, blackbirds and their relatives. In Maryland, they typically include starlings, redwings, grackles, and cowbirds. Of these, the brown-headed cowbird is the most interesting. As its name implies, males have a brown head, and also a black body and a short bill; the birds feed mostly on seeds in the winter.

The brown-headed cowbird is eastern North America's only obligate brood parasite: that is, females do not build nests but instead lay their eggs in the nests of other birds. Cowbird eggs develop faster than the eggs of their hosts and hatch sooner. The young are typically larger than their adopted siblings and so successfully compete for a larger share of the food brought back to the nest. In many cases, the host nestlings die. Thus the host parents expend much time and energy raising a bird of another species, reducing both their own fitness and the future size of their population.

Cowbird parasitism is a problem for songbirds in Maryland and throughout the eastern United States. More than 200 species of birds are parasitized, including many that are uncommon and whose populations have long been declining. Warblers, vireos, and flycatchers seem particularly affected; adults rarely recognize cowbird eggs as foreign. For example, one researcher found 100 percent of worm-eating warbler nests on Sugarloaf Mountain in Frederick County to be parasitized by cowbirds. Similar results have been observed for other warbler species on a variety of study sites throughout the east, prompting one biologist to note that some nesting populations are "raising nothing but cowbirds."

Why haven't warblers and other host species evolved to recognize and destroy the eggs of invaders, given the strong selective pressure to do so? Biologists note that the brown-headed cowbird is a native of the midwestern grasslands and prairies. As the eastern forest was converted into farmland, the cowbird's range expanded; it is now common everywhere between the Rockies and the Atlantic northward to the boreal forest of Canada. Warblers may not yet have had enough time to evolve a response to this recent stress on their population. However, other birds, like robins, catbirds, and blue jays, do reject cowbird eggs. One ornithologist notes that these larger birds frequently renest if disturbed; warblers are less likely to renest, because of either their smaller size or their shorter nesting season.

The last refuge of these wood warblers seems to be large tracts of unbroken forest. Cowbirds, being birds of open fields and edges, mostly parasitize nests near forest borders. Indeed, the farther one ventures into a large tract of forest, the fewer cowbirds are seen and the fewer nests are parasitized. However, these tracts must be exceptionally large to ensure a true refugium from brood parasitism; although a study deep in the interior of virgin forest in the Great Smoky Mountains found no cowbirds, they have been seen in the middle of a patch of forest almost a mile from the nearest edge. Nevertheless, many scientists feel that the single most important factor in the decline of songbirds is the fragmentation of our forests, exposing vulnerable species to the depredations of brown-headed cowbirds and other predators that frequent forest openings. Most ornithologists agree that preserving public land in the largest contiguous blocks possible holds the best chance for conserving dwindling populations of warblers and other migrant songbirds. ⚲

Gettysburg National Military Park

Section: Battlefield tour

County: Adams County, Pennsylvania

Distance: 18.3 miles, with an optional 2.5-mile loop

Type: Lightly traveled park roads

Surface: Asphalt

Difficulty: Rolling to hilly

Hazards: Traffic

Highlights: Battlefield site, rolling farmlands

More Information: Gettysburg National Military Park, (717) 334-1124

GETTYSBURG, PENNSYLVANIA: the site of the battle that marked the turning point of the Civil War; a college town; the nation's premier battlefield park; the classic example of an overdeveloped tourist trap. The National Military Park at Gettysburg is many things to many people. It is on the "must see" list of most visitors to Washington, D.C., and environs. But to those of us living less than a hundred miles away, it is a fine recreational resource. Large chunks of the 1863 battlefield belong to the National Park Service and are crisscrossed with a variety of small roads on which traffic is generally light and speed is limited to 25 mph or less. This makes the park perfect for cycling, and it has long been a favorite destination.

Gettysburg National Military Park

Carlisle Rd
(Route 34)

Harrisburg Rd
(Bus. Route 15)

Mummasburg Rd

Buford Ave

Chambersburg Pike
(Route 30)

Double-
day Ave

York Pike
(Route 30)

Reynolds Ave

Gettys   burg

Lutheran
Seminary
*

Hanover Rd
(Route 116)

Hagerstown
(Fairfield) Rd

(Route 116)

Gettysburg
National
Military
Park

National
Cemetery

*

*   Culp's Hill

Seminary Ridge

West Confederate Ave

*
visitor
center

P

*   Spangler's
Spring

Hancock Ave

Cemetery Ridge

Baltimore Pike
(Route 97)

Granite School
House Lane

Eisenhower
Farm National
Historic Site

Wheatfield Rd

Taneytown Rd
(Route 134)

N

Devil's
Den   *

*
Little
Round
Top

Emmitsburg Rd
Bus. Route 15

South
Confederate
Ave

*Big
Round
Top

1 mile

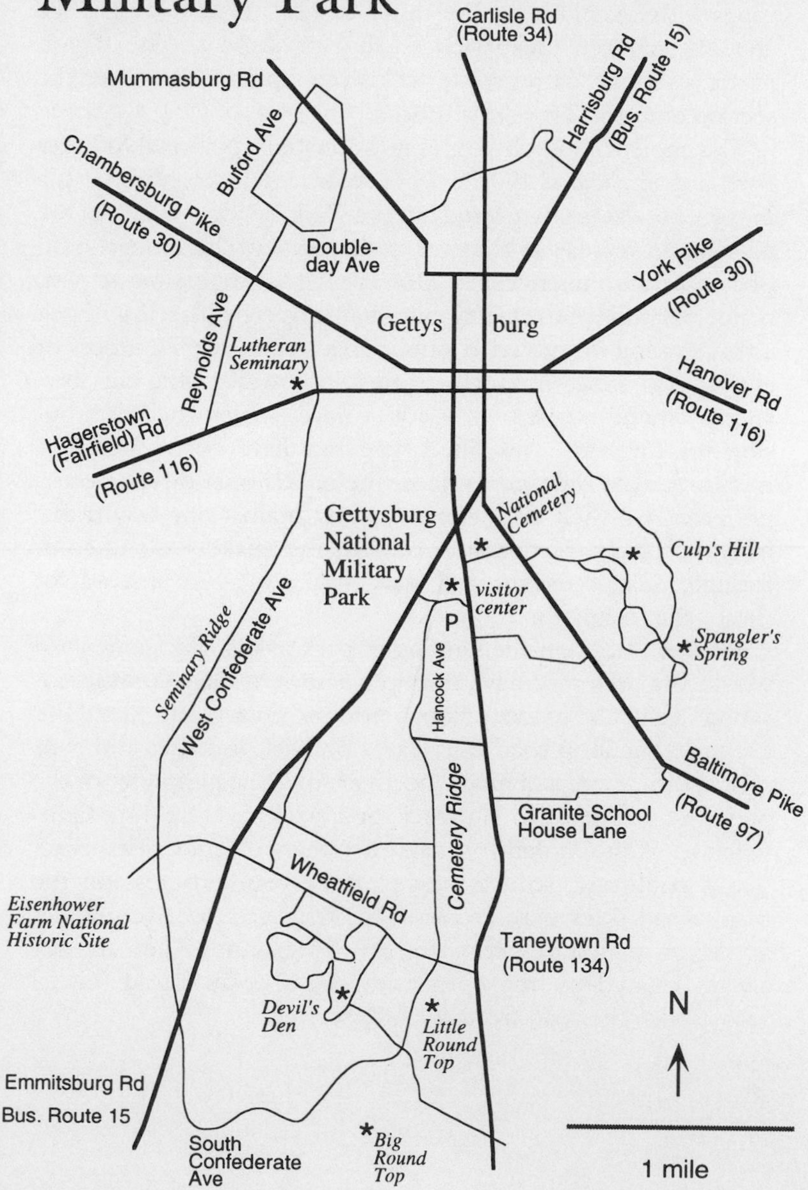

The Gettysburg battlefield is broken terrain and in a few places has rather steep hills. In two short sections (0.7 mile total) of the cycle route described, the route follows public roads with lots of traffic. For these reasons, this is not a trip for children or even inexperienced, out-of-shape adults. If you prefer a shorter, flatter route exclusively on park roads, see the section after the Trip Description.

The choice of bicycle routes in Gettysburg National Military Park is complicated by the legal requirement to observe the many one-way signs posted by the Park Service. Bicycles are considered vehicles in the eyes of the law and therefore should obey all traffic restrictions. However, it is impossible to visit major portions of the Gettysburg battlefield by bicycle without either cycling on crowded public roads that lack shoulders or cycling for short distances against one-way traffic on low-speed, limited-access park roads. I have chosen the latter option for the route described here but have been careful to minimize such mileage. Indeed, the park's own bicycle route, published on their visitor map, travels against one-way traffic in some places. If this sort of pedaling makes you uncomfortable, just dismount and walk with your bike instead for these short segments.

Finally, a note on the naming of park roads. The same road within the park may have multiple names, usually commemorating generals whose troops fought near that site. For example, the loop road that leaves the visitor center and runs south, then west, and finally north around the perimeter of the park is variously called Hancock, Sedgwick, Sykes, South Confederate, West Confederate, and Seminary Avenue. This practice is confusing, so it is best to track your progress on the map. Road signs here are built for the ages: bronze plaques sitting on pedestals a few feet off the ground. They are not always located on the corner but are usually found several yards down the road from the intersection.

TRIP DESCRIPTION

The National Park Service visitor center is found in the heart of the park on the south side of the town of Gettysburg. It is the best place to begin your trip, despite being crowded. Here you will find information, a museum, a bookstore, wheelchair-accessible bathrooms, and the Electric Map. The latter is a fascinating way to learn about the events that took place here on July 1–3, 1863, and it should not be missed even if you're just here for the bicycling. There is an admission charge for the 45-minute presentation. Located adjacent to the visitor center is the Cyclorama, an immense mural that stretches around the circumference of a circular room, giving you the impression of being in the eye of the battle. It is also worth a visit. Across the road is the Gettysburg National Cemetery, dedicated by President Abraham Lincoln in his famous Gettysburg Address, delivered here on November 19, 1863. In the other direction is a large selection of fast food joints, wax museums, junk shops, and other business establishments catering to the removal of dollars from the wallets of visiting tourists. Parking is available around the visitor center; an overflow lot is located 0.1 mile south on Route 134 (Taneytown Road).

After viewing those exhibits of interest, begin your bicycle trip from the visitor center parking lot. The route described here is just over 18 miles long; the optional Culp's Hill loop adds another 2.5 miles. It is possible to lay out shorter and longer trips using the map. However, the route described here visits most of the landmarks of significance on the battlefield and minimizes the mileage on Gettysburg city streets and high-speed public roads.

From the visitor center parking lot, pedal west toward the far side of the Cyclorama building and make an immediate left onto Hancock Avenue. This route brings you quickly to the heart of what was the Union line during the battle of Gettysburg. Just ahead is a large statue of General George Meade, the commanding general of the Union forces, seated on his horse and looking west toward the Confederate lines on Seminary Ridge. Another hundred yards brings you to the Angle and the Copse of Trees. They constitute perhaps the most famous few acres of American landscape, for it was here that the final Confederate assault of July 3, 1863, was repulsed. The Copse of Trees was one of the few landmarks visible from the Confederate lines, and the 17,000 men forming Pickett's Charge were told to aim for it. The advance reached this point and hand-to-hand fighting ensued, but the outcome was never in doubt. The rebel army had lost so many many men in reaching this point that the battle was brief and conclusive. This line of advance has been called the high water mark of the Confederacy; after it, the Army of Northern Virginia never again took the offensive. Contemplating the bravery and foolishness of these men is unavoidable as you look out over hundreds of acres of open fields.

Continue on to the Pennsylvania monument, the largest on the Gettysburg field. It honors the 34,530 Pennsylvanians who fought here in their home state. Of these men, over 5,000 were killed, wounded, or missing at Gettysburg.

Hancock Avenue continues downhill, still following the Union lines. Military historians refer to this area as Cemetery Ridge, but the prominence in the landscape is hard to discern.

Pass United States Avenue and turn right on Wheatfield Road at mile 1.8. Coast downhill, cross Plum Run, and pass an unnamed road banned to bicycles because of cattle guards in the road surface. Just ahead, turn left onto Ayres Avenue. This road encircles the Wheatfield, the site of intense and inconclusive fighting on July 2. This bloody struggle was precipitated by an incompetent Union politician-general, Daniel Sickles, who placed his troops more than a mile to the front of the Union lines for no obvious reason except sheer pugnacity and a thirst for glory. This road dead-ends back at Wheatfield Road; turn left. As the road proceeds west toward the Confederate lines, it passes through the Peach Orchard, also a part of this phase of the battle. An orchard has been planted here recently in an effort to recreate the landscape existing at the time of the battle. Carefully cross Business Route 15, the Emmitsburg Road, and pedal to West Confederate Avenue. Turn right (north).

West Confederate Avenue runs along the crest of Seminary Ridge and marks the Confederate line on July 2 and 3. The ridge is shaded by trees for its entire length and bordered by stone walls where cannon look toward the Union lines a mile away; its strategic significance is obvious even to the untrained eye. The Virgina monument, topped by a statue of the mounted General Robert E. Lee, is very striking and is found at mile 4.7. Another 0.4 mile brings you to the North Carolina monument. Perhaps the most expressive on the field, this monument is frequently photographed. West Confederate Avenue runs another 1.2 miles to Route 116, the Hagerstown (Fairfield) Road.

At this point, the road enters the battlefield of the first day's conflict at Gettysburg. Northwest of the town of Gettysburg, this field was the scene of much hard, back-and-forth fighting on July 1, 1863.

Turn left on Route 116 and follow it for 0.5 mile. Although a busy road, there is a good paved shoulder. Turn right onto Reynolds Avenue, cross the railroad cut, and proceed to the Eternal Light Peace Memorial at mile 8.1. Seventy-five years after the battle, 1,800 surviving Civil War veterans dedicated this impressive monument, erected on the site of fierce fighting.

The park road crosses the Mummasburg Road at an observation tower. The view here from atop Oak Ridge is toward the town of Gettysburg, and it appears little changed despite the passage of over 130 years. On weekends, an excursion train powered by an old steam locomotive passes on the nearby railroad tracks, providing another touch of authenticity. The road continues on, forming a loop that brings you back to Reynolds Avenue and Route 30 at mile 9.3.

Turn left on route 30 and pedal 0.2 mile along a good shoulder to Seminary Avenue. The road is unmarked, but it is the first right turn, opposite the General Lee Restaurant.

Seminary Avenue runs for one long block through the Lutheran Theological Seminary. The seminary was founded in 1863, and several of the large buildings that you see were already in existence when the winds of war blew through

Gettysburg that same year. These buildings were used as ob-servation points from which commanders could see and un-derstand the terrain, troop movements, battle lines, and action. The seminary was used by Union generals on July 1, looking northwest to the developing battles along McPherson and Oak ridges. Overrun by the Confederates late in the day, it served General Lee and other southern commanders on July 2 and 3 as they observed Union lines to the south and east along Cemetery Ridge.

As you leave the seminary grounds, carefully cross Route 116 at the traffic light. The road now resumes as West Confed-erate Avenue. Retrace your outbound route along Seminary Ridge past the North Carolina and Virginia monuments to the observation tower just past Wheatfield Road.

The view from the high observation tower encompasses the Eisenhower Farm to the west and the jumbled terrain of the second day's battle to the east. Most prominent to the south-east are two conical hills, Big Round Top and Little Round Top. The latter was of major strategic importance in the battle. Cleared of vegetation in 1863, it commanded the southern half of the battlefield and anchored the Union left wing. Its loss would have necessitated a Union retreat from Gettysburg.

Follow West Confederate Avenue to the south, east, and then north as it circles the perimeter of the battlefield. The road soon runs along the edge of Big Round Top, which played no significant role in the battle. If you visit in winter-time, keep an eye out for the hundreds of black and turkey vultures that use the treed slopes as a roost. Legend has it that these vultures appeared here just after the battle in 1863 to feast on the carnage of war; a primitive form of racial memory keeps them here in hopes of another such windfall. The scien-tific explanation for their presence is that they are protected from harassment within the battlefield park.

In the spur between Big Round Top and Little Round Top, turn left on Warren Avenue. This road leads downhill to the Devil's Den, a jumble of rock outcrops facing Little Round Top and used by Confederate sharpshooters. The maze of rocks here never fails to capture the imagination of children, and it is one of the most popular spots on the battlefield. Small boys can usually be seen wedged among the rocks using imaginary guns to ambush tourists on distant Little Round Top. Bathrooms, drinking water, trash cans, and a bike rack are located here, and it is a fine place to dismount, walk around, and explore.

Return up Warren Avenue, retracing your path to the top of the hill. Turn left onto what is now called Sykes Avenue and climb steeply to Little Round Top. The view from atop this knoll is an impressive one, looking down on the Devil's Den and the Wheatfield. Amazingly, neither army realized the strategic significance of this point until midafternoon on July 2. As Confederate troops advanced up the hill, the Union 20th Maine Regiment reached the field just in time to meet them in intense, sometimes hand-to-hand combat. Finally, the rebel troops were driven off, and the position was reinforced.

Leaving Little Round Top, coast downhill to Wheatfield Road. If you're thirsty or hungry, a right turn here will bring you within 200 yards to a small drive-in featuring excellent ice cream. Otherwise, continue north on the main park road, now called Sedgwick Avenue, eventually passing the Pennsylvania monument, the Copse of Trees, and the Angle again and returning to the visitor center parking lot after 18.3 miles.

Cyclists with any energy left, or true devotees of the battle at Gettysburg, should not miss the Culp's Hill loop, a rolling 2.5-mile route on the east side of Taneytown Road. From the visitor center parking lot, pedal south on Taneytown Road (Route 134) for a hundred yards or so, turning left onto Hunt Avenue. After 0.5 mile, turn right on Route 97, the Baltimore Pike. Go 0.3 mile on a wide shoulder, and then turn left at an unnamed but obvious park road. Running for 0.6 mile through dense woods, the road emerges at Spangler's Spring. Here wounded soldiers from both sides congregated for relief from the hot July sun.

Take the left fork, Geary Avenue, to avoid a steep hill. Just beyond where Geary Avenue rejoins Slocum Avenue, the road branches again. The right fork winds very steeply to the top of Culp's Hill; those not already in cardiac arrest when they reach the top have another chance to precipitate it by climbing the observation tower. Fine views of the surrounding countryside and mountains reward the climber.

The alternative is the left fork, Williams Avenue, which is narrow, woodsy, and flat. It rejoins Slocum Avenue at the large statue of Major General Henry Slocum atop East Cemetery Hill. From here, it's a short trip back to Route 97. Pedal 0.1 mile uphill on the shoulder of this road to the National Cemetery. Ride through the cemetery back to the visitor center.

This short loop encompasses the biting end of the fishhook-shaped Union lines at Gettysburg, where heavy fighting occurred on July 2 and 3 for possession of Culp's Hill.

Traffic on the park roads described here is generally light. Keep a wary eye out for cars, however, as drivers are often distracted by scenery, monuments, and restless children. Traffic on public roads, in contrast, is usually heavy. Exercise care to stay on the shoulder, obey all traffic signs and vehicular laws, and be generally vigilant.

A SHORTER, FLATTER ALTERNATIVE ROUTE

For those not up to the 18-mile trip described here, a shorter, flatter out-and-back loop that covers many of the most interesting monuments, landscapes, and areas of military significance is feasible. From the visitor center parking lot, cycle south on Hancock Avenue past the Copse of Trees and the Pennsylvania monument. Turn right at Wheatfield Road, then left at Ayres Avenue for the loop of the Wheatfield. A side trip to the Devil's Den is possible from here; consult the map. When the Wheatfield loop joins Wheatfield Road, turn left. Make your first right on Sickles Avenue, and then right again on United States Avenue. This leads you back to Hancock Avenue, where a left turn will bring you to the visitor center. Total distance is about six miles.

HIKING TRAILS AT GETTYSBURG

The battlefield at Gettysburg has a number of cleared, marked hiking trails. The rangers at the visitor center can give you specific details on routes, distances, and difficulty. A paved, wheelchair-accessible path leaves the Cyclorama and visits the Angle and the Copse of Trees. A brochure describing this High Water Mark Walking Tour is available; it notes that not all of the trail is wheelchair accessible, but that detours are clearly marked around those sections without a paved surface.

DIRECTIONS

From the Capital Beltway, take I-270 north. In Frederick, it becomes Route 15; continue north. Just over the Pennsylvania line, bear right so as to avoid Business Route 15, which goes through the heart of Gettysburg. Exit Route 15 onto Route 97, heading northwest. Follow signs for the visitor center.

From the Baltimore Beltway, take I-795 northwest. When the interstate ends, get onto Route 140 heading toward Westminster. On the north side of town, exit to Route 97, still going northwest. Cross into Pennsylvania, pass Route 15, and follow signs to the visitor center.

OTHER OUTDOOR RECREATIONAL OPPORTUNITIES NEARBY

The hiking trails of Catoctin Mountain Park and Cunningham Falls State Park are located about a 30-minute drive from Gettysburg. They are described in the chapter entitled "Blue Ridge Duo" beginning on page 152 in this book.

Vultures

Look up to the sky almost anywhere in rural areas of Maryland and you stand a fair chance of seeing one of our most common but least-loved birds: a vulture. Soaring on unseen thermals and air currents, seemingly without effort, the vulture looks down with haughty disdain on all of our activities, sure and confident that they will yield his next meal. Vultures are scavengers and carrion feeders; they actually provide an important service in recycling dead animal material.

There are two species of vultures in Maryland: turkey vultures and black vultures. Turkey vultures (often referred to as TVs by birders) are the larger of the two, with a wingspan of up to six feet. In the sky, they are easily differentiated from other large birds by the long duration of time between wing flaps and

Turkey vulture

the set of the wings at a dihedral angle above the horizontal. TVs also seem to rock back and forth unsteadily as they soar. At closer distances, the trailing edge of the wings is seen to be lighter in color, the wingtips fingerlike, the tail narrow, and the head small and red in color. Black vultures are smaller and chunkier birds, with a maximum wingspan of less than five feet. They have a wider tail and wings, white may show at the wing tips, and they have black heads. Because of their less efficient aerodynamic shape, black vultures have to flap much more frequently between bouts of soaring.

During most of the year, vultures roost communally in dead or sparsely leaved trees, often with a southeastern exposure so as to facilitate warming in the morning's first rays of light. These roosts can be quite large; one in Talbot County numbered over 500 birds, who in addition to trees perched on rooftops, windowsills, and automobiles. In spring, breeding pairs disperse to find nesting sites, the most favored of which are in tree cavities, under cliff overhangs, and in dense scrub. Between one and three eggs are laid, and the young are tended by both parents. Although predators no doubt take a toll on nestlings, their repulsive habit of projectile vomiting deters most human disturbance.

Turkey vultures locate dead animals primarily by using their sense of smell. Research has shown that a very fresh kill is often ignored by TVs, as is very rotten meat; a certain amount of decay is necessary to release odors, whereas too much can endanger the bird by introducing heavy bacterial loads into the meal. Black vultures, on the other hand, locate food primarily by sight, often keeping visual track of turkey vultures. ☙

CANOEING

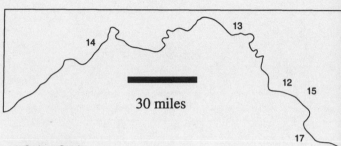

30 miles

1. Corkers Creek
2. Nassawango Creek
3. Pocomoke River
4. Janes Island
5. Watts Creek
6. Kings Creek
7. Tuckahoe Creek
8. Nanjemoy Creek
9. Mataponi Creek
10. Gunpowder Delta
11. Otter Point Creek
12. Potomac River: Dam Number 4 Cave
13. Potomac River: Fort Frederick
14. Potomac River: Paw Paw Bends
15. Monocacy River
16. Upper Gunpowder River
17. Virginia Canal
18. Middle Youghiogheny River

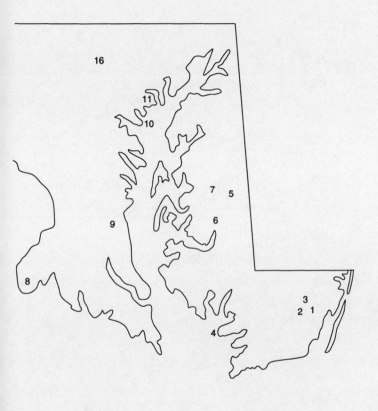

CANOEING WITH KIDS

O F   T H E   T H R E E   K I N D S   of outdoor activities covered in this book—hiking, cycling, and canoeing—
paddling a canoe is enjoyed by the smallest
constituency. Yet I get more questions by far regarding where
and how to go canoeing than about any other outdoor activity.
There is a mystique about canoeing that calls up our pioneer
heritage, a powerful cultural myth that speaks to most Americans of untamed wild land, adventure, and excitement. Indeed, like all myths, this one possesses an underlying kernel of
truth, for the expertly paddled canoe leaves no mark or sound
on the landscape and penetrates into places that not even a
hiker can reach.

The purpose of this chapter is to address those particular
aspects of canoeing that are specifically pertinent to paddling
with children. It is not a comprehensive treatment of canoeing
in general. A number of good books can supply you with more
information regarding the sport of canoeing; consult your
public library or bookstore.

BASIC SKILLS FOR SAFE CANOEING

Canoeing with children requires a significant amount of skill
and practice. Canoes do turn over, and the consequences of a
capsize, even on a lake, can be significant when children are
along. Although two adults in a canoe are sometimes willing to
accept the possibility of a capsize, they should not be when

small children are passengers. Each canoe needs a minimum of one adult in it with basic canoeing proficiency: the ability to steer the canoe in a straight line, the capacity to keep the canoe upright, and the knowledge of what to do in the event of a capsize. Before one ventures into whitewater, a number of additional, more advanced skills must be learned and practiced. Until you have these abilities, you should not take children canoeing. Unfortunately, most beginning canoeists do not have these skills; they just hope to muddle through, relying on a beneficent Providence to ensure their safety. I strongly recommend that every paddler take a good basic canoeing class, taught by the Red Cross, the American Canoe Association, or a local canoe club. At the very least, seek out instruction from an experienced and competent paddler who spends at least a dozen days each year in the canoe.

JUDGMENT

Once you have the necessary paddling skills to handle a canoe with children safely, there is one final, supremely important ability that you must have: good judgment. Judgment on the river comes from experience, but it also comes from mental preparation. Before you go on a canoe trip, consider all the possible things that might go wrong and decide in advance what you're going to do about each of them. For example, under what weather conditions will you cancel the trip? What water level is too high? What sort of rapids will you portage rather than risk paddling through, keeping in mind that the answer to this question will be different with and without children aboard? What happens if a child gets sick or injured? Among the paddlers on the trip, who will be the leader in an emergency situation? What will you do in the event of an electrical storm that arises halfway through the trip? There are no hard and fast answers to such questions, but the mere act of considering them prepares you for the situation and acts as a supplement to good judgment.

WEATHER

The canoe glides silently over crystal-clear waters, the lake reflecting the deep blue of the sky overhead. The sun is shining, the birds are singing, and all is right with the world. Some canoe trips are like this, but you can't reliably expect such benevolent weather in Maryland. Even if the weather cooperates, the water in spring and fall can be downright cold; a capsize in such water is serious business, especially with children along.

Until you have absolute certainty of your skills in a canoe, and until you've been out on a number of trips, it is best to confine your paddling season to mid-May through mid-September. During this period, the water is typically warm enough to swim in, and hypothermia is rarely a problem. As a general rule, add the water temperature and air temperature together; if the sum is less than 140, inexperienced paddlers with children along should opt for a hike or a bike ride instead.

Canoeing in the rain is tolerable, but just barely. But riding in a canoe as a passenger is absolutely miserable on a wet day. If the morning dawns rainy or with a reasonable chance of precipitation, I recommend that you stay home. Remember, you want children to enjoy canoeing as much as you do, so they should experience its pleasures before putting up with its pains.

A windy day on open water can make a canoe frustratingly difficult to paddle. When you check the weather report, listen for wind speed and direction. If the day promises significant wind, choose a sheltered canoe trip on a narrow, tree-lined river.

Finally, recent weather can affect paddling conditions. On narrow coastal plain streams, expect trees to be down across the creek after a major windstorm. Recent heavy rains can raise water levels on flowing rivers, creating fast water, rapids, strong currents, and unexpected eddy lines. If the water at a put-in is muddy and moving quickly downstream, consider aborting your trip.

SPECIALIZED CANOEING EQUIPMENT FOR CHILDREN

Personal Flotation Devices

The most important piece of equipment needed for canoeing is not the canoe or the paddle but the personal flotation device (PFD), otherwise known as the life jacket. PFDs *must* be worn at all times on the water; not only is this the law, but it is simply stupid not to do so. I know of no competent paddler who does not wear a life jacket. Children and adults both should wear PFDs in the water during swim breaks. This practice is mandatory in flowing water and recommended in flat water. Kids and nonswimmers should wear PFDs even on shore, in case they should fall in while playing at the water's edge.

PFDs for children must be comfortable or kids will object to wearing them. Avoid buying "horse collar"–style life jackets; they're awkward and uncomfortable and will be taken off at the least excuse. Look for form-fitting jackets of nylon-covered foam from a reputable, well-known manufacturer. A tag indicating Coast Guard approval should be found sewn into the lining of the PFD. In most of these quality vests, the foam flotation is in the form of broad panels. Such PFDs are fairly expensive; just remember that there's a reason they're called life preservers.

Life jackets should be adjustable so that they fit snugly. At least one adjustable nylon web (two for older, taller children) with heavy plastic snap closures should encircle the chest and waist on panel-type jackets. PFDs for children should have a crotch strap to keep the vest from riding up when the wearer is in the water. Children may object to this crotch strap, but it is an important safety feature. Most PFDs (for both adults and kids) are too large or too loosely fitting to be effective. To test the fit of a PFD, have a friend grab it by the shoulders and pull violently upward; if the PFD rides up around your ears and the front panel covers your mouth, it is not only too loose but may actually endanger you in a crisis situation. A crotch strap prevents this. Some vests have a pad behind the head that will keep an unconscious child's head out of the water. Although this is probably a useful feature, it will not return an unconscious, face-down child to the face-up position.

The foregoing advice is especially important to heed when purchasing a PFD for a child. A number of flotation aids available in toy stores and variety stores are unacceptable or even dangerous. One design from twenty years ago was effective in floating a child; unfortunately, it sometimes kept the child afloat with head down and feet in the air. Purchase your child's PFD from a canoe specialty store, and discuss the various models with a knowledgeable salesperson.

Getting a child to wear a PFD is sometimes difficult. The best tactic is to compare it to riding in an automobile: just as the car doesn't leave the driveway until seat belts are fastened, the canoe doesn't get launched until all PFDs have been put on.

Paddles

Most children who go canoeing want to paddle for at least a portion of the trip. If they try to paddle with an adult-sized paddle, they will only become frustrated with something you want them to enjoy. Most canoe shops have child-sized wooden paddles available at inexpensive prices. A paddle for an older child (or adult) should reach from the floor to the chin. A paddle with a T-grip handle is preferable because it allows better control.

Seats

Each child who is not paddling from the bow position should have his or her own seat. This seat gives a child a "home base," a reference point in the canoe that is uniquely personal. Having the center passenger sit in the bilge on the bottom of the canoe is understandably not an option for either kids or adults. An adult-sized beach chair is acceptable, especially if adult and child switch between the bow paddling position and the riding position amidships. Such a chair must be stable, however, and should have as low a center of gravity as possible. For small children, a better alternative is a small box or flat-topped cooler because it gives them more space and permits a variety of sitting positions. Some outfitters sell a "third seat" similar to the bow and stern seats, that can be hung from the gunwale amidships. I cannot recommend these; they leave the center of gravity too high, making the canoe less stable.

Very young children may be less apprehensive if placed in front of the bow paddler. Don't expect much power from up front, however, because there will not be much room to stroke!

Miscellaneous

A few items are so important to the success of a canoe trip with kids that they are worth a reminder even though they are not child-specific:

- Food and drink: bring more than you think you'll need, in a wide variety.
- Clothing: bring waterproof rain gear for every participant. Be certain to include rain hats. Bring one complete set of dry clothes for each person along in the canoe, wrapped in several plastic trash bags. Have another set in the car at the take-out.
- Sun protection: bring sunscreen, sunglasses, and a hat for each participant.
- Toys: a bailing bucket and sponge are necessary for canoeing and make great playtoys too. Squirt guns are popular while underway; shovels and buckets are favorites during shoreline rest stops.
- Emergency equipment: a first aid kit, duct tape, toilet paper, a knife, and extra rope are all useful to have.

PADDLING

A canoe should have only two paddlers at any time. Two adults and two small children (or one older child) is the maximum safe load for a canoe; if you have more than two kids, you will need to recruit a friend who has a canoe! When a child wants to paddle, I recommend that you allow her or him to do so, as long and as often as the child cares to. Paddling gives kids a sense of participation (although children under 10 years old will probably not give you much help) and an opportunity to burn off energy. The child should paddle from the front seat; it is frustrating to try to paddle from amidships. How much a child will choose to paddle is highly variable. Many will only lilydip for a few minutes; on the other hand, I've seen a four-year-old paddle continuously for nine miles of white-water.

However much you go canoeing with children, your trips will doubtless affect their development and outlook on life. Paddling is a noncompetitive outdoor skill; children learn its nuances almost without effort and find themselves proud of being able to do something well that very few of their peers can match. By the time they reach late adolescence, you may find that they want to borrow the canoe in addition to the family car!

Corkers Creek

River Section: Shad Landing marina upstream to head of navigation and return

County: Worcester

Distance: About 2 miles

Difficulty: Tidal flatwater

Hazards: None

Highlights: Cypress swamp

Nearby Canoe Rental: Pocomoke River State Park, Shad Landing area, (410) 632-2566

More Information: Pocomoke River State Park, Shad Landing area, (410) 632-2566

CORKERS CREEK IS A narrow tidal stream on which the Shad Landing area of Pocomoke River State Park is located. Corkers has many assets to recommend itself: it is scenic, it is wild, and it is convenient to the campsites at Shad Landing. On top of that, it is short, for those with limited time or active children, and canoes can be rented at the Shad Landing marina. For these reasons, it's probably the most heavily traveled canoe river on the Eastern Shore. Even so, it is remarkable how a sense of wildness pervades the creek and its banks as soon as that flotilla of Boy Scouts disappears around the next bend.

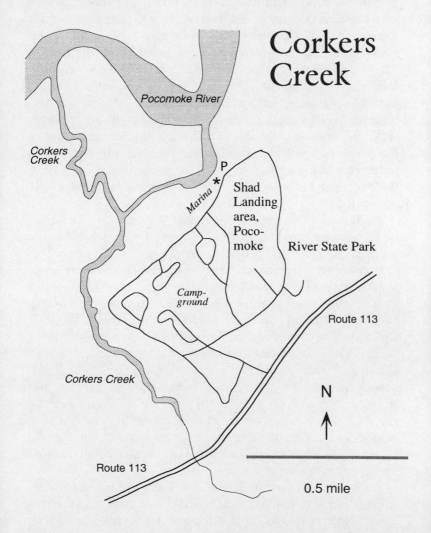

Corkers
Creek

Pocomoke River

Corkers
Creek

P

* Marina

Shad
Landing
area,
Poco-
moke

River State Park

Campground

Route 113

Corkers Creek

N

↑

Route 113

0.5 mile

TRIP DESCRIPTION

Begin (and end) your trip at the Shad Landing marina of Pocomoke River State Park. There's plenty of parking, as well as wheelchair-accessible bathrooms, water, telephones, trash cans, and a campstore (with wonderful, cheap ice cream cones!). It's also a great place to camp, perhaps the best in Maryland; the wind whispers in the tops of 100-foot-tall loblolly pines shading the campsites, and there's a pool for the kids. Rent a canoe from the park if you must, but be forewarned: you'll have to wear an uncomfortable horse-collar-style life jacket and paddle a noisy aluminum canoe with a heavy plastic paddle that's more suitable for use as an industrial-duty pry bar. A few trips in rental canoes are effective in convincing anyone of the substantial advantages of ownership.

Dodge the power boats and fishing lines as you paddle out of the marina into the creek. Although Corkers is tidal, the range is not great, so it's easy to paddle against the current.

Immediately opposite the marina on the far shore are some semisubmerged logs and tiny hammocks of vegetation, and it is here that you'll have a fine chance to observe sunning turtles. Despite the heavy river traffic, they usually frequent this spot. The turtles you see here are most likely to be painted turtles. The painted turtle has the widest range, and is perhaps the most common, of any turtle in North America. It has yellow, orange, or reddish stripes on its neck, legs, and tail, and similar colors typically show at the edges of the plates forming the shell. The smallest turtles in a group seem to be the most skittish and will usually dive first as you approach, whereas the larger ones seem the most loathe to move. Adult painted turtles are herbivorous.

Paddle upriver (to the left as you leave the marina; sometimes it's hard to tell on a tidal creek!). This section of Corkers was dredged years ago to provide access to the marina; you can tell by the arrow-straight nature of the river channel, and the now well-forested spoil banks on the left shore. The branches of riverside shrubs and small trees hang far over the water in their search for sunlight, and many are decorated with plastic bobbers from errant casts by fishermen.

After about 200 yards, the canal enters the true Corkers Creek. Head to the left (upstream); the right branch will take you out to the Pocomoke River. You now enter a natural wooded swamp. Although there are trees and vegetation along the banks, a close examination of the ground will reveal that the soil is as much water as solid earth. About the only firm footing is around the little hammocks of vegetation growing at the base of a root or tree stump. For this reason, it's difficult to get back into an overturned canoe, so do your best to stay upright.

The natural river here winds back and forth in broad, sweeping turns. The channel is usually deepest on the outside of a turn, whereas mudflats build up on the inside as particulates fall out of the more slowly moving water. As a result, rivers tend to meander, forming ever-widening, snakelike bends. During floods, these turns buffer the shores from the erosive effects of water by slowing the current. Inexplicably, the Soil Conservation Service has spent hundreds of millions of dollars to channelize and straighten small creeks and streams. The result is the loss of soil, not its conservation.

Emergent vegetation populates the muddy shallows. The most common plant is spatterdock, a round, tropical-looking leaf that appears to float on the water's surface at high tide. Its yellow, lotuslike flower prompts many people erroneously to call it a water lily. Summertime paddlers may also notice a blue spike of flowers from a plant with arrow-shaped leaves; this is pickerelweed.

Many kinds of trees line the shore. Oak, ash, alder, sweet gum, and red maple are common. But it is the unusual trees that are most interesting. Three species grow here on Corkers Creek that are on the northern edge of their distribution: the fringe tree, the sweetbay magnolia, and the bald cypress. The fringe tree flowers in May, and its white, ribbonlike petals (from which it gets its common name) make it unmistakable. In June, the sweetbay magnolia unfolds its large, fragrant blossoms. But it is the bald cypress that is the dominant tree in

Sweetbay magnolia

this swamp. The high water table in the swamp keeps most tree species under 40 feet in height, but this uniform canopy is punctuated by the occasional very tall bald cypress. Unusual as a deciduous conifer, it has feathery needles that are lime green in early spring and rusty reddish brown in fall. Outcroppings of its root structure, aptly named "knees," form little islands of soil and herbaceous vegetation around the base of the big trees.

Corkers Creek is a great place to see birds, especially in the early morning and again at dusk. You're very likely to see great blue herons, green-backed herons, various woodpeckers, mallards, kingbirds, and other less easily identifiable forest-dwelling birds. Look for turkey vultures soaring high overhead, accompanied on occasion by the scream of a soaring redtail hawk.

In spring and summer, you'll undoubtedly see prothonotary warblers. These engaging denizens of wooded swamps have bright yellow chests and heads and blue-gray wings.

They're completely oblivious to humans; I've been so close as to feel the brush of air from their wingbeats and I have seen them glean a branch for insects within a paddle length of my head.

As the creek winds toward its source, it narrows considerably until it is overhung by trees. Water snakes drape themselves on these branches on hot summer days, and park naturalists enjoy spinning partly true tales of these tubular reptiles dropping into the canoes of unsuspecting paddlers. Since water snakes can be pugnacious, it's best to keep your eyes open and not interrupt their reptilian siestas. The poisonous cottonmouth, or water moccasin, is not found in Maryland, despite the wide-eyed attestations of many canoeists on Corkers Creek.

Soon after narrowing to only a canoe width, Corkers Creek passes under Route 113. Look under the bridge for the nests of phoebes and swallows. On the far side, trees temporarily recede from the river banks, leaving a nice freshwater marsh. Here you can find vegetation of a type not heretofore seen on the trip: cattails, blue irises, jewelweeds, tearthumbs, and smartweeds. Lacing many of these herbaceous marsh plants together is dodder, an orangish vine twining through the vegetation. It has no true roots but gains nourishment from the vascular systems of the plants on which it grows. A few old wildflower texts refer to dodder as mother-in-law plant. Why? Because it is parasitic and the stem resembles a long, red, wagging tongue!

Continue upriver, poling your way through the shallows and parting the vegetation with your paddle. The stream will be only as wide as your canoe here, and at all but the highest tide you may have to retreat. But at high tide, you can reach an enchanting forest dell of bald cypress that Dr. Charles Stine of Johns Hopkins University calls the Hobbitt's Glen. It is cool and shady, with only the occasional shaft of sunlight penetrating to your canoe. Moss and ferns abound; cypress knees poke up everywhere. This is the end of the line, even at high tide, so back your way out to a point where the canoe can be turned around.

Return to Shad Landing. Keep an eye peeled for birds and turtles on the return trip, as they tend to resume their riverside haunts rather quickly after disturbance. The total distance of this canoe trip is only about two miles; allot two to three hours for the moderate pace needed to poke about, admire the scenery, and really enjoy yourself.

DIRECTIONS

From Baltimore or Washington, cross the Bay Bridge and continue south on Route 50 into Salisbury. Turn right on Route 12; the exit is situated in the downtown area. Continue south on Route 12 through the town of Snow Hill to Route 113. Turn right. The Shad Landing area of the Pocomoke River State Park is found on Route 113 about two miles south of the southern "suburbs" of Snow Hill. Once in the park, follow signs to the marina. An admission fee is charged on weekends in spring, summer, and fall.

OTHER OUTDOOR RECREATIONAL OPPORTUNITIES NEARBY

Nassawango Creek and the Pocomoke River, located within a 15-minute drive, are both superb canoeing streams. Hiking is possible on the Paul Leifer Trail, located within a 15-minute drive, and on Assateague Island National Seashore. Paved bike trails are available on Assateague Island National Seashore and at Chincoteague National Wildlife Refuge, both about 45 minutes away by car. All of these places are described elsewhere in this book.

Conservation and Preservation in Maryland

The fate of publicly owned lands in Maryland depends in large measure on citizen opinion and input. With an ever-expanding human population, we face a future in which such lands will become increasingly more valuable for both aesthetic and economic reasons. The dichotomy between utilization of such lands for resources by logging, mining, trapping, and hunting, and preservation through a ban on such activities, is a tension that can be expected to increase as society debates the question.

We have long recognized that certain locales should be preserved exclusively for nonconsumptive uses. By reason of their scenic beauty or the opportunity they present for recreation, parks and wilderness areas ban the harvesting of minerals, plants, and animals. Such areas are under increasing strain, however; in many places, especially near metropolitan centers, parks are literally being loved to death. Recognizing the value of such lands, the Maryland legislature established Program Open Space, a pool of money derived from a surtax on real estate transfers, to fund future purchases of parklands. Unfortunately, the fund has been diverted in recent years to supplement general state revenues. This action is shortsighted for a number of reasons, but the most obvious one is that land is a finite and increasingly scarce commodity.

The majority of state lands are managed for conservation rather than preservation. Conservation can be broadly defined as the wise use of land and its living resources on a sustainable basis. Although the words sound simple and reasonable, the institution of these concepts is difficult, complex, and subject to widely differing interpretations of such words as *wise use* and *sustainable*.

For example, wise use has always implied an economic benefit. Profits from the sale of timber off state lands revert to the state treasury; activities and sales of gear associated with hunting generate economic benefits to the local business community. From this viewpoint, forests are merely tree farms and lands are free-range game ranches. The problem with this belief is that the majority of living organisms have no direct economic value but do play a significant role in maintaining the eco-system. The entire range of organisms that form the ecological community, especially unobvious or poorly appreciated ones like bacteria, fungi, and insects, provide ecosystem services to us free of charge. They filter pollutants, retard the loss of soil, buffer streamflow, recycle nutrients, purify the air, and stabilize the environment against natural and artificial extremes. Simi-larly, charismatic organisms like wildflowers and warblers are among the most beautiful inhabitants of forests, but their value, although aesthetically priceless, cannot be quantified.

What our society needs, therefore, in order to decide upon the proper balance between use and preservation of state lands, is a widespread appreciation among citizens of what Aldo Leo-pold calls a "land ethic." A land ethic changes our role in the ecological community from one of dominance, in which we decide the future and fate of the land and all the species that inhabit it, to one of cooperative equality, in which our actions promote the long-term diversity, complexity, and stability of the natural world. Our relation to the land will now impose obliga-tions as well as confer privileges. We will continue to manage, use, and alter natural resources, but we will also acknowledge our responsibility to do so as a last resort and for the good of all rather than for the self-interest of a few—especially on our public lands.

Our human society operates under such ethics as a matter of course. For example, all taxpayers, even those without school-age children, contribute to the operation of public schools because education is recognized as an important benefit to the society as a whole. A land ethic merely extends such coopera-tion and mutual respect to include the natural world that we share. ⤙

Nassawango Creek

River Section: Red House Road to Nassawango Road

County: Worcester

Distance: 2.3 miles

Difficulty: Tidal flatwater

Hazards: None

Highlights: Cypress swamp

Nearby Canoe Rental: Pocomoke River Canoe Company, (410) 632-3971

More Information: The Nature Conservancy (Maryland Field Office), (301) 656-8673

T HE POCOMOKE RIVER drainage basin on Maryland's lower Eastern Shore abounds with superb canoeing streams. Corkers Creek, Pitts Creek, Dividing Creek, and the upper reaches of the Pocomoke itself are all wild, intimate little aquatic gems. In large measure, this bounty is due to unusually high depth-to-width ratios that lead to narrow but passable watercourses. The geological origin of this characteristic is uncertain, but the result is certainly fortunate for paddlers. Nassawango Creek, still another of the Pocomoke's tributaries, is no exception to the rule.

The Nassawango is the largest subbasin in the Pocomoke drainage, and a great deal of the swampy land has been bought by the Nature Conservancy for preservation. Renowned for its unique ecological character, Nassawango Creek is home to a number of species of plants and animals at the northernmost

Nassawango Creek

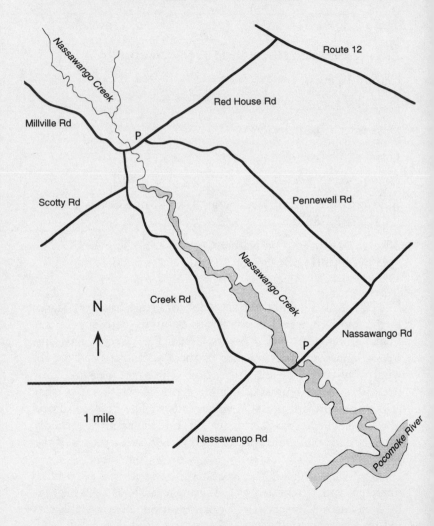

Route 12

Red House Rd

Millville Rd

P

Nassawango Creek

Scotty Rd

Pennewell Rd

N

↑

Creek Rd

Nassawango Creek

P

Nassawango Rd

1 mile

Nassawango Rd

Pocomoke River

extension of their ranges. A canoe trip down the Nassawango is guaranteed to be a day filled with wildlife and scenery.

TRIP DESCRIPTION

The put-in for Nassawango Creek is the river crossing at Red House Road, where there is plenty of roadside parking. This point marks the head of navigable waters; just upstream, the creek dissolves into a braid of shallow, vine-choked passages frequently blocked by downed trees. Red House Road is also the head of tidal action, so that a long stretch of dry weather will have no effect on water level. Many paddlers choose to do Nassawango Creek as an out-and-back trip, returning to Red House Road and thus requiring no car shuttle.

The river is only about 20 feet wide at the start, and it is overhung with trees that give the impression of paddling through a shady green tunnel. Red maple, river birch, sweet gum, ash, and bald cypress form a diverse canopy. Closer to the ground, southern arrowwood, conspicuous by its clustered blue berries, hangs over the river. As its name implies, the shrub has long, straight twigs, which were used by native Americans for arrow shafts.

As with many small coastal plain streams, fallen trees often block progress downriver. Even if paddlers have not sawed out a passage, smaller trees can frequently be bypassed or slipped under. Such a "strainer" lies just around the first bend on Nassawango Creek; by ducking low, you can avoid portaging. Twisted in the branches of this tree, and on several others along Nassawango Creek, is crossvine, an unusual plant on the northernmost edge of its range. Flowering in late May, it has large, tubular orange flowers tipped with yellow at the edges. Crossvine takes its common name from the X-shaped pith revealed when the twig is cut in cross section.

Within a few hundred yards, Nassawango Creek widens enough for sunlight to penetrate to the river. A few clumps of spatterdock and pickerelweed begin to appear at the inside edges of bends where the river is shallow; these will form more

Wild iris

extensive marshes in the creek's lower reaches. A few clumps of the rare and beautiful wild iris are also found. Sloughs branch out to either side, and this complex maze of water, marsh, and swamp almost always hides a few ducks (mallards or wood ducks) and heron (great blue or green-backed). Indeed, this middle section where the river is neither too narrow nor too wide is the most likely place to surprise birds, sunning turtles, snakes and insects, and even the occasional raccoon foraging for dinner.

After many bends and about a mile and a half of paddling, Nassawango becomes wider still, and wind may become a factor on a blustery day. Many paddlers elect to return to Red House Road at this point, content in having visited the best of Nassawango Creek. If you continue downstream, Nassawango Road is a possible take-out, which of course requires a car shuttle. River distance from Red House Road to Nassawango

Road is 2.3 miles. It is possible to continue paddling 1.0 mile to the confluence with the Pocomoke, and then to turn either left and proceed upstream for almost two miles to the Snow Hill City Park or right and proceed downstream for just over two miles to the Shad Landing area of Pocomoke River State Park.

DIRECTIONS

From Baltimore or Washington, cross the Bay Bridge and continue south on Route 50 into Salisbury. Turn right on Route 12; the exit is situated in the downtown area. Continue south on Route 12 for about 15 miles, turning right onto Red House Road. The river crossing is one mile down this road.

OTHER OUTDOOR RECREATIONAL OPPORTUNITIES NEARBY

For canoeists, the Pocomoke River and Corkers Creek are located just a few miles away. Bicycling trails at Assateague Island National Seashore and at Chincoteague National Wildlife Refuge are each about a 45-minute drive from the Snow Hill area. A hiking trail through these same swamps and just minutes away is to be found at the Nature Conservancy's Nassawango Creek Preserve. All of these places are described elsewhere in this book.

Managing for Biodiversity on Public Lands

Preservation of biodiversity is a new paradigm for conservation biology in particular and for science in general, having reached the literature only in the 1980s. Contrary to the paradigms for physics and chemistry, we have so far discovered no universal rules that govern the operation of ecosystems and the direction of the evolutionary process. For this reason, conservation biology is only in its infancy as a predictive science. Policymakers are ever more often wanting to know how to preserve biodiversity on public lands; science has no certain answers, but a consensus is emerging on a number of management practices that should be successful:

- *Save habitats in large, unbroken tracts.* Island biogeographical theory has clearly demonstrated that the larger is a parcel of habitat, the more species it harbors, and that this relationship is synergistic rather than linear.
- *Avoid fragmentation.* Fragmentation creates edge, and edge reduces the effective size of a particular habitat type. A diversity of habitats are acceptable and even desirable at the landscape level, but keep habitat types as unfragmented as possible.
- *Connect these large unbroken tracts with broad habitat corridors.* Greenways of natural habitat promote genetic exchange between populations and promote recolonization in the event of localized extinctions.
- *Preserve areas of critical importance in sustaining biodiversity first.* In the past, public lands have been purchased for their scenic beauty, recreational potential, commercial potential, or perceived lack of any other value at all. Identify species-rich assemblages, critical habitats, rare communities, and genetically diverse populations through scientific study, and make them the priority for conservation.
- *Limit the influence of human activities on the landscape.* The primary force driving species toward rarity and extinction is the actions of humans. Preserve "hotspots" of biodiversity

as reserves closed to the general public except for passive recreation like birding.

° *On lands managed for multiple use, preservation of biodiversity should be the overarching priority and not just a competing use.* When biodiversity is lost from public lands, it will not grow back like trees or return like game animals. Harvesting of plants and animals for commercial gain should take place only on those tracts of public lands not critical for the preservation of biodiversity.

The principles enumerated here may seem extreme, especially to those who are accustomed to utilizing natural resources on public lands rather than conserving them. But this final decade of the twentieth century is the first time in history that we have understood the importance of biological diversity for the proper functioning of our biosphere and for the preservation of the raw material of evolution. It is time for a new way of thinking. ✦

Pocomoke River

River Section: Section 1: Whiton Crossing to Porters Crossing
                   Section 2: Porters Crossing to Snow Hill

County: Worcester

Distance: Section 1: 5.0 miles
              Section 2: 5.1 miles

Difficulty: Section 1: Flat, flowing water
                Section 2: Tidal flatwater

Hazards: Section 1: Trees down across the river
             Section 2: Windy weather possible in lower half

Highlights: Cypress swamp

Nearby Canoe Rental: Pocomoke River Canoe Company,
   (410) 632-3971

More Information: The Nature Conservancy (Maryland Field
   Office), (301) 656-8673

WHAT'S THE BEST canoe trip in Maryland? Paddlers will debate this topic endlessly, but one river keeps coming up on everyone's list: the Pocomoke. This little river on the lower Eastern Shore has it all: great scenery, frequent glimpses of wildlife, and a remote, intimate quality difficult to find in a state as populous as Maryland. The logistics of a canoe trip on the Pocomoke are easy, too. You can run a 5-mile, half-day section or continue into the afternoon for a 10-mile trip. There's a friendly and informative outfitter right at the take-out for those who need to rent a canoe. Campsites are available nearby in one of the prettiest

Pocomoke
River

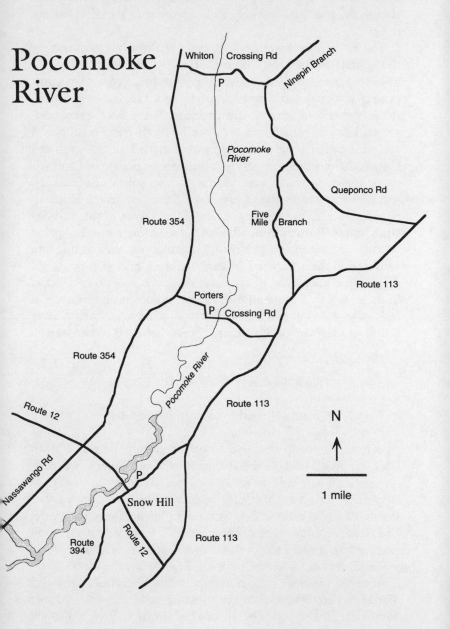

Whiton

Crossing Rd

P

Ninepin Branch

*Pocomoke
River*

Queponco Rd

Route 354

Five
Mile   Branch

Route 113

Porters

P

Crossing Rd

Route 354

Pocomoke River

Route 12

Route 113

N

Nassawango Rd

P

Snow Hill

1 mile

Route
394

Route 12

Route 113

state park campgrounds in Maryland. Yet despite all these attributes, you'll be unlikely to see any other paddlers on the river.

The Pocomoke River drains a large, shallow basin occupying the central part of the lower Eastern Shore. Much of it is a low-lying swamp, dense and impenetrable, seemingly composed of equal parts water, mud, and tangled vegetation. Although the fringes of the drainage basin have been converted into farmland, much of the heart of the Pocomoke is still wild and remote. It is the most northerly of the southern hardwood swamps, harboring a number of plants and animals more typical of river systems far to the south. At least 18 species of warblers nest here, and there are more kinds of breeding birds than on any similarly sized tract in the mid-Atlantic states. Birders from all over the state gather in the spring to look and listen for Swainson's warbler, an elusive and rare songster more typical of North Carolina and points south. Among the mammals, the shy and reclusive river otter is found in these waters. In recognition of the ecological significance of the swamp, The Nature Conservancy has purchased over 6,000 acres, some of which have been conveyed to the state.

TRIP DESCRIPTION

Whiton Crossing to Porters Crossing

The put-in is deep in a bald cypress swamp where Whiton Crossing Road bridges the Pocomoke. There's plenty of roadside parking here but no other facilities. The first mile of river is pretty, but it is nothing special. This portion of the Pocomoke was channelized years ago, so it is straight, wide, and deep, with an almost imperceptible flow. But it's a good place for beginners to work on canoe strokes and teamwork, while birders can take the opportunity to scan the trees.

After the first mile, the character of the Pocomoke changes. The river narrows, the current picks up, and the trees close in overhead. You're paddling through a green tunnel, and soon that tunnel begins to twist and turn. In places, the river itself may be only six to eight feet wide, and in many others vegetation constricts the passage. Fortunately, downed trees spanning the river have been partially cut away so that a canoe can pass. But it's not always easy! On occasion, you may have to duck below the gunwales to clear a branch; in other places getting into position to hit the slot may be challenging. But unless you venture down the Pocomoke immediately after a major storm, there is always one obvious passage.

After a few hundred yards of this, keep watch beyond the right bank for the wreckage of a small airplane. It is well back in the forest, about 50 yards from the river, but it is visible even in summer. Between the force of the crash and scavenging by visitors, there's not too much left except twisted metal and burned plastic. Two people were killed in the crash.

Just in case you've forgotten where you are, a large road sign indicating that this is the Pocomoke River has been nailed to a tree about a half mile farther downstream. Obviously stolen from a nearby bridge crossing, this sign and a few abandoned duck blinds are the only indications of human presence on the river.

These woods are known as bald cypress swamps, for their dominant tree species. Bald cypress trees, although not the most numerous species, are the largest in the swamp, with a stringy bark, feathery short needles, and an exotic, southern appearance. The most noteworthy feature of these trees is their "knees," aptly named protruberances that surround the trunk. Scientists are still uncertain about the function of cypress knees. Some believe that they provide a way for tree roots to exchange oxygen with the atmosphere, since the muddy soils of swamps tend to be rather anaerobic. Other scientists feel that the whole network of knees provides support, much like the pontoons on an outrigger canoe. Some knees may be found at quite a distance from the tree, and several have been discovered lurking just under the surface of the water in the main channel. If you should ride up on a cypress knee or other log, just relax, try to keep your weight in the center of the canoe, and work your way off the obstacle with gentle shoves.

The water in the Pocomoke is clear and clean, unless there has been a recent rain. It is, however, stained the color of tea from tannins leaching out of the surrounding swamp. Where the bottom is sandy, the colors combine to give an orangish cast to the water.

Despite the fact that this is a fine trip for beginners, it also offers plenty of challenge and excitement. You'll need to know your steering strokes to avoid ramming into the outside bank on a turn. The swiftness of the water and the short radius of many of the Pocomoke's bends make a clean turn hard to accomplish. Fortunately, the river is shallow and there are no rocks, so an unexpected dunking is never much of a problem.

The Pocomoke is a special place in every season. As the warmest place in Maryland, the river is frozen only rarely, and it is a good choice for a winter cruise. Long vistas open up across the swamps, revealing the bare trunks of trees that are hidden at other seasons. For the competent and well-prepared canoeist, the rewards of wintertime paddling are many. Spring comes slowly to the swamps, but when the trees leaf out, wildlife activity becomes frantic. Many species of warblers pass through on their migration north, and some species stay to breed. The most spectacular example is the prothonotary warbler, with its bright yellow chest and head and blue-gray wings. These engaging little birds stake out breeding territories along the river's edge in early May, and they are easily seen chasing each other through the underbrush. By midsummer, wildlife activity has slowed down, languishing in the heat, but the heavily shaded river corridor is still the coolest place around. Finally, fall brings the color of autumn leaves drifting over the river, in a reminder that the cycle of seasons is nearing its end.

Most people associate swamps with biting insects, but this is not always true. Insects are rarely a problem along the Pocomoke, especially if you stay on the water. Gnats and mosquitoes may be plentiful after a rain in late spring and summer, however, especially if you leave your canoe. If it looks like insects are going to be a problem, eat lunch in the boats, tying them up to a tree so you don't drift downriver.

After about four miles of this prime swampland cruising, the current slackens and the banks begin to show a tidal influence. Porters Crossing Road soon appears; it marks a possible take-out. If you have only limited time or restless children, this five-mile trip gives you a good idea of what a bald cypress swamp is all about in an easy half-day of cruising. There is plenty of parking along the roadside at Porters Crossing.

Porters Crossing to Snow Hill

To make a full day of it, continue downstream 5.1 miles more to Snow Hill. The character of the river here is markedly different from that of the upper section. Since it is tidal, there is no current to help you, so the the paddling is more difficult. At first, the river is only slightly wider, and it still twists back and forth in tight turns. Gradually, however, the river widens, and fishermen in motorboats may be encountered, especially in the spring. There is still no development, however, and the adjacent forest stretches seemingly unbroken until a few hundred yards before Snow Hill.

Take out on the left-hand side of the river at a bulkhead forming the lower end of a municipal parking lot, just before the Route 12 bridge in Snow Hill. The Pocomoke River Canoe Company is located here, and it has canoe rentals available.

DIRECTIONS

From Baltimore or Washington, cross the Bay Bridge and continue south on Route 50 into Salisbury. Turn right on Route 12; the exit is situated in the downtown area. Continue south on Route 12 to the town of Snow Hill. Cross the bridge over the Pocomoke and make your first left turn into an alley next to the Pocomoke River Canoe Company. A municipal parking lot is directly ahead of you. There are no public facilities here.

To reach the river access points at Whiton Crossing or Porters Crossing, begin from the same parking lot. Take Route 12 north, crossing the Pocomoke and leaving Snow Hill. At the first major intersection, a blinking light, turn right on Route 354. Porters Crossing Road is on your right 3.4 miles up this road; Whiton Crossing Road is also on your right, a further 4.2 miles north.

OTHER OUTDOOR RECREATIONAL OPPORTUNITIES NEARBY

For canoeists, Nassawango Creek and Corkers Creek are located just a few miles away. Bicycling trails at Assateague Island National Seashore and at Chincoteague National Wildlife Refuge are each about a 45-minute drive from the Snow Hill area. All these places are described elsewhere in this book.

Prothonotary Warblers

Of all the animals that are found in wooded swamps like those along the Pocomoke River, perhaps none is more characteristic than the prothonotary warbler. Noisy, active, relatively unafraid of people, and outfitted in a spectacular plumage, the prothonotary endears itself to everyone who canoes here. Named for a brightly robed official of the Vatican, prothonotaries virtually define wooded swamps on Maryland's Coastal Plain.

Prothonotaries are fairly large as warblers go, reaching almost the size of a bluebird. Their entire head and chest are a golden yellow that may range almost to orange. Their wings are blue-gray, and their backs have an olive shading. Females are similar to males in plumage, although they may be a bit duller.

Prothonotary warbler

The prothonotary is the only eastern warbler that nests in a cavity, typically a hole excavated by a woodpecker in a dead tree. For this reason, the young are protected against such predators as crows, blue jays, and raccoons. However, because they use what are essentially "recycled" nest sites, mites, fleas, and other parasites may take a heavier toll on nestlings than is typical for other warblers. In addition, nest sites may be hard to find; such other species as tree swallows, wrens, starlings, and house sparrows all begin nesting before prothonotaries and thus claim the best sites. Upon their arrival in the swamps in late April, prothonotaries spend the majority of their time searching and inspecting prospective nesting sites. Once a nest is built, the male is quite territorial, aggressively driving off all intruders, whether of the same or of different species.

Cowbird predation can be a problem for prothonotaries; one nest was found containing seven cowbird eggs and no warbler eggs. The farther from agricultural fields, scrub, and other disturbed habitats is the nest site, the less parasitism is likely to occur. For this same reason, there is probably less competition for nest sites in unbroken tracts of swamp forest.

Prothonotaries typically lay four to six small eggs in a lined nest. After a 12- to 14-day incubation period, immobile, blind, naked young hatch. They develop quickly and fledge within 11 days; the young are capable of swimming, an important ability since nest sites are frequently over water.

Prothonotary warblers migrate in early fall, wintering in Central America, northern South America, and the Antilles. We like to think of prothonotaries and other migrants as "our" birds, but in fact they spend about half the year elsewhere. For this reason, the conservation of migratory birds depends on proper conditions and habitat in three places: the summer breeding grounds, the wintering grounds, and stopover places visited during migration. Despite these complexities—as well as the problems caused by deforestation, cowbird parasitism, and competition for nesting sites—prothonotaries are one of the few species of warblers that seem to be holding their own. For Maryland naturalists, that's good news, because there are few animals more colorful in plumage and more charming in behavior than prothonotaries. ✦

Janes Island

River Section: Janes Island State Park Marina to Janes Island beach and return

County: Somerset

Distance: About 1 mile of paddling, then up to 3 miles of hiking

Difficulty: Tidal flatwater

Hazards: Possibly getting run over by a motorboat

Highlights: Tidal salt marsh, Chesapeake Bay beach

Nearby Canoe Rental: Janes Island State Park, (410) 968-1565

More Information: Janes Island State Park, (410) 968-1565

THE MEETING OF land and water seems to create special places. Indeed, many of the walks listed in this book border on creeks, bogs, ponds, and rivers. Nowhere in Maryland is the juncture of land and water more gradual, more ephemeral, more changeable, than the tidal marshes of the lower Eastern Shore. They are Maryland's version of the Everglades, where limitless vistas over shallow bays and low vegetation impart a sense of space and solitude. The absence of solid ground and the incredible hordes of biting insects all conspire to keep man at bay; these marshes may be the loneliest places in Maryland.

A good sense of these salt marshes can be experienced at Janes Island State Park, located just outside Crisfield in Somerset County. The park consists of a 310-acre developed main-

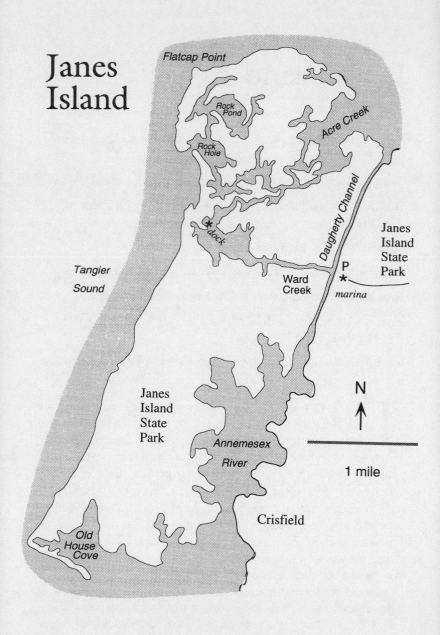

Janes
Island

Flatcap Point

Rock
Pond

Rock
Hole

*dock

Acre Creek

Daugherty Channel

Janes
Island
State
Park

P
*

marina

Tangier
Sound

Ward
Creek

N

Janes
Island
State
Park

Annemesex
River

1 mile

Crisfield

Old
House
Cove

land, known as the Hodson area, and a much larger island of low marshes and tidal guts separated from the mainland by a narrow channel. The Hodson area contains a marina with boat rentals, picnic grounds, and more than 100 campsites, making it a fine base for exploration of the marsh. A channel leads through the center of the island to within 100 yards of the far shore, providing a sheltered waterway for canoeists. Once one is ashore, over two miles of sandy beach fronting on Tangier Sound invite beachcombing and swimming.

TRIP DESCRIPTION

Launch your canoe from the state park marina, where there are wheelchair-accessible bathrooms, trash cans, a soda machine, plenty of parking, and motorboat and canoe rentals. Paddle due west into Ward Creek, crossing Daugherty Channel, where you should watch out for fast-moving powerboats.

As you enter Ward Creek, the only high ground of Janes Island is on your left, featuring a loblolly pine forest. In the 1870s, at the southern tip of this island, a fish processing facility was established, an outlier of Crisfield, then known as the seafood capital of the world. All that remains now is a 50-foot-tall brick chimney, although there were once a board-walk, a dance pavilion, and summer houses here.

As you paddle up Ward Creek, examine the mudflats lining the marsh on either side. The mud is very convoluted, and it is honeycombed with tiny canals and tunnels. If the tide is low, you should be able to see dozens of fiddler crabs scurrying for shelter as you approach. Most are only two to three inches long, but the larger ones seem less skittish and may not enter their burrows if you keep your distance. Use binoculars to view the crabs. The males have one hugely oversized claw. It is used in courtship displays prior to mating, when the crab flexes and extends the pincer and waves the claw up and down. This display is also used to threaten other males competing for territory, but the claw is not an effective weapon despite its size. Fiddler crabs are among the most interesting residents of a marsh, but close observation of them will take time and quiet patience.

A thin layer of *Spartina alterniflora,* salt marsh cordgrass, lines the channel. Farther back, where the ground is slightly higher, black rush dominates hundreds of acres of this marsh. This needlelike grass, about two feet high, often appears dead, lending it a blackish cast.

The deeply invaginated channels of Janes Island provide fine habitat for feeding herons and egrets. In summer, you'll certainly see both the snowy and American egrets, white, heronlike birds in small and large editions, respectively. The snowy egret has a black bill, whereas the American egret has a yellow one, a field mark that is easy to spot if you're unfamiliar with these common summer residents. Colored herons also come in two sizes, the larger great blue and the smaller green-backed. Great blue herons, which some people mistakenly call "cranes," are very common along every watercourse in the state; they stand four feet high on stilt legs with long necks. The green-backed heron, although probably equally common, is more secretive, has shorter legs and neck, and typically stands about 16 inches high. All of these birds feed on minnows and other small fish that inhabit warm shallows at the water's edge; by running a seine net through these same waters, you too can get a feel for the richness and diversity of the piscine life of a salt marsh.

The channel widens after the first half mile. If you're uncertain of the proper direction, follow the numbered triangular channel markers. Your goal is a dock at the far end of the bay. It will be difficult to disembark from your canoe onto the dock, so beach your canoe on a small sand spit to the right, haul it up well into the bushes so that it won't be floated off by a rising tide, and gather the necessary supplies for a beach walk. You'll definitely want to bring insect repellent between late May and first frost, along with sunscreen and whatever else you normally take to the beach.

Wade through the shallows from your landing site to the dock. The *Spartina* here houses a population of marsh periwinkles, small snails up to an inch long that become most evident on a rising tide as they climb the stems of the marsh grass. These hard-shelled snails feed on organic matter accumulated on the stems of the vegetation.

A faint trail leads across a 100-yard stretch of dunes to the windward beach. Use insect repellent here, or make the trip at a fast trot. Fortunately, the mosquitoes rarely venture out onto the beach, so you will have a safe haven when you reach the shores of Tangier Sound. Unfortunately, here you face different kinds of winged terrors. By late summer, deerflies, greenheads, and an ankle-bitng relative of the housefly patrol the beach. Because of the prevailing breezes, however, they stay low and typically alight only on immobile sunbathers. For this reason, active beachcombing rather than passive tanning is the recommended pastime out here. If all this sounds unpleasant, it's really not; the beach is actually a very enjoyable place.

Northward, the beach stretches for only a short distance, about a third of a mile. At Rock Hole, several tidal guts connect Tangier Sound with the interior of Janes Island. It is possible to wade or swim across these narrow channels to gain access to the more remote beach near Flatcap Point.

To the south, the beach runs for several miles to the southern terminus of Janes Island at Old House Cove. This is prime Chesapeake country, and it gives the impression that if you're not at the end of the world, you can at least see it from here. Tangier Sound is located at the widest part of the Bay, and no land is visible for a full 180° sweep. Behind you are the seemingly endless marshes of Janes Island. Only the abandoned packing houses of Crisfield, far to the southeast, disturb the horizon.

The beach on Janes Island is rather narrow, perhaps 25 feet wide in most places. Windrows of eelgrass, dislodged from the Bay bottom by storms, pile up on the beach. The hand of man is clearly visible as well, despite the feeling of solitude. Trash, especially plastic items, lies half buried in sand or decorates the shrubbery that backs the forebeach. Such detritus, which nature cannot decompose, is unfortunate but not unexpected; studies of the most remote islands in the world show similar kinds of human flotsam.

Walk as far as you like and then return to your canoe and paddle back to the mainland. Canoeing distance is only about a mile. Energetic paddlers can explore as many of the saltwater guts dissecting Janes Island as they choose to in order to extend the trip. It is also possible to gain access to Tangier Sound from the beach dock by paddling northward and staying left at all forks. This route brings you out at Rock Hole. Circumnavigation of Janes Island is possible, but it is a long trip over exposed water, where tides and wind can make for slow going. Renting a motorboat is probably a better choice for such a trip. On weekends, the park will ferry you from the marina to Janes Island on their boat; check with the park for availability and schedule information.

DIRECTIONS

From Baltimore or Washington, take Route 50 over the Bay Bridge to Salisbury. After passing through the business district, take Route 13 south. Exit Route 13 onto Route 413, following the signs for Crisfield. Once the highway becomes separated by a grassy median in "suburban" Crisfield, look for the brown Janes Island State Park sign. Turn right at this sign onto Route 358, and go 1.5 miles to the park entrance.

Blue Crabs

If there is any one animal that embodies the essence of Maryland, it is undoubtedly the blue crab. Inhabiting Chesapeake Bay in a plentitude that recalls the historic bounty of our great estuary, blue crabs play an important role in the ecology and economy of the Bay. The crab fishery is by far the most important one in the Chesapeake, and more people eat more crabs here in Maryland than anywhere else. A truly democratic cuisine, crabs are enjoyed by everyone, from the richest blueblood in Potomac or Greenspring Valley to the poorest chicken-necker in Baltimore or Crisfield. Even the Latin scientific name, *Callinectes sapidus,* says it all: *callinectes* means "beautiful swimmer," and *sapidus* means "tasty" or "savory." Yet there is much that we do not know about blue crabs and their management and conservation, so that we cannot be certain that our grand-

Blue crab

children will enjoy these tasty crustaceans in the abundance we do today.

Blue crabs mate in mid-Bay, mostly in early summer. Females then move down the Bay into the high-salinity waters of Virginia, where the eggs are extruded. The yellowish orange egg mass clings to the underside of the female, and after several weeks the eggs hatch to release the earliest larval form, the zoeae. These pinhead-sized planktonic larvae are at the mercy of currents and tides, and they are often swept out into the Atlantic Ocean. Survivors eventually molt into the next larval stage, called the megalops, which look like tiny lobsters. Megalops sink to the bottom, where the heavier, saltier water generally trends back into the Bay, carrying them along. The success of any year's spawn depends in great measure on these poorly understood life history stages and the factors that control their movements. After a few more molts, tiny crabs emerge, growing slowly as they feed in the sheltered waters of eelgrass beds and shallows.

After 12 to 16 months of precarious existence, blue crabs have grown to reach sexual maturity. Crabs are easily sexed by the shape of the apron, or the abdomen on the underside. Males have a "Washington Monument" shell section bisecting the apron, whereas females have a more rounded "Capitol Dome." The tips of the largest claws are red in females. Crabs typically live for two years, rarely three. Winters are spent torpid, buried in mud in deep parts of the Bay.

When Chesapeake Bay was clean and relatively pristine, before World War II, blue crabs were just one of several fisheries that supported watermen. Since then, however, the numbers of oysters and anadromous fish like shad and striped bass have declined precipitously, so that crabbing is today the only way to make a living on the Bay. And the crab fishery has generally held up; the crab harvest reached record highs in the 1980s. The cloud around this silver lining, however, is that the effort needed to hold the harvest constant has been steadily increasing. Scientists know that this trend is usually the first evidence of a fishery on the edge of a decline. At present, there are no significant controls on the crab harvest, although the state has begun to discuss this possibility with concerned parties. The blue crab fishery is our last best chance to get it right in Chesapeake Bay and to institute controls that will ensure an adequate sustainable harvest. Whether we have the foresight and force of will to do so remains to be seen. ━

Watts Creek

River Section: Martinak State Park upstream to head of
navigation and return

County: Caroline

Distance: 4.5 miles

Difficulty: Tidal flatwater

Hazards: Windy weather possible

Highlights: Freshwater marsh

Nearby Canoe Rental: None

More Information: Martinak State Park, (410) 479-1619

SUNDAY AFTERNOON on a holiday weekend, returning from the beach: you creep along Route 404 in an
interminable rolling backup that stretches from the Bay
Bridge well into rural Delaware. The sun blazes down on the
tarmack, sending up baking waves of heat. Tempers flare, and
your blood pressure rises almost as fast as the temperature
gauge on your car. For the seventeenth time today, you try to
remember why you ever thought a weekend at the beach
would be fun. And fail.

Just ahead, a little wooden sign denotes Martinak State
Park. A haven of rest, a refuge of greenery, a chance to relax
and let the world (and much of the traffic) go by. You go for it.

Down by the boat ramp, powerboats are launched and
loaded, parading to and from the wide expanses of the
Choptank River. This is good bass fishin' country, and a lot of
anglers know it. But off to the left, Watts Creek leads away in

Watts Creek

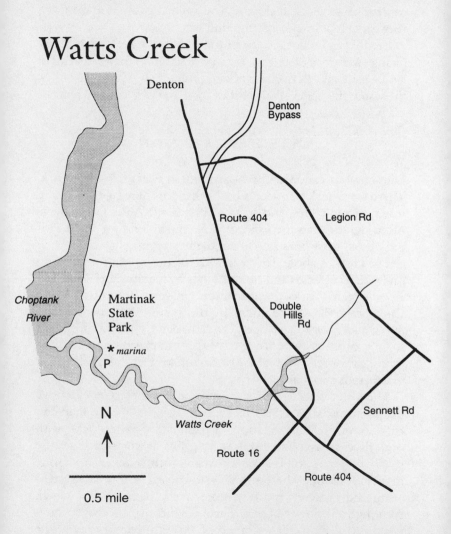

Denton

Denton
Bypass

Route 404

Legion Rd

Choptank

River

Martinak
State
Park

Double
Hills
Rd

* *marina*

P

N

Watts Creek

Sennett Rd

Route 16

Route 404

↑

0.5 mile

a few broad, lazy turns, promising ever-narrowing reaches and a beckoning unknown waiting to be explored: canoe country. For the first time today, a smile creases your face and cares start to drop away. Back at the car, you unload the canoe from the roof rack. It's time to get the hull wet.

Even if you're not caught in traffic, Watts Creek is a pleasant paddle. Martinak State Park is a fine destination for a weekend of family camping. Between canoeing, fishing, and just relaxing by the water, this spot is truly part of the Land of Pleasant Living.

TRIP DESCRIPTION

Launch your canoe at the boat ramp in Martinak State Park. There are wheelchair-accessible bathrooms here, with drinking water, picnic tables, and sufficient parking. Watts Creek bears off to the left, past the fishermen lined up along the bulkheading. Avoid their lines as you paddle upstream.

The creek is about 100 feet wide at this point, bordered on one side by uplands and on the other by marsh. The Choptank River system marks the transition between upper and lower Chesapeake Bay tributaries. In the upper Bay, marshes are fewer and poorly developed, and the land typically drops off steeply into the water. To the south, land elevations are sometimes measured in inches rather than feet, and extensive marshlands surround waterways.

The lower reaches of Watts Creek are bordered by extensive freshwater tidal marshes. As with most Chesapeake marshes, there is an obvious zonation of plant life. Spatterdock—with oval, flaccid leaves and a yellow, lotuslike flower—occupies the shallows, where soil is always covered with water. At a slightly higher elevation, where the soil is exposed at low tide, arrow arum and pickerelweed dominate many acres of this marsh. Although the flower of arrow arum is inconspicuous, pickerelweed has a blue, showy spike of flowers that brightens the marsh for much of the summer. Cattails occupy a slightly higher portion of the marsh, where the soil is submerged by only the highest of tides.

Birds abound in these marshes. Most common are red-winged blackbirds; the males display conspicuously from reeds as they mark their territories. Should you get too close to a nest, a male may make a few dive-bombing passes at your head, but this action is mostly bluff. Great blue herons are very common as well.

A few bends in the creek bring you to a very steep forested cliff about 30 feet high, on the right as you paddle upstream. A few huge old oaks tower over this bank, although hickory, ash, tulip poplar, American beech, and scrub pine are also found. Several large hemlock trees lend a deep shade to this bank; they are mostly northern trees, and their healthy presence this far south on the coastal plain is unusual. In early June, an understory of mountain laurel graces the slope with clouds of white blossoms. Bank swallows have made holes in the cliffside.

After about two miles of paddling and within earshot of the Route 404 bridge, Watts Creek finally begins to narrow. Above Route 404, it is less than 50 feet wide, and marshes soon disappear. By the next road bridge (Route 16), the stream becomes shallow. The main channel is sandy gravel rather than mud, indicating the scouring effects of heavy rains and providing nesting habitat for breeding fish. At a high tide, it is possible to continue a short distance beyond this second bridge before the creek gives way to tangled swamps. At this point, it's time to turn back; round trip distance is 4.5 miles.

DIRECTIONS

From Washington or Baltimore, cross the Bay Bridge and continue south on Route 50. Turn left at Route 404. Just past the town of Denton, look for the entrance to Martinak State Park on the right.

OTHER OUTDOOR RECREATIONAL
OPPORTUNITIES NEARBY

A different, nontidal canoeing experience can be had on Tuck-ahoe Creek, about 10 miles away and described beginning on page 417 in this book. Campsites are available at Martinak State Park.

Red-Winged Blackbirds

Every visitor to the marshes of Maryland is familiar with the red-winged blackbird. Males of the species are entirely black except for conspicuous red epaulets on the wings. Females are smaller, with brownish striping over their entire bodies. In winter, red-wings form huge flocks with other blackbird species, roosting in marshes but traveling out to agricultural fields during the day to forage. By spring, these flocks break up, and the birds disperse to marshes across the state to set up breeding territories. In late March, it seems as though even the tiniest patch of roadside wetlands becomes enlivened by red-wing

Red-winged blackbird

birdsong. Ornithologists feel that red-winged blackbirds are probably the most numerous land birds in the United States as a whole, and the same may be true for Maryland as well.

In addition to being abundant and conspicuous, red-winged blackbirds exhibit a complex and easily observed repertoire of behaviors that reflect their mating system and evolutionary success. Red-wings are polyandrous; that is, one male mates with more than one female, but a female mates with only a single male. A male red-wing establishes and vigorously defends a territory; each female chooses a territory in which to nest, probably based on the amount of food and other resources available there. The richer the territory, the more females it can accommodate and the more successful they are likely to be in raising young. However, there are trade-offs; a female must decide if she will be better off in a rich territory that may be crowded with other females or in a poorer territory where there is less competition for resources. Availability of resources drives the mating system, but it also has consequences for evolutionary success. The richer the territory, the more dominant a male must be to defend it against all comers. Thus females tend to mate with the strongest and most dominant males, perpetuating the most vigorous and adaptive traits into future generations.

Male red-wings establish territorial boundaries by singing and displaying their crimson wing patches. Although the territory must be maintained in order to ensure that enough food is available for the survival of nestlings, time spent in boundary defense is time taken away from foraging. In a polyandrous mating system, males must ensure that they eat enough to defend their territories vigorously; in red-wings, males help feed the young and so must devote time to this task as well.

Epaulets are important social signals among red-wings; males use them to indicate their intentions. The entire red patch is exposed when a male is defending territory. Conversely, if a male is searching for an open territory within a colony or wants to forage without attracting attention, he covers the epaulet to signal submission. Although this ploy is not always successful in preventing attacks from birds defending a territory, the severity of the quarrel is reduced when both participants know the outcome in advance. ᔕ

Kings Creek

River Section: Kingston Landing to Kings Creek to head of navigation and return

County: Talbot

Distance: Kingston Landing to Kingston Road, 3.0 miles one way

Difficulty: Tidal flatwater

Hazards: Windy weather possible

Highlights: Boardwalk through a freshwater marsh

Nearby Canoe Rental: None

More Information: The Nature Conservancy (Maryland Field Office), (301) 656-8673

L OOKING FOR A PLEASANT, easy canoe trip on Maryland's Eastern Shore, but still within a 90-minute drive from Baltimore or Washington? Kings Creek is your answer. This freshwater tidal tributary of the Choptank River combines good scenery and a sense of remoteness with easy access. Best of all, you can explore the innards of a marsh from the dry comfort and convenience of a boardwalk through a Nature Conservancy sanctuary. Kings is truly regal among tidewater canoe trips.

The mid–Eastern Shore of Maryland is a place of contrasts. Most of us know only the rampant strip development of Kent Island, Grasonville, and Easton along Route 50. Sailors, fishermen, crabbers, and powerboaters see another side of this area: the huge patrician homes, both old and new, with lots of

Kings Creek

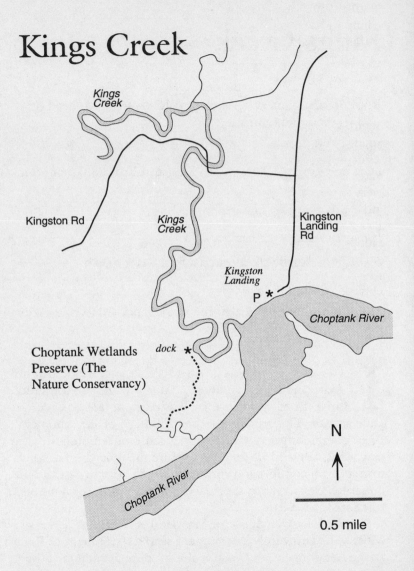

Kings
Creek

Kingston Rd

Kings
Creek

Kingston
Landing
Rd

Kingston
Landing

P *

Choptank River

dock *

Choptank Wetlands
Preserve (The
Nature Conservancy)

N

Choptank River

0.5 mile

ground and private docks and boathouses, that line the Tred Avon, Miles, Wye, and other rivers. But most of the mid-Shore is still heavily agricultural, with fields of corn and soybean rolling to the horizon. Tucked away in an unexpected wrinkle in this pastoral landscape is Kings Creek.

TRIP DESCRIPTION

Begin your trip at Kingston Landing on the wide and sometimes windy Choptank. The road into the landing looks like a residential driveway, but keep going until you hit access to the water. There are no facilities whatsoever here, so arrive with everything you are likely to need. The oyster shell shoreline and rotting pilings speak of older, more commercially active days here at what is now just a sleepy backwater. Put in and paddle downstream (to the right).

The river is quite shallow unless you're in the channel, which here lies well offshore. Low tide reveals a narrow beach littered with the flotsam and jetsam of our throwaway society. The sandy bottom, studded with rocks, is a fine place to run a seine net.

The entrance to Kings Creek appears on the right about 200 yards downriver. The shallows at the mouth of Kings are filled with saltmarsh cordgrass, the single most important species of plant in the Chesapeake Bay estuary. This innocuous-looking grass, one to three feet high, collects and traps water-borne sediments, thereby building up the marsh. Its extensive root system is a buffer against erosion, and cordgrass is planted on suitable eroding shorelines as an alternative to the construction of expensive bulkheading. The presence of cordgrass indicates that the Choptank here is slightly saline; saltmarsh cordgrass requires at least a minimal amount of salt in the water and cannot compete with other plant species in fresh water. As you paddle up Kings Creek, saltmarsh cordgrass quickly disappears as the freshwater influence of runoff begins to dominate.

The creek is about 100 feet wide near its mouth and winds back and forth in broad meanders. A few hunting blinds are the only evidence of human activity, as the marsh vegetation grows up to 10 feet high by midsummer. Shut out from the surrounding world, Kings Creek seems remote and wild. This perception is only enhanced by the flights of ducks and herons that can be observed overhead almost all the time. This little estuary clearly supports a bountiful and diverse population of birds.

For an interesting view of the marsh, poke the nose of your canoe into one of the side channels that appear every so often. Although only 10 feet or less in width, all of them are deep enough to float a canoe, and they extend fingerlike into the depths of the marsh. This is perhaps the best way to appreciate how rich in plant life the marsh really is, and also the best way to see wildlife. Most of these tidal sloughs shelter ducks, usually black ducks or mallards, which explode from the water as you drift quietly around a bend and onto them. Muskrat houses, trails, and slides are also common. Check the mud banks for snakes and frogs, and the vegetation for spiders. The most common birds you're likely to scare up are female red-winged blackbirds (which do not have red wings and are more reclusive than their territorial male harem masters).

As you paddle and pole farther into these tiny streams, they narrow to a width just greater than the beam of the canoe. Vegetation, seed heads, and spiders drop into your boat, and you begin to realize what it's like to live in a marsh. Eventually, there will come a point where a turn is too tight for your canoe, and it will be time to retreat, the bow paddler turning around to become the stern. Obviously, high tide is the time when the greatest progress can be made.

Return to the main portion of Kings Creek and continue paddling upriver. Note an isolated dock on the left, marking the first point at which one bank of the stream abuts solid ground. The dock, some of the adjacent abandoned farmland, and a large tract of marsh are owned by The Nature Conservancy, and the area is known as the Choptank Wetlands Preserve. Disembark, walk through the fringe of trees, turn left, and follow a trail to a signboard erected by the Conservancy. Register and then walk through a gap in the trees. Here begins a boardwalk through the heart of this freshwater marsh, winding for about a half mile to an observation tower. Extraordinarily diverse, the Choptank Wetlands Preserve harbors many common and uncommon plants, and it is a superb outdoor classroom for anyone interested in botany. The best time to visit is late summer, when the greatest number of species of wildflowers are in bloom. However, biting insects can sometimes be a problem.

Marsh birds inhabit this area in high densities. Red-winged blackbirds are very common, and your presence in nesting season may provoke an irate male to a diving attack. Listen for the beautiful, complex song of the marsh wren, a tiny, secretive bird whose nests are sometimes visible from the boardwalk. The marsh wren twists strands of vegetation together to form an enclosed shelter with an opening on one side. Males often build dummy nests in their territory; the ones you see are probably these dummy nests. The nests where the young are raised are far less conspicuous. Ducks like to dabble in the small pools of open water, although what you see is mostly a view of their backsides as they flee. Of course, great blue herons are common sights, and their copious droppings whitewash the boardwalk and observation tower. Ospreys and vultures soar over the distant Choptank. Occasionally, you may see a marsh hawk, or northern harrier, coursing low over the marshes in search of prey. This habit, coupled with a conspicuous white rump patch, easily identifies this efficient predator. Finally, several species of rail inhabit this marsh, but they are almost never seen. The best (and only effective) way to spot rails is to play a tape recording of their call. The territorial males may respond with calls of their own or move toward the sound. However, even competent birders find rails difficult to see until the birds are literally at their feet.

Allow plenty of time for exploring from the boardwalk; you'll find the life of the marsh fascinating. Take the time to think small; look carefully at flowers and plant stems to see associated insects; get down on your belly and watch the surface of the mud alongside a tidal gut as it swells with water; or pretend you're a muskrat viewing the marsh from the

Delmarva fox squirrel

elevation of one foot. Atop the observation tower, soak up the thin winter sun or enjoy the cool summer breezes that keep bugs away. Scan the horizon for birds, or just enjoy the immense quiet of this remote corner of Maryland. We're fortunate to have this creek and this sanctuary available to explore, recreate, and restore the spirit.

Return to your canoe and continue upriver. A thin band of forest separates the creek from surrounding farm fields and houses birds different from those of the marsh. You're likely to see or hear woodpeckers, cardinals, sparrows, and towhees. Kingfishers perch atop dead tree limbs overhanging the river, dashing off with a rattlelike call and a flash of blue color. These small patches of woods are also inhabited by Delmarva fox squirrels, an endangered subspecies confined to four counties on the mid–Eastern Shore. Adult Delmarvas are almost twice as large as the familiar gray squirrels, and this is the easiest way to tell them apart.

About 2.5 miles and many turns from the mouth of the creek, the marsh all but disappears; it is present only as a thin, occasional fringe. Trees reach down to the water's edge on both banks, and Kings Creek becomes a sheltered river incising its way through the landscape. Pass under the Kingston Road bridge and continue upstream. The forested slopes adjacent to the river are beautiful in the fall, as frost turns the leaves various shades of red and yellow.

Several trees near the Kingston Road bridge support small colonies of mistletoe, visible once the branches are bare. This parasitic evergreen plant embeds its roots into the vascular system of the host tree, obtaining water, minerals, and nutrients. Mistletoe is fairly common on the Eastern Shore, especially the more southerly portions. Only rarely is it found within reach of a hand or extended paddle, for it usually occupies the tops of trees.

The creek continues for at least another mile, although it becomes very shallow at low tide. It ends in an impenetrable tangle of branches. Return the way you came. It is theoretically possible to leave a car at the Kingston Road bridge and take out there. However, the landowner has posted the only dry shoreline (even though local fishermen still use and trash it). For this reason, it is a better option to return to the public landing on the Choptank.

DIRECTIONS

From Baltimore or Washington, take Route 50 over the Bay Bridge. Once in the strip development that marks Easton, turn left on well-marked Route 331 (Dover Road). After 2.0 miles, turn left on Black Dog Alley and then make an immediate right onto Kingston Road. Follow this road 3.7 miles to a T intersection. (There is no legal river access where this road crosses Kings Creek on a wooden bridge.) Turn right and follow the road to the water.

Rockfish: An Emerging Success Story in Fisheries Management

The Chesapeake Bay is famous as a food source for many regional culinary delicacies, including oysters (stewed, fried, and on the half shell) and blue crabs (steamed, soft, and in crabcakes). For more than a century, the striped bass (called the rockfish here in the Bay region) was an equal partner in this tasty triumvirate. But no longer; its populations overfished and its reproduction severely depressed by pollution, *Morone saxatilis* was placed on the state of Maryland's list of officially threatened species in 1985, and a moratorium was declared on all fishing. The fate of the rockfish in Chesapeake Bay—its management fraught with controversy generated by competing interests—now hangs in the balance.

The rockfish is a beautiful creature, its silvery scales flashing in the sun, its streamlined body racing through the water. Called striped bass for the seven or eight dark lines running latitudinally from head to tail, these fish can grow up to five feet in length and weigh nearly 100 pounds. Rockfish spawn in the fresh to slightly brackish tributaries of Chesapeake Bay but spend most of their adult life at sea just off the Atlantic coast, mostly between North Carolina and Maine. Although some fish spawn elsewhere (most notably in the Hudson River), about 90 percent of all rockfish captured in the 1970s were born in Chesapeake Bay. Females first reproduce at about six to eight years of age, when they are about three feet long. Older, larger females are even more prolific; a robust 15-year-old may lay three million eggs.

As with most fish, mortality is heavy between the time eggs are laid and adulthood at one year. Predation and the vagaries of early spring weather all take their toll. But something has changed in Chesapeake Bay since the mid-1970s, something that has resulted in very few young rockfish reaching adulthood. Each year since 1954, scientists have conducted a young-of-the-year population census at prescribed locations around the Bay to measure the survivorship of the spring's hatch. For 20 years, the survey yielded census data that had their ups and downs, but there were never two bad years in a row, and a good year would reliably interrupt a run of several mediocre years without exception. But from 1975 to 1988, the census was well below the previous average, interrupted only in 1978 and 1982 by mediocre survivorship. Correspondingly, the commercial catch declined from a high in 1973 of 14.7 million pounds to 400,000 pounds in 1987. What could have caused this drastic decline in a once abundant and very lucrative fishery?

Many fishermen and some scientists at first believed that rockfish declines were part of a natural cycle or a series of random fluctuations and that the population would soon recover. Once it became clear that the decline was real and that recovery was unlikely without action, such factors as acid rain, agricultural herbicide runoff, release of toxic metals from sediments, and the lingering effects of Hurricane Agnes (1972) on egg, larval, and immature stages were all invoked. But a survey of the breeding stock in the early 1980s demonstrated that almost no females less than 11 years old were present. Clearly overfishing was responsible for this severe reduction in the breeding stock. If the rockfish was to be saved and the fishery allowed to recover, drastic steps would be needed to conserve all of the remaining breeding stock.

A moratorium on striped bass fishing, both recreational and commercial, was declared in Maryland and Delaware in 1985 and in Virginia in 1989. Other states along the coast placed major restrictions placed on catches. Fishermen howled in protest, but fishery managers, scientists, and government officials rightly held firm, their positions clearly supported by the data. Their actions may have been taken just in time to avert disaster. Fortunately, the 1989 young-of-the-year census reached its second highest level ever, thanks almost exclusively to incredibly successful survivorship in the Choptank River. The 1993 data were equally encouraging, and they came from a number of tributaries. When these fish reach maturity after 1995, a more stable breeding population composed of fish of several different age classes should be at hand.

Today, a limited catch of rockfish in Chesapeake Bay is allowed. The fishery is monitored closely, and if too many fish are taken the season is closed. Scientists now have a better understanding of how to manage the fishery so as to preserve the species in reasonable numbers, although harvests such as those of the past may never be seen again. Indeed, management of rockfish in Chesapeake Bay is one of the few success stories in our efforts to restore the living resources of a damaged estuary. The lessons learned from this long-standing, divisive, and bitter debate can provide us with the perspective and precedent for taking management action in future controversies based on sound science rather than unenlightened self-interest and political pressure. ⤴

Tuckahoe Creek

River Section: Section 1: Crouse Mill Dam upstream to head
of navigation and return
Section 2: Crouse Mill Dam downstream to
Hillsboro

County: Queen Anne, Caroline

Distance: Section 1: About 5 miles
Section 2: 5.2 miles

Difficulty: Section 1: Flatwater
Section 2: Flat, flowing water; tidal flatwater

Hazards: Section 1: None
Section 2: Trees down in river, poison ivy

Highlights: Section 1: Nontidal freshwater marsh, riparian
forest
Section 2: Riparian forest

Nearby Canoe Rental: Tuckahoe State Park, (410) 634-2810

More Information: Tuckahoe State Park, (410) 634-2810

AMONG THE EARLIEST signs of a Chesapeake springtime is the migration of anadromous fish from the ocean to their breeding grounds in narrow headwater streams. All around the Chesapeake Bay drainage, fish crowd the shallows, congregating at rapids, dams, and other obstructions. Seining, dipnetting, and fishing for shad, white perch, yellow perch, rockfish, and river herring at these places is a Chesapeake tradition, still another way for Marylanders to connect with the cycles of the natural world. The numbers of

Tuckahoe Creek

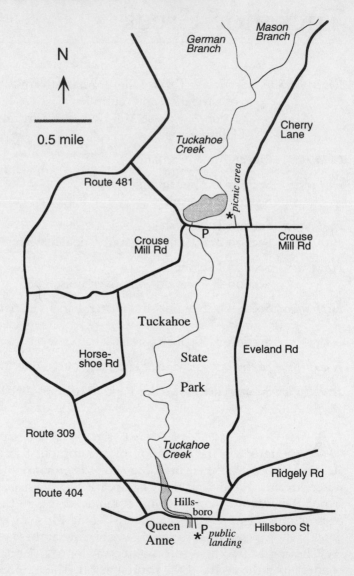

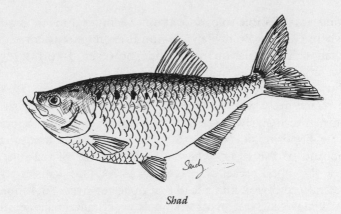

Shad

all these fish species have declined precipitously in the last 30 years, but even today a few creeks and rivers play host to ever-dwindling stocks. Tuckahoe Creek, forming the border between Queen Anne and Caroline counties, is one of the best of these places. Blessed by good water quality and protected by wooded buffers over much of its nontidal length, the Tuckahoe is a wild and beautiful river.

Canoeing the Tuckahoe is a fine way to spend the day in almost any season. Set amid a vast expanse of the mid-Shore's mostly agricultural landscape, it is a haven for wildlife. Canoeists can choose to paddle a narrow, intimate stream, flowing quickly through forested bottomlands to tidewater, or explore a drowned swamp forest where sunlight has created a rich and diverse open marsh. And despite its close proximity to the metropolitan areas to the west, Tuckahoe Creek is still mostly undiscovered.

TRIP DESCRIPTION

Crouse Mill Lake Upriver

This segment of Tuckahoe Creek is the section of choice if you do not want to run a vehicle shuttle or in the unusual event that section 2 is too low owing to extended drought. As of this writing, it is possible to paddle about 2.5 miles upriver, almost to where German Branch and Mason Branch unite to form the Tuckahoe. This situation may change, however, if storms bring down large trees that span the creek.

Put your canoe in the water at the Tuckahoe State Park's lake picnic area, where there are wheelchair-accessible bathrooms. Alternatively, there is a launch ramp with no facilities on the opposite side of the 60-acre lake. Paddle across the pond and to the right, where a wide expanse of marshland forms the upper reaches of the lake. Explore gaps in the vegetation until you find a lead that opens upriver. Tuckahoe's inlet is mazelike, but many channels eventually coalesce into the main creek.

In late fall and winter, the lake is home to large flocks of ducks and geese. Dabbling ducks like mallards, pintails, and widgeons feed on vegetation in the shallow waters; geese loaf here in safety before flying out into the nearby agricultural fields to feed. Even in summer, a few families of mallards and geese hang out in the little millpond, attracted by the open water and plentiful food. Numbers of Canada geese nesting in Maryland rather than on their traditional Arctic nesting grounds have been on the increase. Although a few of the birds may have been wounded by hunters and thus may be unable to make the journey north, others have no such obvious reason for forgoing the rigors of migration.

Within a few bends of the stream is a beaver lodge, constructed mostly of sticks. It is quite large, about eight feet in diameter and almost four feet in height above the waterline. Beaver are now common in most streams in Maryland after being reintroduced by the Department of Natural Resources. In areas such as this one, where there is no significant flow to the river, beaver can exist happily without building dams.

This section of the marsh once had a number of trees, but construction of the dam and lake inundated the roots and killed them. Thus, there are many dead snags, which form lookouts for kingfishers, herons, red-winged blackbirds, kingbirds, and hawks. Woodpeckers have drilled holes in some of them for nest cavities, which are also utilized by starlings.

Other snags look almost alive, as tangles of poison ivy vines have climbed them to great heights. At water level, a number of hammocks of vegetation have organized around old stumps; swamp rose, with pink flowers, and water hemlock, with clusters of white umbrella-shaped flowers, predominate here. Along the edges of the creek, water dock and lizard's tail form the herbaceous layer. Spatterdock, pickerelweed, and cattail, the predominant vegetation of most freshwater marshes on the Eastern Shore, are present but are of lesser importance, probably because this marsh is nontidal.

Ater several hundred yards of paddling, more trees begin to encroach on the marsh, and the creek becomes partially shaded. Red maples are the dominant tree, although there are plenty of specimens of green ash and black gum. Silky dogwood, a water-loving shrub with leaves that look like the more familiar dogwood of lawns and forest, lines the banks. Although the flowers are small and clustered rather than singular, each has the same four petals. Bluish berries form later in the season. Wood ducks and prothonotary warblers like these forested swamps.

The creek soon narrows to about 20 feet in width and becomes shallower. In a few places, it may become so shallow that your canoe scrapes the bottom, but continue onward since the stream soon deepens. Aquatic grasses of several types line the riverbed, indicating good water quality. Bottom sediments are gravel and coarse sand rather than mud; this well-oxygenated substrate is favored as spawning beds and nest sites by anadromous fish.

After almost two miles of upriver travel, several concrete steps appear on the right. These lead to the campfire area of the state park's youth group campground. Another half mile or so of paddling brings you to a tree spanning the entire river and blocking further passage. Although you can portage it, strainers appear ever more frequently upriver, making this a good place to turn around.

Crouse Mill Dam to Hillsboro

This 5.2-mile section of the Tuckahoe begins at the foot of Crouse Mill Dam, just downstream from section 1. It is remarkably different in character, flowing tight and twisty through a deep swamp forest and then emerging into the sunlight at tidewater. The Tuckahoe is runnable all year long, although the water is low in dry summers and it may then be necessary to carry your canoe over a few shallow gravel beds and submerged logs. The rangers of Tuckahoe State Park periodically cut out trees that fall across the creek; judging by all the work they've done in the past, this little stream would be an impassable tangle if not for their efforts.

Unload your canoe where the creek passes under Crouse Mill Road. There is roadside parking here but no other facilities. This is an extraordinarily popular place for fishing in late March through mid-April, when anadromous fish migrating to their upstream spawning grounds cluster at the base of the dam's fish ladder. Shad, perch, and river herring all use the upper Tuckahoe; to see their silvery forms dashing upriver over gravel beds is one of the classic harbingers of a Chesapeake spring.

The Tuckahoe flows off into the swamp at a slow but steady pace; only at high water could the current cause problems. Only a few yards wide, the creek twists around sharp turns and under a number of overhanging tree limbs and fallen trunks. Every one is festooned with a dense covering of poison ivy, without a doubt the most dangerous feature of this trip. Poison ivy is easily identified by its leaves in groups of three; in winter, avoid touching any hairy vine. Vireos, wood thrushes, cardinals, and other woodland songbirds abound in the adjacent forested bottomlands. Hawks and owls nest in these riparian greenways, flying out to feed in nearby abandoned fields. In the summer, butterflies brighten the gloom as they flit through the understory, and dragonflies patrol the river. Mosquitoes, deerflies, and horseflies are common, especially in late spring and early summer, so bring along insect repellent.

After about two miles of narrow river, the stream runs up against a high, steep cliff bank, scoured smooth and free of vegetation, on the right-hand side of the river. This marks the entrance to a wider, deeper pool section of the river. Turtles, including huge old snappers, abound in this area. Within a few hundred yards, the river reverts to its narrower, more winding character, persisting like this for about another mile and a half.

A unique aspect of the Tuckahoe is its river bottom. Large portions of it are covered with small black stones, rounded and water worn, larger than gravel but not big enough to be called rocks. Such stones are unusual on the coastal plain, where unconsolidated sands and gravels are the rule. High water probably flushes away the gravel and sand but is not strong enough to move the rocks, leaving portions of the river bottom with a cobbled effect. Freshwater clams also abound on the Tuckahoe. Small shells, less than an inch in diameter, accumulate in the eddys, but large empty shells up to three inches long litter the river bottom in other places. The shells, with their animals long dead, are testimony to a flourishing mussel community in the Tuckahoe's riverbed.

The Tuckahoe eventually reaches tidewater, where the river noticeably widens, from 20 feet to 20 yards. However, this size is still relatively intimate for a tidal stream, and so the creek remains a pleasant paddle. With sunlight hitting the river, the vegetation changes; shrubs and small trees like sweetbay magnolia, buttonbush, and alder line the banks; a few pocket marshes feature wild rice and wild iris. In the last quarter mile, the Tuckahoe passes under two abandoned railroad bridges and two road bridges. Take out at the public landing at Hillsboro.

DIRECTIONS

From Baltimore or Washington, cross the Bay Bridge and continue on Route 50 south. Turn left onto Route 404, and continue east for 6.8 miles. Turn left on Ridgely Road, at a stoplight. Go 100 yards and turn left on Eveland Road. Go to the end, and turn left on Crouse Mill Road. Follow this road to the dam and lake. To reach Hillsboro, return to Ridgely Road but continue across Route 404. The road ends within 150 yards, in Hillsboro. Turn right; the landing is on the left just before crossing the bridge.

OTHER OUTDOOR RECREATIONAL OPPORTUNITIES NEARBY

Watts Creek, in Martinak State Park, is located about 10 miles east of Tuckahoe Creek. It is described beginning on page 400 in this book.

Acidic Deposition in Maryland

Few people are aware that Maryland has some of the most acidic rainfall in the United States. The average pH of rain in Maryland is about 4.3, approximately 12 times more acidic than the typical pH of 5.6 for unpolluted rain. In addition to acid rain, acidic solids from power plants and automobile exhausts also fall on Maryland, and all three together are referred to as acidic deposition. This process has some important effects on aquatic organisms across the state.

The source of much of this acidic deposition lies outside Maryland. More than 50 percent of acidic deposition in the mid-Atlantic states comes from just 50 coal-burning power plants located to our west and concentrated along the Ohio River. Nevertheless, we residents are not without blame; the failure of Baltimore and Washington to meet federal air quality standards is primarily due to the level of pollution from automobile exhaust.

In some areas of Europe, acidic deposition has affected the trees growing in remote forests. Maryland's forests have not yet been significantly affected as far as we know; most of the damage has been to aquatic ecosystems, especially small streams. About one-third of all headwater streams in Maryland, more than 2,600 miles of such streams, are either sensitive to potential acidification or already acidic. Most of these creeks are located on the Appalachian Plateau in Garrett County or on the coastal plain surrounding Chesapeake Bay.

What makes a stream susceptible to damage by acidic deposition? In addition to the pH of rainfall and the amount of dry acids deposited, the single most important factor is the buffering capacity of the soils through which the water flows. The limestone-containing soils of the ridge and valley province, for example, have almost unlimited buffering capacity and can neutralize precipitation of any acidity.

Stream organisms exhibit differing levels of sensitivity. Mussels and some aquatic insect larvae like stonefly larvae need water of pH 6 or better. Brown trout and some salamanders die off at pHs less than 5. Scavenging beetles like water boatmen and whirligig beetles can persist down to pH 3.5, although they may be indirectly affected by damage to the food chain. In western Maryland streams, the presence of a diverse fish community is correlated with water pH and buffering capacity.

In coastal plain streams, ephemeral pulses of acidic water, rather than a continuous low pH, have had biological effects. During the winter, acid deposition can become trapped in snow. When the snow melts suddenly, the solubilized acidity is released as a sudden pulse. If this occurs late in the winter, the acid spike may reach the spawning grounds of anadromous fish like shad, rockfish, blueback herring, and white perch. Embryos of these fish have been shown to be killed by such pulses of acidity, and the decline of these species is due at least in part to such acid effects. ⬅

Nanjemoy Creek

River Section: Route 6 to Friendship Landing

County: Charles

Distance: 6.0 miles

Difficulty: Tidal flatwater

Hazards: Windy weather possible

Highlights: Freshwater marsh, forested borders

Nearby Canoe Rental: None

More Information: None

CANOEING THE TIDAL rivers and creeks of the Chesapeake Bay drainage can be a surprising delight. Most people look out over a vast expanse of marsh or into a tangle of fallen trees in a wooded swamp and think one thing: bugs. For the most part, they're wrong. Oh, there are plenty of insects out there, but relatively few are of the biting variety. Only in the salt marshes of the lower Eastern Shore are bugs a major problem, and then only on dead calm days near the vegetation. Freshwater marshes and swamps have much, much smaller populations of mosquitoes, and they are most bothersome in late spring, with their numbers declining significantly with the onset of hot, dry weather. Furthermore, such insects seem to avoid the cooler air over water, so that the route you, as a canoeist, want to take will be the least buggy. So don't let an irrational fear of insects keep you from the joys of paddling the dense green jungles of our freshwater swamps and marshes.

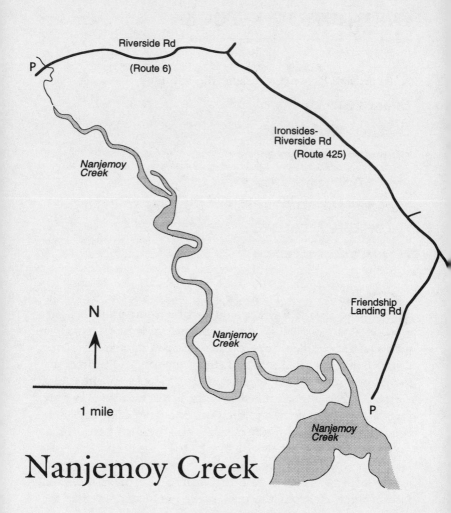

Nanjemoy Creek

Nanjemoy Creek, in Charles County, is just such a place. From the road bridge at the put-in, only a narrow dark stream—choked with submerged logs, half-fallen trees, and twisted vines—is visible. It appears to be at the limit of small-stream navigability, and you wonder what sort of boot camp experiences lie ahead. In fact, this closed-in character persists for only a short distance downstream, and all of Nanjemoy can be paddled without much trouble at all. So go! You'll be pleasantly surprised by the many and diverse joys of canoeing a marsh or swamp.

TRIP DESCRIPTION

The trip begins within a few yards of tidewater, above which passage is not possible. Park where Route 6 crosses Nanjemoy Creek; there is room for about six cars, but there are no facilities. The put-in is underneath the road bridge, and at low tide the bank is several feet above water level, making entry to your canoe difficult.

For the first quarter mile, Nanjemoy runs narrow and twisty through the wooded bottomland, within sound of the road. The mixed hardwood forest arches overhead, making a complete canopy, sunlight filtering down through small openings. The water is shallow, only a few inches deep, with a sandy bottom. There may be one or two downed trees requiring a portage, so the shallow water is a blessing. Very soon, however, the stream widens to 20 feet or so, and strainers no longer pose a problem.

This wooded swamp is alive with birdlife. In addition to the usual swampland species, a pair of bald eagles are frequently seen here. A heron rookery is nearby, so great blue herons are commonly seen, especially during nesting season (March and April). Your best chance of seeing birds is to arrive early in the morning, before anyone else is on the creek.

As Nanjemoy widens, trees become less dense and are replaced by the herbaceous vegetation that characterizes a marsh. In another half mile, the marsh becomes quite wide, and the creek begins to wind in wide turns that abut wooded shoreline only at the outside edges. These attractive uplands, composed mostly of pine and oak, always remain in sight to form a pleasant border to the marshland vista.

Nanjemoy is not wilderness. It is very popular with bass fishermen on weekends, enjoying a reputation as one of the finest tributaries of the Potomac for fishing. For this reason, a weekday visit yields the most enjoyable paddling. The fishermen are all friendly, so if you don't mind the occasional roar of a motorboat, it will still be a pleasant weekend trip.

Nanjemoy Creek averages about 100 feet in width for much of its course, maintaining its narrow character for quite a long way. Only in the last turn does it increase in size, before emerging at Friendship Landing into a wide estuary. There are a few houses occupying patches of high ground, most of them near the end of the trip. Take out at the landing, where there is parking for about 20 cars but no other facilities.

DIRECTIONS

From the Capital Beltway, take Route 210, Indian Head Highway, south. After crossing into Charles County, turn left on Route 225. After crossing Mattawoman Creek, turn right on Route 224 and then make a left within about 100 yards onto Route 425. Route 425 dead-ends at Route 6; turn left and drive just over a mile to the bridge crossing at Nanjemoy Creek. To reach the take-out, retrace your steps up Route 6 to Route 425, and up Route 425 to Friendship Landing Road. As of this writing, Friendship Landing Road has no sign, but it is the only large unmarked road in the area.

Great Blue Herons

Of the more than 300 species of birds native to Maryland, none is more familiar than the great blue heron. This large wading bird of marshes and rivers is found in every season in every obscure corner of the state. Indeed, the noted environmental writer Tom Horton advocates replacing the northern oriole with the far more common and easily observed great blue heron as our official state bird. Although awkward and far from

Great blue heron

handsome, these ungainly birds are somehow undefinably endearing.

Great blue herons stand about four feet tall and have a six-foot wingspan but weigh only five to eight pounds. In large measure, their light weight is due to bones that are hollow, to allow a lighter payload during flight. Herons (and other birds) sometimes have trouble getting airborne after a particularly large meal. Spindly legs and a long thin neck add to the elongate image.

Great blue herons are predators, eating small fish, snakes, frogs, aquatic insects, and soft crabs captured from shallow water and muddy river banks. Far less commonly, and typically during very cold weather or just by accident, herons will take small mammals and insects from adjacent fields. Great blues usually stand immobile, waiting for prey to pass, but they may also stalk slowly through shallow water.

Although herons are very familiar to people, they conduct their breeding activities in private, and relatively few people have visited a breeding colony. Such colonies are scattered around tributaries of the Chesapeake Bay, where food is plentiful, often with both tidal and nontidal waters nearby. Perhaps the best-known breeding colony is on the headwaters of Nanjemoy Creek in Charles County. There are almost a thousand nests here, and birds arrive reliably within a few days of Valentine's Day. Males claim old nests, the dominant individuals getting the most stable ones. At first, they may fight off the amorous advances of females, but eventually a pair bond is formed. Mating occurs, between one and six (typically three) eggs are laid, and both parents incubate for about 28 days.

When the eggs hatch, the heronry becomes a chaotic place. The young must be fed regularly, and as soon as one parent gets back to the nest with a full crop, the other leaves. Because nests are close together and herons landing are such large and clumsy animals, territories are vigorously defended with posturing and squawking. Feeding is by regurgitation. Young herons fledge after about two months on the nest. They disperse but are sometimes accompanied and fed by a parent as they learn to hunt. Despite this practice, mortality is high during this "early adolescent" stage.

The period between hatching and fledging is a time when the colony is easily disturbed by visitation. The young sometimes become agitated; if they fall from the nest, they invariably die. Fortunately for the survival of the birds, the ground below a heronry reeks with detritus from the colony: rotting fish parts, regurgitant, huge quantities of droppings, and the occasional dead heron. The unique bouquet of this gumbo tends to keep humans at a distance. In fact, trees that support heron nests eventually die of this guanotrophy; the lifetime of a heronry is about 30 years.

Unlike much of our native fauna, great blue herons are doing well despite an ever-expanding human population. Only disruptions to the heronry, by people or by beavers that girdle and kill trees, are significant threats. Hawks, owls, and eagles rarely bother the nests or adults. Given their adaptibility, resilience, and cosmopolitan distribution, great blue herons should remain a well-loved and commonplace part of Maryland's natural landscape for some time to come. ⤜

Mataponi Creek

River Section: Selbys Landing to head of navigation and return

County: Prince Georges

Distance: About 3 miles

Difficulty: Tidal flatwater

Hazards: Windy weather possible near the beginning

Highlights: Freshwater marsh, forested uplands

Nearby Canoe Rental: Patuxent River Park, (301) 627-6074

More Information: Patuxent River Park, (301) 627-6074

THE CHESAPEAKE BAY is an endangered estuary, and there's probably not a citizen of Maryland who isn't aware of it. From nutrient enrichment to toxic chemicals to habitat loss, each new scientific study seems to send a fresh message of gloom and doom. Oftentimes, however, we forget that the Chesapeake is still a vital and enchanting place. Mataponi Creek, a small tributary of the Patuxent River, is evidence that such special places still exist, and that they can be preserved if we have the foresight, leadership, and force of will to do so. Mataponi is a symbol of all that is right with the Chesapeake.

Mataponi Creek is a short, tidal arm of the Patuxent, located about halfway up the watershed in lower Prince Georges County. It is protected for much of its length by Patuxent River Park (managed by the Maryland-National Capital Park and Planning Commission) and Merkle Wildlife Sanctuary

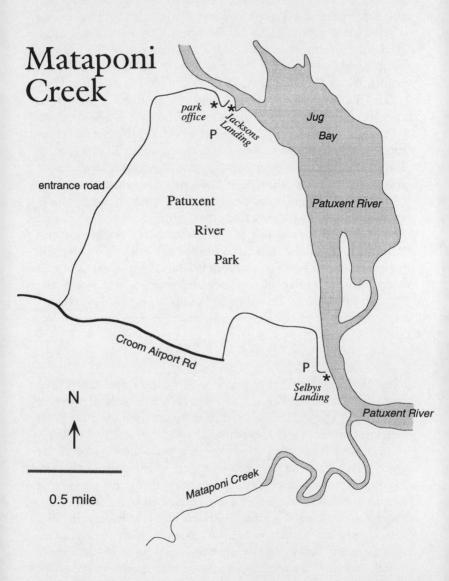

Mataponi Creek

park office

Jacksons Landing

P

Jug Bay

Patuxent River

entrance road

Patuxent

River

Park

Croom Airport Rd

P

Selbys Landing

Patuxent River

N

0.5 mile

Mataponi Creek

(managed by the Maryland Department of Natural Resources). Land for Patuxent River Park was acquired in the 1960s when this portion of the county was still very rural. Each year sees more houses built and more strip developments established, so that the area is swiftly becoming a bedroom community of Washington, D.C.

The Patuxent River is the only major river in Maryland contained entirely within the state. As such, it is a microcosm of the Chesapeake Bay. Its headwaters drain the fast-developing Baltimore-Washington corridor around Columbia in Howard County. Two major reservoirs check its flow almost as soon as it is wide enough to become canoeable. Below the dams, the Patuxent's waters enter the coastal plain, where tangled swamps with downed trees, infrequent water releases from upstream dams, and restricted lands at Fort Meade and the Patuxent Wildlife Research Center all conspire to keep the paddler at bay. The river becomes tidal near the town of Upper Marlboro and is flanked by wide marshes. At this point, the Patuxent becomes interesting and easily accessible by canoe.

TRIP DESCRIPTION

This trip begins with a required visit to the office and visitor center of Patuxent River Park, where a use permit must be purchased. The naturalists on duty here are friendly and a great source of information regarding almost anything you're likely to see. An observation tower gives a panoramic view of the river, which has widened into extensive marshes and is known as Jug Bay. Paddlers who rent canoes from the park must launch at the boat ramp just down the hill from the park office, known as Jacksons Landing. However, if you have your own canoe, a better choice is Selbys Landing, located two miles downstream. Selbys opens up the more intimate Mataponi Creek and shortens the trip to a more manageable distance for novice canoers. Of course, if you have all day and really want to stretch it out, launch at Jacksons Landing here by the park office. This description is based on a launch from Selbys Landing.

(To reach Selbys Landing, leave the park the way you came in. At the park entrance on Croom Airport Road, turn left and drive about two miles to the site of the old airport, now a group camp for Patuxent River Park. Turn left again, and follow the road to the parking lot for Selbys Landing. There are parking places for about 40 cars and a portable outhouse here, but no other facilities.)

Begin your paddling trip from the boat ramp, heading downstream (to the right). Ahead is the wide expanse of Jug Bay. This is a good place to look for the large, conspicuous birds of the Patuxent: turkey vulture, osprey, red-tailed hawk, great blue heron, and several types of gulls. Canoeists paddling in Jug Bay are subject to winds on blustery days that can make paddling difficult. Fortunately, you'll be in this exposed area for only about a quarter of a mile.

About 300 yards below Selbys Landing, turn right into the mouth of Mataponi Creek. If the tide is going out, its force can be quite strong here at the junction of Mataponi and the main Patuxent. Within a few hundred yards upstream, however, the tidal bore seems to slacken off, and paddling becomes much easier.

In summer, tall ranks of vegetation close in on both shores of Mataponi. Beyond the front ranks of lotuslike spatterdock, the common reed (also frequently known by its Latin generic name, *Phragmites*) dominates the right bank. A plant of world-wide distribution, common reed spreads aggressively, especially on sites where the marsh has been disturbed. Reaching heights of up to 12 feet, it has low value as a food source for wildlife but is effective in controlling erosion. The left bank, in contrast, is dominated by wild rice, a high-value food source for many resident and migratory marsh birds. Unfortunately, these birds typically strip the plants of rice grains while they are still immature, so that we humans have to buy our wild rice at the grocery store. The feathery inflorescence, or flower spike, rises high above the rest of the vegetation.

Wild rice

As you paddle farther up Mataponi, two species of flowers that are extraordinarily pretty appear in large numbers. In July, swamp rose mallow, a hibiscuslike flower with huge white petals, studs the marsh. Relatives of the more famous marshmallow, from which colonists extracted the mucilaginous treat of the same name, swamp rose mallows attract hordes of pollinating insects. The fruit, a dried capsule, extrudes brown, shiny seeds. By late summer, the swamp rose mallows have died back, and tickseed sunflower takes over. Growing in rows just behind the spatterdock, the brilliant yellow flowers of *Bidens laevis* make a spectacular show in September.

A half mile or so up Mataponi is a small landing with picnic tables, a portable toilet, and plenty of space. A dirt road leads to an upland area, part of the Merkle Wildlife Sanctuary, that features lots of summer and fall wildflowers. The scrubby habitat here is also well suited for birding.

Continued paddling upriver brings the shoreline trees closer as the marsh narrows. Several interesting marshland shrubs grow at edges where the junction between water and land is sharply defined. Arrowwood has elliptical, widely toothed leaves with unusual blue fruits. Alders have similarly shaped leaves but with flowers that look like small cones. Male flowers are long and thin, giving off a yellow pollen as early as February. Female flowers harden into rounded, woody cones that resemble tiny editions of those on pine trees. Buttonbush has striking white flowers in fuzzy, ball-shaped heads. All are common along the wooded banks of Mataponi.

As the creek narrows, a wooden road bridge crosses it, connecting the two sanctuaries. Just beyond the bridge, in the middle of the marsh, is a nesting platform for osprey. Such platforms have helped reestablish this large, graceful fish hawk. Decimated by the pesticide DDT in the 1950s and 1960s, populations have rebounded to the point that ospreys are now common in the Chesapeake region.

Within a hundred yards of the upstream side of the bridge, Mataponi narrows quickly to less than a canoe width. Strangely, the sound of rapids is soon heard on this, a tidal creek. The final bend yields the solution to this conundrum: beavers have dammed the stream. At low tide, the pile of logs and branches is over a foot high.

The beaver dam has raised the water table here in the marsh, flooding areas that previously were wet only occasionally. The result is that all the trees sparsely dotting the marsh have died, leaving only skeletal remains outlined against the sky. The dead trees, in turn, have attracted new inhabitants: in 1990, a pair of bald eagles constructed a huge, seemingly tumbledown nest atop one of the trees. A sighting of one of these magnificent birds is a never-to-be-forgotten experience.

Most paddlers turn around here, but anyone willing to brave a portage through knee-deep mud and thorny vegetation can squeeze out a few hundred feet more of paddling. When you can't go any farther, return to Selbys Landing via the same route.

DIRECTIONS

From Washington or Baltimore, take Route 3/301 south beyond Upper Marlboro. Turn left onto the well-marked Croom Station Road. Go 1.6 miles and turn left onto Croom Road. After another 1.6 miles, turn left again onto Croom Airport Road. Go 2.1 miles to the park entrance, passing through (not surprisingly) Croom, Maryland. The park office is another 1.6 miles ahead, at the end of the road.

OTHER OUTDOOR RECREATIONAL OPPORTUNITIES NEARBY

Several walking and hiking trails exist in Patuxent River Park. Perhaps the nicest is the Black Walnut Nature Study Trail, originating from the park office. Here a boardwalk leads through the heart of some small wetlands, giving you a dry-shod and close-up view of what you had seen previously from the canoe. This boardwalk trail is wheelchair accessible. For the more serious hiker, a network of trails honeycombs the 600-acre park. Organized groups can make reservations for camping, canoe rental, or a natural history tour in a motor-driven pontoon boat.

Oysters

What comes to mind at the mention of the words *Chesapeake Bay?* Crabs? Sailing? The Orioles? Fishing? The Naval Academy? Watermen? For decades, the Chesapeake was also synonymous with oysters, those tasty bivalves that were a staple of colonial diets and a gourmet's delight in the first half of this century. But now, fully grown oysters are uncommon. The story of the oyster's decline is also the story of Chesapeake Bay's twilight, for the two are necessarily but unfortunately linked.

At the time Captain John Smith sailed into Chesapeake Bay, oysters were an incredibly abundant natural resource. Oyster bars were hazards to navigation and covered immense portions of the Bay's bottom. Prehistoric middens have yielded shells up to 10 inches long, and early travelers reported that they had to cut oyster meats in half to eat them. Oysters are filter feeders, and by one estimate the oyster population of Chesapeake Bay at that time could filter (and thus purify) all the water in the Bay in less than a week. In contrast, the oysters remaining today would require almost a year to perform the same task. As of this writing, there have been suggestions for a complete ban on oyster harvesting in order to allow the resource to recover. This proposal is almost irrelevant, however; harvests are by now so low that many watermen cannot even cover the cost of leaving the harbor.

Oysters are in decline in Chesapeake Bay for three reasons: overharvesting, pollution, and disease. For almost a century, watermen strip-mined the Bay's shallows for oysters. Harvests reached a peak in 1884 at almost 15 million bushels and slowly declined thereafter to a steady-state harvest of about 2 million bushels annually between 1935 and 1980. Since then, harvests have continued to decline, falling to about 120,000 bushels in 1993. The same kinds of pollution problems that plague other organisms in Chesapeake Bay have an even greater impact on oysters. Nutrient enrichment that results in oxygen-depleted water spells trouble for immobile oysters, as do increased sediment loads, which cover suitable habitat. Finally, levels of two oyster parasites, MSX and Dermo, have worsened of late and forestalled any possible recovery. MSX, a protozoan, and Dermo, a fungus, both prevent oysters from spawning. These parasites prefer saline waters, and only in the more northerly, mid-Bay portions of the oyster's range are the molluscs unaffected.

The decline of oysters has had a ripple effect on the ecology of Chesapeake Bay because oysters are keystone species. Reduced populations of oysters mean that algal blooms become larger and last longer, since oysters feed on these phytoplankton. Correspondingly, the amount of oxygen-depleted water has increased, a development that has affected fish, crabs, and other species. Oyster bars are distinct habitats in Chesapeake Bay, harboring a rich assemblage of other species dependent on the bar for shelter and food; but by now untrammeled oyster bars are almost nonexistent. Finally, watermen can no longer extract a sustainable harvest from what is left of oyster populations, making these colorful Maryland citizens what has been called "the Bay's most endangered species." The long-term outlook for Chesapeake oysters is poor; only their prolific rate of reproduction and resilience to environmental insult give any cause at all for hope. ↢

Gunpowder Delta

River Section: Mariner Point Park and environs (loop)

Counties: Harford and Baltimore

Distance: About 6.5 miles, depending on route taken

Difficulty: Tidal flatwater

Hazards: Windy weather possible, powerboat traffic

Highlights: Freshwater marsh, forested borders

Nearby Canoe Rental: None

More Information: Gunpowder State Park, (410) 592-2897.
  Mariner Point Park, (410) 679-1867

IN THE SEVENTEENTH century, central Maryland was a very different place. Farms carved from the primeval forest grew tobacco, the colonies' single most important crop. The fields were tended by slaves and indentured servants. Roads served only to link backcountry farms to tidewater ports, where hogsheads of tobacco were shipped to the Old World. The colonies were united by their waterways, and nowhere was this more true than in Maryland. The ports of Joppatowne and Elkridge were preeminent; Baltimore was still a small town, growing in importance only slowly.

Today, the focus of life has changed in many ways. Agriculture is only a minor part of the economy, especially in the heavily populated central part of Maryland. Road and air transportation bring people, goods, and services to other parts of the state. The old colonial ports are no longer bustling

Gunpowder Delta

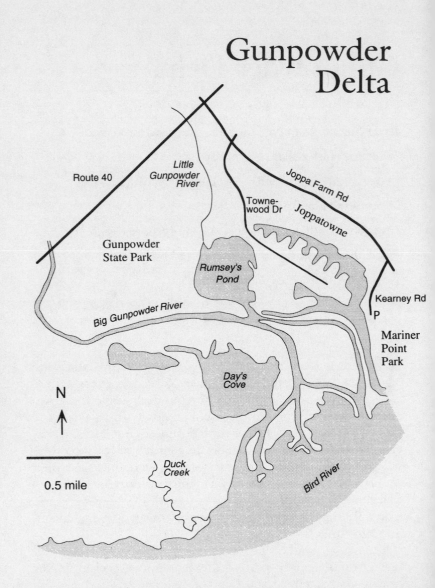

Route 40

Little Gunpowder River

Joppa Farm Rd

Towne-wood Dr

Joppatowne

Gunpowder State Park

Rumsey's Pond

Kearney Rd

P

Big Gunpowder River

Mariner Point Park

Day's Cove

N

Duck Creek

Bird River

0.5 mile

centers of commerce; indeed, Elkridge and Joppatowne are no longer served by ships.

No trace of colonial Joppatowne exists; it is now a quiet residential community of neatly kept homes in the best suburban tradition. The reason for this change? The tidal Gunpowder River, once serving Joppatowne's 12-foot-draft ships, has silted in. Extensive islands of sediment, carried downriver by floods and storm events, dot what was once the deep, open water of the Gunpowder Delta. Marshes and wooded swamps cover the islands.

The sources of all this sediment are the two Gunpowder rivers, the Big and Little, which converge here. The rivers drain much of the northern and eastern parts of Baltimore County and the western part of Harford County; development has made them more susceptible to flooding and the accompanying loss of topsoil. This is not just a recent development; accounts of siltation reach back to the eighteenth century. Indeed, with much of the Big Gunpowder watershed held back by dams, the river's contribution to sediment inflows has been greatly reduced since their construction in the first part of the twentieth century.

All this is good news to canoers looking for a place to paddle. The Gunpowder Delta is nearby, especially for Baltimore-area boaters, and surprisingly pristine. The tangle of waterways offers many opportunities for exploration. Although powerboaters, especially fishermen, use these same rivers, there are a few shallow areas where you can experience a sense of isolation and remoteness unusual for a paddling trip so close to civilization.

TRIP DESCRIPTION

Put your canoe into the water at Mariner Point Park in Joppatowne. There is plenty of parking, and trash cans, outhouses, and a picnic pavilion are available at the park. Paddle downstream (to the left). This body of water is a dredged arm of the river, which provides access to backyard boatslips for upstream residents. For this reason, motorboat traffic is heavy on this part of the river. However, both the traffic and the scenery improve quickly.

The canal dumps you out onto the wide expanses of Bird River. Turn right, staying close to a line of marshes. Continue paddling across the face of these marshes, keeping open water and the Amtrak line on your left. After more than a mile, you'll reach the forested mainland.

Just a few hundred yards farther along you will come to an opening in the curtain of marsh grasses. This is Duck Creek, so obscure and tiny that it is not even named on topographic maps. Despite its anonymous nature, Duck Creek is a little aquatic gem. As it winds its way deep into the freshwater marsh for about half a mile, you'll be likely to scare up herons, red-winged blackbirds, muskrats, beavers, and the creek's namesake ducks. Although shallow in its upper reaches, it can be navigated; stay near the outside of turns to keep in the deeper main channel. When you reach the head of navigation, lie back on the deckplate of your canoe and marvel at how quiet and naturally pristine such a place can be when it is so close to suburbia.

Return to the mouth of Duck Creek, turn left, and follow the wooded shoreline north. The channel becomes narrower; it is actually one of the four mouths of the Big Gunpowder River. At the first opening in the treeline, paddle left into Day's Cove. This bay, about a half mile in diameter, is very shallow, and this characteristic serves to keep motorboats out and ensure that you'll have the cove all to yourself. Like Duck Creek, Day's Cove is also pristine, the uplands on its east side being protected by Gunpowder State Park and the Eastern Sanitary Landfill. The state has recently developed this area into an environmental education facility for use by school-children.

Leaving Day's Cove by its only exit, turn left and continue paddling upstream. A copse of large pines stands alone in a sea of marsh grasses; this ribbon of high ground separates Day's Cove from the main river. Occupying the largest tree in the center of the group is the nest of a bald eagle—a huge, careless

Canada geese

pile of sticks wedged into a triangular crotch about a dozen feet below the topmost bough. The nest can be hard to spot from the water without binoculars, even though it is clearly visible once found. A pair of eagles have nested and successfully fledged young here for the last several years. Adults begin courting in early winter, and eggs are laid by February. It will be early to midsummer before the young eaglets leave the nest, so a patient vigil in late spring is likely to be rewarded with a look at our national bird. This is one of only three eagle nests (as of this writing) in Baltimore County.

Continue up the Big Gunpowder. The marshes are soon left behind, and the Gunpowder takes on the look of a true river, with well-defined banks thickly forested. When an opening in the trees appears on the right, paddle through it. This channel connects the Little and Big Gunpowders, separated here by only a few feet of intervening forest. Do not take the Little Gunpowder either upstream or downstream, but continue north on the channel through a chain-link fence that has been partially torn down. You are now in Rumsey's Pond, a flooded gravel mine only recently opened to boaters. It is one of many active or abandoned gravel mines in the area. Explore the pond as you wish; it is not as large as Day's Cove.

As you exit from Rumsey's Pond, paddle downstream on the Little Gunpowder a hundred yards or so and disembark on the left shore. A very short portage will put you into the dredged canal leading to Joppatowne. Mariner Point Park is about a half mile downstream. Alternatively, you can continue down the Little Gunpowder to its junction with Bird River and bear left and then left again to return to the park. If all this sounds confusing, check the map for clarification.

Finally, a note about nomenclature. The Gunpowder is one of the nation's most colorfully named rivers. Local lore has it that when the colonists first arrived, native Americans were greatly impressed with the noise, smoke, and killing power of the settlers' firearms. Obtaining some gunpowder in trade, they planted it along the banks of the river in hopes that, like corn, it would grow and produce more of itself.

DIRECTIONS

From Baltimore, take I-95 north. Exit at Route 43 east (White Marsh Boulevard). Route 43 ends at Route 40 within a mile; take Route 40 east. After traveling 4.7 miles on Route 40, cross both Gunpowder rivers and turn right on Joppa Farm Road. Go 1.6 miles and turn right on Kearney Road (there is no street sign as of this writing; recognize it by the High's store and gas station on the corner). Follow Kearney Road to the park entrance.

OTHER OUTDOOR RECREATIONAL OPPORTUNITIES NEARBY

Otter Point Creek is another fine freshwater marsh suitable for canoeing. It is located about 10 miles northeast of Mariner Point Park and is described beginning on page 451 in this book.

Chesapeake Bay: Origins

The morning mist curls and boils as it rises from the water; the sun edges above the trees, filling the world with diffuse light. The water is alive with ripples and little splashes, and over by the shore a heron rises, flapping off silently on pterodactyl wings. The coolness of dawn lingers on your skin, and the cares of past and future seem irrelevant to the pleasures of today. So it has been on Chesapeake waters for hundreds of years; the timelessness of this experience extends across the generations. For many of us, the Chesapeake Bay is the essence of Maryland, and this emotional attachment has been the driving force in the campaign to "Save the Bay."

Chesapeake Bay, as we know it, has existed for about 12,000 years. Its origins, however, are far older, dating back almost two million years to the time when Pleistocene ice sheets covered much of northern North America. During this ice age, the colder global climate caused a recession of the oceans from the continental land masses as water became tied up in ice. What is now the Susquehanna River drained meltwater from the southern edge of these glaciers, flowed southward in its channel, and emptied into the sea near the point where the continental shelf is now found. Eventually, the climate warmed, sea levels rose as glacial ice melted, and the sea drowned the lower parts of the Susquehanna. This alternating pattern of cold ice ages and warmer interglacial periods continued for almost two million years. Glaciers advanced three more times; the last ice age ended about 12,000 years ago. Thus man has populated the Bay area only in the most recent interglacial period, a time when the Atlantic Ocean has flooded the lower reaches of the Susquehanna to create the modern incarnation of Chesapeake Bay. Indeed, if you examine a nautical chart of the Bay, the old riverbed of the Susquehanna is readily apparent as a deep channel. The sea level has risen sufficiently to fill the old riverbed to the top, and then some; water has spread out onto the Susquehanna's floodplain. Thus the Bay is much wider than the historical riverbed.

For this reason, Chesapeake Bay is known as a drowned river estuary. But what is an estuary? Scientists describe it as a semi-enclosed body of water open to the ocean and measurably diluted by fresh water. Chesapeake Bay fits this definition exactly: it is surrounded by land on three sides, but it is open to the Atlantic at its mouth near Cape Charles, and at the opposite end the Susquehanna pours in millions of gallons of fresh water every day, even during the most severe drought. Salt and fresh water mix in a complex fashion and spread out over the shallow pan of the Bay.

Yet as one views the Bay from a small boat in a sheltered cove on a summer morning, its dynamic geology and hydrology pale to insignificance against the sensory attractions of the here and now. For most of us, it is the tug of freedom and changelessness and natural beauty that brings us back time and again to enjoy the simple pleasures of life in the "Land of Pleasant Living." ⤝

Otter Point Creek

River Section: Otter Point Landing upstream to head of
  navigation and return

County: Harford

Distance: 4.0 miles

Difficulty: Tidal flatwater

Hazards: Windy weather possible

Highlights: Freshwater marsh, swamp

Nearby Canoe Rental: None

More Information: Chesapeake Bay National Estuarine
  Research Reserve, (410) 638-3903

IN THE EVER-EXPANDING sprawl of development
that characterizes the Boston-Washington corridor, a few
places get left behind, bypassed by roads, cut off by
railroad lines, and encircled by housing tracts. These little
backwaters of natural landscape are often pleasant retreats of
surprisingly pristine beauty and a haven for wildlife that has
been pushed out of surrounding areas. So it is with the region
between Baltimore and the head of Chesapeake Bay to the
east of old Route 40. Both Otter Point Creek and the Gunpowder Delta are pleasant freshwater marshes with forested
wetland borders. At the more northeasterly Otter Point
Creek, a wide estuary bifurcates into narrow passageways that
eventually become closed over by trees. This diversity of
scenery makes Otter Point Creek a fine area to explore by
canoe.

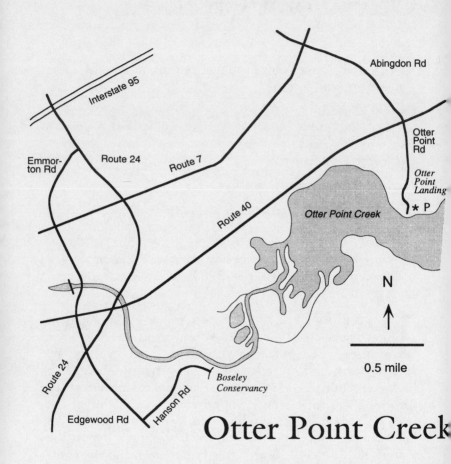

Otter Point Creek

Large sections of the upper stretches of Otter Point Creek are protected through an unusual consortium of agencies. The estuary is a component of the Chesapeake Bay National Estuarine Research Reserve, administered by the National Oceanic and Atmospheric Administration, which employs a site manager. Harford County owns a small park on the more open part of the bay, which has hiking trails through 50 acres or so of hilly upland forest and is used for environmental education. Finally, a large tract of forested wetlands that borders the upper reaches of the creek was the farsighted gift of Melvin Bosely to the Isaac Walton League. This area is known as the Bosely Conservancy, and it has a pleasant but usually muddy trail through a swamp forest with some really big old trees.

TRIP DESCRIPTION

Put your canoe into the water at Otter Point Landing. There is only limited parking here, and there are no facilities at all, but in an emergency you could ask to use the bathrooms at the nearby yacht club. You may feel a bit silly launching a canoe among all the powerboats anchored at the adjacent marina, but they're headed downstream toward the Bush River and Chesapeake Bay, whereas you'll be paddling upstream into the shallows and marshes. Bear right (upstream) from the launch ramp and cross Otter Point Creek, aiming for a wooded knob of land on the far shore. As you go around this corner, the estuary of Otter Point Creek opens to view: a wide, marshy expanse filled with lots of green emergent vegetation.

To the left is a shallow bay that always has several great blue herons. The still, warm waters of this embayment, less than a foot deep, attract all sorts of small and juvenile fish that form the principal prey of these graceful birds. When not actively fishing, the herons congregate in trees along the shore; it is not unusual to have a dozen of them in sight at any one time.

The southern portion of the Otter Point Creek estuary is a maze of small channels that twist and turn through beds of spatterdock and cattail. The far left channel, marked by an extensive line of wooden duck boxes, appears open on topographic maps, but vegetation blocks the way in summer. Similarly, the rest of these waterways are blind, so you can't get very far. However, these little sloughs are good places to surprise herons, mallards, and wood ducks.

Paddle across the face of the marsh toward a small island of trees located in the center of the bay. This is Snake Island, a privately owned oasis of high ground that has, unfortunately, been severely trashed. Paddle down the channel that keeps Snake Island on your right; this leads into the true riverbed of Otter Point Creek and will give you access to the more distant reaches of the stream.

A number of mallard nesting structures are scattered across the marsh and are visible near here. These are wire mesh tubes set atop poles and intertwined with compressed foliage to provide shelter from the sun. Most people think of mallards as very common and tame ducks (they are), but North American populations have been in decline for a number of years. These nesting structures help deter predators and increase hatching rates.

Are there otters in Otter Point Creek? Probably so, although these beautiful mammals are shy and elusive. On most canoe trips, you'll be likely to hear an occasional loud splash, but it could also be caused by a member of the several families of beaver that occupy the marsh. Count yourself lucky if you are ever fortunate enough to see river otters.

Much of the vegetation lining Otter Point Creek is five or six feet high, cutting off long views over the marsh. Cattails dominate, although, as the creek approaches the upland areas, richer and better-drained soils allow herbaceous plants like joe-pye weed and other late-summer composites to grow. The common reed is also prevalent here, growing up to 12 feet tall. It is easily distinguished by its flower head, which is sometimes used in autumn for decoration. Eventually, small trees like red maple and box elder appear along the shores, and soon the open expanse of marshland gives way to wooded swamp.

Otter Point Creek narrows slightly as the canopy closes overhead. The impression is that of paddling through a green

Common reed

tunnel. Some of the trees are very large, and this swamp
harbors a number of songbirds, judging by the evening chorus. Peepers and other frogs abound in spring; plagues of
deerflies sometimes come out in June.

On the left, a well-worn trail appears, with wooden bridges
over side streams and wet spots. This is the trail system of the
Bosely Conservancy, and a walk here makes a nice diversion
from canoeing. The easiest place to get ashore is at the designated canoe launch site, where a ladder off a tiny pier reaches
water level. (Although it is theoretically possible to start your
canoe trip from here, such a route requires a 700-foot portage
through the forest from the parking lot.)

Returning to your canoe, paddle upstream just a bit farther.
A series of fallen trees spans the narrow creek; several can be
paddled over or passed under. Eventually, these strainers block

farther progress upstream. This is unfortunate for canoeists, because at least a half mile of otherwise paddleable river lies upstream. However, there are sound ecological reasons to leave downed trees undisturbed. Their underwater branches provide shelter for fish and aquatic insects and slow the passage of floodwaters. Algae and bacteria grow on the limbs, forming the base of the food chain. This increased structural complexity, both aquatic and aerial, leads to a greater abundance and variety of species.

When you can go no farther upstream, return the way you came. For variety, you can bear left at Snake Island to explore a different channel of Otter Point Creek. It too will lead you out into the broad embayment, passing by the northwest edge of the estuary.

DIRECTIONS

From Baltimore or Washington, take I-95 north. Exit onto Route 24 south. Make an immediate right onto Emmorton Road. Turn left onto Route 40. After passing the Otter Point Creek overlook, make the first right onto Otter Point Road. Follow it to the end.

OTHER OUTDOOR RECREATIONAL OPPORTUNITIES NEARBY

The Gunpowder Delta is a similar freshwater marsh that is suitable for canoeing. It is located about 10 miles southwest of Otter Point Creek and is described beginning on page 443 in this book.

Algal Blooms and Massive Fish Mortality

Among the several problems affecting water quality in Maryland's Chesapeake Bay, the most significant and intractable involve algae. Simple, single-celled aquatic plants that float in the water column, algae seem innocuous enough. But under conditions of nutrient enrichment, they can undergo massive growth spurts, known as algal blooms, that disrupt both the chemistry and the biology of our great estuary. A newly discovered species of algae may be responsible for at least some of the enormous fish die-offs that affect the Chesapeake from time to time.

Scientists have known for some time that the input of excessive loads of nitrogen and phosphorus into Chesapeake Bay is at the heart of many of its problems. These nutrients stimulate the growth of algae in the water, much as fertilizer stimulates grass growing in lawns. The resulting excessive densities of algae inhibit light penetration and coat underwater plants, sometimes killing this submerged aquatic vegetation. The algae eventually die, sink to the bottom, and decay. During the process of decay, oxygen is consumed, and Bay waters may become anoxic. This oxygen-depleted water kills any animal that cannot swim or move elsewhere. A number of fish die-offs over the years have been attributed to just this cause.

But there have always been some anomalies that scientists could not explain, situations in which fish died but there was plenty of oxygen in the water. A 1992 report from North Carolina may explain these findings.

Researchers discovered a dinoflagellate, a kind of alga capable of directed movement, that causes fish mortality. Most of the time, this unnamed organism lies torpid in the sediments of the estuary as a cyst. However, in response to the high concentrations of nutrients in fish excrement, the cyst breaks open and the active vegetative cell is released. The dinoflagellate releases into the water a potent poison that causes neurotoxic symptoms and death in fish. The alga then attaches to and feeds on the dead fish. Within hours, the dinoflagellate reencysts and sinks to the bottom, where it again lies dormant.

This "phantom" alga has only recently been discovered because it has such a short active life span. Only when researchers sampled water at the early stages of a fish kill were they able to find the dinoflagellate. By the time a kill becomes evident, the alga is no longer present in the water column. Scientists have now found this alga in Chesapeake Bay, and they will look for its presence during future fish kills.

The discovery of this toxic dinoflagellate points up the many gaps in our knowledge about the organisms in Chesapeake Bay. Only through continued research will we be able to understand how the Chesapeake functions and ultimately how to "Save the Bay." ⊷

Potomac River: Overview

River Section: North Branch: Headwaters to Oldtown
Paw Paw Bends: Oldtown to Hancock
The Great Valley: Hancock to
  Dam Number 3
The Blue Ridge: Dam Number 3 to
  Point of Rocks
The Piedmont: Point of Rocks to Great Falls
The Fall Line: Great Falls to Chain Bridge
Tidewater: Chain Bridge to the Mouth of
  Chesapeake Bay

County: Garrett, Allegany, Washington, Frederick,
  Montgomery, Washington, D.C.,
  Prince Georges, Charles, St. Marys

Distance: North Branch: 100.0 miles
Paw Paw Bends: 49.2 miles
The Great Valley: 65.9 miles
The Blue Ridge: 13.5 miles
The Piedmont: 33.4 miles
The Fall Line: 10.4 miles
Tidewater: 114 miles

Difficulty: North Branch: Very difficult rapids
Paw Paw Bends: Flat, flowing water
The Great Valley: Flat, flowing water
The Blue Ridge: Difficult rapids
The Piedmont: Flat, flowing water
The Fall Line: Large waterfalls,
  impassable rapids
Tidewater: Tidal water

Hazards: Major rapids in some stretches, high water, windy weather

Highlights: Riparian forest, birds

Nearby Canoe Rental: See individual trips

More Information: C & O Canal National Historical Park: Georgetown to Edwards Ferry, (301) 299-3613; Edwards Ferry to Cumberland, (301) 722-8226

THE POTOMAC: the Nation's River. So it is known by many Americans, this most beautiful and diverse river flowing through Washington, D.C. Although most tourists see only the wide Potomac near the Tidal Basin, looking over to National Airport, the Pentagon, and the low hills of Arlington National Cemetery, Marylanders know it in far more faces and moods: the pastoral river flowing past farms and fields in the western part of the state; the untamed wild beauty of Great Falls and the Mather Gorge; the long, peaceful vistas of the lower estuarine Potomac. The Potomac is one of Maryland's great resources, for recreation, for scenery, for commerce. Every mile in Maryland has been paddled in a canoe, from the southwesternmost border, where the tiny creek floats a boat only in floods, to the lower reaches, where its fresh waters gain the salty tang of the sea at Point Lookout. And all of this river, over 400 miles of it, is part of Maryland; the border with Virginia is not midstream, as with most rivers, but at the high water mark on the Virginia shore.

That's not to say you should load up the canoe and visit just anywhere along the river for some paddling. Significant portions of the river are often too low to paddle, just plain tedious, or even dangerous. Elsewhere, this guidebook describes the best of the Potomac in some detail; here is a quick guide to the rest of the river and an explanation of why some portions are not recommended. In the following descriptions, the Potomac has been divided into sections of varying lengths that, although arbitrary, correspond to logical segments for outdoor activities or to physiographic zones.

TRIP DESCRIPTION

North Branch of the Potomac: Headwaters to Oldtown

The Potomac officially starts from a small spring in West Virginia at the Fairfax Stone, an ancient boundary marker noting the westernmost reach of Lord Fairfax's huge domain. The purist paddler may want to visit the stone, but it's not easy to find—the quest entails a long expedition in the mountains on dirt roads infested with a plague of coal-hauling dump trucks. This is prime strip mine country, and acid mine runoff pollutes the Potomac right from the start, the first of many insults to the Nation's River. Within a few miles, it has gathered enough water to float a canoe in the wettest weather. However, the next 26 miles are strictly high-water runs, paddleable only after heavy rains. Rapids are significant and continuous; this is no place for any but teams of experienced whitewater experts.

The breakneck downhill pace of the Potomac slows behind Jennings Randolph Dam in Garrett County. Built in the 1980s, the reservoir is already gaining a reputation for good fishing, confounding the critics who felt it would be too acid to support a community of organisms. The construction scars on the canyon walls are beginning to heal as well.

The section of river from Jennings Randolph Dam to Bloomington, Maryland, is always unfloatable except during specially announced whitewater recreational water releases, which are scheduled several times each year. Extensive whitewater canoeing experience is a prerequisite for participating in these events: a memorable series of standing waves swamps most open canoes, and there are several more hard rapids.

Downstream, the adjacent communities of Bloomington, Luke, and Westernport hug the banks of the Potomac and are the site of the Westvaco Corporation, the largest employer in western Maryland. Westvaco produces high-quality paper from wood pulp at its riverside plant. Despite the expenditure of millions of dollars on pollution control equipment, the plant dumps enormous quantities of pollutants into the river, giving it a gray, dishwater appearance and a distinctive odor for miles downriver. And water pollution isn't the worst of it; paper mills in general have a distinctive scent, and Westvaco fills the valleys with the peculiar aroma of its smokestack effluvia. If the wind is right, you can get a whiff in Cumberland, 30 miles away. For this reason, paddling the Potomac between here and Cumberland is not recommended, even when there is enough water in the river.

Below Cumberland, the river is bordered by the C & O Canal National Historical Park, providing a greenbelt on at least one side of the river all the way to Washington, D.C. However, summer low water may make the river impassable until the junction with the South Branch of the Potomac; from this point, there is always enough water to canoe. The South Branch, originating in West Virginia and flowing northward, is actually larger and longer and drains a larger basin than the North Branch, but it is not considered the main stem of the Potomac.

Paw Paw Bends: Oldtown to Hancock

This is the best of the upper Potomac, passing through the mountains of western Maryland. The 50 miles of river between Oldtown and Hancock are described specifically under Paw Paw Bends beginning on page 484.

The Great Valley: Hancock to Dam Number 3

The Potomac just below Hancock is still pleasant enough, with a flowing current, but I-70 parallels the river, and it is noisy. The interstate leaves the river near where Licking Creek enters from the north. The 6.3-mile stretch from Licking Creek to McCoy's Ferry, with a stop at historic Fort Frederick (especially during reenactment days) is recommended and is described in detail beginning on page 475 in this book.

Much of the next 23 miles downriver is reservoir, backed up by the Williamsport Dam and Dam Number 4. There is lots of second-home development of an unattractive sort along the banks, and the roar of small engines dominates the sounds of nature as fishermen troll the flats.

From Dam Number 4 downriver to the mouth of Antietam Creek (15 miles), the river again resumes its natural state, flowing slowly with even a few small riffles. The most interesting trip on this section, featuring a stop to explore a cave, is listed beginning on page 466 in this book. Below the mouth of Antietam Creek, the river backs up behind Dam Number 3, and the amount of motorized river traffic increases. The final access is 4.5 more miles downriver, at a national historical park site called Dargan Bend. Be sure to take out here, as significant rapids appear below in the vicinity of Harpers Ferry.

The Blue Ridge: Dam Number 3 to Point of Rocks

The section of river extending 16 miles downriver of Dargan Bend is not recommended unless you have had a good whitewater canoeing class and lots of experience and are part of a strong crew of several canoes. Just upstream of Harpers Ferry is a set of difficult rapids called the Needles. At higher water levels, there are waves and a very fast and powerful current typical of a big river like the Potomac. Canoeists have died here, even at normal water levels. Below Harpers Ferry and the confluence with the Shenandoah River are still larger rapids; White Horse Rapid will flip canoes even at summer dead low water. Most canoeists could handle the smaller rapids between Brunswick and Point of Rocks, but the scenery is only fair.

These rapids were created where the Potomac has carved its way through the Blue Ridge. These parallel lines of north-south–trending ridges are a narrow but distinct physiographic zone, with a unique geological history. The scenery is spectacular along the river, but it is best viewed from the safety of the C & O Canal towpath. A walk in this area (Harpers Ferry) is described beginning on page 141 in this book.

The Piedmont: Point of Rocks to Great Falls

Pleasant cruising on mile after mile of clear flowing water. Big trees—silver maples, sycamores, and box elders—shading the banks. Birdsong and whispering breezes. Does life get any better than this? The Potomac has broken from the mountains and proceeds amiably on its way to the sea. For most of this stretch, islands split the river into narrower, more intimate channels. These islands make fine campsites, although they are almost never used. There is nothing spectacular about this section of the river; it's just an attractive place to canoe, near to home, at any time of year. Among the highlights are the Monocacy River Aqueduct, 560 feet in length and built of white granite, a triumph of the stonemason's art; White's Ferry, the last operating car ferry across the Potomac; and Ball's Bluff, where one of the earliest engagements of the Civil War occurred. The remains of Dam Number 2 back up the river's flow near the end of this section; you'll recognize the area by the increase in powerboaters and water-skiers.

Running the rubble remains of Dam Number 2 is not recommended, since at low water canoes tend to get hung up, while sufficient water makes the dam and the mile of Seneca Rapids just below it dangerous for novices. Two alternatives are possible: on river right, the Virginia shore, you can paddle into the Virginia Canal (described beginning on page 511 in this book); on river left, carry your canoe over to the C & O Canal, which is rewatered between here and Great Falls. Below Seneca Rapids, the river resumes its slow pace for six more miles.

If you choose to canoe the river below Seneca Rapids, be certain of the location of your take-out. As you near the end of this stretch, stay near the Maryland shoreline. The Washington, D.C., water supply dam spans the river just above Great Falls and marks the mandatory take-out. Even if you survived the plunge over the dam, certain death would lie just below in Great Falls.

The Fall Line: Great Falls to Chain Bridge

Some of the most specatcular scenery in any of our national parks lies in this 10-mile stretch of river, but it is no place for canoes. Every year, a dozen or so deaths occur here, at least one or two of which are of people in canoes. Invariably, lack of knowledge of the river, inexperience in canoes, failure to wear life jackets, and alcohol consumption contribute to these deaths. Don't be one of these statistics; see the area safely, on foot. The C & O Canal towpath parallels the river and is described beginning on page 69 in this book.

Tidewater: Chain Bridge to the Mouth at Chesapeake Bay

The Potomac reaches tidewater at the foot of Little Falls, approximately where Chain Bridge crosses the river. Within a short distance, the river becomes wider and is subject to wind, waves, and motorboat traffic. For this reason, it is not recommended. If, however, you want to see Georgetown or the Washington monuments from the water, choose a warm, calm day. Thompson's Boat House in Maryland, at the foot of the Rock Creek Trail, or Theodore Roosevelt Island, reached from the Virginia shore, are your best bets for access. They are described beginning on pages 261 and 331 in this book.

For most of tidewater, the Potomac is a wide river. Stretching over 100 miles from Chain Bridge to the mouth, it is several miles wide in most places. As such, it is no place for an open canoe. But if you have a powerboat or a sailboat, enjoy!

OTHER OUTDOOR RECREATIONAL OPPORTUNITIES NEARBY

The C & O Canal towpath runs parallel to the Potomac River from Cumberland to Georgetown. It is a superb recreational resource, especially for hiking and cycling. All 184 miles are suitable for walking; the terrain is flat and even, and the towpath is for the most part well drained. Most of the towpath is suitable for bicycling as well; the exception is the short stretch between the Old Anglers Inn and Great Falls. Campsites are located about every five miles and may be used by backpackers, bicycle campers, and canoe campers on a first-come, first-served basis.

Potomac River: Dam Number 4 Cave

River Section: Dam Number 4 to Snyders Landing

County: Washington

Distance: 8.0 miles

Difficulty: Flat flowing water and elementary whitewater

Hazards: Windy weather possible, high water

Highlights: Riparian forest, cave

Nearby Canoe Rental: None

More Information: C & O Canal National Historical Park, (301) 722-8226

T HE STATE OF MARYLAND is sometimes referred to as "America in Miniature" because of its wide range of topographic features. Indeed, Maryland has been blessed with a barrier island coastline, an extensive inland bay, rolling countryside, ridges and mountains, swamps and marshes, well-drained uplands, and flowing rivers. However, when it comes to caves, most people think of Kentucky or New Mexico. Surprisingly, Maryland does have a few caves, all tucked away in obscure corners of the state. There are several in far western Garrett County, the biggest of which are preserved by the Nature Conservancy and permit only limited access because of their unique animal life and fragile nature. A few more caves are sprinkled throughout the limestone strata of the Maryland extension of the Shenandoah Valley. Crystal

Potomac River: Dam Number 4 Cave

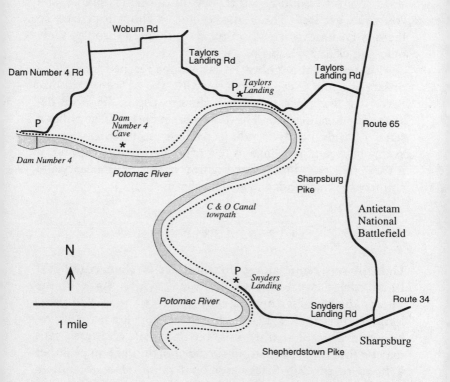

Grottoes, a commercial cave, is the biggest. Less well-known but very accessible is Dam Number 4 Cave, located in a rocky bluff overlooking the Potomac River. The entrance to this cave is on public land, part of the C & O Canal National Historical Park.

Dam Number 4 Cave is perfect for first-time visitors to a natural cave, especially children. It is only about 150 feet long, but a dogleg near the far end puts you out of sight of the entrance and any last vestige of sunlight. There are several small rooms to explore, but the layout of them is simple, and you can't get lost. The lowest ceiling is about four feet, so there is no need to crawl on hands and knees through slimy mud and claustrophobic passageways.

Although Dam Number 4 Cave can be reached by walking or bicycling the C & O Canal towpath, the adjacent Potomac River is a fine place to canoe, and this trip is therefore described as a canoe trip. The Potomac in this area inscribes a series of wide bends trending generally southward, flowing evenly between low banks. A few riffles enliven the trip, but it is the serene and unpopulated nature of this central Maryland countryside that lends the area its charm.

TRIP DESCRIPTION

Unload your canoe along the shoulder of Dam Number 4 Road where it parallels the Potomac within sight of the water. The shoulder here is wide and more than 100 yards long, so there is always enough space. There are no facilities, however. Portable bathrooms, picnic tables, and trash cans may be found by continuing further north on Dam Number 4 Road to the Big Slackwater boat ramp. (Do not put in here, because this approach would necessitate an awkward portage around Dam Number 4.) Carry your canoe across the dewatered C & O Canal and then down the trail to the river. Make sure you put in at least 100 feet downriver of the dam; at high water, turbulent currents at the dam's base can be dangerous.

Dam Number 4 was built between 1832 and 1835 to supply water to the C & O Canal. Like so much of the construction of the 184-mile canal, it was a difficult task for the laborers. Mostly recent immigrants, these hardy men endured epidemics of cholera and other diseases, floods, and ethnic and racial strife in addition to the usual assortment of feuds, personal vendettas, and exploitation by management that was typical of the times. The present dam was completed in 1861.

The Potomac initially flows quickly for a few hundred yards below the dam and then settles down to its more typical placid pace. Pass under a set of high-tension lines and then look downstream for an island splitting the river. Pull over on the left (Maryland) bank at the exact level of the head of this island, 1.1 miles downriver from your put-in. Tie your canoe to a tree, gather what you will need to enter Dam Number 4 Cave, and scramble up the steep bank to the C & O Canal towpath. The cave opening will be obvious in the limestone cliff adjacent to the towpath.

A few preparations are necessary if you're going to enter Dam Number 4 Cave. Bring along one flashlight per person, and make sure that all of the lights have fresh batteries. In all but the driest weather, a small stream flows along the floor of this cave, so suitable footwear is necessary. Most caves, including this one, have a constant temperature in the mid-50s, so bring along a jacket; a raincoat is a good idea also, because you may brush up against the wet walls of the cave.

As you enter, give your eyes time to adjust to the increasingly dimmer light. This area of a cave is known as the "twilight zone" and is favored as a refuge by crepuscular animals. The most common creatures you may encounter are geometrid moths, cloaked in gray and black, estivating on the ceiling. Cave crickets are also fairly common. Long-tailed salamanders are sometimes found in crevices; bring along a small stick to sweep them out so you can examine them. As its name implies, this is the only species of salamander whose tail is longer than its body.

Finally, everyone wants to know about bats. Yes, bats do sleep in Dam Number 4 Cave, hanging upside down from the ceiling in protected places and issuing forth at dusk to catch insects. They also hibernate here in winter. However, as this cave has become better known and more people have begun to visit, sightings of bats have become rarer; there is just too much disturbance for any self-respecting bat to tolerate. If you should see one, pass on quietly and try to disturb it as little as possible.

Within 50 or 60 feet of the entrance, the cave narrows and the ceiling closes in so that adults will have to walk in a crouch. Eventually, the cave doglegs right and opens into a room where several people can stand. On the ceiling, little nubs of stalactites are beginning to form as water percolates downward through the surrounding limestone, carrying saturated solutions of calcium carbonate that precipitate out into these icicles of rock. This is a good place for everyone to turn off their flashlights and experience absolute darkness.

From here, you have two choices. To the left, a narrow passageway leads within 30 feet to another small room. Further progress is possible only down a long tube that gets increasingly more compact; exploration of it should not be attempted by casual visitors. To the right, another small room is reached by scrambling over a boulder. Two tight passages leave this room at higher levels, and once again significant progress is best left to experienced cavers with proper gear. Even so, Dam Number 4 Cave is a good introduction to the joys and discomforts of caving, and it offers the only real opportunity in Maryland for visitors to enter a natural cave.

Returning to your canoe, proceed downriver. In another mile, look for a "Tarzan" swing attached to a huge old sycamore limb on the left river bank. Whoever constructed this swing built it to last; it is made of steel cable, not rope, and the tree limb is protected by a rubber sleeve so that the cable does not cut into it. A rider who lets go of the swing at its apogee drops into a deep spot in the river with a resounding splash; only good swimmers should try this swing.

Continuing downstream, the Potomac resumes its slow flow to the sea. Big silver maples and sycamores line the shady banks; hawks and vultures wheel overhead. The ubiquitous great blue heron stalks the shallows and the occasional fish jumps, but nothing else disturbs the quiet. When the current slackens and the river becomes deeper, Taylors Landing is just ahead.

You may elect to pull out at Taylors Landing if you're looking for a short trip. The distance from Dam Number 4 to Taylors Landing is 3.5 miles; that's sufficient if you've spent lots of time in the cave and had several swim stops. If you're interested in doing more paddling, continue for another 4.5 miles to Snyders Landing, the next convenient access.

The rest of the trip is more of the same, very pleasant but uneventful. Below Taylors Landing the current picks up and dances again over a few small riffles. The last of these, visible only at low water, is truly unique; outcrops of rock ledges run parallel to the river's flow, rather than perpendicular to it. This creates several aisles for canoes, each separated from the adjacent one by rock fins. Just past here, the current slows, and the last mile of paddling to Snyders Landing is in deep, flat water.

The shuttle between Dam Number 4 and Snyders Landing is a long one, although the pastoral countryside eases the ride. For this reason, consider carrying a bike along with you in the canoe, assuming that you have the space. You can then pedal back to your car on the canal towpath, a very easy and direct route.

DIRECTIONS

From Baltimore or Washington, take I-70 west. Exit at Route 65, also marked for Antietam National Battlefied, heading south. Turn right on Route 68, Lappans Road. Turn left on Route 632, Downsville Road, which turns into Dam Number 4 Road. Continue on this road until you reach the put-in, within sight of the Potomac. To reach Taylors and Snyders Landings, see the map.

OTHER OUTDOOR RECREATIONAL
OPPORTUNITIES NEARBY

The C & O Canal towpath in this area is well suited for bicycling, with a smooth surface unmarred by roots or rocks. It is also one of the prettier sections of the towpath, especially in autumn, when the dry leaves lend a smoky aroma to the air. Nearby is Antietam National Battlefield, described beginning on page 308 in this book, which is also a fine venue for bicycling or walking.

Bats of Maryland

Among the diverse and wonderful collection of animals that roam Maryland, few are looked upon with as much fear and loathing as bats. These little mammals have long been associated with evil, but in fact a more benign and beneficial animal would be difficult to imagine. All of the 10 species of bats found in Maryland eat insects exclusively and provide a natural form of population control of mosquitoes, midges, flies, and moths.

Bats are likely to be seen in Maryland only between midspring and midfall. In this warm weather, they roost in dark, sheltered areas of caves, barns, houses, and hollow trees during daylight hours. Bats emerge at dusk to feed on night-flying insects, and they may continue to capture and eat their prey until dawn. Indeed, a bat may eat up to half its own weight in

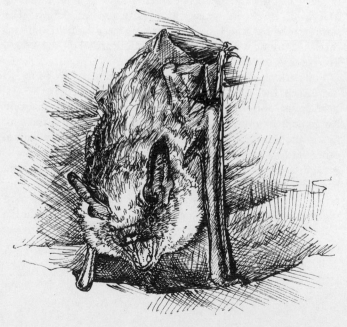

Big brown bat

insects daily. Most people know that bats find their prey by echolocation, but less well appreciated is how the insect is captured. Bats found in Maryland have an interfemoral membrane enclosing the tail and anchored against the two legs. Insects are captured in this netlike structure and then immediately removed by mouth as the bat curls into a shape resembling the letter C. The bat then resumes its normal flight pattern. The most reliable place to see bats is around the lights illuminating stadiums on hot summer nights. As cold weather arrives with autumn, insect prey begins to get scarce, and bats prepare for hibernation. Some migrate southward, but typically only up to a few hundred miles. Caves, with little variation in temperature and humidity, are favored hibernacula.

The most common bat in Maryland is the little brown bat, found throughout the state. Its head and body are only two inches long; the tail adds another inch and a half. It has a wingspan of about 10 inches, making it look much larger than it really is. Among the other nine species of bats found in Maryland, three only pass through during migration. The state's rarest bat, the Indiana myotis, is known only from two caves in extreme western Maryland and is carried on the federal list of endangered species.

Populations of most species of bats in Maryland are probably decreasing, owing to loss and disturbance of hibernating sites, inadvertent poisoning by pesticides, general habitat loss, and harassment by humans. Although bats can carry and transmit rabies, the disease is probably no more prevalent in bats than in other wild mammals. Conservation measures depend primarily on education and a change in attitudes by citizens. Avoid harassing bats at all times of the year. If one gets into your house, merely darken the room and open a window; by midnight, it will probably be gone. Finally, you can put up a bat roost box, available in many nature-oriented stores, to attract these useful little mammals to your property.

Potomac River: Fort Frederick

River Section: Licking Creek to McCoys Ferry

County: Washington

Distance: 6.3 miles

Difficulty: Flowing flatwater and elementary whitewater

Hazards: Windy weather possible, high water

Highlights: Riparian forest, historic fort

Nearby Canoe Rental: None

More Information: Fort Frederick State Park,
(301) 842-2155. C & O Canal National Historical Park,
(301) 722-8226

WHEN THE MISTS OF early morning trail across the river, rising on the convections of cool air and humidity, and sunlight slants down through the maples, you can almost imagine a colonial soldier crouching by the flowing river to fill his waterskin. He lays his long musket down in the dewy grass, warily checks upstream and down, and bends to drink, a part of the forest, like the deer and bear and wildcat. This scene from two and a half centuries ago seems as close as yesterday at Fort Frederick, a colonial fort built in 1755 as a defense against the French and Indians. After Braddock's defeat and Washington's surrender in that year, Fort Frederick was suddenly the frontier, a rallying point for settlers colonizing the wilds and a bastion against the incur-

Potomac River: Fort Frederick

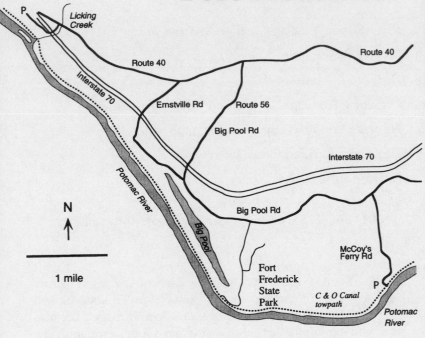

sions of the enemy. The fort has been beautifully restored and is now the focus of a state park where reenactments and demonstrations of colonial skills occur on weekends. Although you can drive in to visit, Fort Frederick marks the halfway point on a short, pretty canoe trip, and it makes a great lunch stop on which the kids can run around and exercise not just their legs but their imaginations as well.

The Potomac River has many canoeable stretches, a number of them scenic, quiet, and lightly visited, so the choice of a day's trip can be confounding. The 6.3-mile section described here may be one of the best in the midwatershed. It is relatively short, perfect for novices who don't want to make an all-day marathon out of a canoe trip. A long lunch stop at Fort Frederick makes the route unique. Check with the park office; if you choose a weekend when there is a reenactment, black powder shoot, or other demonstration, you'll be doubly rewarded.

TRIP DESCRIPTION

Unload your canoe just a stone's throw from I-70 on a little access road adjacent to Licking Creek. This unpromising spot is reached by turning left off old Route 40 immediately after the bridge over the stream. Pass under the twin spans of I-70, proceed about 100 yards, and park at a wide spot in the pavement. A dirt road (unsuitable for vehicles) leads down to the creek. The bank is steep here and may be slippery if muddy, so use care in loading and launching. Be reassured that the worst of the trip is now behind you. There are no facilities here.

Licking Creek has a reputation as a very fine fishing stream. Although narrow and small in volume, it has a relatively undeveloped watershed with little pollution. Numerous riffles over gravel bars and small ledges alternate with deep green pools shaded by overhanging hemlocks. If the water is higher, as in spring after a rainy spell, you might consider starting farther up this scenic stream, especially if you like fishing.

Paddle under an old railroad bridge and then the Licking Creek aqueduct of the C & O Canal. Completed in 1838, this single-arch span of native stone is in poorer shape than many of the others along the 184-mile-long canal. Just beyond, Licking Creek enters a small slough of the main Potomac, separated from the main flow by a narrow island. The current picks up, and you join the parent river as it flows over a tiny ledge, creating a few riffles.

The first two miles of river are slow, with a barely perceptible current. Trees border both sides of the river, broken only by a few fishing camps on the West Virginia side. Keep an eye out for wildlife on this trip, especially in the vicinity of the railroad bridge at mile 2. The shallow, slow waters are favored by green-backed and great blue herons, kingfishers, ospreys, and ducks. Indeed, on a late summer trip I saw more wood ducks and green-backed herons here than on any other comparable stretch of river I've been on.

Just below this railroad bridge, the gradient picks up a bit. This is a good spot to float with the current, as you make progress without any effort. The river bottom, just a few inches away from the bottom of the canoe, alternates between striated bedrock and softball-sized cobbles deposited during floods. Most impressive are the numerous small black snails clinging to the river-bottom rocks, most easily noted when they contrast with white rocks. The bottoms of rivers with good water quality are a rich if specialized habitat. In addition to the snails, the Potomac is home to large numbers of tiny, thumb-nail-sized freshwater clams, as evidenced by the shells that constitute a major fraction of the gravels found in back eddys.

Fort Frederick is encountered about a mile and a half below the railroad bridge on river left. A set of stairs made from railroad ties leads up the considerable bank to a campground. Water and outhouses are available here, and thankfully so, since there were no such facilities at the put-in. Tie the canoe to a tree and follow the road about a half mile uphill to the fort, museum, parade ground, and gift shop. The very scenic grounds, studded with isolated, mature shade trees, present a neat and picturesque setting.

Green-backed heron

After seeing the fort and environs, return to your canoe. Just downriver, a large rock outcrop on river right marks another small riffle, and this dancing water continues for most of the next mile. The last shallow turn in this stretch reveals the landing at McCoys Ferry and marks the transition to flat water, deep pools, and the playground of powerboats. The final half mile to the boat ramp makes a good swimming hole, assuming that you like deep water. Take out at the concrete ramp. There is parking for about 50 cars here, as well as picnic tables, trash cans, outhouses, and a campground, but no water.

This paddling trip is possible even if you have only one canoe. Although normally you need two cars to set up a shuttle, leaving one at either end of the trip, the presence of the parallel C & O Canal makes a bicycle shuttle feasible in this case. Just load a sturdy bike into your canoe and pedal back the six miles on the towpath to retrieve your car.

DIRECTIONS

From Washington or Baltimore, follow I-70 west beyond Hagerstown. Exit at Big Pool (Route 56). Proceed north for 1.5 miles. The road ends at Old Route 40; turn left. Continue west for 2.5 miles, until you cross over Licking Creek. Make an immediate left at the far side of the bridge, pass under the twin spans of I-70, and park at the first wide spot on the pavement just beyond. To reach the take-out at McCoys Ferry, return the way you came, passing over I-70 on Route 56. Continue another 2.9 miles past the interstate, passing the entrance to Fort Frederick, and turn right on McCoys Ferry Road. The boat ramp is at the end of the road.

Biopollution

The native flora and fauna of Maryland are a diverse and wonderful collection of organisms, but when a plant or animal makes headlines, it is frequently an exotic species introduced into the state by man. The new immigrant, whether introduced accidentally or on purpose, invariably gains notoriety as a damaging, unpleasant nuisance. Consider this rogue's gallery of well-known foreign organisms that plague Maryland: crabgrass, starlings, gypsy moths, Norway rats, thistles, and HIV virus.

Ecologists have long known about the devastating effects that nonnative invading species can have on ecosystems. Their populations, uncontrolled by the normal checks to unlimited expansion—predation, parasitism, competition, and disease—invaders frequently displace native organisms, alter the ecology of the community, and may even cause extinctions. Less well understood are the characteristics that make a place susceptible to invasion in the first place. In general, ecological communities already placed under stress seem to be the most fertile breeding grounds for outbreaks of what is now being called biopollution. These stresses are almost invariably caused by humans: plowing, logging, damming, development, elimination of native species, single-crop farmlands, and habitat loss. In addition, it is usually our activities that introduce new immigrants to these stressed ecological communities, by either transporting exotic species inadvertently over geographical barriers or transplanting them purposely.

Perhaps we should have learned our lesson by now; yet the introduction of exotic flora and fauna goes on apace. The public at large *likes* exotics; witness the popularity of zoos and aquariums. Crops, ornamental plants, game birds, and fish are regularly stocked into new habitats throughout the United States. For example, there are at least 69 species of exotic fish in United States waters, 158 more that have been stocked outside their native range, and countless transplantations of different genetic stocks within the same species. In Clear Lake, California, there are now 20 species of fish—but only 5 of the original 12 native species still survive.

The reason for our fascination with exotic biota, of course, is that some introductions are pleasant or useful. For example, sika deer were introduced into Maryland near the turn of the twentieth century and have flourished in the counties of the lower Eastern Shore. They are a popular game species and apparently do not compete with native white-tailed deer, whose numbers increase every year. Some scientists want to introduce the Japanese oyster into Chesapeake Bay because it resists diseases like Dermo and MSX better than our native species. If this introduction is approved and successful, it could spell the salvation of one of Maryland's oldest and most famous industries. The best way to control population outbreaks of exotic pest species is deliberately to introduce a predator. For example, wasps that prey on gypsy moth larvae were transplanted from the moth's native range in Asia and have succcessfully controlled yearly outbreaks of the moth in New England to the point that the spraying of pesticides has been abandoned.

Some exotics have both positive and negative qualities, and the jury is still out on them. Hydrilla is an underwater flowering plant that colonized the Potomac River below Washington, D.C., in the 1980s. It has dramatically increased water clarity and created a world-class bass fishery. However, hydrilla mats are all but impenetrable by boat, and they may be preventing the return of native underwater grasses wiped out by pollution in the 1950s and 1960s. Multiflora rose, popular with game managers because it supplies cover and food and prevents erosion, also aggressively displaces native vegetation. *Phragmites,* the common reed towering over freshwater marshes and roadside ditches in Maryland, also displaces native vegetation and has no wildlife food value, but at least it prevents erosion and provides cover.

In general, however, nonnative species cause problems. With continued development in Maryland, coupled with the increasing frequency of global travel, we can expect more problems with exotics. As of this writing, scientists are worried about the zebra mussel, a thumbnail-sized mollusc first discovered in the Great Lakes in the mid-1980s. In 1991, the mussels were found clogging the water intake pipes of a power plant on the Susquehanna River in New York. They will almost certainly spread down the Susquehanna as far as the upper Chesapeake Bay; whether they can withstand the salinities of the middle and lower Bay is uncertain. Possessed of a fabulous rate of reproduction (females devote half their body weight to egg production) and hardy, motile larvae, zebra mussels displace native

Indeed, navigational buoys have been observed sinking under their accumulated weight.

Although scientists and managers remain worried about the zebra mussel, other introductions continue, inadvertently and on purpose. Unfortunately, the ecology of invader species is not a predictive science, so we cannot tell which of these introductions will be detrimental and in what way. The best course is probably to minimize such introductions, and to preserve undisturbed large blocks of land where the stresses that mankind places on the environment are at least minimized. In this way, perhaps we can hold the line against the continuing assaults of biopollution. ✦

Potomac River: Paw Paw Bends

River Section: Paw Paw access to Little Orleans

County: Allegany

Distance: 21.7 miles

Difficulty: Flat, flowing water and elementary whitewater

Hazards: Windy weather possible, high water

Highlights: Riparian forest, historic tunnel

Nearby Canoe Rental: Hancock Outfitters, (301) 678-5050

More Information: C & O Canal National Historical Park, (301) 722-8226

T HERE ARE FEW places in the eastern United States where you can load up the canoe with food and camping gear and paddle downriver for two, three, four, or more days, secure in the knowledge of finding good campsites and sufficient water in the river. The Potomac River in western Maryland is just such a place, and although it is well used by canoeists, it is never too crowded. Wilderness it is not, but a surprising degree of solitude can be found. And the scenery is most pleasant: rolling hills, green forests, and little development. Although the upper Potomac is not outstanding in any single way, the sum of its many parts makes it a unique place.

The Potomac in western Maryland owes much of its primitive character to an accident of history. The C & O Canal parallels the river's Maryland shore; it served as a route for hauling freight between Cumberland and Washington until 1924. After that, the canal was abandoned, and large parts of it were destroyed or dewatered by storms and floods. The canal slumbered in a backwater of history and geography for years, until it caught the eye of developers and planners, who envisioned it as a fine site for a highway. Fortunately, preservationists led by Supreme Court Justice William O. Douglas prevailed, and the canal and towpath were made into a national historical park. The towpath was converted into a trail for foot, horse, and bicycle travel, and campsites were established every few miles. Thus a greenbelt of recreational park land protects one side of the river for 184 miles.

This section of the Potomac gets its name from the winding path the river has taken in carving its way through the ridges and valleys near the tiny hamlet of Paw Paw, West Virginia. You will often find the sun in your eyes, then later at your back, and then again on your face in the course of a few short river miles. Progress, measured as the crow flies, is slow, but the idea of canoeing is to enjoy not just the final destination, but the getting there as well.

The trip described here is a 21.7-mile, two-day canoe camper, a typical weekend trip. It begins at Paw Paw and ends at Little Orleans. At the conclusion of the trip description, sections upstream and downstream are described so that shorter, longer, or different trips can be planned.

TRIP DESCRIPTION

The put-in is at a National Park Service river access site downstream of Paw Paw. Picnic tables, outhouses, and plenty of parking may be found here; overnight camping is prohibited. The portage from the parking area to the boat launch is about 200 yards, quite a long distance when you're loading a canoe with camping gear. Also at the boat ramp is a metal river gauge divided into three sections: safe, caution, and danger. Although you should heed it, the gauge alone is insufficient since it does not predict future changes in water levels. The Potomac

Potomac River: Paw Paw Bends

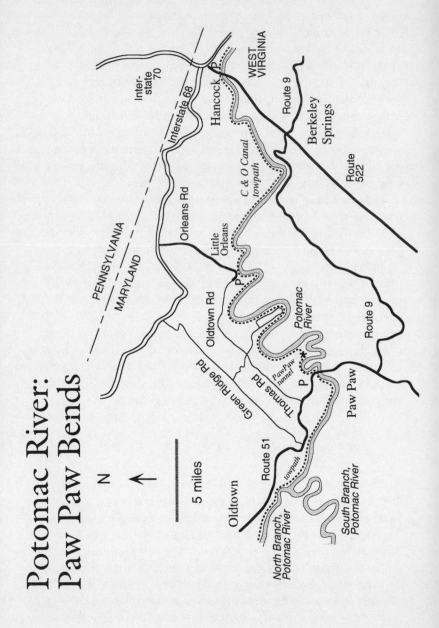

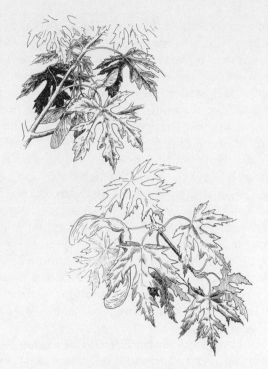

Silver maple leaves

has a large watershed, and widespread rainfalls of an inch or more may well bring the river to unsafe levels. Get a good two-day weather report before you leave, and use caution and good judgment during high water.

The current in the upper Potomac is continuous but not swift. It pushes the canoe along at about 2 mph, even in calm portions. A few small riffles, widely spaced, are found on this trip, but none is likely to cause trouble. Merely avoid rocks and keep the canoe pointed downstream, and you'll have no problems. At high water, the rapids do not get larger but merely wash out.

As you leave the canoe landing at Paw Paw, civilization drops behind. The steep forested hills of the Green River State Forest reach down to the river on the Maryland side. An impressive outcrop of reddish sandstone protrudes into the river within about a mile of the start. There is good deepwater swimming here, and it is one of the few places where a swimmer cannot touch bottom. It's easy to see how the sand forming the rock was laid down in successive layers and subsequently folded and twisted. Much of the rock underlying this entire area is sandstone and its derivatives, yielding thin, rocky soils poor in nutrients. Ridgetops and steep slopes have the least-developed soils; look for small, twisted Virginia pines growing here, where little else can. In contrast, the river floodplain and hollows between hills boast a diversity of large, healthy trees because the soils there are richer and retain water better.

This section of the Potomac is notable for its many train trestles over the river. It would seem that several railroads are converging on some important center of commerce, judging by the number of trestles spanning the river. But a glance at the map shows that the railroads run straight, cutting directly across the many bends in the river. Trains are frequent, but they don't really detract from the river experience.

Most overnighters stop at the Sorrel Ridge hiker-biker (and canoer) campsite about eight miles into the trip. It is on river left about a mile below two consecutive railroad bridges. Although it is not easy to spot, the outhouse and a cleared flat area beneath the trees can usually be seen if you keep a weather eye peeled. The site covers about 200 yards of shoreline, so there is room for several groups.

Camping at Sorrel Ridge allows you to take a day hike westward on the C & O Canal towpath. The trail leaves the river and enters a narrow cut in the living rock blasted out with black gunpowder. Known as Tunnel Hollow, it is the entrance to the 3,118-foot-long Paw Paw Tunnel. This brick-lined tunnel houses the C & O Canal and towpath on its route through the bowels of the mountain. By constructing this tunnel, canal builders avoided the longer route along the sinuous curves of Paw Paw Bends. Just beyond the western end of the tunnel lies the put-in parking lot—a handy location in case you left some vital piece of equipment in your car! Bring a flashlight for hiking through the tunnel.

Downstream, the river resumes its meandering, although the curves are now much wider. Bonds Landing on river left is an access point, and a local canoe outfitter often puts day trippers onto the river here. Nevertheless, the river is wide enough to space out the canoes. Ospreys and even the occasional bald eagle frequent the wide, shallow places, sweeping over the water in search of fish.

The final bend reveals a beehive of activity around the river access at Little Orleans. Between canoeists, picnickers, fishermen, and campers, there is always noise and commotion—a marked contrast to the peace and quiet of your last two days of paddling. The aqueduct at Little Orleans is well preserved and very beautiful; paddle your canoe up into the mouth of Fifteen Mile Creek to see it up close.

A word to the wise: leave any cars parked at Little Orleans on the uphill side of the riverside lot. This lot is covered with water when the river rises to even moderately high levels. Many a paddler has completed a Paw Paw Bends trip only to find his or her shuttle vehicle half submerged in the muddy Potomac.

Finally, no trip here would be complete without a visit to Bill's, the country store in Little Orleans, just on the uphill side of the railroad tracks. Although the interior has been cleaned up in recent years and is now a restaurant and bar, it is still worth a visit. Sodas, candy, and snacks are available, as are a pool table and video games in an adjacent room. Check out the dollar bills tacked to the ceiling by customers from far and near who wished their visit recorded for posterity. The exterior, a ramshackle place of weathered boards with swinging chairs out front, comes straight out of the West Virginia hills.

ALTERNATIVE TRIPS

If you have a three-day weekend or longer, consider continuing downriver to Hancock, a further 16.6 miles. The scenery is similarly fine, and there are even fewer people on the river. Or put in at Spring Gap (17 miles upriver from Paw Paw) or

Oldtown (11 miles upriver). However, avoid these upper put-ins at very low summer water, as they are above the point where the considerable flow of the South Branch of the Potomac enters.

DIRECTIONS

To reach Little Orleans from Washington or Baltimore, take I-70 west. At Hancock, exit onto I-68 west. Continue west on I-68, through the spectacular Sideling Hill road cut. At the top of the next hill, take the well-marked exit for Orleans Road. Follow this road south (left) to its end. To reach Paw Paw from here, driving will be mostly on dirt or gravel roads, so use care in wet or freezing weather. From the Little Orleans store, turn west on Oldtown Road. Cross Fifteen Mile Creek on the low water bridge, turn right, and stay with Oldtown Road by going right at the fork. Follow this road for a long distance through Green Ridge State Forest. The road ends at Route 51, an asphalt road. Turn left and proceed downhill to the well-marked Paw Paw river access. When you return to do the shuttle to Little Orleans, this road leading up into Green Ridge State Forest is labeled Thomas Road, not Oldtown Road, but it is the same road.

Sideling Hill Road Cut

Maryland is not a state notable for its geological formations. Compared to the wonders of Yosemite Valley or the wind-sculpted rock of the Colorado Plateau, Maryland is a geological wallflower, where soil and vegetation cover the bones of the earth. Only Calvert Cliffs, with its layers of fossil beds, is well known. But the recent construction of Interstate 68 west of Hancock has exposed a geological site of national significance, where the road cuts through Sideling Hill. Even tourists with no interest in or understanding of geology marvel at the multi-colored layers of rock. In response to this newfound fame, the state has constructed a visitor center and pedestrian bridge from which the cliffs can be safely viewed.

The Sideling Hill road cut offers a unique and rare glimpse into the geological past. The first and most obvious feature to note is that the rocks form a number of distinct layers, much like layers of cake and icing in a Black Forest cake. Each layer corresponds to a deposit of mud, sand, silt, gravel, or organic matter that was subsequently compressed into stone. All of the rocks visible at Sideling Hill were laid down between 330 and 345 million years ago. At that time, the ancestral Appalachian Mountains occupied what is now the Blue Ridge near Frederick. The area to the west of the Blue Ridge, including Sideling Hill and extending as far west as a line running between Pittsburgh and Charleston, West Virginia, was an alluvial floodplain receiving material eroded off the mountains. Farther west still was a shallow inland sea. Changes in the level of this sea also resulted in deposition of fine-grained material.

All the rocks at Sideling Hill are therefore sedimentary in nature. The type of sedimentary rock formed depends, in large part, on the size of the particles deposited. Clays or claystones form from the finest particles, shales and siltstones from mud, sandstone from sand. Conglomerate is a mixture of the largest particles: sand, pebbles, and cobbles that occur where rivers deposit these coarse-grained materials. Coal beds form from decaying plant material in swamps. Of course, these distinctions are artificial, and, although useful, obscure the fact that all these types intergrade with one another.

The second obvious feature to note about the cliffs is that the layers of rock, or strata, are folded into a U shape. This formation is called a syncline, and it contrasts with an anticline, in which the strata form a shape similar to the letter A. The forces needed to fold and bend these rocks were immense. About 230 to 240 million years ago, long after the sediments had been laid down and compressed into rock, the folding began. Largely as a result of the stresses created by the collision of the North American and African continents far to the east, the pressure folded what had previously been horizontal layers of rock. Mountains thousands of feet high were formed, occupying what is now the Ridge and Valley Province. In Maryland, this province extends from the western edge of the Blue Ridge near Middletown westward to the Allegany Front near Cumberland. This same period of orogeny, or mountain-building, lifted the similar rock strata of the Allegany Plateau west of Cumberland, but the forces were not strong enough to fold them. Thus the rocks in this more westerly region (which also includes the Poconos and Catskills) are still mostly horizontal, although of high elevation.

In the last 200 million years, erosion has greatly reduced the size of the mountains in the Ridge and Valley Province, resulting in a series of north-south–trending ridges. Easily erodable rocks like shales, siltstones, and limestones have been removed, while hard rocks like sandstones, which are less easily eroded, still remain. Thus most of the ridges seen today, like Sideling Hill, are capped by sandstones, whereas the valleys contain softer rocks. This is the explanation for the seemingly contradictory observation that a syncline, the lowest part of the strata, occupies the highest topography.

In summary, three major processes are responsible for the appearance of the rock exposed at the Sideling Hill road cut: deposition (in which the rocks were formed by settling and compression of sediments); orogeny (in which pressures folded the rock strata and uplifted the region into mountains); and erosion (in which water cut away the rock).

Fossils are present but not common in some layers of Sideling Hill. They consist primarily of the shells of marine invertebrates. Climbing on the cliff faces to search for such fossils is prohibited. The rock is very crumbly, and there are frequent minor rockfalls. So confine yourself to viewing the road cut from the pedestrian bridge near the visitor center. ⤆

Monocacy River

River Section: Lilypons Road to Mouth of Monocacy boat ramp

County: Frederick and Montgomery

Distance: 6.3 miles

Difficulty: Flowing flatwater, elementary whitewater

Hazards: High water

Highlights: Riparian forest

Nearby Canoe Rental: None

More Information: None

THE MONOCACY may be the quintessential Maryland river; neither tidal nor montane, it runs through the rich heartland of well-kept farms and low rolling pasturage. The Monocacy seems moderate in all its aspects: of medium volume with only a slight gradient; with little streamside development but not wild either; having few major environmental problems but accumulating a variety of minor insults. A canoe trip down the Monocacy will never be the most scenic, the most exciting, the most pristine, but the river will impress you, much like an old friend, with its quiet good nature. There is much to appreciate in the Monocacy, and for that reason it has been declared an official Scenic River by the state of Maryland.

The Monocacy drains several counties in south-central Pennsylvania, as well as parts of Frederick, Carroll, and Montgomery counties in Maryland. From the time its waters enter

Monocacy River

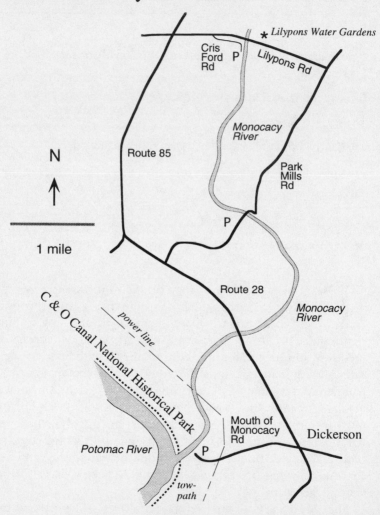

the state near Emmitsburg, it flows slowly for 57 miles in meandering bends southward toward the Potomac. Fine agricultural fields line most of the river, although a border of riparian habitat in the form of big old trees invariably buffers the river corridor and gives a sense of isolation to the paddler. Very little of the riverbank is publicly owned, but access is good at a variety of road crossings. When water levels are moderate, you can choose whatever section of river appeals to you, making judicious use of a good map. In summer, however, low water limits your paddling possibilities to the lowermost portion of the Monocacy. The trip outlined here runs from Lilypons Road to the mouth near Dickerson; these 6.3 miles almost always have enough water to float your canoe, although in dry years you may have to get out and haul your boat over a few rocks or gravel bars.

TRIP DESCRIPTION

Begin your voyage on the Monocacy just downstream from the high bridge at Lilypons Road. Cris Ford Road leads down to the river via a turnoff just west of the bridge; it is a gravel road and looks like a residential driveway, but it is clearly marked. The road reaches the river in the deep shade of tall trees at an old bridge crossing; this is a cool and pleasant place on a hot summer's day. There are no facilities here at all, however, so bring along everything you might need. The river dances as it flows fast over a gravelly bed but soon becomes a slow-moving pool, settling down to its typical pace.

The Monocacy runs fairly straight for several miles. Just before reaching the first bridge crossing at Park Mills Road (about 2.3 miles into the trip), the river runs over three small rapids, one after another. At low water, these can hang up your canoe, especially if it is made of aluminum. However, the rapids are not dangerous (unless the river is very high), and they may provide some spice to your trip if you can get through. For a shorter trip, you can access the river here at the road crossing (there is a fisherman's parking lot), thus avoiding the little rock garden.

The Monocacy is admirably adapted to a summer canoe trip with kids because it's a great river for wading, dabbling, and just generally messing around in water. Choose a gravel bar on which to pull out your canoe, and get wet! The river's depth averages only a foot or two, even near the center; there is no well-defined channel. The flow is continuous but never fast, and even small children are not overwhelmed by the current. The bed—of cobbles, sand, and gravel—gives a fairly good footing, although everyone should wear old sneakers and use care when wading. Bring along a surf mat or old truck inner tube for the kids to float in; adults can even position a low-slung beach chair in a foot or so of flowing water, sitting in water-cooled comfort while the children romp. You might even try "rapid sitting." This oxymoronic activity involves finding a small rapid or riffle, positioning yourself on a flat river-bottom rock, and trying to avoid being swept downstream by the current. If you park yourself in the lee of a larger rock, the turbulence formed by the aerated water gives the feeling of being in a jacuzzi. When the temperature hits 90 and you're tired of sitting at home in the air conditioning, this is the only way to beat the heat outdoors!

While you're sitting in the river, pull up a rock from the riverbed wherever there's a good current. In the Monocacy, you'll find it loaded with snails and aquatic insects. Most common are caddis flies, insects that are wormlike in shape but possess legs, with which they squirm over the rocks. Caddis flies cement together tiny stones to form rude huts, which help to protect them from predators; a square foot of rock surface may have dozens of these curious structures. Caddis flies spin a web of fibers that they set out in the current much like nets, capturing whatever drifts downstream and happens to get caught. Although caddis fly larvae are the most common aquatic insects on the Monocacy, you may also find a few water pennies and mayflies. Together, the number and diversity of these insects are an index to the water quality of any flowing river or stream, and they are used by scientists for that purpose.

Mallard

What does the aquatic insect index say about the water quality of the Monocacy? It's a mixed verdict: somewhat degraded, but not extremely so—about what you might expect of a creek running through mostly agricultural land. The input of nutrients from animal feces enriches the water and encourages the growth of algae on rocks. Fencing in pastures could go a long way toward curing this problem. At certain times of the year, pesticides and herbicides can get into the river, especially after heavy rains or during the spring thaw. Overall, however, the Monocacy is in pretty good shape, and its water quality will not negatively affect your trip.

Another two miles of paddling will bring you to the second road bridge of this trip. A shallow ledge of rocks spans the river almost under the bridge, making a pleasant riffle at higher water and a possible drag at low water levels. In another mile, the river seems to disappear, as an island occupies the middle. There are routes through on the right and in the center, but the passage on the left is more pleasant, featuring a quick, deep current. Protected by a gravel bar, this left chute is not visible until you're almost on top of it.

Signs of civilization now mark the end of the trip. The river passes under a sizzling high-tension line, carrying electricity from the nearby Dickerson generating plant. The ruins of an old bridge piling appear at a turn, and just past this the C & O Canal aqueduct and Potomac River emerge from the haze. Take out at the National Park Service boat ramp and parking lot on the left; there are trash cans but no other facilities.

Finally, the Monocacy is a fine fishing river. Sunnies and smallmouth abound, and they are usually easy to catch. Angling seems about equally divided between bank fishing, wading, and casting from a canoe or small boat, so take your pick. Once again, it's not the best fishing in the state, but it can be fun, especially for novices.

DIRECTIONS

From Baltimore, take I-70 west to Frederick. Exit at Route 355 south, going only for a hundred feet or so, and then branch right on Route 85 toward Buckeystown. Turn left on Lilypons Road. Go 0.4 mile and turn right on Cris Ford Road, to the put-in.

From Washington, take I-270 northwest toward Frederick. Take exit 26, Urbanna, getting on Route 80 west. Continue on Route 80 for a short distance; it ends at Route 85. Turn left, south, and proceed to Lilypons Road. Turn left, go 0.4 mile and turn right on Cris Ford Road.

To reach the take-out from the put-in, return to Route 85. Turn left. At a fork in the road, bear left; Route 85 turns into Route 28. Cross the Monocacy and continue south. Turn right onto Mouth of Monocacy Road; this is 6.0 miles from Lilypons Road. Follow it to the end, parking in the boat launch lot.

OTHER OUTDOOR RECREATIONAL OPPORTUNITIES NEARBY

Birders and gardeners will not want to miss Lilypons Water Gardens, located on Lilypons Road just east of the river. The gardens are situated on a broad floodplain, and the owners raise and sell all sorts of plants, although they specialize in aquatic plants. The water lilies bloom in July. The wetland habitats attract all sorts of water birds; birders should bring a spotting scope. Sugarloaf Mountain, just a few miles away, is a pleasant site for a short walk, and it is described beginning on page 134 in this book.

Riparian Habitat

Of all the different kinds of habitat found across the face of Maryland, perhaps none is as rich with living organisms as riparian habitat. Defined as the land edge of streams, rivers, lakes, and other bodies of water, riparian habitat is almost invariably a wetland, with hydric soils and characteristic plant species. Yet most of us do not consider the miles and miles of Maryland forested riparian habitat bordering our flowing rivers and creeks to be wetland. For this reason, the economic and ecological value of such riparian habitat is only poorly appreciated.

Forested riparian habitat has a great many environmental benefits. Streamside buffers of trees act as filters, removing excess nutrients from groundwater, decomposing pollutants, and removing bacteria. The roots of trees stabilize streambanks and prevent erosion, while the boles and forest floor detritus slow the speed of floodwaters, causing the deposition of sediment. These same trees shade the creek, creating a cooler, more humid microclimate important to organisms in the water as well as those on the land. Indeed, forested riparian zones are incredibly rich in animal life. Amphibians, so dependent on water for much of their life cycles, are obligately associated species. Among the mammals, otter, beaver, and mink are the most common riparian inhabitants. Bird life is especially rich in riparian zones; studies invariably show a higher density of breeding birds there than in nearby upland sites. Migrating forest species, probably using rivers to navigate, stop over here as well. The role of riparian habitat as corridors for wildlife movements between larger reserves has only recently become appreciated.

Historically, about 70 percent of North America's riparian habitat has been lost to forest clearance, drainage for agriculture, and development. Much of what is left, fortunately, will probably remain preserved, since its importance is now recognized. Although some towns in Maryland are built on river floodplains, more often local and state governments have purchased such lands and converted them into parks. Indeed, many of the trips described in this book traverse riparian zones.

Ultimately, the highest and best use of forested riparian habitat may be for the enjoyment and edification of us humans; if it is only by coincidence that such a use is also the most beneficial for wildlife, then so be it. ➤—

Upper Gunpowder River

River Section: Section 1: Masemore Road to Monkton Road
Section 2: Monkton Road to Phoenix Road

County: Baltimore

Distance: Section 1: 7.8 miles
Section 2: 6.8 miles

Difficulty: Flat flowing water, elementary whitewater

Hazards: Trees down in the river, rocks

Highlights: Riparian forest

Nearby Canoe Rental: Monkton Bike Rental,
  (410) 771-4058

More Information: Gunpowder Falls State Park,
  (410) 592-2897

THE GUNPOWDER RIVER gathers its waters from the rich, rolling countryside of north central Maryland and southern Pennsylvania. Rather sparsely populated, with only small, quaint hamlets, the land is dissected by a number of tiny streams, many of which contain viable populations of native trout. Yet almost as soon as these rivulets coalesce into something of size, the Gunpowder's waters are dammed into Prettyboy Reservoir. Between the outflow of Prettyboy Dam and the backwaters behind Loch Raven Dam 16 miles downstream lies a beautiful wooded valley that is one of the Baltimore metropolitan area's finest recreational resources.

Known among paddlers as the Upper Gunpowder, the river flows cool and clear year-round. Even in the driest weather,

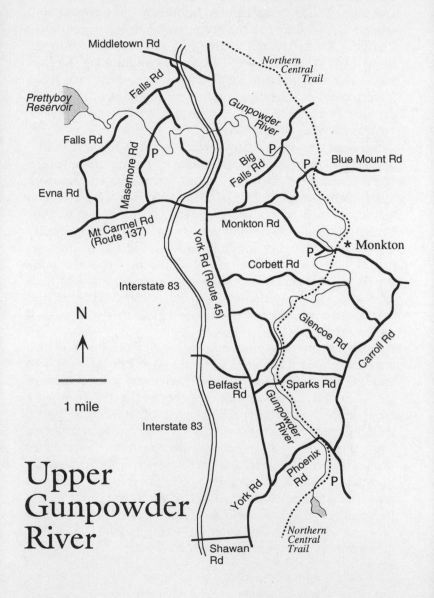

Middletown Rd

Falls Rd

Prettyboy
Reservoir

Falls Rd

Masemore Rd

Evna Rd

Mt Carmel Rd
(Route 137)

Interstate 83

N

1 mile

Interstate 83

Gunpowder
River

Northern
Central
Trail

P

Big
Falls Rd

P

P

Blue Mount Rd

Monkton Rd

P

* Monkton

Corbett Rd

York Rd (Route 45)

Glencoe Rd

Carroll Rd

Belfast
Rd

Sparks Rd

Gunpowder
River

Phoenix
Rd

P

York Rd

Shawan
Rd

Northern
Central
Trail

Upper
Gunpowder
River

there's a minimal flow of water in the river to maintain the fish and aquatic insect populations. In summer, the coolest spot around can be found in the steep, wooded gorge just below Prettyboy Dam. The water coming out of the bottom of the reservoir is in the 40 to 50° range, air-conditioning the river valley. The narrowness of the river (it is never more than about 50 feet wide) and the shade of the overhanging mature trees of the Gunpowder Falls State Park ensure that the water does not heat up appreciably in its flow to Loch Raven.

Although the Upper Gunpowder is canoeable year-round, dry-weather water levels are minimal. During these times, you'll scrape your canoe over gravel bars and riffles that mark the downstream ends of long, deep pools. In a few places, you may even have to get out and walk, dragging your canoe behind you. But on a hot summer day, a fluvial walk is refreshing. In fact, this is a great place to tow an old truck inner tube or two full of kids. Most people who tube the Upper Gunpowder do so only once; the chill waters linger in memory even after bones and muscles rewarm. But with a canoe to haul snacks and beverages and to provide a place to warm up, such a trip is memorable for its easy living.

Finally, keep a low profile on the Upper Gunpowder. Park your car only in designated areas and deal with the locals in a friendly and courteous fashion. There was a great deal of animosity toward tubers and canoeists in the 1970s, when a number of well-publicized incidents of rowdiness, public drinking, and rude behavior justifiably upset the local citizenry. Since then, the establishment of the Northern Central Trail alongside part of the river, and frequent patrols by park police, have been helpful in restoring peaceful relations, but this record of good behavior needs to be continued. So leave the beer and radios at home and carry out a trash bag full of litter on every trip. You'll feel better for having helped to keep this invaluable resource pristine.

TRIP DESCRIPTION

Masemore Road to Monkton Road

With sufficient water—typically in late fall, winter, and spring (into June)—begin your trip at Masemore Road. This is the uppermost easily accessible road crossing, and this upper part of the river is the most pleasantly intimate section. There's room to park about a dozen cars here, with good access to the river but no facilities. Initially, the river flows over shallow gravel bars, with a few riffles thrown in for variety. Vegetation overhangs the riverbanks, so keep to the middle. The flow is constant and fast in this upper section, and the first few miles can be covered quickly and with little effort.

Scenery along the Gunpowder is beautiful. Gunpowder Falls State Park runs along both banks of the river, preserving it from development. Rock outcrops decorated with ferns are common, and hillsides full of large trees stretch up from the river. In some places, rich floodplains on the insides of bends present a riot of vegetation. Spring wildflowers are superb.

On narrow, fast-flowing streams like this, canoers must use caution to avoid trees that have fallen into the river. Known as strainers because they hang up solid objects like canoes and canoers while allowing water to pass through, these hazards can be deadly on flooded creeks. At normal water levels on the Gunpowder, strainers can still result in a flip, a swim, and a broached canoe. Stay well away from downed trees, aggressively paddling your canoe out of the way well before you think you have to. Even on as benign a river as the Upper Gunpowder, strainers deserve a healthy dose of respect. There are a few places where what appear to have been mini-tornadoes have taken down dozens of trees and left them spanning the river in a tangled maze.

Rapids appear at only two locations. About a half mile downriver of York Road (Maryland Route 45), an old rock dam spans the river at a hard right turn. There is an opening near the right shore. The water drops about a foot into a fast, straight chute filled with small waves. The other rapid, about a hundred yards of moderate rapids, is found just below Big Falls Road. At low water, this will be impassible, as the river has been constricted by fill from the adjacent quarry and rock rubble fills the channel. At higher water levels, it will give a bouncy but straightforward ride.

Below the Big Falls Road quarry, the Gunpowder resumes its serene flow through forested parkland. A recommended take-out is at Blue Mount Road, a remote, shady location with limited parking, or further downstream at the Monkton Road highway bridge. Wheelchair-accessible bathrooms, water, picnic tables, trash cans, and information are available at Monkton station, just 100 yards uphill from the river. The distance from Masemore Road to Monkton Road is 7.8 miles.

Monkton Road to Phoenix Road

In summertime low water, the section from Monkton Road downstream to Phoenix Road is recommended. This route avoids the shallow rapids at the quarry described previously, and the river's flow is augmented by input from Little Falls. Although slightly wider and slower moving, the Gunpowder is still beautiful, shady, and cool. By summer, the river banks are a riot of lush vegetation, with jewelweed, coneflower, joe-pye weed, boneset, and New York ironweed flourishing in the rich, moist, alluvial soil. Bees, wasps, and bugs of all sorts congregate on the flowerheads in search of nectar and plant juices. The structural complexity of this herbaceous layer provides prime habitat for web-spinning spiders; the morning dew glints jewel-like along their tracery. Bird life along the river corridor is plentiful, with the young of the year now grown to adolescence. With food plentiful, living is easy, but the shortening days already portend the coming of cold weather, and animals use this time to store winter reserves.

The best take-out for this section of river is at a small wooden fishing platform about 200 yards downstream of the Phoenix Road bridge. Carry up the steep stairs, across the Northern Central Trail, and over to the adjacent parking lot. Do not continue downstream beyond this point, as the Gunpowder soon backs up into the flatwater of Loch Raven Reservoir. Canoeing is illegal here without a permit, and there are no good places to take out. The distance from Monkton Road to Phoenix Road is 6.8 miles.

If you have only one vehicle, or do not want to bother setting a car shuttle, it is possible to use the Northern Central Trail to bicycle back to your car. The trail parallels the Gunpowder as far north as Monkton.

DIRECTIONS

From the Baltimore Beltway, take I-83 north. To reach the Masemore Road put-in, exit the interstate at Mt. Carmel Road (Route 137). Turn left (west). The first right turn is Masemore Road; follow it to the river. To reach Monkton, return to Mt. Carmel Road. Cross over I-83. The road ends at York Road (Route 45). Turn right, go 100 yards, and turn left on Monkton Road. Follow it to the river. Access to the river is on the concrete right-of-way at the southeastern corner of the bridge. Obey the nearby No Parking signs; parking is available about 50 yards up the hill on a spur road.

River Floodplains and Amphibian Breeding Sites

Floodplains like those along Maryland's piedmont rivers provide a unique habitat for certain kinds of plants and animals. Each spring, heavy rains bring the river out of its banks, and silt-laden water spreads out over the floodplain. These irregular but consistent events provide plants growing in the floodplain with a fresh pulse of nutrient-rich alluvial soil, decaying vegetation, seeds, and moisture. Thus the floodplain receives the natural equivalent of a good fertilizing. Of course, a major flood also has a down side: it will scour low-lying areas of vegetation, weaken the root systems of large trees, and

Green frogs

generally subject the flora to erosional stress and localized extinctions.

Seasonal flooding also creates temporary ponds in low-lying areas of the floodplain just beyond the primary banks of the river. These vernal pools usually dry up by midsummer, but over their short lifetimes they provide important habitat for the living organisms of a river valley. Perhaps the most significant role of these ephemeral wetlands is as a breeding ground for several species of amphibians. The vernal ponds along the upper Gunpowder River are among the best local examples.

The first warm, rainy night of late winter or early spring signals the start of the breeding season for many frogs and salamanders. Leaving estivation sites deep in the earth on surrounding hillsides, adult animals migrate toward the floodplain, drawn by some primitive, unknowable urge. Wood frogs are the earliest-breeding species in Maryland. They can sometimes be found in these vernal ponds even when a skim of ice extends outward from the edges, as early as February. A dark mask or line extending horizontally across the face from ear to ear, identifies the wood frog. Sound is the best way to locate breeding frogs; each species has its own characteristic call. The wood frog makes a raspy sound, halfway between a quack and a cluck. Its breeding season is short, ranging from a few days to a few weeks, depending on weather conditions. After eggs are laid in the vernal ponds, adults disperse back into the surrounding forests, leaving the developing young at the mercy of predators and harsh weather.

Breeding almost as early as the wood frog is the spring peeper. It is perhaps the most common of our frogs and is familiar to almost everyone. Its long breeding season and noisy call make it synonymous with the coming of spring. Identified by an X-shaped design on its back, the frog is tiny (with a body less than two inches long) and amazingly hard to find even when it is vocalizing. Its distinctive call is a short, sharp note or peep. Males stake out a territory at the edge of a vernal pond and sing to advertise their readiness to mate.

Still later in the season, after wood frogs have left but while peepers are still active, American toads join the chorus. Their call is a loud trill of closely spaced notes. Once again, males stake out a territory, and they will clasp (or attempt to clasp) almost anything that moves past—a female, another male, or even an otherwise inanimate object. For this reason, males have a second call in their repertoire, a "get-off-my-back" call. If you stay long enough at an active breeding site, you should be able to distinguish this different call.

These breeding amphibians are sometimes active all day at the short peak of their breeding season, but activity really picks up after dark. For this reason, early evening is the best time to visit and observe this fascinating rite of spring. Armed with hip waders and a good flashlight, make your way to the edge of a vernal pond and wait until the animals get acclimated to your presence. You can then use your flashlight to spotlight singing amphibians, find mating pairs, or locate egg masses. Fortunately, most frogs and toads seem to remain oblivious to this intrusion on their sex lives. Since the sounds of breeding frogs are among the earliest signs of spring, a visit to one of these vernal ponds is a great way to reconnect with the natural world after a long winter inside. ⤙

Virginia Canal

River Section: Virginia Canal circuit, using the Potomac River and C & O Canal

County: Loudon (Virginia)

Distance: About 2 miles

Difficulty: Elementary whitewater

Hazards: Rocks, trees down in the river, high water

Highlights: Riparian forest

Nearby Canoe Rental: None

More Information: C & O Canal National Historical Park, (301) 299-3613

MOST OF THE CANOEING rivers listed in this book are scenic flatwater, but here's one with elementary whitewater that can be managed by anyone who is able to maneuver a canoe accurately. It's a narrow, intimate side channel of the Potomac River west of Washington, with good scenery and wildlife. Best of all, the trip requires no shuttle; it's a circuit where you paddle back to your car.

The Virginia Canal, also known as the Patowmack Canal, is a part of a canal system older than the better-known C & O Canal. Built by a company that included George Washington as an investor, this canal permitted navigation around the rapids at Seneca. By about 1830, it had fallen into disrepair, and today it bears no resemblance at all to an artificial waterway.

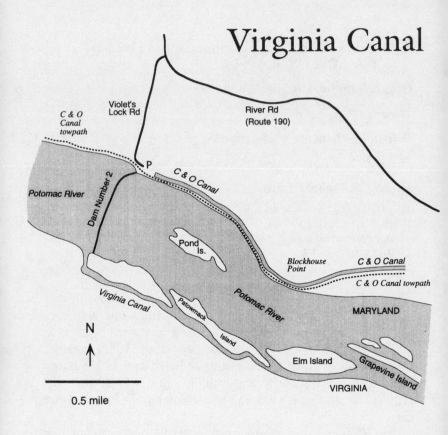

Virginia Canal

TRIP DESCRIPTION

Begin (and end) your trip at the Violet's Lock parking area of the C & O Canal National Historical Park. Neither drinking water nor bathrooms are available here, so arrive with a full water bottle and an empty bladder. Parking places are at a premium; arrive before 9 A.M. or after 2 P.M. in warm weather. Carry your canoe across the C & O Canal's Lock 23, then upstream on the towpath for 50 yards, and finally down to the riverbank. The remains of Feeder Dam Number 2 back up the river here into a long slackwater known as Seneca Lake, popular with powerboaters and water-skiers. Paddle across the wide Potomac well above the rubble of Dam Number 2. On the far Virginia shore, look for an opening in the trees that is located about 100 feet above the rapids formed by the crumbling dam.

Entry into this intimate stream opens up a whole different world. Tall trees arch gracefully overhead; the canal is shady and cool on even the hottest summer days. There is a continuous current here, even at low water, so paddle only to steer, relax in available eddys to enjoy the scenery, and take your time. Stay alert for downed trees in the water and avoid them even before you think you need to. Because the Potomac is such a big river, it carries much debris when in flood. That debris frequently gets tangled up among rocks and along the riverbanks in a chute as narrow as the Virginia Canal, making it more hazardous than would be typical.

Keep an eye peeled for wildlife as you paddle the Virginia Canal. Turtles and herons (both great blue and green-backed) frequent these backwaters, although they tend to be a bit skittish. You're more likely to hear the plop of a turtle diving from a log than to see it and to glimpse the wrong end of a heron as it flaps off downriver than to watch it feeding peacefully. On hot summer days, water snakes are common. These thick, chocolate-brown snakes with obscure patterning are generally harmless, although they can be pugnacious and deliver a sharp bite if provoked. They also give off a nasty-smelling, mucouslike secretion when handled. Finally, these woody sloughs are favorite hangouts for wood ducks. Nesting in cavities in trees, male wood ducks are probably the most beautiful of all our ducks. Count yourself lucky if you see one of these avian jewels.

Several small rapids and riffles punctuate the canal. Local paddling clubs find the Virginia Canal a perfect training site for novices enjoying their first taste of whitewater, and informal classes are frequently encountered. The current flow is fast enough to create visible eddy lines, but not so violent as to flip over the unwary canoeist or kayaker. All the rapids are open down the middle but require some elementary steering skills. A pool for recovery and relaxation follows each.

The Virginia Canal is divided into three visually distinct segments. The first quarter mile runs straight and fairly narrow, with a steep bank on the right side. The final rapid of this section drops about one foot over a ledge over which experienced kayakers drift sideways, into a surprisingly vigorous surf. A large, deep pool follows, marking the start of the second segment of river. Here the water splits among a maze of channels, separated by rock outcrops and small islands. Selecting a route with enough water can be a problem through here at dead low water levels, and a judicious reading of current flow is helpful. The end of this second section is marked by a channel on river left that flows back into the main Potomac around the west end of Elm Island. Continue downstream, however, into the third segment of the canal. Here the river widens, flowing over a shallow bed of stones and gravel unobstructed by rapids or rock outcroppings. If the water is clear, note the many tiny shells of freshwater clams and mussels that litter the bottom; this shallow, cool, sheltered environment with a steady flow of oxygenated water is a nearly perfect habitat for these poorly appreciated animals.

After another third of a mile, the Virginia Canal merges with the main Potomac. Turn left, around the end of Elm Island, and paddle upstream against the current. The goal is to cross the Potomac to its Maryland shore; to do so, you must traverse the western end of Grapevine Island, which here divides the main Potomac for more than a mile. Once you've attained the head of the island, aim for the gap in the trees that marks a

Pawpaw leaves and flowers

pipeline crossing. Do not, however, take out here for the portage to the C & O Canal, because the canal has diverged from the river at this point. Instead, continue upstream 100 yards to a well-used beach for a flat, 30-yard carry.

Once on the rewatered canal, proceed upstream (left). A remarkable number of pawpaw trees line the canal here. In late August, many bear edible fruits that resemble green, fat, stubby bananas. Scoop out the custardlike fruit inside for an enjoyable snack. There are also a few persimmon trees overhanging the water. The fruit, an orangish sphere about the size of a golf ball, requires cold weather to become palatable. Ripe specimens will have a brownish tinge and will virtually fall into your hand when cradled gently. Eating an unripe persimmon, however, is one of life's most unpleasant gustatory experiences, for it resembles nothing so much as a mouthful of raw cotton.

This entire circuit is just a bit over two miles long. If you take your time, loaf, practice eddy turns, and work on your tan, it can be a satisfying half-day trip. Couple it with some good friends and a picnic lunch and you have a recipe for a great day on the river!

A final note of caution: the Potomac is a powerful river at moderate to high water, and at those times it is no place for an open canoe. To find out about water levels before you leave home, phone (703) 260-0305 and listen for the Little Falls gauge reading. If it is between 3.5 and 4.0 feet you should have whitewater experience; above 4.0 feet, you would be wise to curl up at home with a good book.

DIRECTIONS

From the Capital Beltway, take Route 190 (River Road) west. Proceed 11.3 miles, through the village of Potomac, and turn left onto Violet's Lock Road. Follow the road to its end at the parking area.

The drive to Violet's Lock is almost as entertaining as the river run itself. Route 190 runs through Potomac, Maryland, one of the nation's most affluent communities and a hotbed of conspicuous consumption. The houses along River Road are immense, with high-ceilinged rooms and many windows. One of my favorite pastimes is to count the number of fancy cars on River Road between the Beltway and Violet's Lock. See if you can beat my personal best of 13 Mercedeses, 3 Jaguars, and 2 Rolls-Royces!

Mussels

Freshwater mussels may be one of the least-known and most poorly appreciated groups of animals found in Maryland. These shelled animals are molluscs, a taxonomic group that also includes snails, clams, and oysters. They have two shells (and so are called bivalves), a heavy, wedge-shaped foot that they use to move and anchor themselves, and a pair of extendable siphons. Freshwater mussels typically sit half-buried in river-bottom gravel with their shells partly open, filtering the passing flow of water for food.

Because they are immobile and feed by filtration, mussels are exquisitely sensitive to water quality. Pollutants in the water column tend to accumulate in mussel tissues; in fact, analysis of tissue has been used to identify an upstream pollution source via its unique chemical signature. Massive mussel die-offs have been documented in response to major pollution events upstream. Unable to move, mussels are tireless monitors of water quality.

In addition to chemical pollution, mussels are sensitive to sedimentation. Changes in upstream land use, such as deforestation and development, usually cause erosion. Increased loads of silt and mud eventually fill the interstices in bottom gravels that mussels require and make feeding and breathing more difficult.

Construction of dams has also affected mussel populations and their diversity. Mussels require sun-warmed waters to reproduce; many dams release water from the cold bottom of the reservoir. Although this release is often a boon to trout, it means that mussels may continue to exist for years but never reproduce.

In optimum habitat, fertilization results in a free-living larval stage called a glochidium. This tiny, clamlike organism settles to the river bottom and awaits a passing fish. When a fish brushes the open shells of the glochidium, the valves close around a gill or fin. The little mussel obtains nourishment from the fish for a period of time and then eventually drops off. If the glochidium fails to attach to a fish, or falls off in unsuitable habitat, it dies. Some scientists believe that declines in mussel numbers and distribution may be due in part to the decline in anadromous fish populations that serve as glochidium hosts.

North America is host to the greatest diversity of freshwater mussels in the world. Unfortunately, 43 percent of its 300 species are extinct, endangered, or threatened. Unobtrusive and sensitive, freshwater mussels act as canaries in the environmental coal mines, and their continued existence is largely in our hands. ⤙

Middle Youghiogheny River

River Section: Ramcat Launch Site near Confluence to Ohiopyle

County: Somerset (Pennsylvania)

Distance: 8 miles

Difficulty: Elementary whitewater

Hazards: Rocks, high water

Highlights: Forested borders

Nearby Canoe Rental: Contact Ohiopyle State Park, (412) 329-8591, for a list of outfitters

More Information: Ohiopyle State Park, (412) 329-8591

THE YOUGHIOGHENY river begins its life in the high, cool frost pocket bogs and clear-flowing springs at the extreme southwestern end of Maryland. The wet climate of Garrett County ensures that plenty of water runs off the land, and the Yough (pronounced "Yock") is a river big enough to canoe within 10 miles of its origin. The river flows almost due north and begins to cut a narrow, steep-sided gorge when it enters Swallow Falls State Park. For the next 15 miles, the river canyon is one of the most remote and difficult-to-reach places in the state of Maryland. The whitewater here, known as the Upper Yough, is exceedingly difficult (rated as Class V) and appropriate only for teams of expert boaters using every safety precaution.

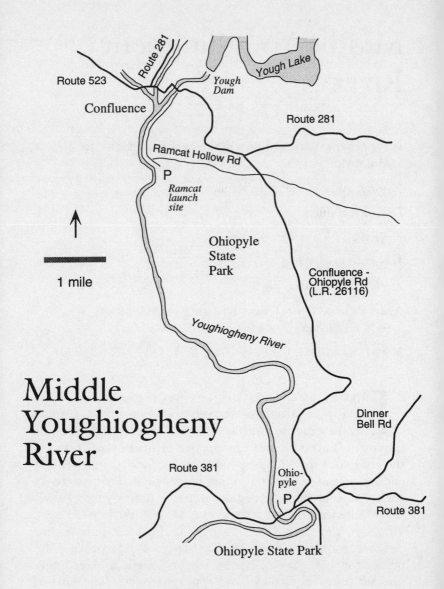

Route 281

Route 523

Yough Lake

Yough Dam

Confluence

Route 281

Ramcat Hollow Rd

P

Ramcat launch site

Ohiopyle State Park

Confluence - Ohiopyle Rd (L.R. 26116)

1 mile

Youghiogheny River

Middle Youghiogheny River

Dinner Bell Rd

Route 381

Ohio- pyle

P

Route 381

Ohiopyle State Park

When the river finally slows down at the little town of Friendsville, it backs up into the long, thin reservoir known as Yough Lake. Here it is the playground of water-skiers, powerboaters, and even the occasional sailboat, and the traffic on the water is always heavy.

At the far north end of the lake, the dam releases at least 350 cubic feet of water per second, 24 hours a day, 365 days a year. It is this reliable flow, unusual from most dams in the east, that makes canoeing, kayaking, and rafting possible downstream. The section just below the dam, running about eight miles downstream to the town of Ohiopyle, Pennsylvania, is called the Middle Yough, and it is the section recommended here for canoeing. It's true that the Middle Yough is not in Maryland. But nowhere in the Free State is there a river for canoeing that features rapids and year-round flow. So, since virtually all the water in the river is Maryland water, visit and have a great time!

TRIP DESCRIPTION

The Middle Yough is an eight-mile trip of flat, flowing water punctuated by several stretches of easy, straightforward rapids. It is most appropriate for canoeists with experience in simple rapids, especially for those who have taken a basic river canoeing course. If you've never been in a canoe before, or if you can't keep a canoe going in a straight line, this is not the place for you. Try instead one of the easier trips detailed in this book.

The trip begins at the Ramcat Launch Site, maintained by Ohiopyle State Park, about two miles downstream from the town of Confluence. Parking for 50 cars is available here, as is a wheelchair-accessible composting toilet. There is no drinking water.

Carry your canoe about 100 feet down the clearly marked trail to the river. A metal gauge here denotes water level. Above four feet, the character of the river changes dramatically, and canoes are not advisable. Here at the put-in the current sweeps along quickly over gravel and small rocks; the water is gin-clear and very cold, as the dam is located just upstream. Launch and you're quickly underway. Within about 200 yards is the first rapid, Ramcat. The Riversport School of Paddling, located on the far shore, has strung a series of hanging poles, or gates, throughout the rapid for use by their kayaking classes, and these clearly identify the rapid. At normal water levels, Ramcat will give you a bouncy, splashy ride on which the occasional wave may drop into the bow paddler's lap. The rapid is wide open and may be run anywhere that there's enough water.

Rapids interspersed with short, calm stretches continue for about another mile. None is more difficult than Ramcat. The deep green pools between rapids are good fishing holes. They're also great places to swim, but only if you're really hot; even in midsummer, water temperature is in the low 50s.

The river now enters a five-mile stretch of very calm, slowly flowing water known as the Flats. At low water, you'll have to look carefully to spot the channel, as the river tends to spread out to 100 yards wide and six inches deep. A wrong decision could lead to a scraped hull, or even a short fluvial walk hauling the canoe behind you. Although the paddling is sometimes tedious here, the scenery is superb. On river left, unbroken expanses of trees march up to the top of large mountains, the tallest of which is Sugarloaf Knob, at 2,640 feet. The only sign of human presence is the occasional train on the B & O tracks paralleling the river on the right.

Rapids begin again before mile 7, as the river narrows. Once again, all are straightforward, but the occasional midstream rock can cause problems for those too slow to react. Large blocks of sandstone scattered along the river banks make fine sunbathing or snacking spots, and the river provides entertainment as you watch other paddlers negotiate the rapids.

The final rapid of the trip is named Elephant Rock, after the large chunk of Pottsville sandstone that stands at midriver. Its resemblance to a ponderous pachyderm crossing the river is uncanny. Run your canoe down the open channel to the right of Elephant Rock.

The take-out is about a quarter mile downstream on the left. It is clearly marked with a wooden sign. If you should miss this obvious take-out, make sure you beach your canoe under the Route 381 road bridge. Just below here, large rapids begin, and these terminate in the 20-foot-high Ohiopyle Falls. Canoes going over the falls most nearly resemble large aluminum pretzels, and bodies fare somewhat worse.

The take-out at Ohiopyle has 80 parking spaces, and water, wheelchair-accessible bathrooms, and information are available at the old train station. Food, gas, and gifts are available in town, a block away, as is more parking. As this parking lot is shared with bicyclists, hikers, and sightseers, it is usually crowded.

In the event of an emergency during your trip, the Youghiogheny River Trail runs along the left side of the river from Confluence to Ohiopyle, and a passing cyclist could no doubt get an emergency notification to park officials in a short time.

Outfitters in Confluence and Ohiopyle rent other watercraft suitable for the Middle Yough in addition to canoes. Families with small children or uncertain canoeing skills may rent a raft and travel this stretch on their own. Although ponderous and slow, rafts are almost impossible to flip over in rapids this small; can haul lots of kids, clothes, coolers, and almost anything else you can think of; and make a great platform for swimming.

More recently, rubber ducky rentals have become popular. A rubber ducky is a one- or two-person inflatable raft shaped like a kayak. It is paddled from a sitting position with a double-bladed kayak paddle. Duckies are highly maneuverable, forgiving, and fun in whitewater, and learning to paddle them requires only a few minutes of practice. They are a poor choice on cold days, however, since the paddler sits in the bilgewater. They provide a good introduction for those who think they might like to try kayaking.

DIRECTIONS

From Washington or Baltimore, take I-70 west. At Hancock, get on I-68 west. About 25 miles beyond Cumberland, take exit 14B, marked Uniontown, Pa. This road will dead-end in about 200 yards, at the Keyser's Ridge truck stop. Turn left on Route 40. After about five miles on Route 40, turn right on Route 523. Follow it for seven miles into the town of Confluence. Turn left at the sign "to Route 281," crossing two bridges. Follow Route 281 west over the Youghiogheny River and make an immediate right. The Ramcat launch area is about two miles down this road.

To reach the Ohiopyle take-out from Ramcat, leave the parking lot and turn right. This road (Ramcat Hollow Road) quickly turns to gravel. Follow it uphill for several miles until it intersects an asphalt road, Confluence-Ohiopyle Road (L.R. 26116). Turn right and drive over several large hills to a T junction in Ohiopyle. Turn right, go three blocks, and turn right again just before going over the river. Enter the train station parking lot and drive to the far end.

OTHER OUTDOOR RECREATIONAL OPPORTUNITIES NEARBY

Ohiopyle State Park is one of the world's finest for water sports. In addition to the Middle Yough, described here, from Ohiopyle downstream for 7.5 miles is the Lower Yough, the most heavily used stretch of whitewater in the world. Peak summer weekends will see almost 2,000 rafters and boaters challenging the many difficult rapids. In addition, a superb bike trail parallels the river for at least 16 miles extending from Confluence downstream. This newly completed trail has already become very popular, and cyclists now outnumber boaters in Ohiopyle. There are a number of excellent hiking trails leaving from "downtown" Ohiopyle; the best are the Ferncliff Penninsula Trail and the Meadow Run Trail. The mob scene in Ohiopyle tends to obscure the fact that the river and its valley have extraordinary scenic beauty. Visit, if you can, on a weekday, when you can truly enjoy the river and surrounding Ohiopyle State Park.

Salamanders, Frogs, and Localized Extinctions

Amphibians like salamanders and frogs play a surprisingly significant role in many ecosystems. For example, amphibian biomass often exceeds that of all other vertebrates combined in moist, mature forests. Although poorly studied and rarely considered in environmental assessments, amphibians make good bioindicators of changes in habitat quality because of their water- and air-permeable skin and their position high on the food chain.

Scientists who study amphibians assembled for the first time in 1990, and they were surprised to find that there were many reports of mortality and extinctions from all over the globe. It seemed that in the previous decade many populations of frogs and salamanders had declined or disappeared. Although local problems could account for some of the declines, others occurred in pristine and protected areas as diverse as national parks in California, Costa Rica, and Australia. Were these amphibians the first signal of some global, as yet unrealized, environmental problem?

Maybe. Scientists continue to collect data in the field that show declines and localized extinctions. Nevertheless, dismay has been tempered by a new understanding and appreciation of the population dynamics of amphibians.

For example, one group of scientists has been studying three species of salamander and one of frog in a South Carolina seasonal pond since 1979. They reported that population sizes varied significantly from year to year. For example, marbled

Red salamander

salamanders showed a high of about 2,600 females in 1986 but a low of 3 in 1981. Tiger salamanders and chorus frogs each went locally extinct during the study, but each time their numbers rebounded in later years. Recruitment (survival of a new generation to metamorphosis) varied even more widely, by over five orders of magnitude.

The causative agent of these fluctuations was water. These amphibians breed in seasonal ponds that accumulate rainfall in the late autumn and winter and dry up completely in the summer. Wet years typically led to large populations and good recruitment, whereas dry years had the opposite effect. Thus the length of time over which water persisted in the pond was correlated with population size. Having evolved over millions of years with these episodic variations, amphibians have adapted to these "boom or bust" cycles.

In addition to dramatic changes in the size of a population over time, animals like amphibians must be examined in the context of their spatial arrangement. Amphibian breeding sites are typically spread widely over suitable landscape; in dry years each site may be disjunct, whereas wet years may connect them with corridors of habitat suitable for migration. Thus a reproductive failure at one site may be offset by a wildly successful year elsewhere that provides excess animals for migration and colonization. Viewed over time and space, then, localized populations may fluctuate widely, winking in and out of existence like the flashing lights on a Christmas tree. This "metapopulation" theory may be helpful in understanding patterns of distribution and abundance among amphibians and other species.

Widespread variation in amphibian populations seems to be the norm, and observers who look at only one or two years of census data from a single location can come to erroneous conclusions regarding the rarity of salamander and frog species. This cautionary tale illustrates the importance of long-term scientific studies (and the money necessary to fund such research) in the examination of our natural heritage. ✦

GLOSSARY

Terms included in definitions that are themselves defined elsewhere in the glossary are *italicized*.

Accipiter　A fast, agile, low-flying woodland hawk with short, rounded wings and a long tail whose primary food is other small birds taken in flight. Three species occur in Maryland: the sharp-shinned hawk, Cooper's hawk, and the northern goshawk.

Alluvium　Clay, silt, sand, gravel, or other similar material suspended in runoff and deposited when fast-running streams lose their velocity.

Altruistic behavior　Consideration of the interests of others without regard to self-benefit.

Anadromous　Of or pertaining to oceanic species that migrate to fresh water to spawn.

Anaerobic bacteria　Bacteria that do not require oxygen.

Barren　Descriptive term for land that lacks trees and where other vegetation is scarce.

Biodiversity　The variety and variability among living things and the ecological complexes in which they occur.

Bioindicator　An organism, sensitive to one or more environmental factors, the health or abundance of which reflects the degree of stress placed upon it by those factor(s).

Bog　A wetland with limited drainage where decomposition of organic material is slow, resulting in peat formation and acidic *pH* levels.

Boreal forest An evergreen, coniferous forest located in the higher latitudes.

Brackish Of or pertaining to ocean water that has been noticeably diluted by fresh water.

Canopy The uppermost layer of leaves in a tree or forest. Canopy closure refers to the appearance of leaves in the spring, which shuts off light input to the forest floor.

Carnivore An organism that feeds on other animals. Compare *detritivore, herbivore, omnivore.*

Crepuscular Active in the twilight of dawn or dusk.

Dabbling duck Any member of several species of duck that feeds by tipping tail-up to reach seeds, vegetation, or animal prey in shallow water. Compare *diving duck.*

DDT A chemical widely used as a pesticide in the 1940s and 1950s. It was later found to exert a number of toxic effects on wildlife. Its breakdown product, DDE, was even more toxic.

Detritivore An organism that feeds on detritus (dead plant and animal material). Compare *carnivore, herbivore, omnivore.*

Diving duck Any member of several species of duck that feeds by submerging completely to obtain food, usually from deeper water. Compare *dabbling duck.*

Endemic Restricted to a particular region.

Estivate To pass the summer in a state of torpor or inactivity. Compare *hibernate.*

Ethology The study of animal behavior.

Fall line The final rapids on a stream or river before it reaches tidewater.

Floodplain A flat or nearly flat area adjacent to a river where floodwaters disperse and deposit sediments.

Forest fragmentation The splitting of large, unbroken tracts of forest into smaller tracts by the construction of such features as roads, power lines, or clearcuts.

Habitat The place where an organism lives and grows. The terms refers in particular to the physical features of that place.

Herbaceous Of or pertaining to a plant that does not develop wood in its stem and that usually dies back over the winter. Compare *woody*.

Herbivore An animal that feeds on vegetable material. Compare *carnivore, detritivore, omnivore*.

Hibernaculum A shelter that is used by an organism during the winter.

Hibernate To pass the winter in a state of torpor or inactivity.

Hydric Having or requiring an abundance of moisture. Compare *mesic, xeric*.

Keystone species A species that occupies a central functional role in an ecosystem.

Lepidopteran A member of the taxonomic order that includes butterflies and moths.

Marsh A wetland with mostly *herbaceous* vegetation. Compare *swamp*.

Mesic Having or requiring a moderate amount of moisture. Compare *hydric, xeric*.

Metamorphic Of or pertaining to rock transformed by pressure and heat. Compare *sedimentary*.

Metapopulation A group of populations that are normally separate but whose members occasionally intermingle.

Monadnock An isolated hill or mountain of resistant rock rising above a surrounding plain.

Montane Of or pertaining to mountains.

Mycorrhizal interaction The association of fungi with the roots of plants in the *rhizosphere*.

Omnivore An animal that feeds on vegetable, animal, and detrital material. Compare *carnivore, detritivore, herbivore*.

Orogeny The formation of mountains by geological processes.

pH   A numeric value that indicates the degree of acidity or alkalinity of a substance.

Pelagic   Of or pertaining to the oceans.

Physiographic province   A region with relief features significantly different from those of surrounding areas.

Physiography   The description and interpretation of the relief features of the earth's surface.

Plant succession   The process by which communities of plants on a given site are replaced over time by a series of different, usually more complex, communities.

Rhizome   A root that spreads horizontally, giving off both stems and other roots.

Rhizosphere   The portion of the soil containing mycorrhizal fungi.

Riparian   Of or pertaining to the land bordering streams and rivers.

Sedimentary   Of or pertaining to rock that forms from the accumulated products of erosion. Compare *metamorphic*.

Shell midden   An accumulation of discarded shells near a dwelling place.

Spoil bank   A site where materials dredged from the bottom of a body of water are deposited.

Stopover area   A place where animals rest and feed during migration.

Swamp   A wooded wetland. Compare *marsh*.

Vernal pool   A temporary pool of water, usually filled by spring rainwater, snowmelt, or floodwaters.

Watershed   The land area that drains into a river.

Wetland   Land that is covered during all or part of the year with standing water.

Woody   Of or pertaining to a plant that accumulates wood in its stem. Compare *herbaceous*.

Xeric   Having or requiring little moisture. Compare *hydric, mesic*.

INDEX

This index lists places, organisms, and concepts to which significant coverage is devoted in the text. It is not a listing of every occurrence of a word. Trip names are listed in **boldface** type.